AF478204

A SAVAGE MIRROR

A Savage Mirror

POWER, IDENTITY, AND KNOWLEDGE
IN EARLY MODERN FRANCE

Michael Wintroub

STANFORD UNIVERSITY PRESS
Stanford, California
2006

Library of Congress Cataloging-in-Publication Data

Wintroub, Michael.
A savage mirror : power, identity, and knowledge
in early modern France / Michael Wintroub.
p. cm.
Includes bibliographical references and index.
ISBN 0-8047-4872-1 (cloth : alk. paper)
1. France—History—Henry II, 1547–1559. 2. France—Politics
and government—16th century. 3. Political culture—France—
History—16th century. 4. Political customs and rites—France—
History—16th century. I. Title.
DC114.W56 2006
944'.028—dc22   2005033153

Original Printing 2006

Last figure below indicates year of this printing:
15 14 13 12 11 10 09 08 07 06

Typeset by Classic Typography in 10.5/12.5 Bembo

Nous ne sommes que cérémonie.

Michel de Montaigne

Contents

List of Illustrations

Figures

Plates

Following Page 114

Acknowledgments

I owe a number of institutions thanks for enabling me to work on and finish this book. The Lynn White Jr. Memorial fellowship from the UCLA Medieval and Renaissance Center and the UCLA Paris Program in Critical Theory allowed me to begin my research in France. The J. Paul Getty Research Institute provided a stimulating intellectual environment within which to write up my preliminary results. The Department of History and Philosophy of Science at Cambridge University, the Maison Française of Oxford University, the Museum for the History of Science at Oxford University and the Max Planck Institute for the History of Science in Berlin all helped me to take my research into new and unforeseen directions. Grants from the NEH for university teachers and from the Horace H. Rackham School of Graduate Studies at the University of Michigan allowed me to finish my revisions. A subvention from the Office of the Vice President of Research at the University of Michigan has supported the publication of this work. I also gratefully acknowledge the Newberry Library and the Weiss/Brown Publication Subvention Award made to commemorate the exemplary career of Howard Mayer Brown. Finally, the Department of History at the University of Michigan not only provided numerous small grants, generous time off from teaching and administrative duties, but invaluable intellectual direction, all of which enabled me to bring this project to fruition.

Footnotes can only point in a very indirect manner to the many individuals to whom a scholar is indebted; in my own case, I would especially like to thank Carlo Ginzburg, whose curiosity, advice, and criticism inspired this work from its beginnings; and Mario Biagioli, who in addition to offering sage advice was invaluable in freeing this book from perpetual imprisonment on my computer's hard drive. Others who have contributed in one way or another to any virtues this book might contain, while being quite distant from its all too many faults, include David Bell, Jim Bennett, Robin Boast, Robert Brain, Gayle Brunelle, Nina Caputo, Yves Cohen, Tom Conley, Alison Cornish, Lorraine Daston, Natalie Zemon Davis, Richard Drayton, Claudio Fogu, Kelly Goode, Tom Green, Mitch Hart, Diane Owen Hughes, Paul Nelles, Juan Pimentel, Craig Rodine, David Sabean, Simon Schaffer, Roberta Shapiro, Nirmala Singh, Paolo Squatriti, and Keith Topper. Maxime Wintroub has taught me more than any book ever could; he is a constant source of delight and inspiration. My parents deserve a special thanks, not only for all their help and support, but for instilling in me the belief that what I was doing was important, while at the same time teaching me that most important of lessons—not to take myself too seriously. Hélène Mialet's contribution to this work has been immeasurable. Her love and support, her subtlety and her curiosity have inspired and informed my own thought in incalculable ways. I do not have the words to thank her, so I'll borrow them:

> Ton regard dans le cœur, dans le sang m'est entré,
> Comme un esclat de foudre alors qu'il fend la nue:
> J'euz de froid et de chaud la fiévre continue,
> D'un si poignant regard mortellment outré.
> Lors si ta belle main passant ne m'eust fait signe,
> Main blanche, qui se vante estre fille d'un Cygne,
> Je fusse mort, Helene, aux rayons de tes yeux:
>
> Mais ton signe retint l'ame presque ravie,
> Ton œil se contenta d'estre victorieux,
> Ta main se resjouyt de me donner la vie.

This book is dedicated to her.

A SAVAGE MIRROR

Introduction

MIRRORS, KINGS, AND CANNIBALS

Brilliant flashes of color burst from the trees—parrots set off like flares by monkeys fleeing arrows shot from below. The naked hunters pursued their prey. They did not see him, or at least they pretended not to. A man and woman intertwined in a hammock shared their embrace with his gaze. He observed others cutting down trees and carrying them to the river to trade for all manner of wonders: iron tools, fishhooks, and mirrors. Then, a commotion and a curious silence . . . men of the Tobajaro huddled around their *Morbicha*, their king, waiting. At first he spoke softly: words of eloquence and passion. Then he roared—words of war. The Tobajaro rose as one and attacked. The unsuspecting Tupinamba—hunting, making love, and peacefully trading with French sailors—were their victims. They were caught off guard, but not for long. They retaliated with a vengeance. The village exploded in an orgy of blood and violence. The fighting was vicious, appalling—marvelous. Silently he observed the battle from above. On a chilly October morning in 1550, in the city of Rouen, Henri II, Most Christian king of France, stood on the edge of the New World and looked in. He was, by all accounts, pleased.[1]

This detailed representation of a Brazilian village was only one of many marvels that Henri II would see on the day of his royal entry into Rouen. There were warring gladiators, elephants, and unicorns; pageants with Roman gods,

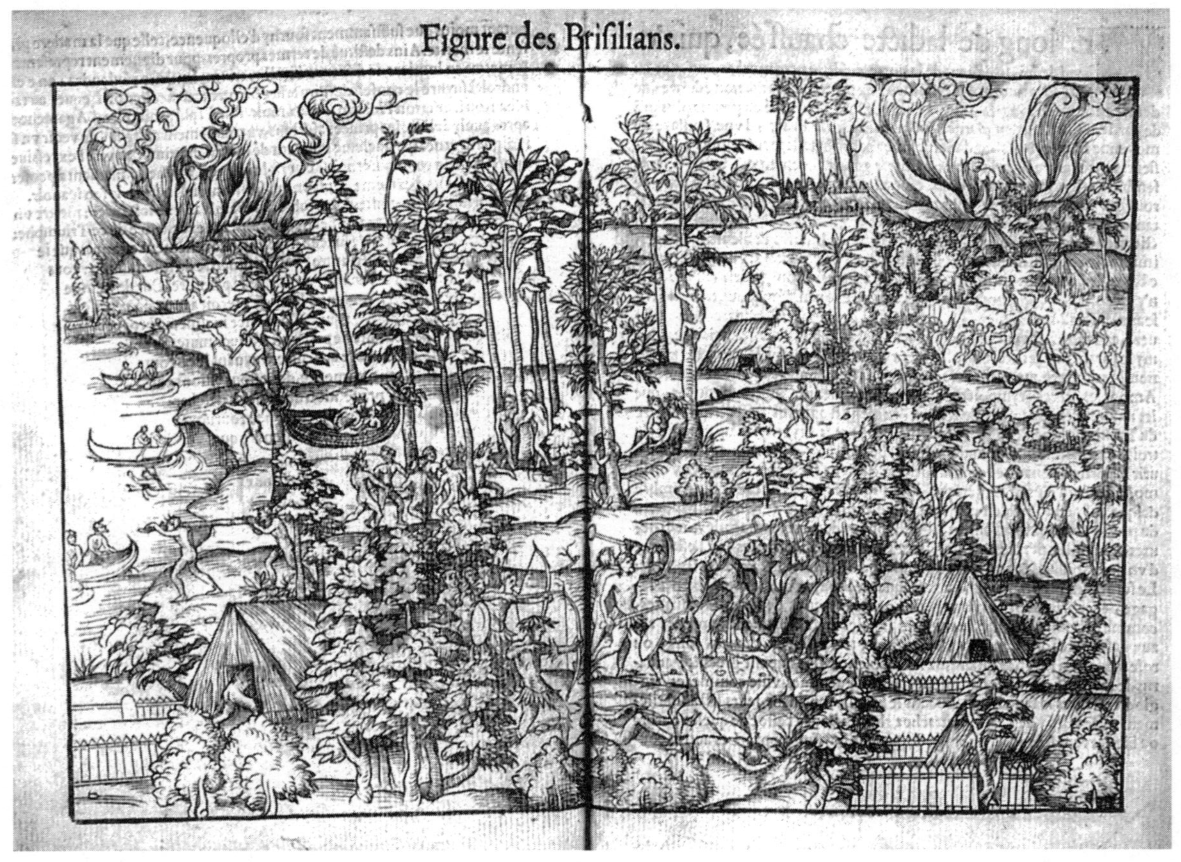

FIGURE 1. Brazil in the Faubourg Saint-Sever. *Cest la deduction du Somptueux ordre* (Rouen, 1551). Courtesy of the Bibliothèque Municipale de Rouen. Photo by Thierry Ascensio Parvy.

nymphs, and muses; a mock sea battle between French and Portuguese ships; a parade of captives from recent victories over the English; and a procession of Henri's ancestors all the way back to Pharamond. So breathtaking was the entry that one chronicler claimed it "would be forever imprinted on the minds of those who had witnessed it."[2]

A King's Mirror

Though few have heard of them today, royal entry festivals were among the most important rites of early modern kingship.[3] Ritual celebrations staged to welcome newly anointed kings at the time of their first visit to a city, entries were structured in terms Marcel Mauss has made familiar—as gifts.[4] Municipalities would spare no expense in organizing magnificent displays to demonstrate recognition of a king's authority. In return, entering kings were expected to reaffirm the customary rights and privileges of a city's citizenry and clergy.

In the Middle Ages entries were relatively simple ceremonies. Clergy, municipal officials, bourgeoisie, and guild members would meet the king at the city's gate and escort him into the town and then to the cathedral. By the end of the fifteenth century, entry ceremonies had become elaborately constructed ritual dramas, with richly produced pageants marking the various stages of a king's itinerary. These pageants were meant to flatter, entertain, and impress. They also aimed to lobby and edify. In this sense, they were explicitly modeled after the medieval literary tradition of the *speculum principis*, or Mirror of Princes, which sought to educate kings in the virtues by which they should live and rule.[5]

As important events celebrating civic culture and identity, entry festivals were not only a means to lobby kings, but weapons in symbolic battles of pomp and consumption staged between rival urban centers of the realm.[6] The entry staged for Henri II in Rouen (1550) was no exception in this regard, for it was meant to surpass the fabulous entries given to him by the cities of Lyon (1548) and Paris (1549). According to its chroniclers, it succeeded in this, being among the most spectacular ever staged.[7] Yet, what is most interesting about Henri II's entry into Rouen for modern day observers is its living display of Brazilians fighting it out on the banks of the Seine. We want to know who these Brazilians were; what they thought; and what happened to them. However intriguing these questions may be, they remain unanswerable. Indeed, the Brazilians displayed in Rouen in 1550 have left no trace of their presence beyond official accounts of the entry. This work therefore focuses on these accounts—that is, on French representations of the Brazilians and their place in the festival. Following from this, my aim in this book is to understand what the French made of these naked New World cannibals; to ask why they put them in their city's festival honoring their king; to examine what motivated them to conceive of and organize such a bizarre display; and to investigate how, when it was enacted, it was understood by those who watched and participated in it. Put another way, if the royal entry presented the king with a mirror upon which he was to model himself and his actions, one cannot help but wonder what exactly it was he saw—and what exactly he was meant to have seen—when he gazed into the naked and savage mirror of the Brazilians inhabiting Rouen's Faubourg Saint-Sever?

A New World Order

The city of Rouen traded extensively with the New World during the sixteenth century, having especially close ties to Brazil. This brought its merchants into violent conflict with the Spanish and Portuguese, who claimed exclusive rights to these newly found lands. At its most basic level, the mise-en-scène of Brazil organized for Henri's entry reflected the interests of the city's merchant community in lobbying the king to support their overseas ventures. This said, the reasons behind Rouen's New World display can be given more subtle meanings than simply economic self-interest. This becomes obvious when the tableau vivant of Brazil is resituated within the larger narrative of the king's entry. Accordingly, the site of Brazil was just the beginning of an allegorical pilgrimage through an elaborate series of tableaux vivants (literally, living pictures) that took the king from the unrestrained savagery of the New World to the humanist ideals of learning, eloquence, and piety represented by his father, François I, in the entry's final tableau, the Elysian fields of the terrestrial paradise.

Crucial to comprehending the entry's narrative, however, were not the differences between the Brazilians and the French—i.e., that the French were "civilized" while the Brazilians were not—but their similarities. France in the sixteenth century was considered by many to be, like the newly found peoples of the Americas, a nation of barbarians. This opinion was widespread, much commented upon, and keenly resented by French men of letters. The royal entry enacted for Henri II—with its mythological allusions, its lightly worn erudition, and its lavish displays of artistic skill—was meant as a clear retort to this characterization. Indeed, it was specifically designed to demonstrate to the king the cultural heights that the French could achieve if only he would do the right thing and patronize Arts and Letters. To this end, the narrative of Henri's entry was constructed as a transformative journey: a journey that took the king (and those who followed him) from barbarism to *civilité*, from the warlike and uncultured savages of Brazil (and France) to an ideal of the humanist prince (Henri's father) reposing in the Elysian fields at the entry's conclusion. We can thus approach the mirror of the Brazilians from at least two different angles. The first reflected the interests of Rouen's merchant community in overthrowing Portuguese commercial and maritime hegemony. The second reflected the interests of its learned community in asserting the independence of France from Italian cultural hegemony. Ultimately, these were not separate stories, but were part of a single overarching narrative that plotted the decline of the Mediterranean world system and the ascendancy of France as the economic and cultural center of a new Northern Atlantic world order.

Savage Mirrors

In the sixteenth century, New World peoples stood on the margins of the known universe. Considered tabula rasa, they were, according to the commonplace dictum, "without laws, religion, or culture whatsoever." Not merely inhabitants of uncharted and faraway lands, they quite literally embodied the presence of the New Worlds from which they came. Whether in tales told by travelers or in court festivities, they acted to efface the distance between here and there, the Old World and the New, and in so doing acted as mediums that transported and translated exotic and unnamed lands without frontiers into coherent and mappable territories, becoming, quite literally, the sites upon which Europeans could stake their conflicting claims to power, status, and authority. In writing the Other and making her "legible," Europeans were less interested in understanding Others per se than in articulating their own interests and concerns. The New World "savages" that inhabited the pages of sixteenth-century texts were little more than reflections of the men who defined, gave meaning to, and used them.[8] The display of Brazil organized in Rouen is particularly relevant in this regard, for it was but one site among many in an unfolding series of tableaux vivants composing the entry's ritual narrative. As such, it was part of a larger story being told to the king about the nature and limits of his power. By analyzing the place held by Brazil in this narrative we can see—in a way that a singular display of curiosities does not permit—the processes by which it was inscribed with meaning and purpose. This, of course, tells us next to nothing at all about who the Brazilians were, what they experienced, or how they understood the strange spectacle within which they were placed. On the other hand, it does tell us a great deal about the French who put them there.

Thus, though the object of this book is the fantastically detailed mise-en-scène of Brazil constructed for the king's entry into Rouen in 1550, its subject is the French who created it.

In the pages that follow my aim will be to illuminate the specific confluence of forces, interests, and practices that contributed to and animated the production of Rouen's mise-en-scène of Brazil. My approach will be a semiotic one whereby symbolic elements are related to one another internally as well as to the economic, political, and social interests that influenced their production, dissemination, and reception. Accordingly, I will not treat Rouen's display of Brazil in isolation from the larger narrative told by Henri's entry or from the overlapping and heterogeneous contexts from which this narrative took shape. Such an historically situated analysis will enable us to see more clearly not only the social and cultural agonistics that organized the symbolic economy of the entry, but the manner in which the articulation of the cultural category of the exotic mediated the construction of French elite identity in the early modern period.

We will begin by following in the king's footsteps as he experienced the entry's spectacle. We will read its symbolism, analyze its clues, and investigate the arcane intellectual and spiritual language of its text and performance; we will then go backstage to observe the social and historical forces that set its stage. We will interrogate the longue durée structures that formed the horizon of expectations, the conceptual tools, and the interpretive skills of those who organized and enacted the entry; at the same time, we will be concerned with showing—on the level of micro-history—how these cognitive and evaluative structures were themselves subject to constant change, revision, and negotiation. The king's entry festival was not (as is often thought) a benign attempt to create civic unity around a common repertoire of themes and ideals, but a strategic act in an ongoing effort to define and demarcate the position of Rouen's new urban elites in the social topography of early modern France.[9]

Ritual Negotiations, Mirrors, and Others

A ritual is not simply a functional reaffirmation of a preexisting way of life, a display of group solidarity, or a celebration of communal harmony, but a medium of social struggle by which specific material, ideational, and spiritual interests are integrated into the perceived structure of the universe.[10] Rituals, in this sense, are highly mediated acts of negotiation, persuasion, and compulsion in which social place, power, and prestige are defined and elaborated in ontological terms, and vice versa.[11] Henri's entry festival was no exception in this regard, for it aimed to explicate the nature of the world and the roles and responsibilities of the individuals and groups who inhabited it. In one sense this world referred to the immutable and transcendent values thought to structure the very cosmos itself. In another, it should be regarded in a very particular sense, as that constructed at a specific time (October 1, 1550), at a specific place (Rouen), and by specific people (not simply the "people of Rouen," but by the groups and networks of individuals involved—whether as participants or observers—in writing and enacting the king's entry). Written in the language of ritual, the entry thus gave voice to a specific dialect: that of the civic elites who conceived, paid for, and organized it. Typically, this elite is associated with the *noblesse de robe*. The *robe*, however, as I will argue, was but a subset of a much larger social grouping that included artisans, merchants, savants, city officials, clergy, and even old nobles. The boundaries of this new elite were, as we shall see, defined less by economic wherewithal, occupation, and title than by certain common cultural and linguistic dispositions, attitudes, and skills.[12] A necessary corollary to the social differentiation of this new elite was the articulation and elaboration of distinct modes of self-presentation and understanding.[13] These can be located, for example, in the emergence and proliferation of works having to do with rhetoric, grammar, eloquence, and courtesy, or as I argue here, in the literary and performative genre of the entry festival.

Though high social status had been traditionally identified with the inherited rights of birth, military prowess, and personal loyalty, Henri's entry attempted to link it with such visible signatures of virtue as eloquence and learning. We can, in this sense, view the itinerary mapped out by the entry's various tableaux vivants as an attempt to symbolically mediate contrasting ideals of what it meant to be noble in the sixteenth century.[14] Please note, however, that I am not arguing that efforts to reconfigure elite identity ought to be seen in oppositional—class—terms, with the old nobility losing out to the new; or that the old nobility was experiencing some sort of deep and fundamental crisis. Recent scholarship has shown not only the substantial cross-fertilization between old and new nobilities, but the continued vitality of the feudal nobility.[15] In either case, the inclusion of new elites among the ranks of the old, or of the old among the ranks of the new—in addition to the clear competition between both groups, as well as internal divisions within each group separately—necessarily involved the strategic working out of highly contested notions of what it meant to be an elite in early modern France. Put another way, the relationship between old and new nobilities was not simply a means to an end—either as a marriage of convenience between capital and rank, or as a strategy for extending (and/or gaining) power through networks of patronage relations, or even as a negative act of self-definition with reference to Others. On its own terms, and much like Europeans' relationship to exotic peoples on the margins of the world, the encounter between old and new nobilities constituted the field upon which the sociocultural articulation of new forms of elite identity and sociability took place. This, I believe, was in large measure what Henri II's entry into Rouen was about.

In reading the narrative of the king's journey through Rouen, then, I will show that the savage warriors from Brazil at its starting point gave consummate expression to the ideals of chivalry and military virtuosity championed by France's old nobility. This meaning, far from being a stable one, was subverted through the course of the entry such that by the final tableau of the Elysian Fields, the king could look back upon the Brazilians as exemplifying a critique of these values as uncivilized and barbaric. In contrast, the entry's final tableau set out such qualities as eloquence and learning as the distinguishing features by which true nobility could be recognized. In this manner, Henri's entry can be viewed as an act of resistance to—and/or co-optation of—the monarchy; that is, as a strategic attempt by Rouen's civic-cultural elite to reformulate the king's identity in terms consonant with its own values and ideals.

Blurred Boundaries: The Political and the Spiritual

The ritual of Henri's royal entry was an expression of the interests of Rouen's civic elite in transforming the king's identity according to their ideals of learning and eloquence. This transformation, however, was only made viable as a strategy of sociocultural legitimization through its linkage with the belief that the New Learning was the principal means by which the unmediated purity of God's Word on earth could be restored. Indeed, just as France was discovering the New World, it was also discovering its own language. And just as the New World was bound up with the eschatological certainty of the world's imminent end and the promise of a new beginning, so too the exploration, mapping, and territorial organization of language was thought to be among the principal means of reconstituting political, social, and moral authority. In this sense, the distinguishing characteristic by which Rouen's new elites sought to assert their status dovetailed with the spiritual justifications underpinning the humanist project as a whole—that is, with the attempt to reestablish the semantic connection to the time before the Fall and to a resurrected Golden Age.[16] At the same time, this humanist ideal, rather than rejecting the values of the old nobility, was conjoined to them, fusing humanist, chivalrous, and dynastic ideologies and placing the French king in the forefront of a civilizing crusade that would extend his—and France's—power throughout the world, both Old and New.

The entry's attempt to mediate between old and new elites was thus accomplished, on the one hand, through the conceptual indeterminacy—hence versatility—of the New World as a vehicle for expressing Old World interests, desires, and needs; and, on the other, through a reformulation of Christian piety as militant, literate, and apocalyptic. The king, cast in the prophetic role of Last World Emperor, was thus to unite the peoples of the earth, and lead them all (by both force and eloquent persuasion) to the terrestrial paradise of Christ's millennial kingdom—a place that some said was to be found in the New World.

At the same time, the entry was not simply a teleological movement from barbarism to civilization, or a simple passing of the baton from the old nobility to the new, for among the manifold meanings associated with the New World were those that undercut this sort of simple linear narrative.[17] The New World was not in any sense limited to these contrasting ideals of elite identity, but was subject to a host of other interpretations and understandings. Among the most common was its association with the Golden Age and/or its identification with the virtues of life lived in simple concordance with natural law. As such, the naked Brazilians inhabiting the banks of the Seine stood clearly in both the tradition of the charivari and the literary genre of the Rabelaisian farce, as well as resonating closely with the growing number of works that spelled out the inherent depravities associated with public life at court.[18] In either case, the Brazilians stood as representatives of natural virtue, of life as it was lived before mankind's fall from God's grace and before the disciplined repression of bodily, gestural, and intellectual comportment by which France's new cultural elite sought to distinguish itself as being civilized and noble. This irony did not escape the observant eye of Michel de Montaigne, who in his famous essay on the cannibals wrote (of the Brazilians he met in Rouen in 1562) that they were wild,

> just as we call wild the fruits that Nature has produced by herself and in her normal course; whereas really it is those that we have changed artificially and led astray from the common order, that we should rather call wild. The former retain alive and vigorous their genuine, their most useful and natural, virtues and properties, which we have debased in the latter in adapting them to gratify our corrupted taste.[19]

Seen from this perspective, the naked savages living in Rouen's Faubourg Saint-Sever represented a naturalistic freedom, a Golden Age, which had escaped the pernicious effects of so-called civilized life. The mise-en-scène of Brazil thus stood as a potent critique of France's new cultural elites, serving to relativize and undercut the artifices of courtesy, language, knowledge, and manners by which they sought to distinguish themselves. Hence the shifting images reflecting from this savage mirror of princes effected a deconstruction of one of the principal social narratives defining Henri's entry; it did this by showing up the supposed superiority of those who would be noble as but a thin veil disguising their truly barbaric and corrupt natures.

Overview

Much was new about the Old World in early modern Europe. This was especially so in France. The New Learning challenged traditional scholastic hierarchies of knowledge. New products—and production methods—came to dominate many of its local economies. New financial institutions contributed to the expansion of trade and new techniques of warfare revolutionized the battlefield. New fashions, new manners, and new tastes came to dominate the conduct of elites; new styles and aesthetic sensibilities governed the building of buildings, the painting of pictures, and the writing of poetry; while new perceptions of time and history isolated the entire era as distinct from that which came before it. No one was more responsible for all these new things than the new urban elites who had risen, through commerce and learning, to positions of status and authority rather than being born into them. And even where these phenomena were not really new, and indeed where, as was usually the case, they were entirely rooted in and mediated by long-standing traditions and practices, there was a perception, as one contemporary put it, of living in "the time of tears and . . . great marvels." The diverse ways that people tried to come to grips with the perception of these vertiginous social and cultural transformations are at the center of this book's concerns.

As a micro-history that is also global, the story told here is about the impact of the(se) "New" World(s) on economies and worldviews; it is about changing social identities and changing attributes of sovereignty, learning, spirituality and etiquette. *A Savage Mirror*, in this sense, is not simply a study of a royal ritual, but an investigation into the intricate and complex relations between social and epistemological change in early modern France. As such, it occupies a unique place at the crossroads of a number of different literatures.

Scholars such as Francis Yates, Roy Strong, and Clifford Geertz have shown that the ritual of the Renaissance royal entry festival played a key role in articulating the early modern mythology of divine kingship. Important as their work has been, it is little concerned with illuminating the specific confluence of forces, interests, and practices that contributed to and animated the symbolic production of monarchical ideology. In contrast, this book is not concerned simply with the hermeneutics of ritual symbolism, but with the social context(s) of a ritual's production, meaning, and use. Though a number of prominent scholarly studies devoted to civic ritual have appeared in the past twenty years, for the most part, they do not attend to questions central to my concerns: most notably, the impact of the New World on the Old, the rise of vernacular consciousness, and the interweaving of monarchical ideology, religious devotion, and identity formation. Much the same could be said regarding works on Renaissance humanism; they do not address—at least as a central theme—the question of the Other, which haunts the esoteric heart of humanist letters. With regard to new historicist works on the encounter with the New World—or with the spate of historical/literary scholarship produced in the wake of the Quincentenary of Columbus's voyage—I do not privilege the literary canon as the site where anecdotes of encounter are put to work. Similarly, though a number of authors have examined the rise of vernacular consciousness in early modern France, they have tended to focus on the canonical literature of the period, reflecting neither on social agency nor on the intertwining filiations of social mobility, literary consciousness, religious and civic ritual, monarchical ideology, and the discovery of the New World. Regarding histories of anthropology and anthropologies of history, though this work touches on many of the same themes, it does not deal with an unconditioned Other, or even with the indigenization of modernity, but with the highly mediated co-construction of selves and Others. The same can be said regarding the analysis of early modern civic elites. While many scholars have examined social change and identity formation with specific reference to elites in early modern France, *A Savage Mirror* attempts to take into account the complex and highly mediated strategies of social and epistemological transformation that defined the social, spiritual, and cultural lives of early modern elites. No one has linked these multifarious acts of identity-formation to the Old World's discovery of the New, or to the connections among the social differentiation of new urban elites, apocalyptic eschatology, and knowledge production. Finally, though a number of scholars have investigated early modern collecting practices and their relationship to the epistemic transformations associated with the Scientific Revolution, relatively little attention has been paid to the religious, ritualistic, and sociolinguistic aspects of these endeavors and how they were bound up in processes of identity formation and epistemic change.

The journey I propose in *A Savage Mirror* is thus a meandering one through multivalent social, political, and cultural contexts normally not seen as being connected. Building detail upon detail, layer upon layer, the different chapters of the book—taken as a whole—aim to present a rich tapestry of intricate iconographic, intellectual, and human associations. The book's aim is to gradually unfold a thickly textured understanding of the entry and the people who wrote and enacted it so as to gain insight into the larger—i.e., global—dimensions of early modern French culture and society. This big picture, however, is kept elusive, vague and distant, so that its coherence only comes into focus gradually, through the cumulative effect of each chapter falling upon the next like so many overlapping layers of bone, muscle, skin, and hair, to form the integral body of the ritual and its historical significance. In other words, the book wants to be read as a whole. This said, a brief sketch of its anatomy is in order.

We will begin by "de-exoticizing" the mise-en-scène of Brazil by placing it back within the narrative frame of the entry festival as a whole. Chapter I simply recounts and summarizes the entry from its beginning to its end. Chapter 2 takes a step back, away from the festival, to the diplomatic context that framed Rouen's presentation of Brazil, by focusing on how Normandy's merchants attempted to draw the king into their battles with the Portuguese over the right to trade in Brazil. The tableau vivant of Brazil will be seen as having the obvious end of lobbying the king to support Rouen's merchant community by translating what was essentially a local battle fought by provincial merchants into a conflict about the honor, prestige, and glory of kings. Chapter 3 returns to the entry to analyze the complex story told by the tableaux vivants that charted the king's itinerary through Rouen. The entry's narrative, it is argued, was not in any simple sense a paean to royal power, but was an act of resistance to—and/or qualification of—this power. Seen from this perspective, the entry was nothing less than an attempt to co-opt—to hijack—the king and all that he represented. Thus, through his embodied performance of the entry's carefully choreographed itinerary, Henri II was himself to become an integral part of the Rouennais attempt to reformulate elite identity in terms they themselves defined. Chapter 4 gives specificity to the entry's narrative by tracing it into the social world of the individuals who wrote and organized it. This is accomplished by focusing on a poetry society, the *Puy de Palinod*, whose participants were prominent members of Rouen's civic-cultural elite. A prosopography of the Puy's membership, along with a detailed examination of their poetry and its relationship to the idea of triumph (which organized the second act of the festival), will demonstrate how the entry expressed this new elite's religious, cultural, and status concerns. Chapter 5 continues the discussion of these Norman poets, many of whom were merchants, sailors, and explorers. The millenarian eschatology that infused their poetry is examined both with reference to the meaning of the New World, and to the role of kingship as it was articulated in the Puy's poetry and in the various royal entries staged in Rouen between 1485 and 1550. Chapter 6 examines the popular milieu that framed the entry through the analysis of another of Rouen's literary societies, the Conards. This chapter sets out the social and epistemic fields within which popular urban traditions, such as the charivari, were linked to Rouen's display of Brazil. It shows, contrary to prevailing views, that the literary and festive work of the Conards was neither a critique of France's established hierarchies nor of its traditional order, but aimed, rather, to satirize the social aspirations of new urban elites, while at the same time valorizing ideals of natural virtue and simplicity, which were associated (by the Conards) with both feudalism and peoples from the New World. Like the Conards' social satire, the verisimilar representation of Brazil found in the king's entry is linked to an "empiricist" response to the social and epistemic instabilities that accompanied the discovery of the New World, the fracturing of religious unity, humanist philological historicism, and the rising power of France's new elites. Chapter 7 examines how absolutist notions of all-powerful kingship were devised as a means of stabilizing the particular "Rouennais" vision of social order put forth in the entry. The question of how such a highly contextualized formulation of divine kingship came to have a life beyond its ritual frame—i.e., as absolutism—is addressed in the book's conclusion. In Chapter 8, I continue to explore attempts by France's new elites to establish social, political, and epistemic order through their distinctive intellectual and cultural dispositions. In doing so, I weave together the three contrasting elements definitive of the entry and those who created it: the humanist valorization of rhetoric, the quasi-empiricism of antiquarians and collectors, and the ritual memorialization of the king as the "one who comes in the name of the Lord." Here my analysis focuses on the relationship between early modern collecting practices—e.g., wonder cabinets—and the form and content of Henri's triumphal entry. I argue on the one hand, that it was through acts of collecting—whether of things or words—that France's civic-cultural elites sought to fashion themselves as a new kind of nobility and to resurrect the lost Age of Gold. On the other, I suggest that insofar as nobility came to be seen as an art to be affected rather than a natural (e)state, the question of how authenticity—in all its social, cultural, and spiritual dimensions—was to be adjudicated took center stage. Attempts to answer this question, both prescriptively and in social practice, came to play an important and often overlooked role in the social history of our own representational practices.[20]

Thus, though this book is very much a work of early modern history, it can also be seen as an intervention into current methodological debates over the aims, limits, and possibilities of representation, for it is an attempt to understand something of the genealogy of our own scientific and historical practices by exploring the social, cultural, and historical circumstances that produced such a thorough—and ethnographically detailed—exhibition of an alien culture in the sixteenth century. Henri's entry—held not a century from the date of production of the first printed book, only a few years after the publication of Copernicus' *de Revolutionibus*, and the same year as the famous debate at Valladolid between Las Casas and Sepulveda about the status of New World peoples—offers itself as an ideal candidate for such an investigation. Why? Because of fifty unnamed, long dead Tupinamba and Tobajaro tribesmen from a land that we now call Brazil who were brought to France and placed in a village that, according to contemporary accounts, was *"un certain simulachre de la verité."*[21]

CHAPTER I

The King's Entry

It was a season of rain. From the time of the king's arrival at the prieuré de Bonnes-Nouvelles on September 27, the downpour had not ceased. The festival planned for his entry into Rouen had to be postponed.

Henri and his entourage crossed over the ancient bridge to the abbaye de Saint-Ouen without fanfare. There he presided over the solemn ceremonies of the knightly order of Saint-Michel. Four days later he retraced his steps across the bridge to the meadow of Sainte Catherine de Grandmont's priory.

The air was clear and calm and there was a soft wind, which the sailors called the *Levant*, blowing from the direction of the Orient. Surely, the chronicler tells us, it was a sign from both God and stars, that on the day set aside for the king's *joyeuse entrée*, the weather had so miraculously changed.[1] On a more earthly plane, the people of Rouen were equally concerned to honor and welcome their king, "not by sham shows or flat paintings, but by the effect of moving and living things."[2] By midday they were ready to begin.

In a gallery elevated on Ionic columns and decorated with his device (a crescent moon) Henri found his throne. From on high he looked down as his city paraded before him. First the clergy, then the royal and municipal officials, the merchants and the tradesmen. It was a chain of being whose end was sealed with a show of force: the civil law dressed in scarlet, followed by three hundred crossbowmen, fifteen hundred soldiers carrying the king's device, a group of Roman gladiators fighting a mock battle with two-handed swords, and fifty of the most esteemed knights of Normandy.[3] From their ranks rose six flags; these were adorned with the insignias of the king and of Normandy interlaced with "the eyes and tongues of immortal glory."[4]

Their passing marked the beginning of the festival's next movement: a triumphal entry modeled after those held for the ancient caesars of Rome. Winged horses, unicorns and elephants; captives, chariots, and Turks; the triumph passed before the king. First, the chariot of Fame holding death enchained; next, Vespa, goddess of religion; and finally, Fortune, balanced on a silver wheel and holding an imperial crown of gold over the head of an actor portraying the king. Then it was the Henri's turn to be seen.

Descending from his throne he and his entourage began their journey into Rouen. Midst the brilliant colors adorning the princes of the blood, the king appeared before the crowds gathered on the prairie. He rode toward the Seine.

Of all the sights that he was to see on his journey into and around Rouen, none was more remarkable than the one he discovered along the banks of the Seine, just outside the city's walls, in the Faubourg Saint-Sever.[5] From scaffolding built specially to afford him an unobstructed view, his vision extended from the Old World to the New, for there, before him, on a small strip of land two hundred paces long and thirty-five wide, was a Brazilian village.

At each end of the meadow were lodges made of rough-hewn tree trunks, roofed with leafy boughs and surrounded by sharpened stakes. Junipers, ash, and stands of willow were painted red to look like trees from Brazil. In their branches parakeets sang and monkeys climbed. The village had no name, but it had three hundred inhabitants—women as well as men—all completely naked: *sans aucunement couvrir la partie que nature commande.*[6] Fifty were "true savages" imported from Brazil by a bourgeois merchant of Rouen. Their cheeks, lips, and ears were pierced and adorned with long polished stones of white and emerald green. The rest were Norman sailors pretending to be savages. Their portrayal, the king was assured, was entirely authentic. Not only had these men frequented the coasts of Brazil, but they had learned to speak the savages' language and affect their manners with such accuracy that they were all but indistinguishable from the "true" savages.

Captivated, the king looked on as the Brazilians shot arrows at birds, relaxed in the shade, rocked back and forth in their hammocks, and chased after monkeys. Others cut brazilwood and carried it to a fort built along the Seine, where they bartered with French sailors for axes, fishhooks, and iron chisels. Anchored just offshore was a ship being loaded with the precious wood. Its sails were adorned with white crosses and fleurs de lys of gold set in fields of azure. They swayed gently in the breeze.

Suddenly, a group of savages—who called themselves *Tabagerres* (the Tobajaro)—gathered around their king. They squatted on their heels and listened to his words with great attention. Speaking passionately and making wild gestures, the savage king harangued and remonstrated with them. When he finished, they jumped to their feet and without a moment's hesitation went to war.

Furiously swinging clubs and shooting arrows, they set upon a rival band of savages, the *Toupinabaulx* (the Tupinamba). The two tribes joined in fierce combat. The Toupinabaulx were soon victorious, routing their attackers and burning their lodges to the ground. So convincing was Rouen's living display of Brazil, that many who had frequented the land of *Brasil* and the *Canyballes* swore in good faith that it was "a certain simulacra of the truth."[7] (See Plate 1.)

Upon leaving Brazil in the Faubourg Saint-Sever, Henri and his entourage moved toward the ancient bridge leading across the Seine and into Rouen. A huge rock, measuring more than 60 feet wide and 150 feet high, blocked their way. Though artificial, it appeared completely natural, for it was covered with moss, ivy, roots, and brambles and was faced with stones of many colors.[8] Deep in this rock was a grotto where Orpheus sat on a polished marble throne. He was dressed in velour the color of sky. Above him a rainbow glistened; its many colors were crowned with a silver crescent. To his right, Hercules, wearing the skin of a lion, battled a many-headed hydra. To his left, nine muses, the daughters of Mnemosyne, played violins. Orpheus accompanied them with his harp. Their music sounded with such sweetness and grace that it "pacified the torments of the sea."[9]

His crossing thus ensured, Henri approached the center of the bridge where Neptune and other, lesser gods of the sea waited to greet him. Neptune presented him with a trident, symbolizing dominion over the oceans. He then saluted the king and jumped over the side of the bridge into the waters below.[10]

In the water, dolphins, whales, and strange sea-creatures swam. In their midst Neptune reappeared. Accompanied by the three daughters of Calliope, muse of rhetoric, he sailed triumphantly across the river in a chariot pulled by two hippopotami.[11] Then, seemingly from nowhere, a Portuguese corsair attacked the French ship anchored offshore the Brazilian village. The battle that ensued was so fierce that it frightened those spectators not accustomed to the savagery of war. In the end, the French were victorious. Henri watched with pleasure as the Portuguese ship slowly sank into the river; he then moved on toward the other side of the bridge—to Rouen.[12]

At the city's entrance a triumphal arch had been built. On its summit two sibyls held a crescent moon. Balanced on the interior curve of the moon, with each foot posed slightly off-center, stood the figure of Saturn. The scene was decorated with verses that explained to the king that he, like Saturn, would usher in a New Golden Age of peace and happiness.

As Henri passed beneath Saturn and the arch and into the city he was met by four of the city's councilors dressed in long robes of black velour. They carried the canopy under which he would remain for the duration of his journey through Rouen. It was made of gold and crimson velour embroidered with the King's insignia: a silver crescent moon. Written into the circumference of the crescent was the King's motto: *Donec totum impleat orbem* (until he fills all the world).[13] The procession then continued toward the Cathedral of Notre Dame where Henri was to meet the founder of his line, Hector. (See Plate 2.)

Henri's Trojan ancestor was dressed in full armor and stood fifteen feet tall. As the king came near, blood from the wounds inflicted by Achilles shot toward the clouds and took the shape of Henri's device, a triple crescent. The display had a written counterpart—a note from Hector to his descendant:

> It pains me not, neither that Troy lay in ruin,
> Nor Achilles' murderous blow,
> For I see that my blood is distinguished,
> By the favor of heaven, to form a triple crescent,
> Which will fill this round machine.[14]

The king contemplated this remarkable display for some time before moving on to the convent of Notre Dame des Carmes, where a sumptuous theater had been erected.

On the lower stage of this theater stood two of the Fates, Clotho and Atropos; they held the figure of eternity—a serpent biting its tail—above their heads. This hieroglyph, the king was told, signified the immortal memory of François I, who was not only the king's father but also the father of the arts and sciences in France.[15] As Henri approached, the scene was transformed, becoming a star-covered globe the color of sky. By subtle means this globe turned on its axis while flames enveloped it. Then suddenly it opened and out from the flames appeared a winged Pegasus, symbol of immortal fame. It moved with such supple agility that it seemed as if nature herself had communicated to it the very means of life. The onlookers stared, captivated—suddenly their attention was distracted by the sound of a lone trumpet coming from high above. When they returned their gaze, the stage had once again been transformed. In place of Pegasus there appeared a likeness of Henri balanced on a silver crescent moon. This silver moon rested on a polished marble stone upon which the word FIDES had been engraved. Beneath king and moon a furious fire raged; in its midst a salamander, the insignia of Henri's father, could be discerned. A symbol of immortal glory, the salamander was immune to the flames. From the king's heart grew a vine that filled the space of the theater with its leaves and fruit. Kneeling on either side and before him were peoples from many nations. They held out their hands and implored Henri to allow them a taste of the grapes on the vine. Above the king, on the second level of the theater, were the seven gods and goddess that gave the planets their names. They offered gifts to him: imperial, royal, and ducal crowns; scepters from antiquity and others more modern. In the king's right hand was the bloody head of a gorgon, signifying the utter defeat of his enemies. In his left hand was a flowering sword, signifying the justice that flourished in France under his rule.[16]

From this remarkable and ingenious display, the king moved on to the final pageant of the entry at the pont de Robec. Here Henri discovered the Elysian fields of the terrestrial paradise.[17] Planted with trees, shrubs, and a variety of herbs, it was enclosed by trellises interlaced with vines and fruit. Placed over the entrances were silver crescents. Standing in the middle of this paradise was Henri's father, François I. Beside him was a representation of Good Memory. She held a book—written in Latin, Hebrew, and Greek—that commended François for his love and support of letters.[18] Behind them stood Egeria, from whose breast came a stream that fed a fountain consecrated to the Muses. At his feet were two men: the first was a chivalrous knight who represented the noble estate, the proud defenders of the republic; the second, a laborer, represented the common people without whom the republic could not have been built. According to the chronicler, Egeria symbolized the profit and renown François derived from his support of the arts. François was here compared to Egeria's husband, Numa Pompilius, king of the Romans, who attained immortality by following Egeria's council and transforming—through education—his barbarous people into virtuous men. Written on the placard accompanying this display were words praising both Henri and François for their support of letters:

> This is the repose of happy paradise
> Of kings enamored with learning,
> François the first is freed and delivered
> And Henri the second will want to follow him
> Good memory has made this place for them.[19]

Another placard spoke of the benefits that would accrue to a republic governed by a just king armed with the arts and sciences. A third placard carried Aeneas' entreaty to his companions to carry on with their voyage despite tremendous hardship and to have faith that what was divinely ordained would come to pass: that they would reach a place of sweet repose, ease, and joy.[20]

Departing from the Elysian Fields Henri passed by the church of Saint Maclou; he then turned back toward the cathedral of Notre Dame. There, before the cathedral, this most Christian king rendered himself unto God, the divine source of his earthly power and majesty.[21] Entering the cathedral, Henri was received by Rouen's clergy. With due honor and reverence, he was dressed anew in the raiments of the church; these were adorned with exquisite metalwork and subtle embroidery and interwoven with pearls and gems of inestimable value. Immediately thereafter Claude Chappuys, *chantre* of the Cathedral, delivered his oration to the king.

Chappuys' words were well-ordered, graceful, and eloquent; indeed, despite their brevity, it seemed to those listening that they were enriched with emblems both divine and grave. Chappuys praised Henri's virtues and implored him to protect and conserve the true faith, his people, and the nation.[22] In conclusion, he predicted that if the king were true to his divinely ordained duty, he would be exalted by God, elevated to a station beyond that of other worldly kings, and ascend to the heavens to receive the imperial crown promised to all just monarchs.

The oration completed, the king knelt before an image of the Virgin and said his prayers. Then both king and congregation sang *Te Deum*.[23] Thus Henri's entry came to an end.

CHAPTER 2

Pleading Their Case in a Silent War

BRAZIL IN THE FAUBOURG SAINT-SEVER

The Brazilian village created for Henri II's entry had a very specific purpose: to lobby the king to support the interests of Normandy's merchant community in their ongoing and long-standing war with Portugal over the right to trade in the New World. Rouen, as the capital of Normandy, and as the administrative, economic, and cultural center of the province, was at the very center of this conflict. Its local economy was deeply implicated in this trade, with many of Normandy's most powerful merchants living—at least part of the time—within its walls. These merchants not only played an important part in the city's economic life, but in the city's vibrant cultural life. This chapter will place their interest in overseas trade into a larger diplomatic context; it will show how Normandy's merchants used the entry to create a bridge between their concerns and those of their king. (See Plate 3.)

First Contacts

According to Desmarquets' history of Dieppe, it was not Columbus, but the Norman captain Jehan Cousin who discovered America. Cousin, he explains, landed in 1488 in Brazil, where the Amazon empties into the sea.[1] One of his ships, he continues, was captained by a Spanish navigator from Palos named Pinçon (Pinzón), who was one of the three famous brothers who was to accompany—and, of course, "advise"—Columbus on his journey to the "Indies."

As La Popellinière was later to lament, Desmarquets' account cannot be verified by any independent means, for the French care less for letters than for deeds:[2]

> The French, and in particular the Normans and the Bretons maintain that they were the first to discover these lands, having traded with savages from Brazil along the river of Saint-Francis at a place called Port Real. But . . . they had neither the wit nor the forethought to leave a public accounting of their travels to assure the status of their discoveries.[3]

The first officially recorded contact between Normandy and the New World took place in 1504.[4] Seeing the spices and other rarities from the *Indes Orientales* in the Lisbon marketplace, the Dieppois merchants Jean Ango and Pierre Le Carpentier resolved to send one of their ships, *L'Espoir*, in search of similar treasures.

Carrying a cargo of hatchets, knives, cloth, mirrors, and beads, and captained by a gentleman of the lords of Buschet, Paulmier de Gonneville of Honfleur, *L'Espoir* departed from Dieppe on June 23, 1503. Blown off course, Gonneville and his crew landed in Brazil. They remained there for six months, making repairs to their ship and trading with the natives.

The Indians, according to Gonneville, lived simple and *joyeuses* lives without travail.[5] Their king was a man of about sixty, of middling stature, with a serious countenance and a welcoming gaze. He agreed to let Gonneville take his son, Essomericq, to France in order to learn artillery, and how to make mirrors, knives, and hatchets. According to Gonneville, "to these simple people such knowledge was like promising a Christian gold, silver, or the philosopher's stone."[6]

Soon after departing from Brazil, the crew of *L'Espoir* took ill. Several men died. Near death, Essomericq was baptized. As it turned out, his baptism was "a cure to both body and soul," for he quickly recovered. Thus reborn, he was given a new name to reflect his new beginning, Binot, which comes from the verb *binoter*, meaning to till the land a second time.[7]

The illness of the crew forced *L'Espoir* back to land. They found themselves in a place where the Dieppois, the Malouins, Normans, and Bretons had been trading for brazilwood, cotton, monkeys, parakeets, and other merchandise for several years.[8] Thus, though Gonneville's was the first recorded contact, his account, given before the admiralty of Normandy, indicates that French merchants had been present in Brazil for some time. Though such evidence does not confirm Desmarquet's claim, it does indicate the possibility of Norman relations with Brazil before Cabral's "discovery" of April 22, 1500.[9]

Meanwhile, Captain Gonneville adopted the reformed savage Binot, gave him his family name, de Paulmier, and eventually even his daughter, Suzanne, in marriage. Binot de Paulmier came to be one of Honfleur's most highly regarded residents; his fellow citizens were said to have remarked that there had never been one from so far away in France before.[10]

Four years after Gonneville's return, Thomas Auber sailed another of Ango's ships, *La Pensée*, to the New World and brought back seven "savages" to Rouen. A contemporary account describes them:

> They came from a region parallel to the seventh climate, far below that of Gaul. They carried bows with arrows tipped with stones and bones of fish. Their boats were made from the bark of trees and were so light that they could be carried on their shoulders. They were dark in complexion, with large lips and hair thick and black like that of a horse. They had neither beards nor hair on their bodies and their faces were decorated with ornamental scars. They wore skins to cover their shameful parts, but they often went about naked. Their meats were roasted flesh and they drank only water, having no use for the essentials of civilized life—bread, wine, gold, and silver. They spoke their language as if they had neither religion nor manner of living reasonably.[11]

Seeing Red: Brazilwood and the Enticements of Trade

In the *Coming of the Book*, Lucien Febvre and Henri-Jean Martin argue that though the New World was "discovered" in the late fifteenth century, its presence in the Old World was still difficult to locate at the end of the sixteenth. As they put it: "Beyond a comparatively small circle of scholars, merchants and courtiers, works on the New World . . . were of no great interest outside the Iberian peninsula until about 1550."[12] Yet in Normandy, the New World was not a vague and distant idea lurking on the pages of obscure and scholarly texts—it was a real presence.[13] From the 1520s trade was extensive.[14] In particular the Normans sought a type of wood used to make brilliant red dyes.[15]

Le bois de braise, as it was known and from which Brazil is said to have taken its name,[16] is a tall tree with gray bark, green leaves, and brilliant yellow blossoms. As depicted in Henri's entry festival, in numerous maps, and in the anonymous wood reliefs that decorated the façade of 17, rue Malpalu in Rouen (c. 1530), the Normans enticed the natives with various goods to carry out the difficult labor of cutting and transporting the trees.[17] (See Plates 4 and 5.)

Once back in France, the logs would be rasped into sawdust that was then soaked in water to produce a luminous red dye. Though the dye was somewhat unstable, *les couleurs joyeuses* were all the rage at court, thus making the potential profits worth the risks involved in overseas trade.[18] By mid-century brazilwood—and Brazil—had become a significant part of the Norman economy, based as it was on the production of linen.[19] This trade was so important that reference to it even found its way into the poetry written for Normandy's famous literary competitions held each year in honor of the Immaculate Conception of the Virgin Mary; thus, the ship captain, navigator, and humanist Jean Parmentier wrote of traveling "to countries far away, to carry full cargoes, of rich red wood (*riche boys rouge*) . . . , to the great profit of all *humanité* . . . ,"[20] while another, lesser known poet, Jean Broise, wrote a poem called "The Land of Brazil, from which *Escarlatte* is made" in which he compared the "precious wood" to Jesus Christ, and the land where it was found to the pure and holy body of the Virgin—"a redolent garden without sin that was discovered by divine science."[21](See Plate 6.)

The right of the Normans to trade in the New World was emphatically challenged by the Portuguese, who claimed exclusive rights (by papal decree and the treaty of Tordesillas) to the land of Brazil. The conflict between Normandy's merchants and Portugal reached fever pitch in the 1520s and 1530s; 1522 was a particularly turbulent year. François I and Charles V of Spain were at war. The Normans gladly joined in, contributing a ship belonging to Jean Terrien, a close associate of Jean Ango.[22] The Norman ship attacked and captured a Spanish vessel returning from Mexico with a cargo of gold, pearls, skins, and other "singular merchandise." On the way back, both ships were seized by the commander of the Portuguese fleet, Pedro Botelho because, according to Botelho, the French ship had engaged the Spanish vessel in Portuguese waters. The French king was not pleased. On September 3, 1522, he authorized Terrien to take whatever action he deemed necessary to recuperate his losses.[23] Terrien was well known to the Portuguese, not as a merchant, but as a pirate. They considered François' letter of marque as nothing less than a declaration of war, for it gave official sanction to Terrien's incursions into waters, lands, and markets claimed as their own. What began as a local conflict between Norman and Portuguese merchants thus quickly escalated into an international dispute between kings.

At roughly the time that Terrien received his letter of marque, Giovanni Verrazano was offering his services to François I. According to João III's ambassador in Paris, Verrazano had promised not only to discover "new realms in the Orient . . . [but] also [to] colonize the [Portuguese] land of Brazil."[24] Shortly thereafter, the ambassador's spies in Normandy confirmed that Verrazano was preparing several ships for departure with Jean Ango's help. This information prompted João to send his special envoy, João da Silveira, to the French court to complain about the "silent war" being carried out by Norman merchants against Portuguese shipping on the high seas. Da Silveira told François that if he wanted to maintain peace and friendship between France and Portugal, he would have to restrain his Norman subjects, restore property stolen through acts of piracy, and prohibit expeditions to "countries already conquered by the Portuguese."[25]

François responded by professing his desire to preserve the ancient friendship between France and Portugal. To this end, he prohibited Normandy's merchants from traveling to the Indies and ordered the restitution of all property "stolen" from the king of Portugal and his subjects.[26] This apparent conversion had little to do with the French king's loyalty to João III; rather, it was a transparent attempt to win a potentially powerful ally against his lifelong enemy, Charles V. Da Silveira was well aware of this. As he put it in a communiqué to his king: "The news that Your Highness was on bad terms with the Emperor" has led François to embargo the ships of Verrazano, "but he did this without informing me, not wanting to tie his hands before knowing how things would turn out between Your Highness and the Emperor."[27]

Nevertheless, da Silveira seemed convinced of François' goodwill. He wrote to his king that a Portuguese galleon recently captured by the French was being returned and that Verrazano's expedition would not take place.[28] But da Silveira was beginning to have doubts about the information he was receiving from his agents in Normandy. Taking no chances, he sent Diego de Gouveia (the eminent doctor and geographer of the college of Saint-Barbe) to Rouen to discover the true status of Verrazano's expedition.[29] Soon after his arrival, de Gouveia learned that Verrazano was still preparing for his voyage.[30] Thus was François' deception discovered: despite promises to the contrary, he had secretly exempted Verrazano from his embargo.[31]

Trading Zones: Between Local and National Interests

François' support of Verrazano's expedition put him at risk of alienating a powerful ally in his ongoing struggle against Charles V. His willingness to pay such a price is perhaps indicative of the value he and his advisers placed on overseas discovery, trade, and colonization. In a culture where elite status was defined by notions of honor and glory, overseas exploration held out the promise not only of profit, but of immense symbolic significance. As we shall see in Chapter 5, the economic interests of Normandy's merchants were closely intertwined with a protonationalist eschatology: that of a military-spiritual quest in which the French king, as Last World Emperor, would do battle with infidels and heretics, unite all the peoples of the world, and prepare the way for Christ's millennial kingdom on earth.

No matter its lofty justifications, João was furious at the French king's about-face. He immediately authorized his subjects to attack any French ships they encountered off the coast of the New World. Armed with François' letter of marque, Jean Terrien responded in kind. Along with Jean Ango, he put together a fleet of eight ships. They set sail early in 1524 under the command of Jean Fleury, one of Ango's most able pilots.[32]

At about the same time François I suffered his humiliating defeat at Pavia. His army was crushed, and he himself captured, sent to Spain, and imprisoned for the better part of two years.[33] Despite their king's predicament and the dramatically changed diplomatic circumstances, the conflict between Normandy's overseas merchants and the Portuguese crown continued unabated. By year's end, Fleury had taken more than thirty Spanish and Portuguese vessels.[34]

In March 1526 François was compelled to sign the Treaty of Madrid. In addition to forcing him to abandon his transalpine claims, it forbade the French from trading in the New World. Shortly thereafter, the king began his voyage back to France and to freedom. As he sailed across the Bidassoa toward Hendaye, his sons, the eight-year-old dauphin and the seven-year-old duc d'Orléans (later, Henri II), sailed past him and on to Spain: hostages to ensure his compliance with the treaty.

Notwithstanding the imprisonment of his heirs, François disavowed the Treaty of Madrid. On the day after his return from captivity, he signaled his defiance by meeting with the amiral de France, Philippe Chabot de Brion, and agreeing to sponsor Verrazano's second voyage (an endeavor in which Chabot and Ango had heavily invested).[35] In response to this about-face, the king of Portugal dispatched Christovão Jacques to interdict French vessels in the New World, giving him the added incentive of exclusive rights to trade in brazilwood.[36] Jacques went about his mission with zeal, capturing three French corsairs at Bahia and then pillaging *La Marie*, a ship owned by two associates of Ango. Following on the heels of this loss, Jean Fleury was captured by the Spanish and brought back to Toledo for trial. At about the same time, da Silveira learned that Verrazano was preparing a third voyage that he believed was "destined . . . to establish a base . . . and continue making discoveries in the lands belonging to Portugal and Spain."[37] In a letter sent to João, da Silveira wrote that "our intention to defend Brazil is regarded here [in Paris] with resentment" and that the French "feel that they are legally entitled to retaliate in kind."[38] Despite mounting Portuguese and Spanish hostility, Verrazano departed for Brazil, having been commissioned by Jean Bonshons, a bourgeois merchant of Rouen, to transport a cargo of brazilwood.[39] Far from halting trade with the New World, Portuguese and Imperial attempts to interdict Normandy's merchants seem to have had little effect. From 1529 brazilwood began to arrive in increasing quantities; in the first half of that year alone over 200 tons were unloaded in Honfleur for Rouennais merchants such as Jean de Saldaigne and Jean de Quintanadoines.[40]

On June 21, 1529—after his defeat in Lombardy—François was forced, at least for the time being, to give up his Italian ambitions. He signed the Treaty of Cambrai on August 3, 1529. His treasury exhausted, he raised new taxes and imposts, but had to turn to João III for a loan to pay the ransom demanded by Charles V for his sons.[41] On the eve of his marriage to João's mother-in-law—and Charles' sister, the former queen of Portugal, Éléonore, François declared himself willing to search for a permanent solution to the conflict over Brazil. He proposed the creation of a tribunal charged with arbitrating the conflict. João responded to François' overtures and his request for a loan by demanding compensation for the 500,000 cruzados and 300 ships that had been lost to Norman acts of piracy. François found the money elsewhere; some sources claim that Jean Ango, conseiller du roi, vicomte-gouverneur-capitaine de Dieppe, bore the debt himself.

Once the ransom was paid and his sons were released, François again showed signs of defiance. He ordered officials in Provence not to oppose Jean Ango's efforts to exact retribution from Portuguese nationals and granted Ango wide-ranging authority to recuperate his losses from the Portuguese.[42] João turned to his brother-in-law, the emperor, for help. Charles responded by sending his ambassador to Paris to persuade the French king to rein in his subjects.[43] In the face of this diplomatic activity, Ango returned to court to defend his interests and to demand the release of Jean Fleury and his crew, held captive in Spain. Charles, to Ango's surprise, agreed, and on June 30, signed an order granting Ango's men freedom. Emboldened by his diplomatic success, Ango pursued the Portuguese with a vengeance, arming a fleet to challenge them on the high seas as well as placing an embargo on all Portuguese vessels sailing along the western Atlantic coast bound for Flanders.[44] Ango's show of force persuaded João to pursue a less orthodox course of action: his ambassador to the French court bribed Admiral Chabot to restrain Ango and his associates. Chabot repaid the Portuguese by persuading Ango, his sometime business partner, to settle with Portugal for 60,000 ducats rather than pursuing the 250,000 to which he was entitled by François' letter of marque.[45] This problem solved, Chabot turned his attention to the larger issue of Norman incursions into territories claimed by Portugal. He counseled François that the sacrifice of overseas trade with Brazil was a small price to pay for the strategically valuable friendship of the Portuguese king; in August 1531, François prohibited his subjects from trading with Brazil.[46] Immediately following this decision, Rouen's merchant community came before the Council of 24 (Rouen's primary deliberative body) to complain that their manner of living depended on freedom of the seas.[47] The council, bowing to the interests of the city's richest citizens, sent a delegation to plead their case before the king. The king, however, refused to reconsider.[48]

Ango's associate, Pierre Crignon, the Norman poet, navigator, and mathematician, summed up Norman resentment; according to him, the Norman pilot Denys de Honfleur had discovered Brazil well before the Portuguese. Indeed, he continued, "the people of this land (Brazil) are free, not having either king or law; . . . [moreover] they love the French better than any other nation with whom they have dealt." Thus,

> if the king would but loosen the bridle on French merchants, in less than four or five years they would conquer the friendships and ensure the obedience of the Brazilians without other arms than persuasion and good conduct. And in this short space of time the French will have penetrated farther into the interior of the land than the Portuguese have in fifty years, and even if the Portuguese tried, they would—in all likelihood—be hunted down and killed by the natives who consider them their mortal enemies.[49]

Elsewhere Crignon commented that

> While the Portuguese are the smallest people in the entire world, the earth does not seem large enough to satisfy their cupidity. They must have drunk the dust of the heart of King Alexander to show such unmeasured ambition. They believe that they can take in their closed fist what they cannot embrace with both hands: one truly believes that they have persuaded themselves that God has made the sea and the land for them alone.[50]

That François' prohibition was unpopular in Normandy is not surprising. Yet, despite Chabot's promise of strict enforcement, the ability of the "central" authorities to implement the prohibition on the local level was extremely limited.[51] The peripatetic nature of the court, competing centers of authority, the morass of local, provincial, and "national" administrative bodies together with a willfully defiant provincialism, combined to diffuse the practical, on-the-ground reality of royal authority.[52] Laws might be written and decrees issued, but compliance was not a matter of course. Thus, the Portuguese ambassador complained that the ban was all but ignored by the Normans. Indeed, when his agent tried to publicize the ban in Rouen, he was met with such hostility that he was forced to flee for his life. Ango seems to have been particularly defiant.[53] Chabot ordered that all "stolen" goods brought to Rouen were to be sequestered.[54] This new directive was no more effective than the first. As Portuguese diplomatic correspondence for 1531 and 1532 makes clear, the Normans continued in their commerce with the New World. In the autumn of 1531 alone, there were more than ten ships at Honfleur and six at Rouen bound for Guinée and Brazil.[55] Crignon made the Norman position clear: "Certainly, the Portuguese have it in their power to close off the seas from Cape Finistere to Ireland. . . . However, they have no more right to impede French merchants from going to lands . . . where they have done no good, and where they are neither loved nor obeyed, than we have the right to block them from going to Scotland, Denmark or Norway."[56]

While João continued in his efforts to interdict the French from going to Brazil, François turned a blind eye to the activities of Normandy's merchants. In October 1533 João sent a new envoy to the French court, ostensibly to congratulate François on the marriage of Henri, duc d'Orleans (the future Henri II) to Catherine de Medici, Pope Clement VII's niece. His real motive, however, was to bribe Montmorency, Du Prat, and Chabot to stop François delivering new letters of marque against Portugal.[57] João made his position on the matter of Brazil explicit: "The seas where anyone can—and ought—navigate, are those which have always been known and common to all, but the others, which were never known and did not seem navigable and which were discovered at the cost of considerable effort on our part, are ours alone."[58]

François replied to this claim by having his *grand almoner*, Jean Le Veneur, persuade the pope, now tied by blood to François, to declare that Alexander VI's Bull of 1493 applied only to "known continents, not to territories subsequently discovered by other powers."[59] The day after the pope departed Marseilles for Italy (November 13, 1533), François delivered a new letter of marque that guaranteed his subjects liberty of the seas.[60] The Venetian ambassador commented that a silent war raged between Portugal and France over the matter of Brazil. The French, he continued, "make a show of having the right to navigate . . . as they please. The Portuguese contest this, and when they meet them at sea, wanting to prove themselves the strongest, they fight and sink them."[61]

In January 1536 François invaded Savoy and by March he had conquered it. The Emperor was furious. On Easter Monday, in the presence of the pope, he publicly challenged the French king to personal combat; by mid-May any pretense of peace had given way to war. On July 13, Charles invaded Provence. The next day, François and João swore fidelity and friendship to one another against the Emperor.[62] Again, Portuguese agents bribed Chabot; he reciprocated by convincing François to interdict attacks on Portuguese vessels coming from the Indies. In late September, Charles was forced to retreat. But in response to a French attack on his Flemish territories, he launched a counteroffensive in northern France. François, wanting to maintain his alliance with João, banned navigation to Brazil (May 30, 1537).[63] This ban was renewed on August 26, 1537.[64]

For François and Admiral Chabot, ceding to Portugal's claims in Brazil appeared a small sacrifice compared to the possibility of an alliance with João III against the growing power of Charles V. Early in October that same year François arrived in Lyon, where he prepared to invade Italy. Soon he was in possession of the whole of Piedmont as far as Montferrat. A truce was signed, but the peace was tenuous. The ban on overseas trade authorized by François on December 22, 1538, can be attributed to the continued tension between France and the empire.[65] As a communiqué to the Portuguese king put it:

> François I, by the grace of God . . . to the ambassador of our dear brother, ally
> and confederate, king of Portugal, we confirm . . . here that we have forbidden
> and interdicted all our subjects from going to the land of Brazil . . . on pain of
> confiscation of their vessels, goods and merchandise, and each and everyone of
> their wares, as well as by corporal punishment.[66]

The king's decision to ban overseas trade with Brazil brought a quick response from Rouen's merchant community. They immediately sent a delegation of seven merchants to vigorously protest it.[67] They no doubt reminded the king of the services they performed in the recent war against the Emperor.[68] Though there was now a truce of sorts between Charles and François, the alliance with Portugal had to be maintained; in the king's view, an official ban on trade with Brazil seemed a small sacrifice to ensure this.

Portuguese friendship—or at least neutrality—was important to François, not only as a precaution against renewed violence with the empire, but also because of Henry VIII's increasingly hostile stance toward France. Henry, it seems, was worried about the possibility of a truce between France and Spain. He feared an entente that aimed at deposing him and reinstating Catholicism in England. His fears were well founded; in July 1538 François and Charles met and agreed to unite against the enemies of Christendom: the Turks, the Lutherans, and the heretical English king. In January 1539 the ban against trade with Brazil was renewed.[69] On February 1, 1539, a truce was signed between France and Spain. Rumors of an imminent offensive against England caused Henry to make frantic preparations for war.

A secure peace established between France and the empire allowed François to renew his open support of overseas trade in Brazil; on February

19, 1539, the king hired a ship to transport a cargo of brazilwood and other exotic items to Paris.[70] These developments coincided with the trial of Admiral Chabot for corruption and lèse-majesté.[71] His alleged crimes included illegally selling licenses for maritime expeditions and taking bribes from the Portuguese ambassador. After its principal advocate was discredited, the ban against trade with Brazil was revoked on November 13, 1540.[72] With the conviction of Chabot in February 1541, Normandy's trade with the New World exploded.[73] In 1541 alone forty ships made the crossing.[74]

Charles was furious and ordered his ships to interdict and destroy French vessels going to or coming from the New World.[75] To Charles' insistence that François stop his subjects from trespassing on New World territories, François famously responded: "Is it to declare war and contravene my friendship with His Majesty that I send my navy onto the seas? The sun shines for me, as it does for others; I would very much like to see the clause of the testament of Adam that excludes me from my share of the world."[76]

João III also found the situation intolerable; in October he sent a new envoy to France to complain about the continuing harassment of his subjects by Normandy's pirate-merchants. This, combined with the heightened political tensions between France and the empire, led Rouen's merchants to believe another ban on overseas trade was imminent. The Rouennais immediately sent another delegation to plead their case before the king.[77] Perhaps owing to their efforts François did not act on either the Emperor's or João's demands.

In 1542 François declared war on Charles. Early the next year the Emperor turned to Henry VIII for help. In these circumstances François had far more need of ships and money—both of which Normandy's powerful merchant community had—than in an uncertain alliance with the Portuguese. Reflecting these changed conditions François issued an edict guaranteeing his subjects freedom of the seas (June 7, 1543).[78]

The following summer Charles invaded Champagne and Henry landed at Calais. By fall, the emperor's army had collapsed; he signed the Peace of Crépy on September 18. The next day Boulogne fell to the English. François was unable to retake it. He therefore turned to Jean Ango and Normandy's merchant community for help in fighting the English. With Ango's assistance François assembled a fleet to invade England. An anonymous poet from Dieppe wrote about Ango's valiant efforts against the English:

> He, and he alone armed
> The grand fleet [that] put to sea, expressly
> To make visible to English conceit
> That François is king on both land and sea.[79]

François rewarded Ango for this help with a new letter of marque (February 4, 1544) that authorized him to attack the Portuguese because of the "many great inhumanities, depredations, murders and violence" committed against his ships.[80] A little book, said to be authored by Rabelais, entitled *Bringue-narilles, cousin germain de Fessepinte* and published in 1545 by the brothers Dugort (the same men responsible for publishing the prose account of Henri's entry, *Cest la deduction . . .* in 1551), sums up the attitude of the Normans towards Portugal. In it, Bringuenarilles encounters the Portuguese on the open seas:

> they fired their artillery at him, but he caught their bullets in his hand as if they were little balls, and threw them back with such force that they burst their ship asunder. And just to spite them, because they were proud and said they were the kings of the sea, he took their ship between his teeth and swallowed them whole . . . , which he found most disagreeable, for the ship contained more than 500 marmots and as many monkeys, all of which incessantly jumped around in his stomach . . . [which made him feel most ill]. Thus he was constrained to see his doctor who counseled him to sweep and clean them out with a sturdy birch rod. Forthwith, he did, with a few great strokes in the hole of his bum, force them out . . . and threw them all into the sea.[81]

The invasion of England ended without consequence, except for Ango who, for all his efforts, was left bankrupt. Letters of marque were little compensation compared to loans never repaid by the royal treasury. To make matters worse, François agreed to suspend all letters of marque (February 28, 1547) for two years if João would do the same. During this period commissions seated in Paris and Lisbon were to settle all claims. A month later, François I died and Henri became king. Ango died some years later, his merchant empire ruined.

A New King and an Old Policy

Henri II, like his father, wanted to maintain an alliance with the Portuguese. In a concerted effort to win the goodwill of Portugal he asked João to be godfather to his newborn son. At about the same time he recalled Montmorency who was described by Rui Fernandes, a Portuguese agent in Paris, as a "good servant of João III."[82] Shortly thereafter, João sent a special ambassador to Henri's court in Paris to congratulate him on his accession. Henri gave João's envoy a magnificent welcome.[83] There can be little doubt that the new king was trying to bolster his friendship with the Portuguese king (just as he was trying to form a new defensive alliance with the pope and the Venetians) against the possibility of renewed conflict with the emperor over France's possessions in Italy. João had every reason to be optimistic about Henri's rise to power. This optimism was repaid. On October 20, 1547, Henri forbade his subjects from going to "any lands discovered by the Portuguese."[84]

Despite increasing centralization of administrative and juridical power, effective means for ensuring compliance were either lacking or required such a degree of violence that they were only employed in instances where social order was severely threatened (as in the case of the 1549 rebellion against the *gabelle* in Bordeaux).[85] Portuguese diplomatic correspondence for 1547 and 1548 testifies to the defiance of Henri's ban, for it indicates that French corsairs continued to assault Portuguese shipping and trade in the New World. Thus João was advised by his agents in France to put "the *capitaineries* of Brazil in a state of defense against the French."[86]

João responded to the continued belligerence of the Normans by having his ambassador warn Henri that if he wanted to maintain good relations with Portugal he must "instantly give the order that attacks on Portuguese shipping cease and that the guilty be punished." He also requested that Henri confirm the treaty signed by François in 1547 for another two years.[87] Henri acceded to these demands.[88] The following year, on September 10, he prohibited any importation of spice and drugs (*drogueries*) by way of the Atlantic into France except through the port of Rouen, where they could be strictly regulated.[89] On November 19 he extended the treaty of February 1548 for another 3 years;[90] on December 13, 1549, he agreed to extend it for a period of ten years.[91]

Ritual Persuasion and the New King: Naumachia

In May 1550, after a long siege, the English agreed to give up Boulogne. Claude d'Annebault, amiral de France and governor of Normandy, notified Rouen's city council of the king's intention to make his triumphal entry into their city at the end of August.[92]

Henri, like his father before him, seemed quite willing to sacrifice the interests of Normandy's merchant community in the name of larger diplomatic concerns. The king's entry presented Rouen's merchants with a perfect opportunity to persuade him to support their overseas ventures. Many of Normandy's most prominent New World merchants (e.g., Civille, Cossart, Du Couldray, Du Mouchel, Hallé, Le Prevost, Saldaigne) were recruited to help pay for the entry.[93] That their interests found expression in Rouen's representation of Brazil is clear; but these interests needed to be convincingly portrayed as the king's as well. While the economic benefits of peaceable trade in brazilwood might seem, on the face of things, persuasive, such benefits were far too narrow to interest the new king. Presented in the larger context of a global war with the Portuguese, however, this trade was something that would surely capture Henri's attention. He was, after all, seeking to present himself as a warrior king coming to Rouen fresh from his triumph over the English at Boulogne. This larger context was given explicit expression in the entry's *naumachia* (a mock naval battle) staged shortly after the king left the simulated land of Brazil.

In this naumachia French and Portuguese vessels fought a pretend battle. At first, given recent events, the battle was thought to be between English and French ships but, as the English ambassador Sir John Masone observed, it turned out to be "a representation of a fight between the Portugals and the French about the old quarrel for the Isle of Brazil."[94] As seen in an engraving accompanying *Cest la deduction*, a French ship was anchored just offshore from the site of the Brazilian village peacefully trading with the natives for brazilwood.[95] The battle began when a Portuguese caravel suddenly appeared firing its canons, as would an "African pirate." The French responded by lifting anchor and returning fire. Moments later they boarded the caravel and battled her crew. They fought furiously—with pikes, lances, arrows, grenades, and other weapons. Some in the audience were horrified by what they were seeing; others marveled at it. The sailors seemed to be fighting to the death. Soon the Portuguese caravel began to sink: its hull breached, its masts and sails on fire. As the vessel burned, those on board desperately tried to save themselves by leaping into the Seine. This, according to the chronicler of the entry, caused a great commotion among those spectators who were "not accustomed to the furies of war." The French victory, however, was never really in doubt; indeed, it was a confirmation of the promise made only moments before by the ocean god, Neptune, when he gave Henri a trident symbolizing France's undisputed dominion over the world's seas.

Naumachiae were something the new self-styled warrior king loved. Whereas his father might have been enamored with arts and letters, Henri directed himself toward the more noble goals of "honor, warfare, virtue, action, courage, [and] strength."[96] Above all else he considered himself a man of action—a man of war. His contemporaries made much of his disdain for effete intellectual activities and his preference for hunting, chivalric sport, and warfare. He was known as *le Belliqueux* and was considered by many to be the very embodiment of the military virtues with which the old nobility so closely identified.[97] Designers of entry festivals were well aware of their king's predilections, and they used their entries to appeal to them. Elaborate

FIGURE 2. Detail of the Naval Battle enacted for Henri II's entry into Rouen. *Cest la deduction du Somptueux ordre* (Rouen, 1551). Courtesy of the Bibliothèque Municipale de Rouen. Photo by Thierry Ascensio Parvy.

naumachiae and *seyomachiae* (land battles) were organized for several of his entry ceremonies, as for example that held for his coronation entry into Rheims (1547),[98] and for his entry into Lyon (1548). This latter entry featured a naval battle between Greek and Roman ships.[99] Unlike Rouen's naumachia, however, there were no sides to be taken in the Lyon spectacle, for it was so carefully choreographed—and the rival fleets so evenly matched—that no one seemed to be in danger at all.[100] Though the Rouennais clearly borrowed from their Lyonnais rivals in constructing their naumachia (so much so that the author of *Cest la deduction* lifted part of his description word-for-word from the Lyon account),[101] the two displays were very different. Whereas Lyon's naval battle had all the appearance of a staged spectacle, the Rouennais presented so realistic a battle that observers actually feared for its participants' lives. More important, while the naumachia in Lyon was a self-contained battle for show—that is, a display lacking any and all reference to reality—the Rouen spectacle was an enactment of the violent war being fought between Normandy's merchants and the Portuguese on the high seas.

Ritual Persuasion and the New King: Seyomachia

The role of the Brazilians in this naumachia is somewhat ambiguous. Masselin's text says that the Portuguese ship was sacked and pillaged by *les sauluages.*[102] The prose account makes no mention of Brazilian participation, however. Sir John Masone gives a slightly different account: the "savages," he says, came not to attack, but to defend the Portuguese:

> there was on both days a fight upon the river between two ships, the one garnished with white crosses, and the other with red; and on both the days the red-crossed ship had the worst, and was burned. Many thought, and so did I, at the beginning, the same had been made for an English ship; but it was afterwards known that it was a representation of a fight between the Portugals and the French about the old quarrel for the Isle of Brazil, which appeared openly, for that to the defense of the Portugals' ships came many naked men, their bodies all colored with red, in which sort the saying is the people used to go abroad in that country.[103]

That the Brazilians acted spontaneously in coming to the aid of the Portuguese is a distinct possibility. The Tobajaro were closely allied with the Portuguese and fierce enemies of the French. Yet if the "savages" did take an official part, Masselin's account would be more consistent than Masone's with the aims and design of the festival. That this was the case can be seen by returning to the scene which opened Henri's journey into Rouen, for in a sense, the battle between the French and the Portuguese had already been fought by the two opposing tribes inhabiting the Brazilian village. Accordingly, just as the French ship responded to the unprovoked attack by the Portuguese caravel, the Tupinamba, who were allied to the French, responded to the attack of the Tobajaro, who were allied to the Portuguese. And just as the French viciously defeated, burned, and sank their foe's ship, so too the Tupinamba overran their enemies and burned their lodges to the ground. Thus, the naumachia between the French and the Portuguese mirrored the seyomachia fought just moments before between the Tupinamba and the Tobajaro.

This parallel is not mentioned in any of the texts of the festival; the knowledge that the savages were distinguishable on the basis of their relationship with the sovereign kings of France and Portugal was perhaps imparted to the king by one of the many observers present said to have frequented the land of Brazil.[104] These alliances were common—indeed, crucial—knowledge for those who traveled there. For example, the German gunner, Hans Staden, when captured by Tupinamba (c. 1552), claimed to be allied with the French who were their friends. The Tupi's king, Konyan Bebe, did not believe Staden: "I have," he said, "already captured and eaten five Portuguese and every one of them has pretended to be French."[105] Similarly, the Tamoyos were also allied to the French. Antoine Knivet reported that when he was captured, the Tamoyos did not hesitate to massacre his Portuguese companions. Knivet was spared because he greeted his attackers in French. "You have nothing to fear," they responded, "because your ancestors have been our friends . . . , the Portuguese," however, "are our enemies and we make them slaves and that is why we have treated them as you have seen."[106]

The Tobajaro, on the other hand, were the traditional allies of the Portuguese.[107] The native Brazilians took such alliances very seriously. Jean de Léry described the Margaia—who like the Tobajaro and Tupinikin were allied to the Portuguese—as being "such enemies of the French that if they had us at their mercy, we would have paid no other ransom except being slain and cut to pieces and serving as a meal for them."[108]

The naumachia, like the seyomachia that preceded it, was a clear allusion to the struggle of Norman merchants and sailors to maintain their rights to navigate and freely trade on the open seas. More particularly, the Rouennais wanted to assert their right to trade in the land of Brazil, which they insisted was discovered by the Normans. Though Henri, like his father, harbored imperial ambitions, he was content to pursue them on European ground. In searching for profit and glory across the seas, Normandy's pirate-merchants took the lead in persuading—indeed, forcing—French kings into new spheres of conflict and competition.

By presenting the French/Portuguese naumachia and the Brazilian seyomachia to their king, the organizers of the entry were raising their particular local interests to a "national" level. Insofar as they were successful, it was by appealing both to Henri's perception of himself as a soldier king and to his dynastic ambitions as Most Christian king of France, as exemplified by his motto: *Donec totum impleat orbem.* In fashioning their festival to lobby their king, they hoped that Henri, taking their cause as his own, would reward their elaborate preparations. As they put it to him:

> You see there under your name and port
> Brazilians anchored in our harbor.
> One sees that through you all danger
> Is put to rest, so that strangers
> Can, without fear, come to our shores
> While we can go to theirs to trade.
> You see in them a heart that is equal to ours,
> To make the enemy, Portugal, flee.
> As to the country of *Guynée*
> For the glory of your great renown.
> Sire, it is not until the *caniballs,*
> Islands most disloyal to all but us,
> That we are not in good assurance
> Of the favor of your authority.[109]

As with their delegations of 1538 and 1541, the merchants of Rouen used the entry to persuade the King to support their overseas ventures in the face of the fierce opposition waged by the Portuguese and their Tobajaro surrogates. It is therefore not surprising that one of the men sent by Rouen's city council to remonstrate with François I over his ban on trade with Brazil in 1541,[110] Joseph Tasserie, was also one of the local notables singled out in the municipal archives to organize the festivities in honor of Henri's entry,[111] or that another of Rouen's most notable citizens, Pierre du Couldray, a prominent merchant involved in New World trade,[112] was recruited both to help pay for and organize the king's triumphal entry. It was perhaps a measure of the success of the Rouennais attempt to integrate their provincial war with a militantly imperial representation of their triumphant king, that shortly after his entry, the king extended and reinforced his edict of the previous year, making the importation of spices and drugs by sea the exclusive right of the port of Rouen.[113]

CHAPTER 3

Civilizing the Savage and Making a King

As we have seen, the mock war staged between the Tupinamba and the Tobajaro for Henri's entry presaged a mock naval battle enacted only moments later between French and "Portuguese" ships.[1] This narrative doubling made explicit the military alliance between the French and the Tupinamba against the Portuguese and their allies, the Tobajaro. The French-Tupinamba alliance was not simply one of strategic expediency vis-à-vis a common enemy, however, for the French saw much to be admired in their "savage" friends.

According to the chronicler of the entry, Henri was very pleased by the staged battle of the Brazilians.[2] His pleasure derived from not only the victory of the French and their New World surrogates over the Portuguese, but from his identification with the martial spirit his New World allies so consummately exemplified. Indeed, the mise-en-scène of Brazil must have appealed to Henri on an immediate and visceral level, for he too was a warrior. As the seigneur de Brantôme put it, the king was "*tout martial,*" he "ardently loved to make war";[3] or, as Blaise de Monluc matter-of-factly declared, "he was the best king whom God has ever given to soldiers."[4]

Like their king, France's nobility closely identified with chivalrous ideals, as reflected by the fashionability of works such as the *Roman de la rose* and the *Amadis de Gaule* at court.[5] The Brazilian cannibals brought to Rouen for the king's entry excelled in many of the same ideals celebrated by these influential books. As the chronicler of the entry explained, the skill and bravery of these New World barbarians surpassed even that of the ancient heroes of Troy from whom the French were said to be descended.[6]

Accordingly, Rouen's Brazilian savages were not simply displayed as a means of lobbying the king to intervene on the side of Rouen's merchant community in their ongoing conflicts with Portugal over Brazil (though, of course, this was an important reason for their inclusion), but as a mirror ideal reflecting the most deeply held values of France's nobility. This becomes clear if we view their inclusion not as an isolated event, but as part of the larger narrative of the king's *joyeuse entrée*.

FIGURE 3. Portrait of Henri II in full armor. André Thevet, *Portraits et vies des hommes illustres*. Courtesy of the Clements Library, University of Michigan.

FIGURE 4. Detail of the Figure of the Brazilians.
Cest la deduction du Somptueux ordre (Rouen, 1551).
Courtesy of the Bibliothèque Municipale de Rouen.
Photo by Thierry Ascensio Parvy.

Living Pictures and Social Narratives

The narrative of the Rouen entry was structured through a series of tableaux vivants, such as Hercules fighting a hydra, Orpheus playing his harp, and Hector bleeding from wounds inflicted by Achilles. Like the stations of the cross, or the succession of beads on a rosary, the living pictures of Henri's entry served not only as mnemonic devices that evinced a range of topical rubrics (e.g., classical texts, scriptures, genealogical myths), but as foci of image-assisted meditation that directed Henri's (and his entourage's) attention beyond the singularity of each individual display to the more profound emotional and spiritual essences informing the entry as a whole.[7] It was the king's role, in traveling from one tableau vivant to the next, to link them all together—to activate them through the connecting thread of his experience—into a coherent narrative program. Thus, the entry's tableaux vivants were more than simply discrete elements in a theatrical event meant to entertain; they were essential components in a didactic program meant to teach, and a ritual act meant to transform. The king's movement through Rouen, in this sense, can be viewed as a rite of passage, with his physical progress through the city being paralleled by an allegorical journey through a narrative that aimed to adapt the political characteristics definitive of just rulership to the particular social, intellectual, and material concerns of the provincial elites responsible for the entry.

The tableau vivant of Hercules immediately following Henri's departure from Brazil, and preceding his crossing the bridge into Rouen, played a crucial role in this regard. Half man and half god, emblem of savagery as well as of civilization, Hercules was known for his heroic strength as well as for his powers of eloquence. Like the Brazilians, he stood for—and mediated between—contrasting ideals of what it meant to be an elite in early modern France (ideals well known in literary terms as "the battle between force and eloquence").[8] Both the Brazilians and Hercules embodied values central to the identity of France's nobility, values such as bravery, strength, and skill in battle. At the same time, they evinced the humanist critique of the nobility as lacking in the most basic rudiments of civilized life. In this respect, the symmetry between the Brazilians and the military/feudal nobility points to their interchangeability in humanist strategies of self-promotion and social reform, for both were considered to be barbarians who needed to be civilized. As I will argue, it was by symbolically civilizing these objectified representations of the nobility's value system that those responsible for the entry sought to recalibrate the normative basis of elite identity and thereby their own position within French society and culture.

Civilizing the Barbarian

The meaning of the word *barbarian* derives from the Greek for one who stutters. Closely intertwined with linguistic propriety, the word was defined negatively in opposition to native fluency. From its beginnings, the category of the barbarian was defined through a xenophobic lens that characterized the foreigner as one fundamentally lacking the requisites of civilized life.[9] In the early modern period, the absence of written culture was among the principal features defining the barbarian. From the time of their discovery at the end of the fifteenth century, the warlike and savage beings from the New World were readily classified as barbarians. This is not surprising; what is, however, is that the French were as well.[10] This was especially true on the Italian peninsula.

From Charles VIII's expedition of 1494, the French repeatedly invaded and brutally conquered large portions of Italy. Powerless to thwart them on the battlefield, Italian commentators excoriated them on the field of culture.[11] As descendants of the ancient Romans, they considered themselves unquestionably superior to the warlike "barbarians" from beyond the Alps.[12] In his *La Deffence et illustration de la langue françoyse*, Joachim du Bellay explicitly refers to the Italians' low opinion of the French. As he put it, the envy of the Romans conspires against our "martial glory, the brilliance of which they cannot endure; and not only have they done us wrong by this, but to render us still more odious, *they have called us brutal, cruel and barbarous*."[13] That this charge extended to the French language was implicit in the title of du Bellay's defensive treatise.[14] Indeed, du Bellay's was but an echo of a commonly held view.[15] Castiglione, for example, expressed a similar opinion about the French; mainly, that they "recognize only the nobility of arms and reckon all the rest naught; and thus not only do they not esteem, but abhor letters, and consider all men of letters to be very base." [16]

The charge of barbarism, however, was not simply due to what Lemaire de Belges called the *mesprisance accoustumée* of the Italians, but was widely shared among elites in Europe.[17] In his influential book, *De pueris statim ac liberaliter instituendis declamatio,* Erasmus wrote that a German boy could easily

> learn French in a few months quite unconsciously while absorbed in other activities. . . . [And] if one can learn with such ease *a language as barbarous and irregular as French, in which spelling does not agree with pronunciation, and which has harsh sounds and accents that hardly fall within the realm of human speech,* then how much more easily should one be able to learn Greek and Latin?[18]

The notion that the French language was uncivilized and barbarous was also an opinion shared by the French themselves. Thus the great humanist and moving force behind the Collège de France (also known as the Collège Royal), Guillaume Budé, came to lament that his compatriots believed themselves to be "unsuited to letters, in contrast to the Italians, whose sky and soil enabled even infants to wail eloquently and poetically."[19]

Yet, despite its sting, or perhaps because of it, the charge of cultural barbarism provoked a strong nationalist reaction among the French; this proved to be an energizing force in the rise of vernacular consciousness.[20] Men such as Tory, Dolet, Lemaire de Belges, Estienne, Budé, du Bellay, and Rouen's own Pierre Fabri, took it upon themselves to reform, standardize, and, more generally, to "civilize" the orthography, grammar, pronunciation, and usage of their mother tongue. Dolet, in his book *La Maniere de bien traduire d'une langue en aultre,* summed up the tenor of this quest: "Take my labor joyously in hand and completely reform our language, for by this means and this beginning we will, in the end, succeed such that *foreigners will no longer call us barbarians.*"[21]

A Barbarous University and a Civilized College

Though the movement to reinvent French culture on a humanist model was embraced at the upper levels of the courtly aristocracy under François I, it was not exclusive to court circles, to famous debates between well-known figures, or to the capital, for it was clearly manifested in the narrative of Henri II's provincial entry into Rouen. Thus, for example, in the final pageant of the entry, François I was depicted as finding lasting peace and repose in the Elysian Fields through his support of arts and letters.[22] A placard decorating the tableau explained:

> This is the repose of happy paradise
> Of kings enamored with learning,
> François the first is freed and delivered
> And Henri the second will want to follow him
> Good memory has made this place for them.[23]

Not only did François restore the ancient knowledge of Greek, Latin, and Hebrew books, the chronicler of the entry explains, but he supported men capable of understanding and expounding upon them. Among his most virtuous deeds, he continues, was the building of a large and magnificent college at the University of Paris.[24] Henri was similarly lauded for his support of learning and for having increased by half the number of readers at his university.[25] The allusion here is not to the University of Paris, however, but to the Collège de France; thus the goddess of Good Memory handed Henri II a book commemorating the good deeds of his father written in the three languages that formed the core of the Collège's interests: Hebrew, Greek, and Latin.[26]

Depending directly on the patronage of the king, the royal readers at the Collège were granted an unprecedented degree of independence from the University of Paris. It was through this relative autonomy that they were able to turn the disciplinary hierarchy of the university on its head and elevate the status of the inferior disciplines of rhetoric, grammar, and eloquence to a level of importance previously held only by the representatives of scholastic philosophy and theology at the Sorbonne. This change in status contributed to the development of the Collège as a counterweight to the university's monopoly over the study of theology.[27] Not surprisingly, humanist incursions into theology were fervently opposed by the doctors at the University of Paris.[28] This resistance was written into law with the 1542 edict giving the Faculty of Theology wide-ranging powers of censorship. Among those works prohibited were treatises on grammar, rhetoric, logic, or *lettres humaines* that referred to Christian doctrine.[29] Increasingly, the response of the doctors at the Sorbonne to the challenge posed by the Collège was to associate its royal readers with heresy and Lutheranism.[30] On the other hand, the king's readers, their associates, and sympathizers at large characterized the scholastics at the university as barbarians.[31] In the words of Ulrich Zwingli, the scholastics at the University of Paris were "even more cruel than veritable savage beasts."[32] Similarly, Erasmus' *Antibarbarorum liber* consisted in a sustained attack against the representatives of scholasticism. Here, Erasmus' mouthpiece, Jacob Batt, styled himself as nothing less than

FIGURE 5. Theater of the Pont de Robec, the Elysian Fields, from Henri's entry into Rouen. *Cest la deduction du Somptueux ordre* (Rouen, 1551). Courtesy of the Bibliothèque Municipale de Rouen. Photo by Thierry Ascensio Parvy.

Hercules defending the humanist curriculum against the barbarism of the schools.[33]

For humanists, the theologians at the university occupied a position similar to the ancestral warrior nobility: both were likened to barbarians who actively impeded the progress of humanist culture in France.[34] The comparison between humanist struggles in favor of the New Learning and Hercules fighting the barbarians was a commonplace one in polemics against the university. Hercules' appeal, no doubt, derived much of its force from his association with the already well-established and powerful traditions that linked him with the great houses of the feudal nobility.

Indeed, before he became the champion of the humanist cause, Hercules had a long and venerable history. In the early fifteenth century he was held up as an emblem of the warrior prince for the House of Este.[35] In Burgundy, a knightly Hercules was said to be a distant ancestor, founding the royal line through his marriage to Alise, whom he met after departing from Spain.[36] The house of Navarre traced its origins to Hercules' nephew, Hispalus.[37] Toward the end of the century, the emperor Maximilien was portrayed as the ancient warrior, Hercules Germanicus.[38] Similarly, in his royal entry into Vienna in 1490, the French king Charles VIII, was presented as the "worthy Duke" and "knight" Hercules, who fought a dragon plaguing the garden of France.[39] Not long afterward, in 1492, the genealogical connection between the French kings and Hercules was elaborated in detail by Joannes Annius of Viterbo in his *De his quae praecesserunt inundationem terrarum*. Claiming that he had discovered an ancient text by Berosus Babylonicus, Annius' book declares that Hercules founded Gaul through his marriage to Galatea, daughter of a Celtic king and ancestor of the royal houses of France. Some years later, the king's poet, Jean Lemaire de Belges, relied on the authority of the pseudo-Berosus to establish a firm genealogical link between Hercules and French royalty in his widely read ethnogenetic fable, *Illustration de Galle et singularitez de Troye*.[40]

The Hercules who championed the humanist virtues of eloquence and prudence against the barbarians of the universities and the old nobility clearly had very little in common with his more chivalrous counterpart. If he was to become an emblem for the humanist battle against the barbarians, Hercules himself would have to be transformed: he would have to be civilized.

Hercules the Mediator

Hercules represented the man-god-ancestor who embodied the chivalrous ideals of strength, fortitude, and bravery. As such, he became emblematic of the opposition to the rising social power of France's new civic-cultural elite. At the same time, as the status of these new elites grew, they increasingly came to challenge the normative ideals with which their royal benefactors most identified. This can be seen in the appropriation and transformation of Hercules for their own purposes. Deployed strategically, the figure of Hercules became a potent symbolic weapon in the struggles to redefine French elite identity.[41] Thus alongside the Hercules who represented the knightly virtues, appeared a new Hercules who represented ideals of eloquence, civility, and prudence. His presence in the Rouen entry on the bridge immediately following the mise-en-scène of Brazil signified the pivotal importance he had in the king's journey toward the humanist ideal of virtue, as represented by François I in the Elysian Fields at the entry's end. This is not to say that the humanistically conceived Hercules supplanted the chivalrous/feudal Hercules, but that the former undermined the latter's authority to establish definitively the values and qualities normative of elite identity.

A landmark in the transformation of Hercules from the image of a barbarian to avatar of humanist values was the publication of Erasmus' Latin translation of Lucian's *Heracles* (1506). In this work, as in subsequent French translations by Guillaume Budé and Geoffroy Tory, the form and content of Hercules was fundamentally altered. Where in 1464 Raoul Lefèvre wrote of Hercules as a chivalrous knight, Erasmus went back to Lucian to find an image of Hercules consonant with humanist ideals of eloquence and prudence. According to Lucian's account, the people of Gaul believed that "the real Heracles was a wise man who achieved everything by eloquence and applied persuasion as his principal force." He then described a pictorial representation of Hercules that he claimed to have seen in his travels through Gaul:

> That old Heracles of theirs drags after him a great crowd of men who are all tethered by the ears. His leashes are delicate chains fashioned of gold and amber, resembling the prettiest of necklaces. Yet, though led by bonds so weak, the men do not think of escaping as they easily could. . . . In fact, they follow cheerfully and joyously. . . . But let me tell you what seemed to me the strangest thing of all. Since the painter had no place to which he could attach the ends of the chains, as the god's right hand already held the club and his left the bow, he pierced the tip of his tongue and represented him drawing the men by that means.[42]

Through Erasmus' translation, this image gained wide currency, especially in France. Pictured in the emblem books of Corrozet and Aneau, written about by Tory, Budé, Rabelais, du Bellay, and Ronsard among others, the eloquent Gallic Hercules was represented as leading the four estates of

FIGURE 6. The Gallic Hercules. Geoffroy Tory, *Champ fleury. Au quel est contenu Lart et Science de la deue et vraye proportion des lettres attiques, quon dit autrement lettres antiques, et vulgairement lettres romaines proportionnees selon le corps et visage humain* (Paris, 1529). Courtesy of the British Library.

France from savagery to civilization by golden chains that extended from his tongue to their ears.[43]

What Erasmus saw as a timely device for reviving the ancient ideal of eloquence—and as emblematic of humanist struggle against scholasticism—was also a didactic attempt to reform and civilize a preexisting symbol of elite identity, and by extension elites themselves.[44] Accordingly, the Gallic Hercules made his appearance in court pageantry early in the sixteenth century, as for example, in the royal entry held for François I in Rouen (1517). François, in particular, was closely identified with the Gallic Hercules—an association that continued even after his death. Thus, for his son's royal entry into Paris in 1549, François was presented as the Hercules "who made flower in his realm Hebrew, Greek, Latin, Italian, Spanish, German and even the French language, which had previously been extremely savage and rude."[45] Reborn as king of France, the Gallic Hercules could now triumph over his nemesis, Fortune, and inscribe the destiny of his reign and his people in immortal memory. He would do this not by force, but by his powers of eloquence and persuasion. As du Bellay implored his readers at the end of his *La Deffence et illustration de la langue françoyse*: "Remember . . . your Gallic

Hercules who drew the nations after him by their ears with a chain attached to his tongue."

It is perhaps not a coincidence that one of the men chosen by Rouen's city council to create something special for Henri II's entry was Claude Chappuys, author of a booklet entitled, *Le Grand Hercule gallique . . .* (1545).[46] Chappuys was a poet, courtier, chamberlain, and librarian to François I.[47] Prior to this, he was a member of the household of Jean du Bellay.[48] From 1537 until his death, he was the *chanoine* of the Cathedral of Notre Dame in Rouen. He nevertheless spent little time in Rouen before the accession of Henri II, preferring to live at court instead. No stranger to either the court or its ceremonial, he wrote the well-known tract, *Discours de la cour*, and penned an account of Charles V's travels through France that was included in a manuscript collection dedicated to Charles' French royal entries.[49] Later, in his capacity as *chantre de la chambre du roi*, he assisted at the funeral of François I, and then witnessed the crowning of the new king, about which he was to write a detailed chronicle.[50] Because of these qualifications, he was an obvious candidate to help organize Henri's entry festival. The choice of Chappuys was particularly apt because of his apparent influence on Henri's royal entry in Paris the previous year. The description of François I as the Gallic Hercules in the Parisian entry (cited above) followed the text of Chappuys' *Le Grand Hercule gallique* word-for-word in its portrayal of François as a new Hercules who revived the study of languages and civilized (the) French.[51] Indeed, it was this same theme of social and linguistic reform that structured the narrative of Henri's entry into Rouen.

A Narrative of Civilization

Immediately following the tableau vivant of Brazil, Henri was presented with the figure of Orpheus seated deep within a grotto at the entry to the bridge leading into Rouen. Orpheus, as the son of Apollo and Calliope, muse of eloquence, poetry, and rhetoric, was closely associated with the civilizing powers of language. Not only was he able to tame wild beasts with the merest touch of his harp, but he was said to have led mankind out of savagery and into civilization through the sheer force of his eloquence.[52] As Jacques Lefèvre d'Étaples said of him: "by means of lute and song Orpheus tamed the passions of wild beasts, which means that by singing to the accompaniment of his lyre he reduced the savage customs and practices of men to those of temperate humanity."[53] In Henri's entry it was the harp of Orpheus that calmed the raging sea, making it possible for the king to cross over the bridge and continue his journey from "Brazil" into Rouen.[54]

Though Orpheus civilized Man, it was Hercules who civilized the most distant ancestors of the French, the Celts. Thus, next to Orpheus, Henri saw himself as Hercules slaying a seven-headed hydra. The poem accompanying the scene explained:

> Your royal majesty, O very Christian King,
> You are, for the good of all, a Hercules on earth,
> Who puts the cruel Adder of Mars into disarray,
> Who honorably establishes peace in place of war. . . . [55]

Though the hydra which Hercules fought was explicitly related to the conquering of Mars, the god of war, and though it was also a clear reference to both Lutheranism and the taming of the often unruly *menu* people (the metaphor of the populace as a many-headed monster being a constant trope in municipal and parliamentary records),[56] the hydra was also commonly associated with sophistry. Among stalwarts of the New Learning, the charge of sophistry was frequently leveled against the doctors at the University of Paris, as for example, in Rabelais' *Gargantua,* or a letter of the Swiss Humanist, Henricus Glareanus, to Erasmus in which he describes the doctors of the Sorbonne as "sophists who impede all progress."[57] Similarly Erasmus, in a letter to Etienne Poncher, bishop of Paris, remarked that Glareanus does battle with no less spirit than Hercules in fighting against those "prickly sophisters," the scholastic theologians of the University of Paris.[58] Or again, in a letter to the Jacques Toussaint, royal reader in Greek at the Collège de France, Erasmus boasts that he was among the first to provoke the vehement attacks of that hydra of the old learning against the study of languages and good letters.[59] Likewise, in Barthélemy Aneau's translation of Alciati's *Emblemata,* the figure of Hercules fighting a hydra was accompanied by verses that explained that the "vain arguments of the Sophists would be confounded more by eloquence than by force."[60]

Upon leaving the grotto, the king continued along the route of his narrative. As he crossed the old bridge leading into the city, he watched the battle between French and Portuguese ships. On the bridge, he met Neptune and other lesser gods of the sea, receiving from them dominion over the oceans, as signified by the gift of a trident. Afterwards, the poet Arion, who is said to have invented the dithyramb (a choral poem performed at Dionysian rites) rode past on a dolphin. Then, Neptune reappeared, this time riding across the Seine in a triumphal chariot/boat pulled by two hippopotami, in the company of Calliope's three daughters—the sirens Ligia, Parthenope, and Leucosia. Henri's maritime power, the Rouennais seemed to be saying, rested not only on the French naval victory over the Portuguese, but on the patronage of ocean gods, ancient poets, and the daughters of Rhetoric.

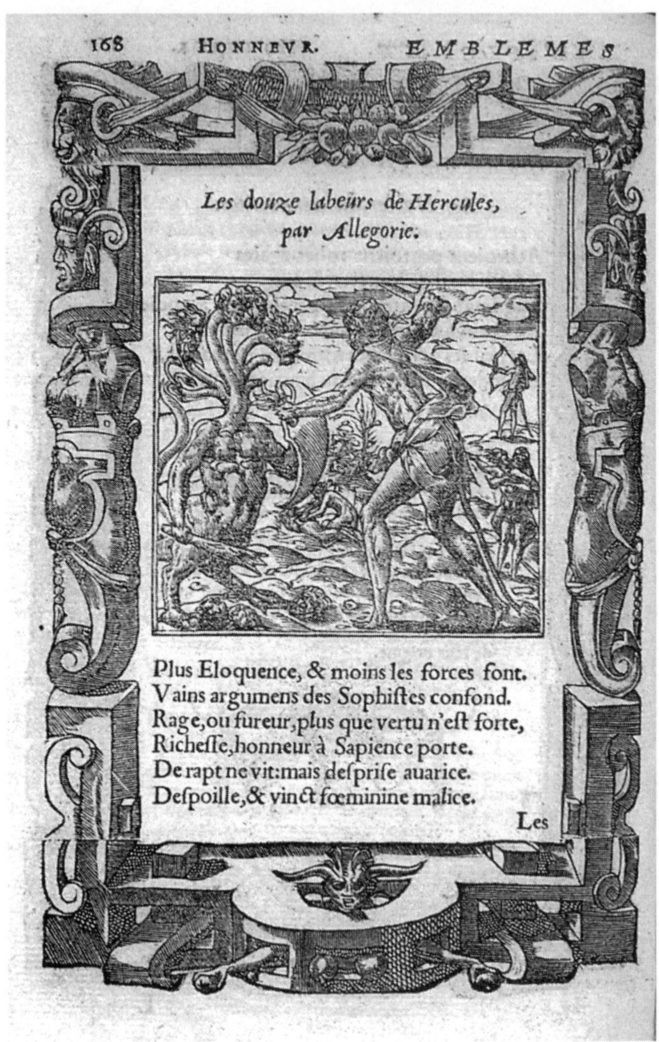

FIGURE 8. Hercules fighting the hydra. Barthélemy Aneau's *Emblèmes d'Alciat* (Lyon, 1549). Courtesy of the Getty Research Library, Los Angeles.

FIGURE 9. Detail of the Triumph of the River from Henri II's entry into Rouen. *Cest la deduction du Somptueux ordre* (Rouen, 1551). Courtesy of the Bibliothèque Municipale de Rouen. Photo by Thierry Ascensio Parvy.

As the king and his entourage crossed over the bridge and approached the city's gate, they came to a triumphal arch. On its summit stood the figure of Saturn, who was made to look like the king. In his right hand was a placard with the following verses:

> I am the golden age
> By honor reinvested
> I am in virtue
> And will be again.[61]

Beneath him were words engraved in gold:

> The golden age, which flourished
> Before the silver, the iron and the
>   copper
> By the virtues of a king will rise into the
>   world
> And begin to live again.[62]

It was then explained to the king that it was through his support of arts and letters that he would—like Saturn—restore the world to a golden age of peace and tranquility.

The first tableau that the king witnessed upon his entry into Rouen depicted Henri's distant ancestor, the wounded Hector, with his blood spouting into the air to form the king's device: a triple crescent. A placard explained that Hector's bloodline would, as heaven had ordained, live on through Henri to fill the world. This was an obvious reference to the king's motto, *Donec totum impleat orbem*, which was stitched into the canopy being

FIGURE 10. Tableau vivant of Saturn at the entryway to the city from Henri II's entry into Rouen. *Cest la deduction du Somptueux ordre* (Rouen, 1551). Courtesy of the Bibliothèque Municipale de Rouen. Photo by Thierry Ascensio Parvy.

FIGURE 11. Tableau vivant of Hector from Henri II's entry into Rouen. *Cest la deduction du Somptueux ordre* (Rouen, 1551). Courtesy of the Bibliothèque Municipale de Rouen. Photo by Thierry Ascensio Parvy.

held above him during the entry.[63] As the physical embodiment of Lemaire de Belges's genealogy of France, Hector was a potent symbol of French nationalism, serving to undercut Italian claims to cultural superiority based on their Roman ancestry. Not only was Hector's Troy chronologically prior to Rome, but its civilization was thought to be manifestly superior. The Romans, after all, only imitated the greatness of the Greeks (and presumably the Trojans); they did not originate it.[64]

The next pageant on the king's itinerary was entitled the "Theater of the Cross." On the lower part of a two-tiered stage his father's insignia, a salamander engulfed in flames, was depicted; according to the chronicler, it signified the immortal glory that François had won as father of arts and letters in France. Above, Henri found a likeness of himself balanced on a crescent moon. A vine grew from his heart and filled the stage's expanse with its fruit. Kneeling on either side and before him were peoples from many nations who gathered to receive the sweet liqueur of *amyable confederation et obeissance* dripping from the fruited vine.[65] Building on the imperial themes illustrated by Hector moments before, Henri was here presented with a vision of himself as the Christ-like king whose blood would bring salvation and redemption to all humanity. The Theater of the Cross thus completed in Christological terms the entry's promise that Henri would

> convert rude and uncivil enemies to gentleness and humanity, either by force or by reason, and being the terrestrial monarch, restore the Golden Age of Saturn, and rise, as the very Christian king, to time everlasting, despite any and all misfortune.[66]

Next, the king moved on to the pont de Robec, where he discovered the final pageant of the entry—the Elysian fields of the terrestrial paradise. One of the poems accompanying this tableau made explicit the relation among Hercules' labors, the king's support of the new learning, and his attainment of immortal glory:

> Through his efforts, Hercules prevailed
> Over loathsome monsters to achieve a
>   victorious end,
> By which he secured immeasurable glory,
> And thus learned kings are by Good
>   memory,
> In sure repose, translated up to the
>   heavens.[67]

FIGURE 12. Theater of the Cross from Henri II's entry into Rouen. *Cest la deduction du Somptueux ordre* (Rouen, 1551). Courtesy of the Bibliothèque Municipale de Rouen. Photo by Thierry Ascensio Parvy.

A Composite Hercules and a New Nobility

According to the Imperial ambassador, Henri's entry praised François I "for having restored letters and saved [Rouen] from barbarism" while encouraging Henri to follow in his footsteps.[68] However, it was not simply Rouen that was being led from barbarism and into civilization, for the entry cast Henri in the messianic role of leading all the diverse peoples of the world toward the Elysian fields of peace, tranquillity, and Edenic repose.[69]

Yet, the entry's message was neither so clear nor so unambiguous as this. Like Hercules, the entry was a hybrid of conflicting values. At a time when the self-perception of large sections of the ancestral nobility maintained a close connection to the feudal values of the warrior knight,[70] it would have been both a dangerous and an ineffective strategy for the organizers of the entry to try to persuade the king simply to forgo his chivalrous/military ideals in favor of the Ciceronian values represented by the Gallic Hercules. The aptness of Hercules for the entry's delicate task of mediation once again becomes evident when we consider that his identity reflected many of the same ambiguities found in the entry's narrative.

In the sixteenth century, there were two different versions of Hercules. The first (often referred to as the Lybian Hercules) was embraced by the feudal nobility; he represented the warrior virtues of prowess, valor, and chivalrous honor. The second, by contrast, was renowned for his ability to persuade through eloquence and was known—after Lucian's description— as the Gallic Hercules. That the Gallic Hercules triumphed in France was at least in part due to the power of his humanist exponents to project their interests onto an established figural form. It was also due to the dynastic competition with François' bitter enemy, Emperor Charles V, who closely associated himself with the Lybian version of Hercules.[71] In this sense, humanists in France mirrored the tactics that their Italian counterparts employed in response to repeated French invasions at the beginning of the century; that is, they responded to Charles' military superiority on the cultural level by depicting François as the Gallic Hercules who—through his support of arts and letters—would, in contrast to Charles (the barbarian), lead mankind to a new golden age.

Despite his many cultural accomplishments, it was François' ignominious defeat and capture at Pavia that must have weighed on his son's mind. Henri paid dearly for his father's failure, for at the age of seven he was sent to Spain as a hostage. He was to remain there for over four years while the king reluctantly negotiated the treaty of Cambrai. François' repeated impotence in the face of the military challenges from Charles V and Henry VIII (to whom he lost the port city of Boulogne) was hardly a legacy that his son wanted to continue. Upon his accession the new king acted quickly to distinguish his reign from that of his father's. In what Baumgartner has referred to as a veritable "revolution at court," Henri decisively rejected the values of eloquence and artistic achievement embraced by François in favor of a policy of war and a revival of chivalric values.[72] From its beginnings, Henri's rule was characterized by the resurgent power of the ancestral nobility—with Henri coming to be known as the "Father of the Nobility,"[73] just as François I had been known as "Father of the Arts and Letters." The very first expression of his reign was that of conquest, war, and vengeance.

He began by reinstating Montmorency, the man who arranged for his ransom and negotiated his release from his Spanish prison. In quick order, he renewed France's alliance with Scotland, sending the Maréchal d'Essé with six thousand troops to rescue the six-year-old Mary Queen of Scots from the English.[74] He then sent Montmorency to Bordeaux to exact brutal revenge for the rebellion against the salt tax—the *gabelle*;[75] and he besieged Boulogne, forcing the English to come to terms and give up the city that his father had lost. Clearly, the eloquent Gallic Hercules, who preferred the force of words to that of arms, was not an apposite model for the new king.

Fortunately, another Hercules had begun to emerge toward the end of François' reign. In Chappuys' *Le Grand Hercule gallique*, for example, François was described as merging the persuasive qualities of the Gallic Hercules with the warlike attributes of the Libyan Hercules. This composite of the chivalric and the humanist Hercules particularly suited Henri's desire to distinguish his reign from that of his father. This was made explicit in Henri's 1549 entry into Paris, for while the late king was presented as the Gallic Hercules, the municipal records explained to Henri that there were in fact

> two Hercules, the one from Libya, who fought a number of monsters with his strength—his valor bringing him praise; the other was from Gaule, who was endowed with eloquence, prudence and justice and who led the Celts from the open fields into enclosed cities, teaching them to live together and how to wage war. But *these two are combined to make a third, perfectly assembled in you*; and that which Libya and Gaule had, and that which they did not have, are recovered for France in you.[76]

Hercules, thus divided and reassembled, was a site of contestation and mediation; as such, he embodied and came to arbitrate the social aspirations and self-understandings of two rival—though increasingly interdependent—groups.[77] Seen from this perspective, the scene from the Rouen entry in which Orpheus and the Muses were juxtaposed with Hercules fighting a

hydra merged the Gallic with the Libyan Hercules in order to present Henri
with an image of kingship that joined military prowess to humanist ideals of
eloquence, prudence, and justice. While he represented a trajectory leading
away from the naked savagery of Brazil and toward a humanistic ideal of the
New Learning as exemplified by the entry's final tableau, the Elysian Fields,
he was also a fierce warrior whose exploits embodied all the virtues of military prowess so admired by the old nobility, as exemplified by the entry's beginnings in the "New World." In other words, Henri's ceremonial itinerary
from the perfect warriors represented by the Brazilians to an ideal of humanist *civilité* represented by the apotheosis of François I, was mirrored by a
movement from the chivalric/military ideals characteristic of France's old
feudal nobility to the Ciceronian/humanist values of its new civic-cultural
elite. This was not a linear trajectory, however, for it was characterized less by
the asymmetries of bipolar opposition than by a kind of mediated ambiguity whereby "civilized" and "savage," "cultured" and "barbarian," "high" and
"low" were dialogically present both as exoticized and as normalized components of French elite identity.[78] It is by paying close attention to these ambiguities and to the various and complex ways they were mediated that we
can move beyond a superficial understanding of the Brazilian mise-en-scène
(e.g., as anecdotal evidence of the sixteenth century "culture of curiosity")
to understand something of its place in the larger social and political context
of early modern France.

The Endless Circle and the Hall of Mirrors

Henri as king, like Hercules of ancient myth, had embarked on a civilizing journey, converting not only his rude and uncivil enemies, but his
rude, uncivil, and divided people into citizens of a common land: France.
Rouen was but one stop on his extended itinerary around his realm. Henri
made over twenty-eight royal entries in the years immediately following his
accession,[79] and just as his physical presence in Rouen acted as the link
connecting the entry's separate tableaux vivants into a coherent narrative
program, so too, his pilgrimage to the various metropoles of his realm aimed
to enact and embody the imaginary of the *patria* that he was said to represent. Yet, as the entry makes clear, just as his civilizing mission aimed to extend his rule throughout the disparate regions of his realm, so too it would
efface the distance that separated the Old World from the New. Indeed, the
national and imperial themes articulated by the entry placed Henri firmly
in the role of the Last World Emperor (the Christ-like Hercules) who would
found a new world order—a terrestrial paradise not unlike the one that

awaited him at the entry's end. Hercules was, after all, as Claude-Gilbert Dubois has pointed out:

> a voyager without frontiers, who united the Orient with the Occident, and who brought together under his name and his authority the entire world. He founded cities, not as capitals of nations, but as universal metropoles.[80]

This point is worth pursuing, for it brings us back, full circle, to the Brazilians who began Henri's journey. Given the close association between the New World, its peoples, and the terrestrial paradise of the Golden Age, the position of Hercules at the bridge beginning Henri's journey can be said to have presaged his return at the end. In this sense, the king's pilgrimage from Brazil to the Elysian Fields was less a linear trajectory moving from the extreme poles of savagery to civilization than the closing of a circle. For both the first and the last pageants represented different versions of similar ideals: Edenic paradise, the return to the Golden Age, a merging of the savage and the civilized and a union of two ideals of elite identity.

If Hercules embraced the fundamentally contradictory dispositions of the Renaissance humanist and the feudal warrior, then peoples from the New World embodied similar contradictions. That the Brazilians were valiant and courageous warriors was amply demonstrated by the battle fought between the Tobajaro and the Tupinamba at the beginning of the entry. As the author of the prose account describes them, they were so accomplished in the military arts that they "surpassed the skills of Meryonez the Greek and Pandarus the Trojan."[81] Some years later, writing about several Brazilians he met while in Rouen (1562), Montaigne affirmed this impression. As he put it, their "warfare is wholly noble and generous, and as excusable and beautiful as this human disease can be; its only basis among them is their rivalry in valor."[82] According to Montaigne, there were only two articles of faith in the ethical economy of the savage: "valor against the enemy and love for their wives."[83] Such chivalric values would surely have struck a resonant chord with nobles who located their social identity in terms of military prowess.[84] As Montaigne said: as "for boldness and courage, as for firmness, constancy, resoluteness against pains and hunger and death, I would not fear to oppose the examples I could find among them to the most famous ancient examples that we have in memories of our world on this side of the ocean."[85]

Naked but for his lion skin and club, Hercules appeared every bit the savage, yet as an emblem of proper governance, he symbolized not simply the ferocity of brute strength, but power derived from eloquence. Even in this respect, if we accept Montaigne's judgment, the Brazilians also embodied many of the ideals championed by humanists and personified by the Gallic

Hercules. As he puts it: the Brazilian's "language . . . is a soft [*doux*] language, with an agreeable sound, somewhat like Greek in its endings."[86] Accordingly, Montaigne seeks to demonstrate the refinement of the Tupi language by quoting from one of their love songs:

> Adder, stay; stay, adder, that from the pattern of your coloring my sister may draw the fashion and the workmanship of a rich girdle that I may give to my love; so may your beauty and your pattern be forever preferred to all other serpents.[87]

Arguing from the authority of his personal knowledge of poetry, Montaigne maintains that this Tupi song—far from being barbaric in its conception—was reminiscent of Anacreon, the much emulated Greek poet whose verse was to inspire members of the *Pléiade* throughout the 1550s and 1560s with its grace, elegance, and delicacy.[88]

Similarly, the Protestant minister, Jean de Léry, who took part in the unsuccessful efforts to found a French colony in Brazil (1555–1560), made a related point regarding the similarity of the Tupi and Greek languages. In his introduction to a dialogue he claimed to have had with a native Brazilian, Léry deferred to the judgment of an interpreter who had lived in Brazil for "seven or eight years and understood the language perfectly." This interpreter, Léry explains, "had studied considerably, and even knew some Greek; therefore, since this nation of Tupinamba has drawn several words from that language (as those who understand it have already been able to observe), he could explain it all the better."[89]

Thus, in a number of respects, the "savages" from Brazil shared key attributes of the antique models associated with elite identity.[90] Significantly, this brought them within the same conceptual space occupied by Hercules.[91] This is remarkably confirmed by the early-seventeenth-century explorer of Brazil, Marc Lescarbot, who described the Brazilians by comparing them to pictures he had seen *"of Hercules, who killed a lion, and put the skin on his back."*[92] As an emblem of kingship, Hercules was related not only to Henri II, but to Henri's counterpart and ally across the seas, the Brazilian king, Quoniambec. Accordingly, in his gallery of history's most esteemed rulers, André Thevet not only included such men as Alexander, Caesar, François I and Henri II, but also Quoniambec, whom he describes as a kind of New World Hercules.[93] According to Thevet, Quoniambec, dressed in the skin of a lion and carrying a club, was "one much esteemed by his enemies, the *Margageas*, the Portuguese and his other enemies for the unbending force of his massive body; but who was feared much more for his prudence and good grace."[94]

FIGURE 13. The Brazilian Hercules, Quoniambec. André Thevet, *Portraits et vies des hommes illustres*. Courtesy of the Clements Library, University of Michigan.

This utterly alien being—a cannibal, a giant, a savage whose body was covered with tattoos and whose face was pierced and set with polished stones of emerald green and white—was also a Hercules, and as such, a mirror, despite his "otherness," of kingship and nobility.

CHAPTER 4

The Social Poetics of the Triumph

The royal entry festival was an enactment of the literary tradition of the speculum principis, or "mirror of princes," which described the virtues upon which the king was to model his actions.[1] As Roy Strong has pointed out, "the fête enabled the ruler and his court to assimilate themselves momentarily to their heroic exemplars. For a time they actually became the 'ideas' of which they were but terrestrial reflections."[2] This was true not only for kings and the members of their court, but also for those who wrote, organized, and directed these festivities. Indeed, mirrors made for princes reflected others as well.

In the previous chapter the image-idea of Hercules was used as a key to unlock the complex semiotic structure of the entry's narrative; this narrative aimed at creating a symbolic bridge between two different—though increasingly interdependent—notions of elite identity: that of the warrior and that of the learned and eloquent prince. Like that image-idea, but of far greater currency, the triumph itself, after which Henri's entry was fashioned, had an analogous function—representing ideals both of France's feudal nobility and those of its new civic-cultural elite. The triumph, like Hercules, was not simply a representation of these conjoined ideals, but a site of strategic mediation—a place where divergent aspects of elite culture were articulated, negotiated, and contested. The triumph's ability to mediate between these different ideals made it a potent resource in ongoing attempts to reformulate elite identity in early modern France. Its significance cannot be underestimated. At the time of Henri's entry, triumphs could be seen at practically every turn in Rouen: in bas-relief decorating the homes of its most prominent citizens; in the windows of its most important churches; in the city's public spaces and monuments; and in the poetry of a local poetry society called the *Puy de Palinod*. If in the previous chapter Hercules was the analytic key used to unlock the narrative sequence plotting Henri's journey through Rouen, in this chapter, the triumph will provide a key to a different door—that leading into the sociocultural world inhabited by the individuals who planned his itinerary and acted as his guides. (See Plate 7.)

Architectures of Triumph: Gaillon

Though triumphs were something of a commonplace in Italy of the late fifteenth century,[3] in France they were practically unheard of. The Normans were the first to incorporate them into their civic and ceremonial practice.[4] The immense interest that the triumph was to inspire can be traced to the influence of Cardinal Georges d'Amboise, governor of Normandy and archbishop of Rouen.

Around the same time that France discovered the New World, it also discovered Renaissance Italy. As with the New World, this discovery also was a conquest. In 1507, Cardinal Georges d'Amboise accompanied his friend, King Louis XII, on a crusading voyage to the Italian peninsula. By all accounts, d'Amboise was impressed by what he saw, and upon his return to Normandy, he systematically sought to translate his newfound taste to his château at Gaillon, filling it with the booty—the paintings, the tapestries, and the books—that he had acquired there.[5] D'Amboise's interest extended beyond books and objets d'art, however, to include Italian architectural accomplishments as well; he thus took great pains and spared no expense to import the best local and Italian architects, builders, sculptors, painters, and artisans to work on his château.[6]

According to Roberto Weiss, Gaillon was the "earliest large-scale example of the Italian impact upon French ways of building. . . . " It was, he continued, meant to demonstrate that the French could "produce buildings second to none in grace and elegance."[7] Arguing that Gaillon marked France's progress toward the cultural achievements of the Italian Renaissance, Weiss has seen the Cardinal's château as a gauge by which to measure Italy's influence on France. In his view, Gaillon was a symbol of French pride: a statement proclaiming that France was capable of mimicking the best that Italy had to offer in art, architecture, and literature. This view, however, misstates the contemporary significance of Gaillon. Far from being a modest assertion of equality, Gaillon was a clear and unambiguous declaration of French superiority—of victory and triumph—over the Italians.[8]

Majestic up on high, Gaillon looks down, across, and over the Eure valley. Its monumental gothic design was syncretically transformed in the early sixteenth century to integrate—and express—Renaissance ideals of classical antiquity—in particular, the idea of triumph. The triumphal arch, which in the nineteenth century was to become a commonplace emblem of French cultural and military power, was first brought to France in the sixteenth. It made its debut at Gaillon, built by the cardinal to greet Louis XII and Anne de Bretagne to his château in October of 1508.[9] Shortly before the king's arrival, the Rouennais architect Pierre Fain transformed the essentially gothic design of the entrance pavilion into an *arc triumphant*.[10] Passing through this arch and into the *avant cour* of the château there was another arch—one specially built to commemorate Louis XII's victory over Genoa. This *arc de triomphe* was called the *Porte de Gênes*. Carved above the arch was a gilded relief depicting Louis' Genoese triumph.[11] This arch formed the entryway into the château's *Cour d'Honneur*; here, according to contemporary accounts, were several friezes reproducing Mantegna's famous *Triumphs of Caesar*.[12] These were not the only referents to triumph in the château, for its interior walls and engaged pilasters were also embellished with triumphal themes and motifs.[13] Clearly the grammar of the château's design was meant to call forth a comparison between the accomplishments of the Caesars of ancient Rome and the triumphs of the French king. To further solidify this association, the cour d'honneur was decorated with forty-two marble medallions depicting ancient Roman emperors, antique warriors, and the most renowned kings of France, including—of course—Louis XII.[14]

Gaillon was an architectural emblem exemplifying the translation of political and cultural power from the decadence of the Mediterranean world to northern France. By integrating Louis' triumphs into its very structure and design, the château was nothing less than a physical monument to French military and cultural superiority. From the time of Louis XII's suppression of the Genoese revolt in 1507, French imperial ambitions in Italy were recast in terms of a civilizing crusade against a less-than-human opponent. Thus the Norman poet, Jean Marot, wrote of the rebellious Genoese in terms that were identical to those used to describe the "savage" inhabitants of the New World; they are, he said, a people "without faith [and] without law—more so than any other nation."[15] Pushing the trope of the savage still further, Marot characterized the Genoese as ruthless and bloodthirsty cannibals who indiscriminately "put to death any French they could find, not only men but women . . . committing upon them acts of perverse inhumanity . . . , eating their hearts . . . and other deeds so evil that I dare not describe them."[16] Utterly dehumanized, the Genoese (and by extension, all Italians) were little better than animals. As such, they were clearly in need of the benefices of French culture.

Seen from the perspective of France's ongoing transalpine ambitions, Gaillon's triumphs were an unequivocal declaration of the preeminence of French "civilization"; they not only justified the use of military force in terms of the moral mission of crusade, but they physically embodied the victory of French culture over the savagery and barbarism of their neighbors to the south.

Translations: Petrarch, Rouen, and Literary Civilization

Savagery and barbarism were to be tamed not only by force, however, but as Henri's entry—and the figure of Hercules—made clear, by the powers of eloquence and learning. No work was more influential in communicating this ideal to France than Petrarch's *Trionfi*. According to the French humanist, Jean Despautère, it was Petrarch who "opened war against the barbarians, . . . recalled the Muses who had fled, [and] . . . vehemently excited the study of eloquence."[17] Petrarch's *Trionfi* was singled out for special praise not simply for its exemplary use of vernacular, but for the moral values it prescribed. French humanists looked upon *I Trionfi* both as a literary model to be emulated, and as a compendium of moral *sententiae* to be studied and followed.[18] As Jean Molinet said in the preface to his French translation, "the one true triumph is that of reason and virtue."[19] Seen through this reading, it is not surprising that the triumphs of the French kings in Italy were viewed not only in terms of military glory, but in terms of cultural and moral victory. Indeed, Molinet explicitly presented his translation of *I Trionfi* to François I so that the king might *"study the proper way to triumph."*[20]

Petrarch's *Triumphs* had an enormous influence on the artistic tastes of Renaissance Italy. It gained a similar popularity in France in the wake of Louis XII's campaign against the Genoese. It was in Rouen that the first notable evidence of French interest in Petrarch's *Trionfi* can be identified.[21] According to Franco Simone, close to a dozen of the extant manuscript copies of Petrarch's *Trionfi* dating from the early sixteenth century were made in Rouen's scriptorium.[22] In part, this can be attributed to the influence of the cardinal at Gaillon. Given his interest in the triumph, it is not surprising that he was an admirer of Petrarch, having imported several elaborate manuscripts of the *Trionfi*. These were among the first to arrive in France.[23] He also commissioned its first translation into French.[24] Two of these elaborately illustrated manuscript translations were subsequently given as gifts to his friend Louis XII; one was presented to the king during his entry into Rouen, the other when he came to Gaillon.[25] As the title page of each manuscript indicates, these gifts were prepared at a scriptorium in Rouen.[26]

Yet the idea of triumph was also communicated to Normandy by those who witnessed and then wrote about or painted the triumphal celebrations that greeted Charles VIII and Louis XII in Italy—as for example, Jean Marot (father of Clément), André de La Vigne, Jean Perréal, Jean d'Auton, and Guillaume Cretin. It was perhaps not a coincidence that all of these men were associated with a poetry society, based in Rouen, known as the Puy de Palinod.

The Puy de Palinod was a literary society whose members devoted their poetry to the doctrine of the Immaculate Conception of the Virgin Mary.[27] Every year on the first Sunday after the feast of Mary's Immaculate Conception (December 8) the Puy's members would gather at the convent of the Carmelites and read their works honoring the Virgin. Its membership boasted some of Rouen's most prominent citizens, including courtiers and priests, magistrates, and lawyers, ship-captains and merchants.[28] Of those named by the city council to organize Henri's triumphal entry, almost all were associated with it.

Literary Forms: The Poetry of Triumph and the 'New Learning'

Jacques Le Lieur, a local notable, royal official, author, and poet, was in many ways representative of the civic-cultural elite that constituted the Puy's membership. He was from one of Rouen's most illustrious *robe* families, members having served important roles in royal, municipal, and ecclesiastical administration. In the early years of the sixteenth century he was closely affiliated with the provincial court of Cardinal Georges d'Amboise at Gaillon; later, he became a city councilor and *secrétaire* and *notaire* to the king, a position he maintained until his death just prior to Henri II's royal entry. A powerful member of Rouen's provincial elite, he also had strong links to both Paris and the king's court. These connections were not only those of office, but of family, being a nephew of Guillaume Budé, the driving force behind the Collège de France.[29] (See Plate 8.)

Budé, as we have seen, championed the cause of the New Learning, helping to institutionalize its program in the Collège de France; his provincial nephew, Jacques Le Lieur, was among the most active supporters of the New Learning in the province of Normandy. Not only was he a prolific writer of verse, but he was intimately involved in both the patronage of the arts and the administration of the Puy.[30] It was perhaps in his capacity as a cultural broker that Le Lieur attempted to recruit such illustrious poets as Jean Bouchet to participate in the Puy's competitions.

The rules and techniques of writing palinodic verse were difficult, to say the least; they required an extremely high level of linguistic competence. The sanctioned genres of poetry—the *chant royal*, the *ballade*, and the *rondeau*—had very complicated structural rules that had to be learned through careful study. Even the much-esteemed poet, Jean Bouchet, cited the difficulties presented by the Puy's requirements as his reason for declining Le Lieur's invitation: "Sir, will you please excuse me, If I do not want to employ in your country *Chants royaux*, for I am not practiced in them. Nor do I know anything of their theory."[31]

The composition of palinodic poetry required not only a great deal of practice, but highly specialized knowledge of rhetoric and grammar. The typical structure of a chant royal is eleven verses in five stanzas with an *envoi* of five verses. The rhyme scheme is normally either A-B-A-B-B-C-C-D-E-D-E* or A-B-A-B-C-C-D-D-E-D-E* for each stanza; the envoi, which repeats themes found in the body of the chant, has a rhyme structure of D-D-E-D-E*. The last verse (E*) of each stanza and the envoi—called the *palinod*—repeats as a refrain, giving the chant a circular quality. The complexity of palinodic verse is demonstrated by the invitation written for the Puy's 1516 competition; it stated that a chant royal should contain "xj lignes pour chacun baston sans coupes feminines silz ne sont synalimphées."[32] In other words, each stanza (*baston*) of a chant royal was required to have eleven lines, while the caesura (*coupes*) structured into each line were to be placed after the fourth masculine syllable (unless the tonic final *e* was elided (*synalimphées*), thus making the syllable feminine. With the publication of *Le Grant et vray art de pleine rhetorique* in 1521 by the Rouennais priest Pierre Fabri, the rules governing the Puy's competitions were set out in excruciating detail. Indeed, the entire second volume of the book was dedicated to explaining the complex structure of palinodic poetry. As he said:

> I am going to treat of the art of rhyming so that the devoted agents of the *champ royal* of the Puy of the Immaculate Conception of the Virgin—having the most ardent desire to compose [poetry in honor of the Virgin]—will understand the manner by which their devotion will thrive.[33]

The concern evidenced by Fabri for the elaboration of—and strict compliance to—a shared system of rules was echoed in a notice made for the Puy's 1533 competition. A chant royal, it said, "…must be of eleven lines, with rhymes of five *couleurs* (moods) per stanza, without "*couppes feminines*," if they are not synalimphées, and with a palinod (a refrain that repeats in the final line of each stanza) that ends in a feminine syllable. This notice, however, went even further, for it required that works "be well written, with correct orthography, diphthongs and grammar; otherwise, they . . . will be rejected."[34]

The strict standards enumerated by this notice, as with Fabri's longer treatment in his *Le Grant et vray art de pleine rethorique*, point to the seriousness with which the Puy's members accorded the formal rules and regulations defining palinodic verse. In requiring submissions to conform to such strict standards, the leaders of the Puy were not just sticklers for arcane and abstruse grammatical details, rather, they were setting out and legislating the literary qualifications and the cultural competencies required of those who would be its members. These standards were rigorously delineated and strictly enforced. The possession of such special skills was not simply the entry price into the Puy's annual competitions, but a sign of belonging to a new kind of intellectual-cultural elite.[35] Thus, what appears on the surface as a bizarre attachment to the demonstration of technical virtuosity in the composition of religious poetry, was, in fact, a form of symbolic address that literally located "people as 'classed selves' according to whether they could participate in an appropriate exchange of recognitions."[36] Put somewhat differently, the cultural practices and the dispositions that informed the Puy's poetry competitions were crucial to the crystallization of specific forms of social organization and identity formation. In this sense, the obscure and extremely complicated literary techniques demanded of—and displayed by—the Puy's poets were less dilettantish exercises in social performance looking to garner prestige and honor, than expressions of a new sort of distinctive urban identity—a kind of civic oligarchy of the cultured, a Republic of Letters *avant la lettre*.

Between Culture and Theology

In his posthumously published work on Normandy's poetry societies, Eugène de Robillard de Beaurepaire argued that the poetry written for the Puy was considered by contemporaries not in terms of art, but in terms of faith and devotion.[37] As he put it: "always and everywhere, theology was of principal importance, while literature was only secondary . . . , playing but an accessory role."[38] However, by the late 1520s it appears that the Puy's members had begun to emphasize literary over and above religious concerns.[39] This is reflected in an anonymous ballad of 1533 in which the Greek god Phoebus is described as addressing the nine muses and directing them to the *Palinod*'s annual competition: "if you are looking for support, follow the . . . Seine to Rouen and celebrate the Puy. Apollo will be gladdened to see orators come from around the world to be heard at the Norman Puy."[40]

Yet despite these overtly "pagan" associations, poetry was not being elevated above the Puy's religious concerns; rather, it was being put on an equal footing. Accordingly, the Puy's statutes specified that theologians, poets, princes, and other confreres were to be given equal voice in determining a competition's winner.[41] Such egalitarianism was hardly typical for the early sixteenth century, when theology reigned as the undisputed queen of the intellectual, spiritual, and social hierarchy of truth. At a time when the theologians at the University of Paris were becoming ever more hostile to humanist incursions into religious matters (see Chapter 3), many among the Puy's members aimed to smooth over these differences by closely intertwining the study of grammar with religious devotion. This is exemplified by a chant royal found in one of the manuscripts commissioned by Jacques Le Lieur signed by Saint Wandrille.[42] This chant describes the writing—and printing—of a book of Latin grammar. It begins by listing grammar's various elements along with their spiritual analogues: grammar corresponds to innocence, error to original sin, the verb to Christ, and scholars to mankind, etc. The aim of this grammar, Wandrille explains, is to provide "scholars with true instruction," so that they might "learn to speak and do good deeds (*bien faire*)." Through an act of substitution readers of the poem, using the legend at its beginning, are meant to discover the many correspondences between grammar and the Virgin Mother, for just as a scholar reading a grammar book is redeemed and enlightened (so that no "interjection of a barbarous word" is permitted), so will Mary, as a second Eve, redeem all mankind.

The Puy's competitions, it seems, provided a site in which the traditional hierarchy of knowledge could be suspended. In the charged atmosphere of the Reformation's early years, however, there were limits to this tolerance. Normandy was the center of support for the Reform in northern France.[43] Even the Puy de Palinod felt its influence.[44] A number of prominent members of the Puy were singled out as heretics.[45] Though it seems paradoxical that Protestants would be writing poetry dedicated to the Immaculate Conception of the Virgin Mary, before the outbreak of the Religious Wars (especially in the first half of the century), religious thought and sensibilities were relatively fluid.[46] One needs to be careful not to read the history of the Reform in France through the lens of subsequent events. Accordingly, despite differences in beliefs that may or may not have been considered heterodox, the Puy's poets shared a common literary culture that valorized the writing of highly technical, formulaic, and abstruse verse. Though orthodoxy had yet to be authoritatively articulated, the Puy was not immune either to the spiritual apprehension and longing of its members, or to the charge of heresy brought by church and university authorities. Rather, alongside the hardening of religious positions in the wake of the Affair of the Placards, and the ever more vigilant surveillance of its contributors' poetical submissions, there was a displacement of religious tensions amongst the Puy's confreres into debates over religious versus literary definitions of the Puy. As one of the Puy's most illustrious members, Baptiste Le Chandelier, came to lament, the Puy's valorization of rhetoric and poetry had opened a veritable Pandora's box:

> In rondeaux, ballads and chants royaux
> Are found only lies disloyal
> So much the better would it have been not
> to have opened
> This science discovered between us.[47]

The battle lines between poetry and religion in the Puy closely mirrored those drawn in the controversy between the Sorbonne and the Collège de France in Paris discussed in chapter 3; this is nowhere more evident than in the famous *querelle* between François Sagon, a poet and priest from Rouen, and the illustrious Petrarchian poet, and soon to be Protestant, Clément Marot.[48]

Paris and Rouen: Symmetries in the Formation of a New Cultural Milieu

François Sagon was a frequent winner at the Puy's competitions in the 1530s. In his 1536 *Coup d'essay*, he viciously attacked his fellow poet and confrere at the Puy, the *valet de la chambre du Roi*, Clément Marot. According to Sagon, Marot was little more than a heretic whose deceits were hidden under the guise of poetic license:

> You say . . . that the arts you defend
> To Christians of pure conscience
> Are permitted to you by the right and the
> license
> Of which one sees the poets use . . . ,
> This you cannot anymore deny than excuse,
> . . . Though perhaps Italy
> Better supports your folly than France
> [Giving you the renown and the name of
> poet]

> Without being in France either an orator
>   or a poet,
> But on the contrary an infidel
> Whose interpretations spread such error
>   among the people,
> That their very memory evokes horror.[49]

Sagon accused Marot of pursuing "antique follies" and of making "a god of Tibullus or Ovide."[50] It was Marot's ardent support of the royal readers of the Collège de France against the attacks of the "ignorant Sorbonne" (in his *Epistre au Roy, du temps de son exil à Ferrare*) that particularly infuriated Sagon.[51] Sagon responded by labeling Marot an apostate who had overstepped his place by interjecting himself—and his art—into questions that were the exclusive purview of the theologians at the university. Echoing Bede's criticisms of the Collège de France, Sagon charged that Marot had "neither the prudence nor the knowledge" to enter into such a "lofty enterprise,"[52] while he—by contrast to Marot's "error and . . . offense"—was an upstanding pillar of loyalty in maintaining "the honor of France, . . . justice and the Sorbonne."[53]

Sagon's family, like that of Marot, was of humble, non-noble, origins. His father, Jean Sagon, was a Spanish merchant naturalized as a French citizen in 1501.[54] His mother was the sister of Jean Ango, the powerful merchant organizer of New World trade, vicompte of Dieppe and counselor to the king.[55] François was closely connected to the tight-knit community of Iberian merchants in Normandy whose fortunes and status had rapidly risen in the early years of the sixteenth century. These men traded extensively in alum, wine, wool, salt, spices, and dyestuffs (e.g., brazilwood). With their accumulated capital they bought land, title, and office, and thus came to play key roles in the city's economic, political, and social life.[56]

In her work on Rouen's Iberian merchant community, Christiane Douyère shows that these Spanish immigrants did not overly concern themselves with such cultural pursuits as the Puy de Palinod until the last quarter of the sixteenth century; she counts only one of them (Albaro de La Tour) as being a member.[57] A more careful analysis of Puy's participants reveals that a number of Rouen's more prominent Spanish residents (many of whom were New World merchants) recited poetry at the Puy's annual competitions. For example, such major merchants as Jean de Quintanadoine, Jean Puchot, and Charles de Saldaigne were members.[58] Having neither the status of noble lineage, nor firm roots in France, these men sought to bolster the standing that their wealth had bought them by participating in the Puy de Palinod. The Puy's competitions were among the most important events on Rouen's social calendar. The mastery of the literary skills required in writing of palinodic verse stood as a demonstrable sign of assimilation into the elite of Rouennais society. Despite Sagon's ardent defense of the forces of reaction at the University of Paris and his uncompromising Catholic orthodoxy, his works evidence a commitment to many of the same Petrarchian ideals and ambitions as his more famous opponent.

In one of the many attacks Sagon launched on Marot, the provincial poet brags of his victories at Rouen's Puy, pointing out that though Marot characterized his poetry as being rude, provincial, and barbaric,[59] he, unlike Marot, "faithfully guarded the laws" of palinodic verse.[60] Moreover, he continues, while he "triumphed in Rouen's Theater" winning Palm, Lily, Signet, and Rose, Marot won not a thing.[61] Sagon's lofty literary ambitions are well summarized by the verses introducing a booklet of his winning poems entitled *Le Triumphe de grace, et prerogative d'innocence originelle*:

> Reader understand this present judgment
> That I make to you of the French poets.
> Merlin [Mellin de Saint-Gelais] writes
>   properly,
> In gracious verse and courteous language.
> Salel's solemn verse makes the time
> Of Hector's Troy, and Achilles' Greece
>   live again;
> And Marot, the first of the three,
> His verse is of such sweetness that it flows without
>   constraint.
> But the Muse of Sagon is much Loftier,
> rendering Him a renown equaling, if not
>   surmounting these three.

For Sagon, Marot was a lightning rod: a means by which he could escape the tensions engendered by his twin vocations as priest and poet. Marot was vilified because he personified the dangers implicit in Sagon's own valorization of poetry. Sagon was not simply a jealous and intolerant provincial priest scoring easy points against the exiled Marot (as many have argued),[62] for his demonization of Marot served to exorcise his ambivalence as to the profane and unorthodox implications of his own commitment to the poetic arts. It was perhaps especially important for Sagon to affirm the sincerity of his Catholic orthodoxy, for Marot had accused Sagon's father, Jean, of being a Jew and a *marrano* (an accusation that was perhaps justified given both the timing of his father's arrival in Rouen at the end of the fifteenth century and the fact that a number of Rouen's other Iberian merchant families—in particular the Quintanadoines—were of Jewish origin).[63] By painting his opponent as an infidel, Sagon was seeking to underwrite his own claims to orthodoxy, while at the same time eliding the tensions implicit in his personal investment in the profane art of writing poetry. In effect, Sagon was trying to straddle the fence. On the one hand, he praised François I for having restored the seven liberal arts to their antique stature; he held up Virgil as a model of poetic virtue, and he claimed to be a faithful follower of Calliope and Apollo. On the other, he excoriated Marot for having possessed "filthy books" and for having sullied the good name of the Sorbonne by defending its enemy the Collège de France.

Peripheries and Centers: Resistance and Assimilation

What is especially interesting about Sagon's attack on Marot is the unexpected light it casts on an apparently unrelated matter—the striking absence among the members of the Puy of the poet, courtier, and chanoine of the Cathedral of Notre Dame of Rouen, Claude Chappuys. In the first instance, this absence can be traced to the cathedral chapter's resentment of the king's imposition of Chappuys as his choice to replace Jean Le Lieur as doyen of the Cathedral of Notre Dame. The resistance to the appointment of this outsider by the king was intense. Despite numerous attempts to force Chappuys' election (including letters of support from Jean du Bellay, the pope, and François I himself), the Rouennais emphatically persisted in their right to choose their own candidate.[64] The intensity of local resistance eventually forced Chappuys into making a face-saving gesture by accepting the lesser post of chanoine. Over the next decade he appears to have spent little time in Rouen, choosing life at court to the hostility of his provincial colleagues. Thus Chappuys' initial exclusion from Normandy's poetry associations can be traced, at least in part, to an ongoing conflict between jealously guarded local rights and the encroachments of royal power.

Yet to this essentially political conflict between the capital and the provinces, we must include a cultural dimension, for coinciding with the controversy over his nomination in 1537 was the heated debate between the Rouennais poet/priest Sagon and the courtier Marot, who happened to be a close associate of Chappuys. Indeed, Chappuys was given a prominent place in Marot's *Le Valet de Marot contre Sagon*:

> Who strikes back against my master?
> I do not see a Saint-Gelais,
> A Heroet, a Rabelais,
> A Brodeau, a Scève, or a Chappuys,
> Writing against him.[65]

Having his name invoked as an ally against one of their own by the poet/
heretic from the capital could not have helped Chappuys' case with the provincial chapter of the Cathedral or, for that matter, with many of the Palinod's
confreres, especially given that the man Chappuys was to replace, Jean Le
Lieur, numbered among the Puy's most illustrious founding members.

By the mid 1540s Chappuys' position had changed substantially. With the
death of his chief patron, François, and the accession of Henri II, he made a
concerted effort to play a more substantial role in supporting Rouen's interests vis-à-vis the crown. His talents as a poet and a courtier were seized upon
by Rouen's civic leaders as a valuable resource in the ongoing negotiations
between the city and the king. When on June 12, 1550, Admiral d'Annebault, governor of Normandy, informed the city's counselors of the king's
intention to make his triumphal entry into Rouen, one of the men that the
council selected to "invent something proper" for the entry was the experienced courtier and chanoine of the Cathedral of Notre Dame, Claude
Chappuys. The importance that the Rouennais attributed to creating a
memorable entry should not be underestimated. Not only was it an opportunity for the city to lobby the king to support their interests, but it provided
the means by which the proud Normans of Rouen could challenge the
haughty superiority of the capital that had staged a spectacular entry for
Henri the year before.

The Parisian entry of 1549 was designed by an associate of Clément
Marot, Thomas Sebillet, author of *L'Art poétique françoys* (1548), as well as by
Jean Martin, an expert in ancient architecture who was responsible for the
translation of Vitruvius' *De Architectura* and Colonna's *Songe de Poliphile*. According to V. L. Saulnier, this entry clearly manifested the neoclassical influence of the *Pléiade* and especially of du Bellay's *La Deffence et illustration de la
langue françoyse*, which was published the same year (1549).[66] Claude Chappuys,
as we have seen, also influenced (either directly or through his *Le grand Hercule
gallique*) the scripting of Henri's Parisian entry.[67] For the Rouennais, Chappuys
was the perfect counter to the arrogant disdain with which the capital viewed
the culture of the provinces.[68] As du Bellay, in his enormously influential treatise on the defense and illustration of the French language so bluntly stated
with regard to Rouen's poets, "Leave all these old French poesies . . . to the
Puy of Rouen: the rondeaux, ballades, virelays, chants royaux, songs, and
other such spices that corrupt the taste of our tongue, and serve for nothing
beyond bearing witness to our ignorance."[69] The narrative of Henri's entry
into Rouen, like du Bellay's treatise, was closely linked to humanist ideals
about the reform of language and its institutional legitimization in the Collège de France.[70] Clearly a spectacle designed to impress, it was perhaps also

meant as a direct challenge to the opinion expressed by du Bellay: that the Rouennais were backwards and ignorant provincials.

The success of the entry was immediate and substantially transformed the social position of its chief organizer, Claude Chappuys, who appears to have been quickly assimilated into the elite of Rouennais society. From 1550 he was frequently cited in the deliberations of the Hôtel de Ville; he was repeatedly elected to represent the church at the *États de Normandie*; and whereas he was noticeably missing from the rolls of the Puy in the decades preceding the entry, after it, he was to take up his place alongside Rouen's other poets in one of the Puy de Palinod's principal offshoots, the *Puy des Pauvres*.[71]

From the Puy to the Entry

Of the nine men mentioned by name in the deliberations of Rouen's city council as being responsible for Henri II's royal entry, only one, Mellon Preudhomme—curé de Corny-en-Vexin, chanoine at the Cathedral and a counselor at the parliament of Normandy—had no apparent connection to the poetry societies of Rouen. Of the others, six were members of the Puy (and/or one of its offshoots). Claude Chappuys, as we have seen, took part in the Puy des Pauvres; Pierre du Couldray, sieur de Fréville, échevin in Rouen's city council, secrétaire du Roy, and New World merchant,[72] contributed to both the Puy de Palinod and the Puy des Pauvres, and was married to Jeanne de Croismare, grandniece (?) of Robert de Croismare, the archbishop of Rouen from 1484–1494 (and one of the Puy's founders). Similarly, Michel Desarpens, a curé licensed in law, Nicole Gallopin, also a curé, and Nicole Malherbe, a lawyer, participated in both societies. Pierre de Croismare, Chappuys' fellow chanoine at the cathedral, was not only a member of the Puy, but was related to a number of other members, including several cousins, his great uncle Robert de Croismare, and his maternal grandfather, Nicolas Osmont (who was one of the Puy's earliest members). The two remaining men charged with organizing Henri's entry—Robert Lefebvre and Joseph Tasserie—were directly connected to the Puy through their immediate families.[73] The marriage of the daughter of Robert Lefebvre to the parliamentarian Antoine Caradas (whose uncle, Jean, was a prominent member of the Puy) placed him squarely in the same sociocultural milieu as the Puy's other members. It also seems likely that he was related to one or more of the other four Lefebvres who were members of the Puy (Jean Le Febvre, for example, seigneur d'Escalles and a counselor in Normandy's parliament from 1544–1571). Joseph Tasserie's connection to the Puy was direct: Tasserie was a merchant whose interest in Rouen's New World trade was discussed in Chapter 2. His father, Guillaume, and his two uncles, François and Pierre, were integrally involved in the Puy from its inception in the 1480s.[74] His father was crowned prince of the Puy no fewer than seven times (a record unmatched until the seventeenth century), and his morality, the *Triomphe des Normands*, was among the first explicit statements of the Puy's syncretic purpose in conjoining the literary virtues associated with the idea of triumph to the Norman religious tradition of devotion to the Virgin Mary.[75]

Norman Triumphs and New Elites

Written sometime in the last decade of the fifteenth century, the *Triomphe des Normands* was one of the foundational texts of the Puy. In it, Tasserie employed the theme of the triumph to justify the establishment of the Puy de Palinod as a means of orienting the religious, literary, and political ambitions of Normandy's civic-cultural elite. The text begins with William the Conqueror calling together his faithful and chivalrous knights to celebrate the Immaculate Conception of the Virgin Mary:

> Loyal Normans and glorious knights
>> Victorious
> As we should be
> [For we carry] on our armor in large letters [the words] *Tota pulcra*,
>> thus is my
> devotion . . . [to] a woman conceived in
>> purity. . . .[76]

According to William, it was through the Virgin's patronage that the Normans were able to triumph over their foes time and time again. So great was their veneration for her, he says, that the day honoring her Immaculate Conception—the day of the Puy's annual poetry competition—was known as the *feste aux Normands*.[77] But just as the duke and his men prepared to offer her thanks, a heretic named Sarquis challenged their belief in Mary's Immaculate Conception. William responded with a challenge of his own—not of swords but of words—a trial to be judged by the wise King Solomon. Witnesses were called for both sides: Mohammed and Satan for Sarquis; Figure, Authority, Reason, Example, and the Common People of Normandy for William. In the end, the faith of William and the Normans was vindicated and Sarquis was banished from the "imperial duchy and noble country of the Normans." Tasserie's morality ends with the triumph of the Normans and Solomon urging William to dedicate himself with renewed vigor to the celebration of the Immaculate Conception. He then commands the Normans to prove their pious devotion to Mary by writing poetry in her honor:

> And you, most esteemed and magnificent
> Proud duke, in sign of victory
> And Perpetual memory
> As is due to such a Lord
> We give the palm of honor.
> Similarly, for just recompense,
> And as sign of good defense,
> . . . The poet laureate . . .
> His crown covered nobly
> With a chapeau of laurel pure and green.
> Thus celebrate with devotion
> This yearly festival
> As much with the science of music
> As in that of rhetoric
> With epigrams and chants royaux
> With Ballads, . . . and rondeaux,
> By orations and with songs,
> . . . In the Latin and vulgar
> tongues. . . . [78]

The "triumph of the Normans" over their enemies in this world as in the next was made possible by the patronage of the Virgin. The imagery of triumph played a prominent role in the annual celebrations of the feste aux Normands held by the Puy. For example, among the prizes awarded to the Puy's literary triumphators were those closely associated with the iconography of the triumph, such as the palm that was given for the best chant royal, and the laurel crown that was given to the runner-up.[79] As Fabri's allusion to the champ royal (royal field) of the Puy's competitions, and as the statutes of the Puy confirm, the Puy's annual meetings were seen as a battle fought on a royal field where the agent (*facteur*) of the Puy, armed only with words, "valiantly and virtuously fought" for the honor of the beautiful and pure damsel, Mary, mother of God. As the statutes put it: "Just as the ancient imperators and other Roman Princes triumphantly wore laurel crowns after victories obtained over their enemies, so too would the Virgin, excellent Mother of God, victoriously triumph over all sin and vice without exception—bestow a laurel crown . . . on the poet with the best epigram."[80]

Triumphal themes were not limited to the prizes offered, but were also incorporated into many of the competitors' poems. At or around the time that Jean Marot, de La Vigne, d'Auton, and Perréal participated in the Puy's festivities, a specific genre of chant royal developed that was known as *Triomphes*.[81]

In a manuscript commissioned by Jacques Le Lieur (BN, Ms. Fr. 379), there
are thirteen chants royaux organized around the theme of triumph, while
many others make specific reference to the triumphs of either the Virgin or
of Christ.[82] In many of these, the Virgin, Christ, or symbols closely associated with them were linked to historical and national myths having to do
with the special status of the French king and the extension of French hegemony to the Italian peninsula—as for example, Nicole du Puy's chant, *To triumph beyond the heavenly empire,* which had imperial election for its main
theme; or another by the same author, *To pass through the mountains in triumph
and glory,* which concerned France's transalpine ambitions.[83]

Among the most interesting of the Puy's poems incorporating the
theme of triumph is by the Rouennais priest, Nicolas Lescarre, titled *Le chariot du fort geant celeste.* This chant royal describes the triumphal procession of
a mighty celestial giant whose chariot was drawn by a unicorn, an elephant,
and a panther. Marching beside this chariot were the allegorical figures of
Victory, Trophy, Pomp, and Triumph. Victory carried with her the symbols
of triumph, the palm and the laurel, while Triumph carried a standard of silk
representing the "honor due a Caesar."[84] (See Plate 9.) A miniature accompanying Lescarre's poem (mis)interprets, or rather, transforms the chant's triumphal themes.[85] In it, the giant is not shown; rather, Victory, carrying a
palm branch, is represented sitting upon a chariot being drawn by an elephant and a unicorn.[86] Setting the stage for the appearance of the triumphal
Virgin, this miniature intimates the strong connection between Victory and
the Virgin Mary, hence the presence of the unicorn—the traditional sign of
the Virgin—drawing the chariot. The transition from the figure of Victory
(or Fame) riding upon a triumphal chariot to that of the Virgin was perhaps
inevitable given the close association between the two in Normandy. (See
Plate 10.) Pierre Avril's poem, *Rondeau en forme de triomphe,* found in the
same collection, explicitly fuses the traditional imagery of the triumphal entry procession with the Norman tradition of veneration for the Virgin:

> Rondeau in the form of triumph,
> To the humble Virgin who triumphs.
>
> In her triumph over the evil serpent
> The Virgin departs,
> The wheels of her chariot
> Crushing her vanquished enemy,
> Thus we see humanly acquired sin defeated
> When in her chariot of Virtue, which
>   cannot be impeded
> The treasures of grace are all recovered.

> She sits high on her chariot,
> Holding palm and Green branches,
> While below diverse prisoners
> Are enchained, for through her
> Force is Converted [to virtue]
>   . . .
>
> Through her, the benefits of peace,
>   hidden
> So long, are rediscovered, and thus is
>   war
> Made to retreat, and the adverse fortune
>   of the Holy Spirit is reversed.
> A triumph celebrated in song and
>   verse. . . . [87]

The movement of Avril's poem recalls the ancient associations of the triumph with martial victory and the *translatio imperii*. The Virgin's battle with Satan was framed both in spiritual and military terms. Mary's triumph consisted in crushing her enemy beneath the wheels of her chariot and taking his followers prisoner. Yet, as Avril points out, Force is converted into virtue through her. And thus, her triumph absolves man of the sin inherited from Adam and Eve, and returns him to an Edenic world without war or faction—to the undisputed reign of the Holy Spirit.

The view of the Virgin as both a military and a spiritual triumphator was closely intertwined with the mythology that surrounded French kingship. The French king, like the Virgin, was cast in the role of a political and a religious triumphator—i.e., as the universal Christian emperor. This ideology developed in conjunction with attempts to recapture the crowns of Naples, Sicily, and Jerusalem, serving to legitimate the extension of French hegemony over the Italian peninsula. This is clearly demonstrated in the chant royal of Jean Maillard found in Ms. 379, titled the *Lily that Rises in Triumph and Victory*, in which François I's invasion of Italy was explicitly linked to the mystical triumph of the Virgin over Satan.[88] Indeed, the illustration of Maillard's poem depicts the Virgin's emblem, the lily, growing midst the carnage of the battle of Marignano, the site of the Franco–Venetian victory over the duke of Sforza. Further complicating the web of political, military, and religious interests defining the meaning of the triumph, we can add the humanist reading, which saw the triumph in terms of the revival of ancient learning (*translatio studii*). (See Plate 11.)

In early modern France, as in Italy, the translatio studii was closely identified with Petrarch and, in particular, with his vernacular work, *I Trionfi*. The triumph therefore represented not only French dreams of reviving the Roman

Imperium on Christian terms (in France, *not* in Rome!),[89] but also the movement by humanists to revive and cultivate ancient knowledge. Accordingly, the meaning of the triumph referred not simply to military and/or religious victory, but to the victory of a new cultural consciousness and the concomitant rise to social prominence of those who embraced it. In this sense, the "triumphal" exploits of the Puy's laureates in honor of the Virgin formed a tight link between one of the chief identifying features of Rouen's civic-cultural elite—their high degree of proficiency in manipulating written and spoken signs—and Normandy's long-standing tradition of Marian devotion. To this link another was forged, connecting the spiritual and cultural interests of Rouen's new elite groups to the ideological foundations of French nationalism. As demonstrated by the narrative of Henri's entry, France's new elite reserved for itself a special role in preparing the king to take on the mantle of universal Christian emperor. The entry thus combined elements of both the translatio imperii and the translatio studii, for it was through Henri's support of the New Learning, as much as by his military prowess, that he was expected to lead the diverse peoples of the world out of barbarity and sinfulness to the Elysian fields of the terrestrial paradise.

Social Compositions

In his important work on Normandy's provincial nobility, Jonathan Dewald states that the Puy's membership was dominated by Rouen's "wealthiest and most cultivated bourgeois."[90] From 1544 to 1554 there were between 12 and 15 members of the Puy who were counselors at Normandy's parliament. In 1548, for example, 46 names are listed as members of the Puy. One is singled out as a nobleman and 14 as seigneurs.[91] Approximately 28 held—or were to hold—municipal or royal offices (including a président of the *cour des Aides*, a secrétaire and receveur général du roi, the city's *maître des ouvrages*, 3 members of the Chancellerie, 4 notaires et secrétaires du roi, 7 city counselors, 3 échevins, 3 counselors in the *cour des Aides*, 4 Deputies of the États de Normandy, 2 lawyers in the court laye, 5 counselors and a lawyer in the parliament).[92] If we extend our gaze over the entire sixteenth century, we find that between 26 and 31 of the Puy's poets were counselors in the parliament.[93] If we factor in members who were officials at Rouen's other courts, who held royal office, and who were active in either Rouen's municipal government or in the États de Normandy, we find that approximately two-fifths of its members were associated with Normandy's robe elite.[94] Especially interesting in this regard is the fact that in the year of Henri's entry, approximately half of the Council of 24 was associated with the Puy.[95] Even more striking is the fact that of the six échevins leading the council in 1550—and thus responsible for assigning the men who wrote and produced Henri's entry—five were members.

Approximately one-fifth of the Puy's members were ecclesiastical officials and priests.[96] This does not necessarily mean that we should place them in a special category devoted exclusively to the clergy, for these men were frequently younger sons, uncles, and brothers of those who were titled and/or who held office, as for example, Rolland DuBosc, prieur de Saint-Lô, Robert Le Goupil, curé de villiers, Pierre Langlois, curé de Saint-André, and Jean Raoulin, *célestin*, who all were from prominent Norman families of the robe. Others were prolific writers and scholars with decidedly humanist leanings. To the already familiar names of Pierre Fabri, François Sagon, and Claude Chappuys, we could add the names of the bishop of Bayeaux, Louis Cannossa, a correspondent of Erasmus; or the Rouennais priest, Guillaume Haudens, who wrote and translated numerous works, including *Le Véritable discours de la vie humaine* (Paris, 1545), *Trois cens soixante et six apologues d'Esope* (Rouen, 1547), and *Les Propos fabuleux moralisez extraitz du plus auteurs tant grecs que latins* (Lyon, 1556); or Jean Maillard, another priest from Rouen, who wrote a book entitled *Le Premier recueil des oeuvres de la Muse Cosmopolite* (Rouen, 1533).[97]

The Puy's members were clearly better off than most. Its yearly entry fee was many times the average for a confraternity.[98] Moreover, the fact that Pope Leo I gave the Puy preference over all other confraternities in Rouen, granting its members permission to have an altar for mass and communion at home, as well as a number of other privileges and distinctions, clearly points to their elevated social status. The cost of these privileges came at the almost unheard of price of 142 *livres tournois*, which was, to say the least, an exorbitant sum in the sixteenth century.[99] Their pride was made manifest by the beautifully illustrated and surely very expensive manuscript of their poetry, commissioned by Jacques Le Lieur, Bibliothèque Nationale Ms. Fr. 379. (See Plate 12.) The Puy's members were thus not just robe officials and ecclesiastics; they had money too. Indeed, over a quarter of the Puy's members were—or were closely related to—local merchants. Many of these played an important role in Normandy's trade with the New World, as for example the parliamentarians and merchants Jean Bonshons, Jean de Quintanadoine, Guillaume Le Seigneur, and Charles de Saldaigne.[100] Others involved in New World commerce included Pierre du Couldray, who helped organize Henri's entry; Jacques Ouyn, who was a master of two ships, the *Loyse* and the *Vallentine*,[101] and Jean Du Hamel and his son Jacques, a counselor at parliament, who organized numerous voyages to Brazil in the 1550s and 1560s.[102] And of course, there was also Jean Parmentier, an intimate of Jean Ango, who not only explored the New World, the Orient, and Africa, but wrote poetry and translated the *War with Catiline* and the *Jugurtha* of Salluste.

Additionally, many in the Puy were connected through marriage and family ties to merchants, such as Jean II Du Four, a city councilor and member of the Puy, who married a sister of the New World merchant Jean Ango.[103] This web of marriage and familial associations could be spun out in great length to encompass a large proportion of Rouen's civic-cultural elite. Even merchants who were not themselves associated with the Puy were often closely connected to it. For example, while Antoine Civille, one of Normandy's most important New World merchants, was not a member, his two daughters, Isabeau and Marie, married merchants who participated in the Puy, Jean Quintanadoine and Jean Durand respectively; while his son, Alonzo II, married the daughter of Charles de Saldaigne. Alonzo's son, in his turn, became a councilor in Normandy's parliament, and married the daughter of François Quesnel, who was both a member of the Puy and a councilor at the parliament.

Additionally, several members of the Puy who helped organize Henri's entry were either involved in overseas trade or were related to those who were. For example, the brother of Pierre de Croismare, Jacques, seigneur des Alleurs, was married to Catherine Ango, the daughter of the New World kingpin Jean Ango.[104] The échevin Pierre du Couldray married Croismare's niece and was related (through his mother-in-law) to Ango's family. It was perhaps through this connection that du Couldray became an investor in New World trade. Joseph Tasserie played an even more important role. Not only did he invest in New World expeditions, but he was one of the men sent by Rouen's city council in 1541 to lobby the king for freedom of the seas (with specific regard to commerce with Brazil).[105]

The membership of the Puy also included ship captains, explorers, and navigators such as Jean and Raoul Parmentier, Pierre Crignon, Jean Broise, and Jean de Seville, as well as artisans, doctors, sailors, musicians, and apothecaries. The poems found in the manuscript collections of the Puy's competitions, though all ostensibly concerned with the Immaculate Conception of the Virgin, are deeply embedded in the material/professional lives of its members. There are poems—by schoolteachers, lawyers, doctors, dyers, cloth traders, and navigators—comparing the Virgin to the printing of a grammar book,[106] to the healing arts,[107] to trials,[108] to dying cloth,[109] building buildings, and using astrolabes.[110] Despite the often considerable social distance separating these men from those members who were councilors at Normandy's parliament, royal officials, or even wealthy merchants, they shared certain common cultural dispositions and literary ambitions that identified them closely with Rouen's new civic elite. Thus, for example, Nicollas Baudry, a master dyer (*taincturier*), was a frequent participant in the Puy's competitions, while Guillaume Dubois, a stonecutter from Dieppe, not only took part in the Puy, but published his collected poetical works.[111]

The Puy de Palinod enabled individuals occupying diverse positions in an extremely hierarchical society to intermingle and compete on the merits of their poetry. Notwithstanding often pronounced social differences, the degree of literacy and the knowledge of versification required of these individuals distinguished them as sharing a common literary culture. In addition to this collective sensitivity to the written and spoken word, the Puy's poets were also adepts in a ritual recitation of poetry dedicated to the Immaculate Conception of the Virgin Mary.[112] The Puy thus acted as a kind of bridge between the cultural skills of Normandy's new elites and the social legitimacy of a religious tradition. No longer were spiritual matters to be the sole purview of the doctors at the Sorbonne; now poets and rhetoricians claimed the right to have their say as well. As Pierre Avril told the princes and confreres of the Puy at its 1525 competition:

> The arrogant logicians
> Do not want to augment belief,
> But true rhetoricians,
> Inspired by good faith,
> See the divine providence
> That was revealed to them
> Which is, and was, manifestly,
> True prognostication.[113]

Social Legitimacy and Civic Space

Triumphs, as we have seen, were extremely popular in sixteenth-century Normandy. The Cardinal d'Amboise's château at Gaillon, though perhaps the first, was by no means the only place in Normandy where they could be seen. The themes and motifs associated with the triumph were prominently displayed on the homes of Rouen's local notables as bas-reliefs, depicted in the stained-glass windows of the city's most illustrious parishes, represented in municipal monuments, such as the *Gros-Horloge* (sic),[114] and written about by local poets of the Puy.

In the church of Saint-Foy in Conches, for example, a chant royal by the author of the *Triomphe des Normands*, Guillaume Tasserie, was turned into a stained-glass window depicting the triumph of the Virgin Mary. The text of Tasserie's poem was even duplicated within the window. It reads:

> Her greatness is represented by the white lily, growing among thorns, by the wild rose yielding its fragrance, by the laurel tree, symbol of victory, by the sun which enlightens the earth. She is the bright and beautiful star of the sea, the pure dove of Noah, the Ark of God, built of mysterious wood, the rainbow of peace, the graceful temple, the most pure and spotless vessel of election, whom we must call, in spite of all (the protests of) the invidious: The only one beautiful in her conception.[115]

Next to this window was another that depicted the triumph of the Virgin. Executed in the early 1550s, this window was donated by none other than the échevin, secrétaire du roi, New-World merchant, and organizer of Henri's entry, Pierre du Couldray and his wife, Jeanne de Croismare. The themes depicted in this window were not original, but mirrored those in Rouen. The windows of Saint-Vincent of Rouen (c. 1522), for example, now at the Church of Jeanne d'Arc, consist of three scenes of triumph: the triumph of Adam and Eve, the triumph of Satan, and the triumph of the Virgin as a new Eve crushing Satan beneath the wheels of her golden chariot. As with the windows at Conches, these windows also recapitulate themes found in the Puy's poetry.

Families of a number of prominent members of the Puy were parishioners at Saint-Vincent in Rouen.[116] This parish was densely populated with well-to-do-merchants—a class of individuals who played an important role in the Puy's activities.[117] Similar windows were also made for the Church of Saint-Nicolas in Rouen. Unfortunately, these have not survived. However, other triumphal windows were made for the Church of Saint-Patrice in the late 1540s or early 1550s. These were donated by the *Puy de la Passion*, a sister literary society of the Puy de Palinod.[118] The membership of the Puy de la Passion closely paralleled that of the Puy de Palinod and the Puy des Pauvres. Like the members of the Puy de Palinod, the parishioners of Saint-Patrice were largely from Rouen's civic-cultural elite. In telling the story of mankind's fall from grace and his eventual (triumphal) redemption, Saint-Patrice's windows recount a story analogous to those of Saint-Vincent.[119] Indeed, all of Rouen's triumphant windows can be seen as figural counterparts of the Puy's poetry.[120] (See Plate 13.)

What is especially intriguing about these windows is the chronological sequence in which they appeared: The translation of triumphal themes from the largely merchant parish of Saint-Vincent to Saint-Patrice, a parish dominated by Rouen's most prominent citizens, indicates—in symbolic terms—the rising social status of Rouen's cultured classes.[121] These individuals actively sought social and political positions commensurate with their economic power and cultural status. The merchant members of the Puy were no exception in this regard, as is exemplified by such families as the Quintanadoines, the Saldaignes, and the Bonshons, who parlayed their commercial success into royal and municipal office. Moreover, as Brunelle has shown, the acquisition of office by Rouen's merchants frequently involved relocation to parishes that reflected this rise in social status.[122] The triumphal windows of Saint-Vincent and Saint-Patrice (and of Saint-Nicolas)[123] played a conspicuous role in glorifying those who commissioned, possessed, and/or donated them. First, they promoted a fervent religious faith in the Immaculate Conception of the Virgin Mary, identifying Mary as the second Eve, who would triumph over Satan and absolve mankind of its sins. Second, as devotional and artistic works, they were—and are—considered exquisite. Their beauty clearly redounded to the honor of the parishes and city possessing them.[124] And finally, their representations of the triumph articulated in a visual language the literary and spiritual ideals that animated the Puy and its oeuvre. The interrelatedness of these three functions served to draw in and closely intertwine the interests of the Puy's members with both the distinguishing feature of provincial Norman piety—its Marian devotion—and the civic honor and glory brought to the city by its possession and display of such spectacular windows. In other words, these triumphal windows played an important role in legitimating the Puy and its members insofar as they physically incorporated the Puy's concerns into the principal sites of Rouen's social and spiritual life. By tracing the movement of triumphal themes from windows located in a merchant parish to a robe parish we have a kind of symbolic gauge by which to trace the growing social power of the Puy's members. (See Plate 14.)

Triumphs, however, not only decorated Rouen's most prominent churches, but were found adorning homes in those areas of the city most heavily populated by wealthy merchants, lawyers, and officeholders. Thus, immediately adjacent to the *Palais de Justice* were three stone reliefs depicting the fall of man and his triumphal redemption by the Virgin Mary on her chariot.[125] Close by was the Hôtel Duval de Coupeauville; its elaborate decorations included twelve panels that depicted the military triumphs of Caesar.[126] Northwest of this location, just west of Saint-Patrice, scenes from the life of Deborah were sculpted in bas-relief. These included a sculpture of *Innocence* sitting on a triumphal chariot being pulled by two angels. Innocence, in the role of the Virgin, carried a branch of palm while her chariot crushed a three-headed dog representing Satan.[127] Embellishing a house just south of the Palais de Justice were wood panels that complemented the fifth verse of Nicolas Lescarre's chant royal, *Le chariot du fort geant celeste*.[128] Southwest of the courts, a number of elaborate stone carvings of Petrarch's triumphs decorated the hôtel of the Bourgtherouldes. Though much damaged, these sculptures can still be seen in the hôtel's courtyard.[129] They were commissioned by the sieur de Bourgtheroulde, Guillaume Le Roux. Le Roux was a prominent member of Rouen's civic aristocracy. He was both a councilor in Normandy's parliament and an active member of the Puy de Palinod. Le Roux was so enamored of the triumph that he had the chapel of his country estate at *Boissey-le-Châtel* decorated with elaborate wooden panels of the Virgin's triumph.[130]

As this multitude of triumphs—carved, painted, etched, and staged—makes clear, the people of Normandy, and in particular those of Rouen, were fascinated by the idea of the triumph. The triumph was among the most powerful symbolic expressions of the status and authority of Rouen's new civic-cultural elite. This enthusiasm is clearly attributable to the Puy and its transposition of the political/military triumph into eschatological terms of the Virgin's triumph over Satan. This complex of ideas was, in turn, recast in terms of the translatio studii of humanist learning, thus giving spiritual and political legitimacy to the literary concerns by which the Puy's members sought to distinguish themselves as members of Rouen's social and political elite. As with the organizers of Henri's entry, the confreres of the Puy sought to link their unique cultural skills to powerful and well-established religious and political traditions. Like the triumphs of Gaillon, which represented not only French military superiority over the Italians, but also the triumph of French civilization over Italian savagery, so too the triumphs found in church windows, on houses, in the poetry of the Puy de Palinod, and most especially in Henri's royal entry represented the triumph of a specific ideal of culture and of civilization. In this sense, the triumphal entry of Henri II into Rouen was also the triumph of Rouen's new civic-cultural elite. Indeed, in the poetic concourse of the *Puy d'Amour* (another of the Puy de Palinod's offshoots), it was not the king whose triumph into the Elysian Fields was greeted by Good Memory, but the most esteemed poets of France and Normandy.[131] Thus seven years before Henri's apotheosis at the end of his royal entry, we find in Pierre Du Val's text, the *Puy du souverain amour*, a description of the muse of Good Memory triumphally conveying such excellent poets as Guillaume Alexis, Pierre Crignon, Jean Marot, Guillaume Crétin, Jean Parmentier, Thomas le Prevost, and others—each "having composed a book of invective against the enemies of rhetoric"—to the Elysian Fields. It will perhaps come as no surprise that of the contemporary poets named in Du Val's text, all had participated in the Puy's poetic competitions.[132]

New Civic Aristocracies

The third movement of Henri's royal entry consisted of a pilgrimage in which the king—following a carefully mapped itinerary of tableaux vivants—physically entered the festival's narrative. From the mise-en-scène of Brazil to the terrestrial paradise of the Elysian Fields, the king's progress consisted in a story about the nature of kingship, nobility, and virtue. This narrative was an

FIGURE 14. Captain of the *Enfants d'honneur au cheval* from Henri II's entry into Rouen. *Cest la deduction du Somptueux ordre* (Rouen, 1551). Courtesy of the Bibliothèque Municipale de Rouen. Photo by Thierry Ascensio Parvy.

attempt to form a strategic link between notions of royal power and the aspirations of Rouen's new civic-cultural elite. In a similar fashion, the triumph enacted as the second movement of Henri's entry encapsulated and foreshadowed the narrative sequence of tableaux vivants of the third. Not simply a spectacular display of the formal elements of the triumph (e.g., chariots, prisoners, booty, palm leaves, and laurel crowns) Henri's triumph was a demonstration of the growing power of Rouen's civic elites. It was their triumph as much as his. As a rondeau in another of the Puy's manuscripts put it: "Triumph a tout, triumphez, Rouennoys. . . . "[133]

This power was not only reflected in the figurative and allegorical terms of the triumph and its motifs, but also through the inclusion of the city's elite as active participants in staging the king's triumph. Thus, following the chariots, the gladiators, and the prisoners, three hundred *enfants de la ville*, representing Rouen's most illustrious—or at least wealthiest—citizens, filed past the king and disappeared through the triumphal arch leading to the simulated land of Brazil.[134] Many among the laurel-crowned boys participating in this triumphal procession were from families closely tied to the Puy de Palinod—the Caradas, the Boyvins, the Deshommets, the du Couldrays, Du Hamels, Dufours, Hallés, Romés, etc.[135] One wonders, given the remarkable symmetries (discussed in Chapter 3) between the "savages" of Brazil and elite groups in France, whether it was by design or coincidence that the number of *enfants d'honneur* marching toward the Faubourg Saint-Sever was the same as the number of "cannibals" to be found waiting just beyond the triumphal arch in its portrayal of the New World.

CHAPTER 5

The Virgin, the Astrolabe, and the Apocalypse

The individuals who designed, organized, and enacted Henri's triumphal entry drew on a well-established ritual vocabulary to construct an eschatological narrative of messianic kingship. This chapter will analyze three component dimensions of this narrative and how they were woven into the complex fabric of myths, symbols, and rites at the center of Rouen's civic and cultural elite's concerns: their Marian piety, their millenarianism, and their devotion to the poetical arts.

As we have seen, the narrative of Henri's entry was based on a civilizing journey. It did not, as many voyages of transformation do, follow a linear trajectory, but a circular one whose itinerary was mapped out with reference to a mirrored polarity between two cross-reflecting ideals of paradise: one at the entry's beginning in the New World, and the other at the entry's end in the Elysian Fields. The voyage between these two separate but closely linked ideals was—as I have argued—an attempt to mediate between two distinct, though increasingly intertwined, ideas of what it meant to be an elite in mid-sixteenth-century France.

In Chapter 4, I traced this civilizing narrative into the social world of the provincials responsible for scripting, organizing, and enacting the entry. The members of the Puy de Palinod were identified as being representative of the cultural elite responsible for organizing Henri II's entry. Their rise in power, status, and legitimacy, though based on knowledge and skill, was also mediated by their commitment to a long-standing local tradition of Marian piety. The millenarian eschatology dominating the Puy's religious concerns was also closely tied to their cultural concerns. The paradise they identified with the triumphant Virgin (who would return at the end of time to redeem mankind) was also the paradise inhabited by triumphant poets who could speak the unencumbered and pure spiritual language of God as it existed in the time before the Fall.

The narrative of Henri's entry charted the movement toward an ideal of a cultured nobility that could, as Pontus de Tyard said, "of equal balance, weigh the pen or the lance."[1] This movement, however, was animated by the urgency of intense religious belief. The New Learning was a religious movement every bit as much as it was a social or an intellectual one. Like the New World so prominently displayed at the beginning of the entry, the New Learning represented in the Elysian Fields at its end was inextricably entangled with the belief in the imminence of the apocalypse and the prophesied role of the king as the Last World Emperor. Indeed, the discovery of the Golden Age of the New Learning required a voyage no less than the discovery of the New World across the seas. When Henri finally reached the end of his travels at the theater of the pont de Robec, he was presented with the words used by Aeneas "to exhort his companions to steadfastly endure the torments of their navigation and proceed, putting aside all fear, in their peregrinations with the hope of reaching a place of repose to which fate had destined them."[2] It is with this idea of the discovery of and/or return to paradise, represented by the tableaux vivants beginning and ending Henri's journey through Rouen that this chapter will be concerned.

Poetic Voyages and Spiritual Longings

Long before the Puy de Palinod was a poetry society it was a religious celebration of the Immaculate Conception of the Virgin Mary. This celebration came to Normandy sometime in the eleventh century. The Anglo-French poet, Robert Wace, put the legend of its origins into verse in the twelfth. He traced the festival to Helsinus, a prelate who was William the Conqueror's ambassador to the Danish king, Suénon II.

Helsinus, after having successfully completed his diplomatic mission, was en route to England when his ship was caught in a terrible storm. Giving up all hope of ever surviving, he began to pray. A strange man clothed in light miraculously appeared to him saying that if he promised to celebrate the feast of the Immaculate Conception of the Virgin Mary, the Virgin would safely conduct his ship home. Helsinus agreed and dutifully promised the mysterious man. Thus, the prelate was saved, the circle of his travels completed, and a tradition founded.[3] (See Plate 15.)

The story of Helsinus' voyage was foundational to the Marian poets of the Puy; but it also had a more general significance. Indeed, the role attributed to the Virgin in conducting his ship safely home made perfect sense, for she was considered to be the patroness of Normandy's sailors. Many of the Puy's members were ship captains, navigators, and traders; many others still were merchants associated with Normandy's overseas trade; and still more were closely related by family and marriage to those involved in maritime trade and exploration.

The Virgin's role in giving aid and comfort to Normandy's merchants and sailors perhaps explains why the verse of the Puy's members is so redolent with the metaphors and imagery of the sea. Even the Virgin's name, *La Mère*, conjured up obvious comparisons that were exploited by the Puy's poets, as for example, Nicolas Osmont, who equated the sea (*la mer*) with the mother of God (*La Mère de Dieu*).[4]

The Virgin, however, was not simply compared to the sea, but also to a ship: a vessel upon which humanity could circumnavigate the distance between "here" and "there," this world and the next. Hence, the merchant, humanist, ship captain, and explorer, Jean Parmentier, compared her to a "sturdy ship completely filled with grace." She will, he said,

> Carry in her firm constancy
> good provision and living substance
> to sustain [humanity's] poor courage
> against the wind, the tempest and the
> storm
> [lending you her support on] the great sea
> and on the misery of the expanses
> So that you come to a good port
> a place of peace and holy efficacy
> in which you will see without leaving
> the sturdy ship completely filled with
> grace.[5]

Piloted by God and manned by the virtues, *La Marie*'s course was of the spirit as well as of the seas. Like the nave of a Church (which in old French was called the *nef*—the same word as that used for a ship), she was the means by which one could navigate the vagaries of the material world to reach the ultimate safety of what Parmentier termed "the perfect port of welcome and joy."[6] (See Plate 16.)

From the time of Wace, the Virgin was not only compared to a ship, but with the "true star of the sea"—the unmoving and fixed pole star by which the mariner was guided on his perilous journeys.[7] As Rouen's church fathers said: "she is the North Star, that most sure guide of the Norman people."[8] She was also a sure pilot in guiding the more mundane affairs of the merchant poets of the Puy. Thus Nicolas Osmont reminded his fellow Palinods:

> Merchants, believe that you will well
>   profit,
> [and] that it will accord you well,
> to frequent this sea (*ceste mer*)
> And even lacking money you will have
> Merchandise in abundance:
> Oil, wheat, wine, azure and gold in
>   mass
> Because God has made her for your
>   utility
> The Sea [*la mer(e)*] which receives and
>   gives all grace.[9]

A similar intermingling of commercial interests and religious sentiment was expressed by Pierre Crignon in his chant royal praising the Virgin for preserving navigators "from deadly shipwrecks" and "dangerous perils" in their selfish expeditions to the Orient in search of gold and other "goods of great value . . . for the great profit of all and the well-being of the public."[10]

The umbrella of the Virgin's protection that began with Helsinus being saved from shipwreck was transposed and extended to voyages to ever more distant lands and to the inclusion of the material interests of Normandy's merchants. The play of similitude and analogy between utility and grace, material acquisitiveness and spiritual hunger, was frequently given expression in terms of the specialized vocabulary of the seagoing traveler. This ranged from the colloquial language of the sailor, exemplified by Parmentier's poem beginning, "*Esbare! Haut! Au quart! Au quart! Au quart! . . . A thiebort et babort! . . . La terre est bort à bort*,"[11] to the highly abstruse and technical language of the professional navigator, as exemplified by Pierre Crignon's poem equating the Virgin with the astrolabe (see Plate 17):

> Our astrolabe where the sphere is
>   comprised,
> This is the humble Virgin in her
>   conception.[12]

In this poem Crignon gives a detailed exposition of the many similitudes existing between the astrolabe and the mother of God.[13] He explains that its dawn meridian line is her inception; its graduated circles are her virtues; its equator is her justification; its tropics are her glory; its zodiac and rete are her beauty and perfection; and its "azimuth," "almicantaratz," and "ligne aurore" are, like her, without error. Every aspect of the instrument's design, ornamentation, and use was compared to the Virgin, for both, he explained, were defined—and created—with reference to the cosmic perfection and virtuous symmetry of the celestial sphere.[14]

"Why," asks Parmentier, Crignon's captain, in one of his moralities, "do I journey to lands so faraway?" The allegorical figure of Reason supplies the initial answer: it is for "the glory of the king, to bring honor to your country, and to yourself."[15] Just as the light of the Virgin's star shines (as a chant royal by Thibault tells us) on "barbarous peoples" living in distant lands, it was through the astrolabe, and the journeys it made possible, that similar distances were to be spanned by the king's temporal power.[16] Indeed, it was through precisely such royally sponsored journeys that the Virgin's presence was to be translated across the seas. Like the Virgin, the astrolabe (or as Crignon called it, the "king's instrument") was an instrument of God's benign will. In making possible the extension of the king's reign to the recently discovered lands of the New World, it initiated the course of events that would end with all humanity being led back to the paradise which had been lost. Here lay the real reason behind such journeys: not temporal glory, but the glory of God. The sphere of the astrolabe was a mirror of the heavens formed in God's own hand; as Mother of God, it charted a course that could take the traveler from this world across the seas to the next—to "a port of grace," to paradise, to "the year in which wars and quarrels end."[17] Crignon concludes, thus addressing the judges of the Puy:

> Prince, the people had then certitude
> Of the port of grace and her longitude
> And the pilot, suspending the astrolabe
>   from his finger,
> said: "Children, have no fear, I see
> the ray of the true sun breaks clear
> This is the instrument that will ensure
>   our safe conduct
> the proof of which is in the using, and
>   now I am sure
> just astrolabe where the sphere is
>   comprised."[18]

The Eve of the End: Crushing the Serpent and Saving Mankind

The immaculately conceived Virgin was the devotional center of the Puy's poetry. She was regarded as the new Eve who would redeem Man's sins, triumph over Satan, and return the world to its prelapsarian purity.[19] Eve, as many of the Puy's poems explain, was responsible for pushing the ship of humanity off from its secure mooring to let it drift, without direction, on a sea of ambition, pride, and corruption. The Virgin, on the other hand, was the redeemer who would safely navigate humanity past the Scylla and Charybdis of Satan and human weakness back to a port of pure and holy grace. What one woman had done, another would return to undo.[20] Through her, mankind would be freed from perfidious sin and mortal exile; thus paradise would be founded anew. As a chant royal by Nicolas Ravenier said: "Adam and Eve, by a voice serpentine, were the cause of our adversity, . . . [but] to repair this offence and ruin, . . . God has pre-elected a benign Virgin, [. . .] the chosen vessel to preserves us from all iniquity."[21] Or as Parmentier said, addressing the princes of the Puy: "Let us all piously board this ship [*La Marie*], . . . to better cross this worldly sea, . . . [to] the place where God is the patron [to paradise], the island where the earth is much higher than the heavens."[22]

The redemptive role assigned to the Virgin in leading Man back to paradise was closely linked to that reserved for the Woman of the Apocalypse described in Revelations.[23] According to John's account, a woman would appear at the end of time, her arrival signaling the beginning of the final battle between good and evil, the destruction of the earth, and the Last Judgment. John describes her as she appeared in his vision: "a woman [who had come from Asia] clothed with the sun, and the moon under her feet, and upon her head a crown of twelve stars."[24] By the mid-thirteenth century this imagery had become closely associated with the Virgin. By the fifteenth, the Apocalyptic Woman was the dominant icon representing the doctrine of the Virgin's Immaculate Conception as championed by the provincial poets of Normandy's Puys.[25]

A striking representation of the Apocalyptic Virgin is alluded to in a contract preserved in Rouen's *tabellionage*. Dated December 31, 1548, it records that a sculptor by the name of Guillaume Tranche was hired by Albaro de La Tour to make a woman crowned with twelve stars, dressed in a golden sun and the moon, and standing upon a serpent.[26] That this representation of the Apocalyptic Woman was also a representation of the Immaculate Virgin ardently championed by Rouen's poetry confraternity becomes clear when we recall that the Spanish immigrant who ordered its fabrication, Albaro de La Tour, was also a member of the Puy.[27]

An interesting detail appears in this description of the Virgin, namely, the dragon beneath her feet. According to Vloberg's "The Iconography of the Immaculate Conception," it was "not until the first years of the fifteenth century . . . [that] we find a certain image of the Immaculate Virgin trampling on the head of the Serpent." He continues: "In 1407 . . . Canon Ugo di Summo ordered a wooden statue of the Blessed Virgin for the Church of St. Mary of Cremona, specifying that she was to be 'crowned with twelve stars and with the ancient Serpent under her feet'."[28] Vloberg explains that this imagery expressed Mary's unique privilege at being born immaculately and without sin; her crushing of the serpent's head was understood as a reversal of Genesis 3:15 where the serpent tried to "bruise" Eve's heel; hence it was an affirmation of Mary's purity and grace.[29]

This account can be supplemented in a number of respects. The first specific reference to this iconographic representation was certainly not in northern Italy in 1407, for as early as 1352, in a ritual pageant at Rouen's cathedral, a procession of merchants playing trumpets and horns carried a representation of the Virgin crushing the head of a serpent beneath her feet.[30] Just as this iconography was indebted to ideas associated with the Immaculate Conception of the Virgin, it was also related to the thirteenth-century miniatures accompanying Anglo-Norman manuscripts of the Apocalypse. These placed the Apocalyptic Woman in close proximity to Satan, typically represented as a hydra, dragon, or serpent who she was depicted as either fleeing from or doing battle with. As Mirella Levi D'Ancona has pointed out, of the biblical texts that influenced the representation of the Immaculate Virgin, that found in Revelations "was undoubtedly the most popular."[31] The depiction of the Virgin stepping on the serpent was not simply an allusion to the passage in Genesis, but—as indicated by her crown of twelve stars and being clothed in the sun—an accretion to the traditional iconography of the Apocalyptic Woman as the Virgin. In addition to the biblical allusion of Eve stamping on the serpent, I would suggest that this imagery was also related to a common classical motif of the Roman triumph: mainly, emperors trampling upon a prostrated barbarian. This iconography can be seen on coins, statuary, and bas-reliefs on triumphal arches; it was also described in written accounts of triumphal entries.[32] It signified an emperor's triumphal victory, both in the specific sense of a particular military achievement and as an abstract quality that defined the legitimacy of his rule.[33] In the context of the iconography of the Virgin Mary, the serpent positioned beneath her feet signified her ultimate triumph over Satan and the salvation of humankind. The negative associations bound up with the appearance of the Apocalyptic Woman—i.e., as the sign of the world's imminent end—were thus tied to the positive eschatology that developed around the redemptive power of the Immaculate Virgin as a second Eve who would triumph over Satan at the end of time and be the vehicle for mankind's redemption.

The association of La Tour's statue with the Puy de Palinod reveals the Apocalyptic Virgin's close connection to the Triumphant Virgin so popular among its members (see Chapter 4). Depicted in Rouen's churches, carved upon the homes of its most prominent citizens, and eulogized in the poetry of the Puy, the Triumphant Virgin was typically shown crushing a serpent or dragon beneath her feet or under the wheels of her chariot. As the Triumphant Virgin, the Apocalyptic Woman was transformed into mankind's militant defender: a champion whose immaculate and unflinching purity enabled her to stare down the devil, do battle with him, and emerge victorious. Thus would men find salvation from sin and be made ready for Christ's final advent on earth.

Signs and Portents

The religious beliefs held by Rouen's new elites were infused with a kind of desperate urgency by repeated wars, famines, plagues, the confusions of unprecedented social mobility, and the tempests of religious controversy.[34] The apocalypse, in this context, was not an abstract idea; it was an inescapable reality.[35]

On June 26, 1522, at midnight, the earth trembled. The plague was rampant that year, as it was the year before. Famine was endemic.[36] In 1523 frost once again killed the crops.[37] People from the surrounding countryside flooded into Rouen in search of food.[38] The earthquake that marked the height of 1522's misery was paralleled by numerous other omens in the years that were to follow. In 1537, a spectacular comet filled Rouen's night sky, provoking apprehensions that the last days had finally arrived; and then, five years later, in the middle of the night, a storm occurred of such unprecedented proportions that upon seeing it, the people of Rouen cried out for mercy, "doubting not the certainty that the day of judgment had come."[39] Such meteorological events, as with the misfortunes of poverty and plague, were seen as portents, signs, and warnings. The end was truly at hand.[40] Numerous examples of this can be found in the poetry read before the Puy. For example, Guillaume Tasserie in the *Triumph of the Normans* recounts how in Revelations Saint John tells of an angel who would descend from heaven and bring "*rigueur et pestilence*" in the last days before the end of the world.[41] Similarly, a chant royal by Nicolas Lescarre speaks of the "bitter pestilence," the "sad tears," and the plague that has afflicted all humanity; while a chant by the apothecary Guynguart tells of "an evil wind full of cruel poison," "horrible famine," and "deadly plague."[42] The real sufferings of famine and plague were thus used by the Puy's poets to invoke the redemptive powers of the Virgin as a curative to the spiritual plague which had beset mankind from the time of Eve's fall.[43]

Along with plague and famine, the rise of Protestant heresy was also interpreted as a symptom of the disease infecting mankind and hence a sure sign that the world's end was imminent.[44] Frequent and elaborate expiatory processions were held.[45] Among Catholics, Luther was commonly viewed as the Antichrist; for Protestants, this role was reserved for the Pope. In either case, religious controversy fed into well-established eschatological traditions articulating the inevitability of the apocalypse at the time of great schisms within the church.[46] However, of all these signs and portents, none more surely augured the coming apocalypse than the discovery of the New World.

The association of the New World with the terrestrial paradise, and the links thought to exist between its discovery and the coming of the apocalypse, have been well documented.[47] Columbus, for instance, was a prodigious collector of prophetic literature, believing that his voyage was divinely inspired and that his finding the New World was a providential sign that the dawn of the Last Age had come. As he put it: "God made me the messenger of the New Heaven and the New Earth of which he spoke through Saint John in the Apocalypse . . . and he showed me to that location."[48] The close association of the New World with the terrestrial paradise drew it toward and entangled it with the eschatological themes of the Puy de Palinod's poetry—that is, the story of the Virgin's triumph over Satan, the redemption of mankind, and the return to paradise. For example, a chant royal by Jean Parmentier describes how a cosmographer, by carefully following his map, was able to evade an evil monster and discover the fortunate islands where gold could be found. (See Plate 18.) Parmentier concludes his chant by explaining his meaning in precise terms: "Princes of the Puy," he says, "I take the most beautiful mines of gold to be Paradise, the cosmographer I call humanity, the monster is the vile Luther, and Mary, without the stain of original sin, is the map of the world (*mappemonde*)—humanity's salvation."[49] She was the ship, the astrolabe, the map, the stars, and the sea; she was the cure, the redeemer, and the means by which Man could make the spiritual and the physical journey to the New World—to the "port of grace of paradise." Parmentier also writes of charging his vessel with *riche boys rouge* (brazilwood) in the "perfect port of welcome and joy"[50] and of the "bread and nourishment, the milk and the honey" that one was to find in the terrestrial paradise of "the New World in which everything is so fruitful."[51] The convergence of the material and spiritual worlds is made even more explicit in a chant by an anonymous poet of the Puy that tells of a "terrestrial paradise" where one finds the "mystical paradise" in which God has put "aromatic smells," "mines of gold," "trees and the fruit of life to decorate an Oriental place. . . . A paradise fed by the waters of grace."[52] Or, as another of the Puy's poets wrote: there is "an island found by cosmography, . . . [where one will find] the tree of life on a fortunate island."[53] Or Parmentier's chant in which he explicitly equates the New World with the purity of the Immaculate Virgin:

> When the uncreated [God] made creation
> A pure world of ornate loveliness,
> Its great beauty was polluted
> By the offense and heinous crime of
>   pride
> That was committed against heaven by a
>   being of angelic nature
> Who deceived man and through mortal envy
> Rendered the earth subject to sin,
> But God, moved by the light of his love,
> So as to restore the world that had been
>   ruined,
> Made in it a beauty which surpassed all
>   others,
> The new world is always pure and holy.[54]

New World peoples were also a sure indication that the end times were at hand. According to Amerigo Vespucci, the inhabitants of the New World were without faith, law, or religion. Most sixteenth-century commentators agreed with this assessment. According to Villegagnon, they "were a savage people, remote from all courtesy and humanity, . . . without religion . . . [or] knowledge of honesty or virtue. . . . "[55] For André Thevet they were "people marvelously strange and savage: without faith, law, religion, or any civility whatsoever; they lived as if unreasoning beasts."[56] According to Pero de Magalhaes de Gandavo, even their language betrayed this absence of Faith, Law, and Royalty, for it was without the letters F, L or R.[57] A strange balance of *withouts* characterized them: they were without kings, but they were also without masters; they were without clothes, but they were also without the artifices of fashionability; they were without laws and, indeed, without writing, but they were also without those affectations which could cloud a more immediate apprehension of truth. Somewhere between beasts and angels, they were less than human and at the same time almost divine. At once the innocent and favored children of God living in Edenic repose, they were also devil-worshiping and lascivious cannibals. But whether they were perceived to live in the terrestrial paradise or in the vestibule of hell, whether demonized or idealized, they constituted a portent and a sign: the end of the world was fast approaching, the Last Days had arrived and a new and Golden Age of peace and tranquility would soon appear.

The prophetic expectation that the New World fulfilled can be traced to the widespread influence of Joachimist and Franciscan thought. It was also bound to the development and elaboration of a monarchical ideology in which the king was cast as the Last World Emperor: as a crusader who would tame the barbarian (whether Moor or New World savage), unite all the peoples of the world, and usher in the millennium of Christ's rule on earth.[58] The French monarchy, like its counterpart in Spain, was closely identified with the eschatology of the conquering Christ who would usher in the Last Days and the universal Christian empire. As Lefèvre d'Étaples said in 1509, such momentous events as the discovery of the New World clearly show that

> Christ intends to seek his lost sheep and to rescue . . . [them] from the jaws of the venomous and bloodthirsty serpent, to bring the unknown [i.e., the New] world to the light of the truth, to cause the victorious sign of the cross to shine forth everywhere, and to subdue not only the Moors but anything whatever that opposes the prince who will bear the names of Christ and bring his wars to a conclusion.[59]

The Golden Age and the Last World Emperor

Golden Age propaganda and its association with crusade derived much of its animus from the fervor surrounding the Italian campaigns of Charles VIII and his successors. For example, the illustrious member of Rouen's Puy de Palinod and poet to the king, André de La Vigne, wrote about Charles's 1495 triumphal entry into Florence as if it were the second coming of Christ himself:

> In great triumph and grand majesty,
> In clamor and praise of the victory
> The king of kings entered Florence,
> Where he gained a glorious renown,
> For he bore the avenging sword.[60]

This homegrown messianism was spurred on and mirrored by the Italians themselves, for having been subjected to one crisis (and one master) after another, many came to place their hopes for salvation on the French king.[61] Marsilio Ficino, for example, like La Vigne, wrote a eulogistic account of the entry of Charles into Florence. Modeling his text after the Adventus of Christ into Jerusalem, Ficino describes the people of Florence greeting Charles as they would the return of the triumphant Christ, with the liturgical chant *Benedictus qui venit in nomine Domini* . . . (Blessed is he that cometh in the name of the Lord . . .). He then merged this biblical imagery with that which was overtly pagan, comparing Charles to the Roman God Jupiter, who "shakes the world with a nod of his head . . . , and accordingly one believes that he must be called not just the ruler of France, but of the whole world."[62] Ficino's text was echoed by Savonarola who incorporated the conquering French king directly into a prophetic view of Florence as the "future city of eternal salvation." He thus identified Charles as the "agent of God's divine justice" who would "humble the proud, raise the humble, destroy vice, exalt virtue and reform all that is deformed, since Charles has been sent by Him who triumphed on the cross to save mankind."[63]

We do not, however, have to shift our attention to Charles VIII's invasion of Italy in 1494 to locate the development of this chiliastic view of French kingship; indeed, there was already a long history of such views, as, for example, in Pierre Dubois' fourteenth-century text *De recuperatione terrae sanctae*, which identified the Most Christian King of France as *Dominus mundi*.[64] Descended from Priam and Francus of Troy, anointed with the holy unction sent down from heaven at the time of Clovis, capable of performing miraculous acts (such as healing of scrofula), the Most Christian King of France played out the role of the Christ-like imperator who would subjugate—and bring together—all the peoples of the earth. By the mid-sixteenth century this mythic role was a commonplace. According to Lefèvre d'Étaples:

> Happy is that prince who shall be chosen for these things and who, once an innumerable multitude has been set free from the dreadful tyranny of this brutal and barbarous sect [the Moors], will hear these words of illustrious praise: '*Blessed is he who comes in the name of the Lord*'.[65]

This mythology gained intensity in the years that were to follow, becoming one of the defining features of François I's reign. As Jean Thenaud, the king's tutor, told his pupil:

> Just as your sign, the *fleur de lys*, contains the essential truth of the Holy Trinity, so too your body carries the shining armor of justice and the restoration of immaculate authority. You are the idea and mirror of virtue . . . an insuperable ruler that other kings call dictator. You are the conserver of peace, the propagator and ardent champion of the catholic faith, to whom in a brief space of time barbarous people, and men of all nations, will obediently submit.[66]

A similar view was expressed in an anonymous treatise that declared

> That a French king, estimated above all
>   others
> Will subjugate, according to prophecy,
> All the peoples of Africa and of Asia.[67]

Yet it was not only the king, but the kingdom of France itself that was imbued with this divine purpose. Joseph Strayer has stressed that this "royal propaganda"

> glorified the kingdom fully as much as it did the king. The basic theme ran something like this: the kings of France have always been pillars and defenders of the faith; the people of France are devout and pious; the kingdom of France is so specially favored by God that it is the most important part of the Church.[68]

Propaganda perhaps, but it was not simply the hegemonic discourse of the court speaking, for there was a strong local tradition among the provincial Normans valorizing their own superior faith and piety. Indeed, Normandy frequently appears in the Puy's poetry as the second Zion.[69] Thus, the Norman poet, savant, priest, and royal reader at the Collège de France, Guillaume Postel, definitively located the New Jerusalem on the Western shores of France—in Normandy.[70] As Postel explained:

> Jesus . . . has come to us [the Normans]. . . . He makes his entrance in but one place, Normandy. . . . When he was suspended on the cross, the Holy Ghost . . . chose this country over all the rest on this round machine because his most holy city [Jerusalem] extends on a direct line along the *maestrale* . . . to the extreme dwelling place of the *Triplicité*, thus he first left his divinity there [in Normandy].[71]

According to Postel, this new Israel would be situated under the *Magistrale Triplicité* (Aries, Leo, and Sagittarius) where Normandy is located:

> This is why Jesus inclined his head towards the *Maestrale* or *Magistrale*—what we call the north west wind: . . . so that he could render his spirit unto it, thereby showing us through this land the spiritual and temporal reign which is the reign of the Most Christian *Israélogallique*.[72]

Postel was clearly influenced by the apocalyptic and prophetic tradition of the Middle Ages—as represented most notably by Joachim of Fiore.[73] Yet there was another tradition with which he, and certainly the members of Rouen's Puys, were familiar: the royal entry festival.[74]

An Apocalyptic Tradition: the Royal Entry

Fashioned after the advent of Christ into Jerusalem, royal entries enacted the Christomimetic mythology of French kingship. These rituals had a clear resonance with the millenarian ideas found in the Puy's poetry. Through their active involvement in scripting, organizing, and enacting entries, the cultural elites responsible for designing them were able to channel civic rituals in directions that reflected their particular social and spiritual interests. This can be shown by a brief examination of some of the most important entries leading up to and including the 1550 entry of Henri II into Rouen.

I. CHARLES VIII

The first-ever printed account of a French royal entry was that of Charles VIII into Rouen, dated 1485. This entry was organized as a morality play. One act stands out as being of particular interest in the present context; called *Ordre politique*, it consisted of a dramatization of Revelations. As the verses for the pageant explain:

> Illumined by rays emanating from the
> Antarctic pole,
> Where the lofty throne of political order
> can be found,
> There one sees by a vision clear,
> That which Saint John saw in all its
> lucid splendor.[75]

The tableau vivant of *Political Order* opens with God seated on a throne surrounded by the four evangelists. These latter, we are told, represent the Four Estates of France (the Nobility, Clergy, Bourgeoisie, and the Common People). Above them two angels stood, supporting the *agnus Dei* (the Lamb of God), which, according to Revelations, represents the honor, glory, and power of Christ.[76] Descending to earth, the lamb welcomed the king to Rouen. It then opened the Book of Life, which was locked with seven seals, and gave it to Charles. Placed around the stage were seven ardent lamps; these represented the seven gifts of the Holy Spirit. The scene was completed by the presence of Saint John himself. He was accompanied by twenty-four elders, all honest men, crowned with gold and chanting a beautiful hymn.

As Robert Scheller has rightly pointed out, this pageant posits a sweeping equation of heavenly and earthly orders, placing Charles VIII squarely in the role of God the Father.[77] The entry also reflected the more specific interests of the Rouennais: it prefigured theories that were to be articulated by

Guillaume Postel some seventy years later in placing Rouen at the geographical heart of the Apocalypse. Thus, for example, the Lamb of God played two simultaneous roles in Charles's entry: while it reenacted the part it played in Revelations by breaking the seven seals, opening the book, and unleashing the end of the world, it also represented Rouen, being the city's heraldic device. Similarly, the seven ardent lamps that surrounded the tableau vivant also had a double signification, for they were not only the "gifts of the Holy Spirit" mentioned in Revelations, but the seven bishoprics of Normandy (Rouen, Bayeux, Lisieux, Evreux, Seez, Avrences, and Contances). And finally, the twenty-four elders described in Revelations and enthroned around Saint John were also, like the twenty-four "just and good councilors" prepared "to do any service for the king," a representation of Rouen's municipal government, known as the Council of 24.

Keeping this double register in mind as we follow the plot of this pageant, we can clearly discern the interweaving of local and national mythologies. Thus the Lamb of God, representing Rouen, opens the Book of Life and begins the sequence of events that will ultimately end with the world's apocalyptic destruction. The presentation of the open book to the king locks the destinies of city and monarch in a tight mutual embrace; just as Rouen was to be the site of the New Jerusalem, so was the French monarch to lead the faithful in a final crusade against the Antichrist and prepare the way for Christ's millennial rule on earth. As the next pageant, *Unction de Roys*, recounts, Charles as God's anointed was destined to possess "the noble and victorious crown and the scepter of excellent renown, carrying above all the ensign of triumphant virtue, the papal standard of battle."[78]

The theme of Christian empire led by the French monarch runs throughout the entry. For example, in the opening pageant, Charles was greeted as was Christ upon entering Jerusalem with the liturgical chant *Benedictus qui venit in nomine Domini*.[79] In the penultimate tableau he was identified as the first Christian emperor, Constantine, who, armed with the cross, was able to defeat the cruel king of the barbarians ("the large brown man") Maxentius.[80] Predating the invasion of Italy by close to a decade, Charles' entry into Rouen articulated—from both local and "national" perspectives—a widespread prophetic belief in the French monarch's claim to be the Last World Emperor, who would conquer the infidel, reclaim Jerusalem, and prepare the ground for the reign of the Holy Spirit on earth.

2. LOUIS XII

The next king to enter Rouen was Louis XII, in 1508. One pageant of his entry is of particular interest, namely, that enacted before the Cathedral of Notre Dame. The stage here consisted of a mountain crowned with a lily. A clear stream flowed from this mountain and into the basin of a fountain. Above this fountain a beautiful girl was enthroned. In one hand she held a balance and in the other a sword. Directly in front of the fountain was a lamb, which by "grand artifice" moved as if alive. The text of the entry refers to this girl as Justitia, and the accompanying poem identifies her with the returning Virgin, Astraea.

The anonymous author of the entry based this pageant on Virgil's fourth *Eclogue*, which prophesied the return of the Virgin and with her the return of Saturn and a new Golden Age. According to Virgil:

> Now is come the last age of the son of
>   Cumae;
> The great line of centuries begins anew.
> Now returns the Virgin, returns Saturn's
>   reign.
> Now a new generation from high heaven is
>   sent
> and a child born with whom the iron race
>   shall perish
> And a race of gold rise throughout the
>   world.

The transfiguration of the apocalypse of Saint John across the classical precedents of Virgil and Ovid was—in the context of Louis' entry—mediated by the identification of the Virgin with the Apocalyptic Woman. Indeed, the Just Virgin and Astraea were only different names given to the Virgin of the Apocalypse championed by the Puy de Palinod.

As with the entry of Charles, these millenarian sentiments were followed by those indicating the central role that the French king was to play in the momentous days that were to come. Accordingly, the entry's final pageant consisted in a representation of the world divided in three parts: Asia, Africa, and Europe. Standing at the center of this world was a beautiful woman who represented the Renown of France. In her hands she held a magnificent crown interlaced with the letter "L." She took this "crown of France" and placed it upon all the world.

The imagery here is not difficult to decipher: Louis is being crowned universal Christian emperor; his reign, and the dominion of France, were to be extended to include all the world and its peoples. It is perhaps in this context that the New World savages brought back by Thomas Auber on Jean Ango's ship *La Pensée* (see Chapter 2), came to be shown to the king.[81] In this sense, the return of the just Virgin Astraea, the dawn of a new Golden Age, and the discovery of a New World were all intertwined in the entry's presentation of the king's eschatological role as the emperor who would come at the end of the world.

While the author of Louis' entry remains anonymous, among the city officials responsible for organizing it were many of the leading lights of the Puy de Palinod. Louis Daré, for example, was the principal force behind the establishment of the Puy and was a key player in Rouen civic government for over four decades. Not only did Daré preside over the city council's debates over the entry's organization and cost, but he had the honor of making the city's oration before the king. Two other members of the Puy, Nicolas Osmont, Rouen's *receveur*, and Roger Gouel, a procurer of the king at the *baillage*, were instrumental in arranging to finance the entry. One wonders, given their interest in the literary pursuits of the Puy, whether these men also had a hand in scripting the entry festival. The incorporation of Astraea strongly hints at this possibility.

Indeed, Astraea, the Just Virgin, abandoned the earth as it descended into the bloody chaos of the Iron Age. According to Virgil's fourth *Eclogue*, she would return and with her the Golden Age would be born again. The parallels with the Apocalyptic Virgin are many and obvious. The connection between them—and the hand of Rouen's Puy—becomes explicit when we turn to François I's 1517 entry into Rouen.

3. FRANÇOIS I

The mythology of a lost Golden Age was among the most popular themes associated with François' reign. His entry into Rouen was a consummate expression of this ideology. Its very title refers to it as occurring in "the year of the redemption of humanity."[82] The penultimate tableau is most revealing in this regard. In it François was presented with a silver globe crowned with a glittering star. As he approached, the star opened to reveal a child king; this child then descended to earth upon one of the star's rays. The starlight then radiated outward, filling the stage and changing the silver globe to gold. This, we are told, signified Saturn's return to reign over "an age . . . of peace, love, tranquility and justice."

The pageant, like the one for Louis XII nine years previously, was an enactment of a passage of Virgil's fourth *Eclogue*; the prophesied child who would usher in the Golden Age was here being equated with François, the king:

> A New clarity has descended,
> From the heavens to the earth and over
> the waves,
> When king François comes into the
> world. . . . [83]

After this pageant the first part of Virgil's *Eclogue* was portrayed, but with a particular local twist. François was led to a "garden of delights." At the base of this garden the mechanical lamb representing Rouen and the Lamb of God from Revelations once again made an appearance. More interesting is what François found within the garden: a beautiful girl portraying the Virgin. In her hand she held a palm branch, which signified the victories she granted to princes and kings (the palm being the traditional sign of triumph)—but there was more to this triumphant virgin than just her palm, for like the Apocalyptic Woman from Revelations she was surrounded by a shimmering halo of the sun and had the moon beneath her feet. Astraea but in name, she was, we are told by the entry's chronicler, the very *"vision of the apocalypse."*[84]

The millenarian eschatology present in Charles's 1485 entry was based on Revelations. This entry took place several years before the Puy de Palinod was founded (about 1489). By the time of the next entry, that of Louis XII in 1508, many of the municipal officials responsible for the organization and enactment of the entry were members of the Puy. The introduction of the Virgin Astraea, or Justitia (who was a classical analogue of the Apocalyptic Virgin to whom they devoted their poetry), hints at the Puy's influence in scripting the festival. François' 1517 entry confirms the association between Astraea and the Apocalyptic Virgin, and strongly suggests that the Puy's members continued to be actively involved in the design, organization, and enactment of Rouen's entry festivals. Not only did Daré play a leading role in the city's government and in the Puy's activities at this time, but he was joined, on both counts, by Jacques Le Lieur, Jehan Le Roux, and Guillaume Auber (all leading members of the Puy and elected as city councillors when the entry was being prepared).

Rereading Henri's Triumph

Henri II's entry into Rouen abandoned the medieval style of biblically based *moralité* in favor of classical-based allegory. Yet despite the humanist overlay, the narrative of the entry remained much the same as that found in the entries discussed above.

The circular voyage that the Virgin—in all her various manifestations (the astrolabe, the map, the ship, the pole star, the sea, the Apocalyptic Woman)—made possible was a transformative journey in which the "mariner" made a pilgrimage from the Old World to the Golden Age of the New. Similarly Rouen's entry festivals, including that held for Henri II, were ritual acts meant to span the spatial, temporal, and spiritual distance between these different worlds. As such, they aimed at transforming the kings who traveled along their procession routes into the universal emperors who would mediate the arrival of the terrestrial paradise of the New Jerusalem. (See Plate 19.)

In the Puy's poetry the Virgin made this transformation possible, but this role was more generally reserved for Saint Michel, who had the job of conducting the souls of the departed into paradise. Whether by accident or by design, Henri's entry into Rouen was scheduled to take place on September 28, thus corresponding to Saint Michel's feast day and to the festivities associated with the knightly order of Saint Michel held at the abbey of Saint Ouen.[85] (See Plate 20.)

The Triumphal Virgin and Saint Michel were bound closely together by the narrative of Revelations, appearing together frequently in illustrations of the Apocalypse. It was perhaps as a consequence of this common reference point that they came to share many of the same iconographical and mystical attributes. For example, both were depicted as being armed, doing battle with and triumphing over Satan (in the form of a dragon, a snake, or a many-headed hydra); both were represented as holding the scales upon which the souls of mankind were to be weighed in the Last Days, or brandishing the sword of justice; both were recognized as healers of the sick; and among the Normans, both were venerated as patrons of mariners. The archangel, however, not only resembled the Triumphal Virgin but the king himself. (See Plate 21.)

From the time of Charles VII, Saint Michel was known as the protector of the French monarchy; he was frequently depicted in print, on canvas, and in miniatures as being the celestial analogue of the terrestrial king.[86] For example, in a manuscript at the Bibliothèque Nationale titled simply, *L'ordre de Saint Michel et du Roy*, the identity of the French king was said to be an exact mirror of his angelic counterpart.[87] The anonymous rhétoriqueur responsible for this treatise spelled out in detail the many points of correspondence between king and archangel: Michel, he says, is the governor of the celestial paradise and the triumphant church, as the king is the governor of the terrestrial paradise and the militant church. Michel, he continues, defeated Lucifer and exiled him to hell as the king vanquished the infidels and expelled them from the land of the faithful. Moreover, just as one triumphed over the Antichrist, the other triumphed over heresy. And whereas Michel led God's chosen people (the Hebrews) to the promised land,[88] so too the king would guide God's newly chosen people (the French) toward peace and the true faith.[89]

This list of correspondences between king and angel recapitulates and conforms closely to the eschatological narratives traditionally told in entry

FIGURE 15. Henri II as a Triumphant Saint Michel vanquishing/trampling the hydra of Protestant heresy. Courtesy of the Bibliothèque Municipale de Dijon, France. Jean Duvet's *Figurations de l'Apocalypse*. Est. 213 bis f° 1m. Photo by F. Perrodin.

festivals, where the prophesied role of the king as Last World Emperor and the scourge of the Antichrist was to do battle with infidels and savages, extend his power over all the earth's peoples, unite them in the one true faith, and lead them into paradise. Henri II, like his father, welcomed the association with Saint Michel. Indeed, in the very same year as his entry into Rouen, he commissioned Jean Duvet to portray him as the incarnation of Saint Michel triumphing over Protestant heresy. This triumph was represented by his trampling a hydra beneath his feet.[90]

The identification of the king with Saint Michel is of special interest given the similarities between the Archangel and the Triumphal Virgin. By association one would also expect there to be a similarly close relationship between the king and the Triumphal Virgin. We find evidence for this in an ode sung to Henri during the penultimate pageant of his entry, at the Theater of the Cross—organized at the *Couvent de notre dame des Carmes*, the site of the Puy's annual competitions—where the king was described as having "around his head a radiant sun" and "his feet placed on a crescent" of silver stone like the moon.[91]

The similarity of this imagery to that typically used to represent the Triumphal Virgin was certainly not an attempt to posit an identity between her and the king; rather, it points to the common thread of ideas weaving together the eschatological role of the Virgin and the prophesied role of the king. Thus, the two-tiered theater, where this ode was sung, portrayed the peoples of the earth kneeling at the king's feet (which rested on the crescent moon) while above him, in the heavens, the gods presented him with "ancient and modern scepters, and with imperial, royal and ducal crowns."[92] (See Figure 12 in Chapter 3.)

The moon-like crescent upon which Henri (like the Virgin) stood was his device; a device that was omnipresent in the entry: woven into uniforms of the entry's participants, into the canopy carried over the king's head, appearing in the grotto above Hercules fighting the hydra, beneath Saturn's feet at the city's main gate, and at the entryway to the Elysian Fields at the entry's end. According to Claude Paradin, the crescent signified the "militant church," for just as the moon waxes and wanes, so the church's fortunes have varied. As he explains, sometimes

> it is supported and defended by Catholic Princes, and sometimes it is persecuted by enemies and heretics, which is to say that it is in perpetual combat; yet nevertheless the Royal Majesty, or the King, as the first son of the church, has promised to take it under his protection, until a time when there is but one God, one King, and One Law.[93]

Less obliquely put, the crescent was a common symbol signifying hope for a future time when the world would be united and the ground prepared for Christ's second coming.[94] According to Etienne Perlin, writing in 1558, the magical properties of the crescent moon guaranteed that Henri II would be "future monarch and emperor of all the world."[95] As the author of *Cest la deduction* explained, Henri took

> For his device a heavenly crescent,
> This is for good reason, in that
> Happiness and good fortune are waxing,
> Such that all obscurity
> Under his hand is understood.[96]

The image of Henri, the sun fiery around his head, balanced within the crescent of the moon, not only recalls Saturn's similar pose (minus the sun) at the entranceway to Rouen, but the iconography and the eschatology associated with the Apocalyptic Virgin.[97] The same millenarian themes represented by the Virgin appear again and again in Henri's entry, just as they did in the entries of his predecessors. And though there were no tableaux vivants in the entry that included the Virgin, she was nevertheless present in the form of a gold statuette of Astraea given to the Queen as a gift from Rouen. On its pedestal were the following words:

> I am the Virgin Astraea
> Who returns to live in this century so
>   fecund,
> Foreseeing that your husband will reign
> By grace evident to all
> As a second Augustus, whose virtue will
> Render unto France illustrious renown.[98]

Henri was also given a gift at the end of the entry: a statue of Minerva, goddess of wisdom, who was crowned with a branch of palm signifying the victory "obtained by the virtuous and prudent Prince over the vices that are *trodden beneath his feet.*"[99] According to the inscription on her pedestal, this victory would be obtained through Henri's knowledge and learning, for it was by this means that "the king would triumph in the world over all [other] kings."[100]

Having largely abandoned the religious allegories of the previous entries, Henri's triumph reflected tensions similar to those occurring in the Puy's poetry. Though it maintained a staunchly religious attitude toward the monarch's identity and mission in the world, these came to be ever more closely tied to the unique cultural capacities, talents, and interests of the entry's organizers. These were given clear expression on the base of the statue of Minerva, where the "epitaph of Apollo *Musagète*" (a "Hercules" who was "tutor and patron of the Muses") was inscribed:

> owing to the magnanimous power and virtue of the noble prince, the learned and studious persons represented by the Muses are liberally supported and maintained in the surety and repose necessary to men of knowledge, who will use their offices to reciprocate by composing learned and elegant monuments to perpetuate the memory of the exemplary acts and heroic deeds of this virtuous prince.[101]

Henri, as the inscription on Rouen's gift makes clear, was being entreated to protect and patronize the arts as the best means of ensuring the immortality of his reign and the glory of France.[102] However, what makes his triumph so interesting is not this unabashed lobbying for support, but the way in which its narrative intertwined the cultural ambitions of Rouen's new elite with the political status and power of the French monarchy, and with an apocalyptic eschatology auguring the end of the world and the return of the Golden Age.

Of God, Kings, and Language

Michel de Certeau has remarked that in the sixteenth century men were obsessed with two biblical images: "the mythic image of paradise lost, and the eschatological or apocalyptic image of the New Jerusalem. From this point of view, rational (political or scientific) production and irrational (spiritual and poetic) ones are inspired by the same utopian vision, the goal of which is a 'great instauration'."[103] Henri's entry reflects this view, for it takes pains to point out that the foundations of paradise, like the foundations of political power, were to be based on knowledge. Thus, decorating the tableau vivant of the Elysian fields situated at the end of the entry were two placards indicating that it was "the repose of happy paradise [o]f kings enamoured with learning," and that "the republic" could only be "well-governed, when its King . . . was adorned, [with the] arts and science[s] and tempered by justice."[104]

The second coming of the Virgin Astraea had a double signification: not only was she associated with the return of a spiritual Golden Age that had been lost and then found again in the New World, but she had come to represent the renaissance of a cultural Golden Age in which language—under the auspices of the king—would be restored to its pristine purity and God's spiritual voice made once again audible to mortal ears. As du Bellay's 1549 eulogy for François I said:

> Oh great François so adored by the nine
> Sisters . . .
> You have vanquished the vile monster
> Ignorance,
> You have remade the beautiful age of
> gold:
> By you the beginnings of the world have
> returned
> The beautiful Virgin known in times of
> old.[105]

The revival, reform, and study of language—evidenced by the Puy's poetry and the text of Henri's entry—were thought to be the means by which the confusion of Babylon would be transcended, the schisms in the Church resolved, and the semantic connections with the age before the Fall restored. Thus would God's creation be *spoken* and *written* in the divine and unmediated language of the spirit.

This restoration of language was not simply a means of social or cultural distinction, or a means of acquiring the patronage of the king, but an act of spiritual devotion. The triumph of the Normans, as Guillaume Tasserie argued, was brought about by superior piety and faith, as demonstrated by their spirited defense of the Virgin. This defense was conducted not with arms but with verse. The triumph of the entry's organizers, like that of their king, was to be a triumph of culture and of faith—of language conjoined with piety to forge a new ideal of civilization and a new ideal of mankind. Thus would they brace themselves for the battles to come so that they might triumph over heretics and Satan and at last reach the end of their long and perilous voyage: to land in "the port of grace of paradise"—in a "new world pure and holy."

PLATE 1. The first part of Henri's entry into Rouen. BMR, Ms. Y. 28. Courtesy of the Bibliothèque Municipale de Rouen. Photo by Thierry Ascensio Parvy.

PLATE 2. The second half of Henri's entry into Rouen. BMR, Ms. Y. 28. Courtesy of the Bibliothèque Municipale de Rouen. Photo by Thierry Ascensio Parvy.

PLATE 3. Rouen's Port (c. 1525). Jacques Le Lieur's *Livre des fontaines*. BMR, Ms. Y. 19. Courtesy of the Bibliothèque Municipale de Rouen. Photo by Thierry Ascensio Parvy.

PLATE 4. Bas-relief in wood of the Isle du Brésil: "La coupe et le transport du bois rouge." From the façade of 17, rue Malpalu, Rouen. Courtesy of the Musée départemental des Antiquités, Rouen. Photo by Yohann Deslandes.

PLATE 5. Bas-relief in wood of the Isle du Brésil: "Embarquement du bois rouge." From the façade of 17, rue Malpalu, Rouen. Courtesy of the Musée départemental des Antiquités, Rouen. Photo by Yohann Deslandes.

PLATE 6. Natives cutting and transporting brazilwood for French traders. Jean Roze of Dieppe, detail of Map XII from his *Boke of Idrography* (1542). Courtesy of the British Library.

PLATE 7. Chariot of Good Fortune from Henri II's entry into Rouen. BMR, Ms. Y. 28. Courtesy of the Bibliothèque Municipale de Rouen. Photo by Thierry Ascensio Parvy.

PLATE 8. Jacques Le Lieur offering his poetry to the Virgin. BMR, Ms. Y. 226a. Courtesy of the Bibliothèque Municipale de Rouen. Photo by Thierry Ascensio Parvy.

PLATE 9. *Le chariot du fort geant celeste.* BN, Ms. fr. 379. Courtesy of the Bibliothèque Nationale de France.

PLATE 10. The Chariot of Victory from Henri II's entry into Rouen. BMR, Ms. Y. 28. Courtesy of the Bibliothèque Municipale de Rouen. Photo by Thierry Ascensio Parvy.

PLATE 11. *Lily that Rises in Triumph and Victory.* BN, Ms. fr. 379. Courtesy of the Bibliothèque Nationale de France.

PLATE 12. The Virgin, Patroness of the *Puy.* BN, Ms. fr. 379. Courtesy of the Bibliothèque Nationale de France.

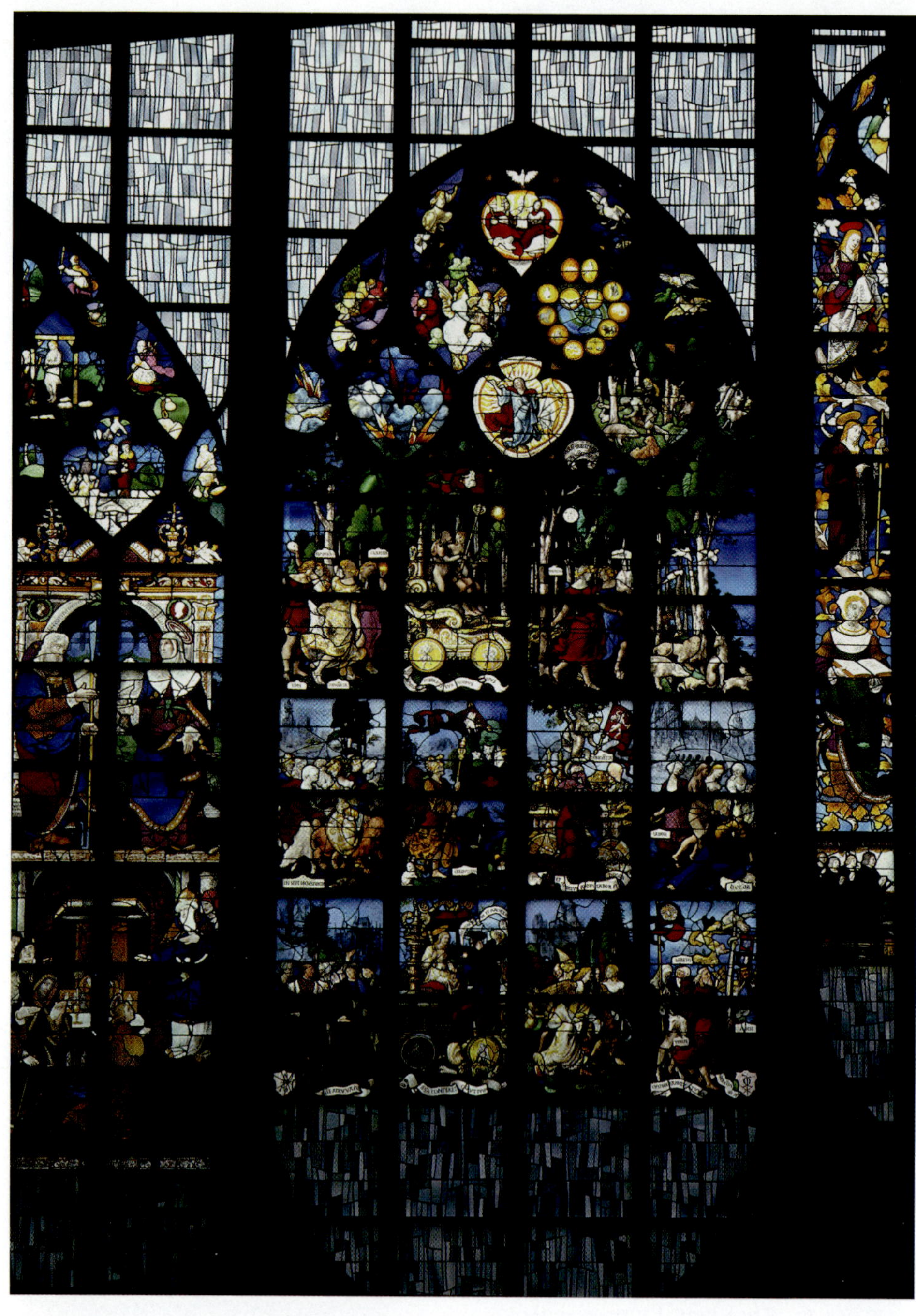

PLATE 13. Windows from l'église de St.-Vincent, Rouen: "Triomphe de la Vierge dit vitrail des chairs." Photo Y. Miossec, ©1993. Inventaire général–ADAGP.

PLATE 14. Windows from l'église de St.-Patrice, Rouen: "Triomphe de Religion." Photo by T. Leroy, ©1991. Inventaire général–ADAGP.

PLATE 15. Helsinus' voyage. BN, Ms. fr. 379. Courtesy of the Bibliothèque Nationale de France.

PLATE 16. Voyage toward Salvation. BN, Ms. fr. 379. Courtesy of the Bibliothèque Nationale de France.

PLATE 17. Making an astrolabe. BN, Ms. fr. 1537. Courtesy of the Bibliothèque Nationale de France.

PLATE 18. Navigating from Sin to a New World pure and holy. BN, Ms. fr. 1537. Courtesy of the Bibliothèque Nationale de France.

PLATE 19. Detail of the Apocalyptic Virgin from l'église de St.-Vincent, Rouen. Photo by C. Kollman, © 1994. Inventaire général–ADAGP.

PLATE 20. Virgin with scales and sword. BN, Ms. fr. 379. Courtesy of the Bibliothèque Nationale de France.

PLATE 21. Windows of St. Michel from l'église de St.-Vincent, Rouen. Photo by Y. Miossec © 1994. Inventaire général–ADAGP.

PLATE 22. A Conard confronts a Learned Man. A marginal illustration in Jacques Le Lieur's manuscript of pious Marian verse. BMR, Ms. Y. 226a. Courtesy of the Bibliothèque Municipale de Rouen. Photo by Thierry Ascensio Parvy.

PLATE 23. Rouen, city of God, most beautiful in the world. BMR, Ms. Y. 226a. Courtesy of the Bibliothèque Municipale de Rouen. Photo by Thierry Ascensio Parvy.

CHAPTER 6

The Triumph of the Conards

In Chapter 3 we found that Henri II's identity as king found its reflection not only in the humanistically conceived mirror of the Gallic Hercules, but in the Brazilian Hercules, Quoniambec. The restoration of linguistic purity—and the recalibration of the relationship between words and things—that was to prefigure the dawn of a new Golden Age had a similarly savage mirror. This mediated hybridity is essential to understanding the place held by the New World at the beginning of the entry; it is also essential to understanding the identity of the new elites responsible for writing and staging it. This chapter proposes a return to the entry's beginning in the light of its ability to deconstruct its end: what Bakhtin might characterize as the laughter that challenges the pretensions and self-importance of learned high culture.

A life of ease, laughter, and plenty; a life without laws or civility; a life of freedom and liberty; a joyous life lived as it ought to be lived: natural, simple, and true—and not just anywhere, or rather nowhere (in utopia), but just over there. There! On a plot of land 200 paces long and 35 wide, just beyond the city's walls, in the Faubourg Saint-Sever. Dressed in somber black, the king was there too, on the outside looking in, his regal gaze wandering with delight over his New World subjects as they rollicked in the brisk Norman autumn wearing not so much as a stitch. But what were these barbarous, naked, and pierced savages doing in Rouen? Why was their antipodean world, so reminiscent of charivaris and *les jours gras*, duplicated with such care and

FIGURE 16. *Les Triomphes de l'abbaye des Conards* (Rouen, 1587), Ms Leber 2612. Courtesy of the Bibliothèque Municipale de Rouen. Photo by Thierry Ascensio Parvy.

precision and then placed at the center of this highly structured and chore-ographed royal spectacle? It is time to approach this question from a differ-ent angle—leaving aside, for a time, the space occupied by the sternly seri-ous Marian poets of the Puy to join in the fun—that is, to examine the role played in the entry by the city's *Abbaye des Conards*.[1]

The Conards were "the most celebrated *société joyeuse* in sixteenth-cen-tury France."[2] So (in)famous were they that the king himself made a special point of asking that they entertain him when he came to Rouen for his royal entry. Rouen's city council promptly granted them permission to put on a triumphant and joyous *chevauchée* (procession) as a kind of addendum to Henri's entry.[3] Thus, "by diverse sumptuous costumes and shows, by cav-alcades of triumphal chariots, by an infinity of torches, by new inventions, subtle and probing sayings and by pleasing moralities, the king and all those who followed in his court [were entertained]."[4]

Un Espace de Conardie

The Abbey of the Conards was organized in mock parallel with the hi-erarchical organization of the church. Wearing red robes and carrying a miter and a cross, their leader, or abbé, surrounded himself with a council of cardinals and dignitaries, such as the Cardinal of Evil Abundance (*Maucomble*), the Bishop of Flat Balls (*Platte Bourse*), the Duke of Slap Ass (*Frappecul*), and the Grand Patriarch of Syphilitics.[5] The preparations for their annual celebrations of carnival—*les hauts jours de l'abbé*—though not quite on the same scale as a royal entry festival, were elaborate.[6] We have no accounts of the Conards' triumph of 1550, but it was probably much like the one that occurred ten years before.[7]

On February 8, 1541, the Conards requested parliament's permission to do what Conards do best—party. Their request took the form of an extended poem in rhyming verse.[8] In making their final appeal for confirmation of their traditional right to celebrate Mardi Gras, the poem ends with a pointed question: "Alas, Good Times, will you ever come back?"[9] Parliament responded two days later, giving the Conards permission to celebrate in their accustomed manner, so long as they did not commit excesses such as masking at night, and that they limit their festivities to Sunday, Monday, and Mardi Gras.[10] This news came as a grave disappointment, so much so that the Conards decided to remove their annual revelries to Fécamp or Saint Gervais, which were beyond the jurisdiction of Rouen's parliament. However, Jacques Sireulde, bailiff of parliament, good Conard, and "protector of communal laughter" that he was, pleaded in verse that the Conards be allowed to mask, promising that if this were to be permitted they would see the abbaye transported on their beautiful chariots into immortal memory.[11]

On February 21, the parliament responded *in verse* to Sireulde's poetic plea, giving the Conards permission to celebrate day and night in exquisite triumph, to go masked and triumphant, with pipes, tambourines, and chariots.[12] A few days later, on February 26, the Conards sent out one of their officers along with "829 masked men on horseback with drums and pipes" to announce the "*grand, gros, gras, haut et magnifique* day of the Abbaye that would take place the next day . . .

> On the part of the *Abbaye* . . .
> and the followers of the cross and miter
>
> . . .
>
> Wanting these days by true and Conard zeal,
> To give pleasure, as much to gentle woman as to girls,
> We will begin to triumph . . .
> Tomorrow at noon, or sooner, not later.
> Otherwise, the Abbé, our Conard prince
> Wants and prays that you be ready at ten,
> Unless, of course, you have better ideas.[13]

La Chevauchée des Conards (1540) Part I

Noon. At the old palace, the site of Rouen's law courts, the abbé met with his minions, who were accompanied by the nine Vices of the Convent and "2400 or 2500 people" costumed and masked in diverse manners. It was, says the published account of the Conard's progress, *Les Triomphes de l'abbaye des Conards* (Rouen, 1587), "a miracle of wine to see their order, which the cardinals of the college of the Conards maintained so well." Banging drums and tooting horns, the boisterous crowd marched by: a wave of cacophonous sound and contagious excitement channeled through Rouen's narrow streets. A solitary figure—an old man on an ass—followed in silence. He was dressed as a phantom. In his outstretched hands he held a severed head (*une teste de mort*).[14] He solemnly read the following poem to the crowd:

> In the season of Conards
> Truth sleeps or does not dare speak.
> The weak have the heaviest burdens,
> Treason goes by land and by air,
> Reason has no place where money wants to be,
> Business is in the cemetery,
> Faith hides and is inconstant,
> Envy rules us, and we call it faith
> Fear wants to conduct all our affairs
> And thus all is contrary to just law.[15]

The season of the Conards, he seems to have been announcing, was not simply a festive rupture in the everyday and normal course of life—a carnival—but a sign of the world's fallen state: a world that no longer made sense, where reason had been supplanted by money, where faith had become little more than envy, and where corruption, fear, and uncertainty ruled. And whereas everyone else was afraid to speak, the Conards, by virtue of their *conardie*, were endowed with the ability—and freedom—to point out hypocrisy wherever they saw it. As they said:

> Under the shadow of acting mad . . .
> More crazy than an astonished goose, . . .
> The Conards are permitted to say all . . .
> Without incurring the ire of the Prince.[16]

More than simply speaking the unspoken truth, however, the Conards championed their celebrations as a didactic mirror in which the Rouennais could see—and thereby correct—their inequities and moral failures. Accordingly, in their request for the parliament's permission to perform their chevauchée, they claimed that their celebrations would be "like the figure of Socrates" who was "a mirror wherein his disciples could see—whether completely naked or clothed—if their natural bodies (*corps Nature*) had been corrupted or falsely decorated."

> If one would perchance see manifest in this Socratic mirror any vice, or moral failing, Socrates would—by humane and subtle reason, prudence, equanimity, sobriety and constancy, and with true words and deeds—rectify these faults. Jurisconsuls, the Abbaye of the Conards wants to put this Socratic mirror into practice.[17]

Not only were the Conards symptomatic of the world's corruption, they were also—at least potentially, they claimed—part of its cure.

After the phantom came the funeral procession of *Marchandise* (commerce). This was led by Alchofribas (a well-known anagram of Rabelais), who was dressed in the black of mourning decorated with silver tear drops.[18] He was pursued by a limping man named Diligence sounding a clarion bell. A cacophony of ringing bells followed as the domestic servants of Marchandise arrived. Written across their backs were the words *Pauvre Commun. La Republique* followed, dressed in mourning. The funeral litter of Marchandise, drawn by two horses and accompanied by pages identified as Avarice and Adversity trailed behind.[19] Bringing up the rear, Hope, wearing a laughing and joyous mask, rode on a chariot covered in black. At the crossroads of the city s/he read out the following poem:

> Hear ye, Hear ye, Hear ye, Hear ye
> And Shut up if you can
> Marchandise who was so strong and free
> And who gave to the poor their lives
> Was tired of seeing herself enslaved and died
> The Abbé Conard and his minions
> Honor her more than is profitable
> And deplore such a lamentable loss
> But what are you going to do? Pray to the heavenly gods
> That laughing hope is favorable to the young
> And brings back that which was lost before your eyes.[20]

After Hope, the abbé followed, garbed in all the pomp and regalia of his office. Indeed, to those looking on, he seemed more like an "Emperor, a Sultan of Babylon or a King of Persia than the Abbé of the Conards."[21] Tambourines, pipes, and trumpets pursued him, followed by the grand patriarch of the Syphilitics accompanied by the most "savage" men one could imagine: with rotted eyes, cheeks pierced clear through, and noses cut open to the light of day. As for the noses, not even Cyrano could imagine such noses: there were thoughtful noses, timorous noses, jar noses, forgetful noses, in-your-face noses, neglected noses, severed noses, hot-tempered noses, despicable noses, terrifying noses, and noses absolutely astonishing. "In short," says the account, "this was the grandest and most horrific spectacle that it was possible to see with two eyes."[22] Then, preceded by a banner "*Sapiens habet oculos*," came sixteen men wearing clothes the color of smoke representing the Shadows of Conardie.[23] Each read out and distributed verses written in *huitains*, as for example, the Shadow of Religion:

> Under the shadow of religion . . .
> reigns [today] hypocrisy
> And Schism, in many regions
> Against God, Faith and Church
> Ravenous wolves in strange guise
> Wear the clothes of simplicity
> Disguised in the Holy Scriptures
> Under the shadow of sanctity.[24]

After the Shadows of Conardie came a cavalcade of seven antique chariots (*faits par bon art d'architecture*),[25] that enacted a farce called *La buée ou laissive* ("Doing the Laundry").[26] On the first chariot, Religion is depicted gathering Rouen's dirty linen with the church putting it to soak. Faith and Truth, accompanied by Ambition, Simony, Avarice, Hypocrisy, Favor, and Riches help wring it out, and then boil, bleach, and wash it. Mad Love dries it and Justice folds it. Accompanying the play was a long poem that explained how the nobility and the church oppress the poor. Both were corrupt and had abandoned their traditional roles (to protect the poor), forcing Poverty to work at the most difficult task of all—hanging the laundry out to dry. Thus, the church profited from charitable donations and assigning benefices while the nobility enjoyed the fruits of exploiting the poor.

La Chevauchée des Conards (1540) Part II

The Conard's triumphal procession aimed to demonstrate the world's fallen state: its passing from an Age of Gold to an Age of Iron. This view was pervasive in the literary/theatrical œuvre associated with the Conards; as another of their plays points out:

> There are more marvels today than ever,
> Everyone and Many-People decide,
> But things are worse than they [ever] were under Saturn's reign,

> When everyone lived as he pleased.
> Laughter, song, feasting, and jests are over and the world is damned,
> Unless God reforms men soon.[27]

No one, except perhaps the poor laboring classes, was absolved of guilt in bringing about this state of affairs. Indeed, there was plenty of blame to go around. Everyone seems to have had a part in the death of Marchandise. Even the virtues associated with doing business (Profit, Hardiness, Enterprise, Assurance) are tied to the vices (Envy, Dissimulation, False Seeming, Ruin, Anxiety, Deception) in forming Marchandise's funeral cortege.

La buée ou laissive gives further specificity to the charges—accusing the church of selling offices and the word of God for a penny and the nobility for ruthlessly exploiting the poor for its own selfish gain. Such accusations were commonplace for the Conards; in another of their farces (*sotties*), churchmen are described as "debauched whoremongers, gamblers and gluttons . . . / lechers full of frenzy . . . / dissolute renegades, apostates and Syphilitic drunkards."[28] As for monks, "may the fires of hell burn them / So green (so horny) are their balls."[29] Neither were the nobles spared as the Conards considered them nothing but a "gang of scoundrels / [and] Evil, good-for-nothing robbers and thieves."[30]

Though the standard accompanying the Shadows of Conardie—"the wiseman's eyes are in his head . . . "—seems to hold out hope for salvation through wisdom, the passage is left dangling incomplete on their banner, its ellipses pointing by omission to the parade of the Shadows (Good Faith, Money, Goods, Ambition, Public Good, Insanity, Law, Love, What You Will) to complete the well-known verse: "the wiseman's eyes are in his head, but the fool walketh in darkness, and yet the same fate overtakes them both." Mixing the good with the bad, the virtues and the vices, order and disorder, the Conards' chevauchée deconstructed and problematized the putative stability of faith, reason, and authority in the light of lived reality. What is, is not an ideal, an abstraction, a universal, but a reality ensconced in shadow and contradiction. Moreover, it was not only the social world that was threatened by the self-centered acts of men pursuing their own interests, but the very structure of the universe itself. This ontological destabilization permeated the very core of reality—to the "officers of the house of Marchandise" (Air, Earth, Fire, and Water), each identifying itself by carrying the banner of its opposite, that is, the sign of its own annihilation.[31]

In the Conards' chevauchée, Church, Religion, Faith, Charity, Justice, Love, and the Nobility were not opposed to the vices of Ambition, Simony, Avarice, and Favor, but worked alongside them. Poverty, on the other hand, dressed in rags and forced to hang out the laundry, seemed the inevitable consequence of the corruption of the traditional order. The carnivalesque world of the Conards was not simply a temporally bounded ludic inversion of the norms and values of everyday life, but an explicit attempt to represent contemporary social conditions. The Conards' critical "sociology," written in the form of a satiric mirror, took aim at those who had abandoned their traditional communitarian roles. They even parodied the pretensions of kings, emperors, and popes to govern the world as a game played among so many fools. Thus, immediately after *La buée ou laissive*, on a chariot drawn by the four Estates, sat a pope, an emperor, a king, and a fool playing with a ball representing the "poor world"; on their backs were placards that read: "Take that," "Give it here," "Laugh about it," and "Mock this." [32]

After this chariot passed by, nine hermits (the Hermit of Red Bum, the Newly Dressed Hermit, the Young Savage Hermit, etc.) came, each carrying a parchment inscribed with two lines of poetry.[33] Next arrived a band with twenty flaming torches [*falots*], four tambourine players, and a pipe player; they carried a standard that said: "*et lux tenebris lucet, et eam non comprehenderut*" [and the light shone in darkness and the darkness comprehended it not (John 1:5)].[34] They were accompanied by a blindfolded figure looking toward the heavens with a banner that read: "Purity renders shadows light." This passage, also from the book of John, is preceded by the famous verses:

> In the beginning was the Word, and the Word was with God, and the
>   Word was God.
> The same was in the beginning with God.
> All things were made through him. Without him was not anything made that has
>   been made.
> In him was life, and the life was the light of men (John 1: 1–4).

The Word, God, and the Light—these were the life of men; yet despite the hope and the promise that light would—through sage men—overcome darkness, God and tradition were being ignored in Rouen. After the blind Conard came a group of twenty-six men wearing masts and sails on their heads with lines of rhetoric written across their backs.[35] Holding a banner saying "Verse Overcome," they perhaps signified that the Word, rather than firmly anchoring man to reality and God, had been overwhelmed by the shifting winds of fortune. Signification, detached from sure ontological ground, is left to its own device to navigate the vagaries of an all too harsh world. Then came a band of *Neuds faits* (knots made), whose standard showed a knot on one side and a rhyme about the good fortune of those who escaped knotty times on the other.[36] Next several other bands marched by: e.g., twelve men dressed in mourning, the Fathers in the Hole (that is,

the burying of tradition in the personified form of fathers) and the Astonished of the World.[37] The procession of each of these troops was accompanied by the reading and distribution of poetry. Last of all came the prophets.
Accompanied by 230 horsemen, tambourine, and pipe players, they arrived
at the pont de Robec and read poetry and passed out candy (especially to
the women). They were introduced with the following verses:

> Horny Conards who wear horny horns
> If you want to understand my device
> Come hear the prophets' pronouncements
> Proclaiming the times which presently divide us
> They have mocked the pride and covetousness
> Which are maintained by all estates
>
> . . .
>
> Of people who are motivated by money and greed
> They have ridiculed . . . without parallel
> They will come to correct malice
> The times of tears and the year of great marvels.[38]

For the Conards, the only chance at regaining the lost paradise of the
traditional order was to hold up their mirror to all the estates—to let them
see what perverse iniquities they had brought into the world. As one of the
poems that accompanied the Astonished of the World proclaimed:

> If the hypocrites were to cease their hypocrisy
> If the Senates cared about justice
> If loyalty and Faith governed business
> The times would come when we would live without
>   care (*sans soucy*):
> For the present, we do not find it thus
> For God exchanges the benefices you trade
> The Men of Justice are marked by vice
> And nothing is left but the Nobles who hurt
> The poor common people . . .
> The three in one, this is nothing: how will all of this end?[39]

The theological allusion to the Trinity is used here to indicate that the traditional order no longer held together. In Christian doctrine the Father, the
Son, and the Holy Ghost are united in the Godhead. The parallel being
drawn by the Conards between the social and spiritual order shows up the
disjunction between reality and tradition and their putative link to religious
justifications and Christian community. The men of law, the clergy, and the
nobility had all abandoned their ideal functions; their actions, moreover, deconstructed the ideological justifications for their power: "the three in one,
this is nothing." How indeed, "will all of this end?"

The Conards were writing and performing their sotties at a time when Protestantism was perceived as the principal threat to social and spiritual order. That they were not accused of heresy for making such statements points to the social register within which they must have been read. Members of the clergy and the nobility were frequently attacked by the Conards for abandoning their responsibilities. The addition of the third member of the Trinity, however, is something of an innovation—one which we will need to examine in some detail, for the men of Justice and Law were the social agents that the Conards held most responsible for the death of Marchandise and the destruction of traditional communal order.

A Conard World

Were the Conards' accusations true; or were they, simply, *conard* accusations? Had business really died? Were the poor in such desperate straits? Had "every man," as *Les Menus propos* put it, "fallen in misfortune and misery"?[40] Was the world, as another of the Conards' plays charged, "forever getting worse"?[41]

Today, Rouen is a small provincial city. Indeed, it has become something of a suburb of Paris. Though it boasts many items of historical interest, it is neither an economic nor a cultural center. In the sixteenth century, however, Rouen was known as the second city of the realm. Only Lyon could vie with it on the level of its commercial and cultural significance. As one poet put it: "*En France, y a trois citez excellentes, / C'est assavoir Paris, Rouen, Lyon.*"[42] Yet there was not just one economy in sixteenth-century Rouen, there were many. For some, the first half of the century brought enormous profits and newfound social status, for others, it brought irredeemable poverty, hardship, misery, suffering, and death.

The century or so after the Hundred Years' War is known as a century of recovery. From the 1470s up until the Wars of Religion, Normandy enjoyed sustained economic growth.[43] Despite notable successes, the combination of demographic upswing and Norman customs of partible inheritance led to the multiplication of smallholdings and the increasing exploitation of marginal lands. Though there were marked advances in agrarian practices and techniques during this period, there was also a decline in agricultural productivity. Subsistence became an endemic problem. For many, already living on the edge of starvation, inclement weather or crop failure had disastrous consequences, as documented in the Rouennais farce entitled *Les Troys pelerins et malice*: "Why does winter come this summer / Which keeps us in poverty/ And from which great suffering comes . . . ?"[44] Moreover, the first half of the century brought a spectacular rise in prices. This inflationary pressure, coupled with the decline in rural wages (according to Guy Bois, by two-thirds to three-quarters between 1500 and 1550), led to the abject poverty of much of the agrarian population.[45] Though decline in real wages made wage labor a less-than-likely solution for the great majority of the dispossessed and marginal landholders, Rouen's expanding textile industry took advantage of the desperation of the surrounding rural population.[46] The cathedral chapter noted, for example, a great influx of country folk into the city at this time; many, they observed, were dying of hunger, others were begging and disturbing the peace. It was not long before Rouen's city council began to legislate against mendicancy and to set up mechanisms to redeem the "worthy" poor. This was something of an innovation, for though there were always poor in Rouen, the city council came to the conclusion that the causes of poverty were not simply moral, but due to external circumstances. As they put it in 1544: *"la marchandise n'a plus cours."*[47] Indeed, there is substantial anecdotal evidence in the records of the Hôtel de Ville concerning the inadequacy of traditional means of coping with the poor; this led to extra-ecclesiastical attempts to solve the problem.[48] In 1534, for example, the city council started an early modern version of a welfare to work program. They gave the able-bodied poor a choice: either do public works voluntarily, or be whipped, put in chains, and be forced to work, or have your ears cut off and be banished from the city upon pain of death.[49]

The dire state of marchandise was, according to many, also due to the constant state of warfare. In 1543, for example, the city council complained that "the open war for the last ten or twelve years had led to the neglect of the state of marchandise." Because of this, they continued, "the greater part of the city's inhabitants who depended for their livelihood on the manufacture of linen and cloth and bonnets had fallen into extreme poverty and begging."[50] Henri's entry was in part a desperate plea for peace: that the king might, as another Hercules, put "the cruel adder of Mars in disarray."[51] Others were more specific, blaming royal taxes for impoverishing the city. According to Fouquet's account, many of Rouen's richest merchants were forced to renounce marchandise altogether because of the *"l'excès des impôts."*[52] The persistent and intense anxiety of the city's council regarding the monies owed to the king (104,000 *livres* in 1550) leaps off the folio pages of their deliberations.[53]

Yet, while many suffered, others thrived. Rouen—as the *avant port* of Paris, the administrative capital of Normandy, the seat of parliament, and an archbishopric—was an important center of commerce and trade, being especially known for printing, luxury textiles (e.g., *les couleurs joyeuses* derived from Rouen's trade in Brazil), metallurgy, and for the import and distribution of salt, alum, linen, and spices.[54] The bourgeois merchants at the center of these industries reaped immense profits.[55]

Though their notable economic success seems to contradict the accusation about the state of marchandise, it also points to another possible meaning of the Conards' mock funeral, for as merchants gained in wealth and power, the question for them increasingly became (as George Huppert has put it) "how to leave marchandise behind?" Which is to say: "how to become a *gentilhomme?*"[56] One extremely effective way was to leave her (Marchandise) for dead and to take up more advantageous social positions by buying up land from poor nobles and peasants and/or pursuing the sinecure of royal or municipal office.

It is beyond question that the sixteenth century brought a substantial infusion of urban *roturiers* into the seignorial class in upper Normandy.[57] As the Conards put it in their chevauchée: "Under the shadow of I don't know who; / Much more than the countryside, marchandise profits from the *taille*."[58] Or as the *Moral de tout le monde* (c. 1535) said:

> By Money more than Combat,
> All the world becomes a gentleman (*gentillatre*)
>
> By money vile laborers
> Succeed in becoming honored nobles
>
> By money many a wicked schemer
> Would be noble who was but a merchant.[59]

According to this farce:

> All the world wants to be noble
> Even the most villainous, such as they are
> Each says himself to be a gentleman
> Even those more foul than a dead rat.[60]

From the turn of the century, declining seignorial revenues and high inflation forced many nobles into the arms of new urban elites who lent them money; this noble debt led to the transfer of both land and title from the nobility to Rouen's wealthy merchant community.[61] Urban nouveaux riches were thus faulted not only for exploiting the poor, but also poor nobles. As *Moral de tout le monde* observed:

> All the world obtains by money
> Dignities, prebendes, offices
> By money it has benefices
> By money the strong and the weak are hurt.[62]

Many of the individuals and families discussed in previous chapters who were associated with New World trade and the Puy de Palinod—e.g., the Romés, the Croismares, the Saldaignes, the Hallés—eagerly bought up both land and offices.[63] Thus, one of the principal organizers of Henri's entry, the New World merchant Pierre du Couldray, in addition to being the sieur de Fréville—and owning the fiefs de Ruffaux, de Boscroger, and du Feugré—[64] was an *échevin* in Rouen's municipal government, *secrétaire du roi, audiencier en la chancellerie du Parlement de Normandie, député aux Etats de Normandie, and vicompte et receveur ordinaire des vicomtés de Conche et Breteuil.*

The Conards' *chevauchée* singled out the "rapaciousness and greed" of such men as the principal cause of the hard times that had overtaken Rouen:

> Under the shadow of money many a novice
> Has become a master or a sir
> I see Benefices and offices
> Traded and sold for wheat and flour
> Favor too much loves money's color
> Now we march without it
> Of money, we have joy and pain
> Under its color, we stagger and reel.[65]

Or perhaps even more to the point:

> Under the Shadow of Beautiful Clothes
> One sees so many vices committed,
> Thus, the poor are killed and the rich robbed.
> By subtle arts and evil deeds
> One sees so many new offices
> Which are the ruin of the people:
> Of which I say—benefices such as these
> To give or to sell is an unworthy thing.[66]

France was clearly no longer living in the Age of Gold. As Saturn said in *Les Quatres ages*, another farce played in Rouen: "My reign is one of tranquility and ease, where the land produces all that is needed without labor, where there is neither property nor the constraint of law, where everywhere the earth blooms and men live without care."[67] Though lost in the distant past, Saturn's Golden Age was preserved by the spatial distance of the New World found across the seas. As Ronsard was famously to write about the Brazilians in his *Discours contre fortune*: "*Ils vivent maintenant en leur âge doré.*" Yet the insatiable greed of Normandy's merchants threatened even this haven. Thus, the Age of Brass in *Les Quatre ages* proclaimed: I want to put ships on the seas, "to navigate to Cailicou, to bresil, to cap, to Perou . . . to ravish (*rauys*) the goods of foreign lands."[68] Similar views are echoed in numerous of the moralités, sotties, and farces played in sixteenth-century Rouen. In these, those held responsible for destroying social order were characterized as *gens nouveaux* (new men), new because they were not part of the traditional order and had no part in the feudal ethic of mutual service and obligation. Innovators were feared and despised in early modern France; this was especially the case for the new men singled out by the Conards' farces.[69] According to them, these new men aimed "to turn this world into another kind"—a corrupt world gone mad that would be judged by God in the final days soon to come.[70]

The Triumph's Mirror

The participation of the Conards in Henri's entry might be understood with reference to the popular sermon exemplum of the fool in the emperor's chariot. The fool's purpose, it was explained, was to remind the king of his mortality. According to the account of Margaret of Anjou's entry into London, a fool sat with an emperor "to schewe clerely [th]at all worldely glorie is transitori and not abidynge and evidently to declare [th]at in [his] estate is none assurance." Thus, the fool might "smite [the] conquerroure euer in [the] necke and uppon [the] hed [so as] to abate the haugtiness which the applause of his countrymen might tend to excite."[71] This freedom was not just the fool's, for on the day of an emperor's triumph, anyone could criticize and mock the emperor without risk of incurring his ire. Bound tightly to the mirror of princes' literature, this comic mirror presented an emperor with a moral lesson: take heed of your mortality and remember that despite the exalted character of your office, you are, like all men, subject to death and corruption. *Nosce te ipsum* (Know thyself), the fool shouted in the emperor's ear along the procession route of his triumph, for despite all the pomp and circumstance of your entry, you are but a man.[72] As we have seen, the mirrors constructed for kings reflected others as well, most notably, in this case, those who wrote, designed, and enacted Henri's entry. The Conards' message was directed at them, as well as at their king.

Eight days after the official entry celebration staged for Henri in Rouen, the Conards played their farce. The king was so pleased with their performance that he extended his personal protection to the abbaye. Whereas the official entry aimed to transform the king into a humanist prince who would protect and patronize the social, intellectual, and material concerns of the new urban elites responsible for staging it, the *Farce des veaux* performed by the Conards was a parody of the city's solemn presentation of this narrative. The parade of *veaux* the Conards presented to the king referred to the expression *veaux de disme* which was at once the name of the tax owed to the abbaye and a descriptive insult, *veau* meaning *sot* (fool) or *conard*. Most often, this appellation was directed at a foolish man, most famously, Georges le Veau. In the case of the farce, it was used to characterize a procession of veaux (composed of representatives from Rouen's various professions: the officers of the law courts, the nouveaux riches merchants, etc.) called up to pay tithes owed to the abbaye.

According to the farce, there were three kinds of fool: those who paid these taxes, those who demanded them, and those who refused to join the Conards in protesting them.[73] The triumphal march of the Conards mocked not only the formal seriousness of Henri's entry, but the self-aggrandizing pretensions of those who designed, organized, and paid for it. The new men—the officeholders, parvenus, and bourgeois merchants—who marched in the procession before the king a week earlier, took the brunt of the Conards' criticisms. According to the farce, the greatest veaux in the world were those nourished by the labor of lawyers.[74] The veaux of the sovereign courts, on the other hand, were far too skinny because they were nourished by avarice;[75] equally underfed were the veaux of the vicompte, which needed to be left out to fatten during the *mession* (a vacation taken by lawyers and scholars).[76] The veaux of the courts, who estimate themselves knowledgeable without knowledge, on the other hand, are "nature's perfect veaux."[77] The veaux of the men of labor, ennobled by the power of money, followed; they were, as could be expected, scrawny little veaux, for after all, one cannot easily make "a little bird into a buzzard."[78]

The New Men

Despite their scatological, impious, and irreverent spectacles, the Conards were not, as is commonly thought, in any simple sense anti-hierarchical.[79] Rather than posing a challenge to the official high culture as represented by the king and the high nobility, they took as their principal target Rouen's new civic elites, whom they accused of usurping traditional authority, destroying the Golden (feudal) Age, and delivering the world to the uncertainties of the bloody Age of Iron.

Much of the Conards' œuvre was concerned with criticizing the scheming pretensions and dissimulating affectations of those whom they labeled gens nouveaux; that is, men who had risen to stations for which they had no right by either birth or tradition. These were the men the Conards held most responsible for the destruction of social and moral order. Yet, the Conards were not lowly outcasts criticizing Rouen's elite from the margins, but were themselves central players in Rouen's civic life. This is perhaps demonstrated by their participation in penitential processions such as that held in 1542 when the city council decided to organize a *procession générale* to combat the "pollution of sins and heresies that could anger Our God."[80] From what little we know about the Conards, and from what we can glean from their highly literate output, they were not altogether different from the members of Rouen's Puy de Palinod; which is to say, many were themselves part of Rouen's new civic-cultural elite.[81]

A number of the Conards were arrested by the parliament in 1542 for publicly defaming the character of the city's échevins, whom they accused of "cupidity, treason, and injustice."[82] The list of those arrested, though small, is the closest thing we have to a membership roster.[83] Two of those named (Noel Cotton and Jehan Delacroix) were cited in the records of the Hôtel de Ville in 1550 as being among the "*plus riches et plus notoires*" of Rouen's citizens,[84] while others, not quite so well off (Nauldin Baillart and Ysaac Jehan), were—along with Cotton and Delacroix—selected as members of Rouen's leading families to participate in Henri's entry as *enfants d'honneur*.[85] Ironically, then, these Conards (of 1542) took part in the very same procession of civic elites parodied by the Conards' parade of veaux staged shortly after the 1550 entry. Others arrested included Jehan Crepel, a joiner (*menuysier*), Jehan Baillart, who like his brother Nauldin, was to be a *quartenier* (neighborhood representative), a city counselor, and an échevin; Philippe Cayeux (Cailloux) who became a city counselor; Guillaume Lejeune, the Conards' abbé, who was a merchant, and Jacques Langlois, who also became a quartenier of one of the city's arrondissements.

Jacques Sireulde, the man responsible for the published account of the Conards' triumph, was a bailiff (*huissier*) of Normandy's parliament. He, along with another of the men found on the list of those arrested in 1542, Robert Fouquet, was a member of the Puy de Palinod. In addition, Jonathan Beck has suggested that Pierre Tasserie, author of one of texts collected in the *Manuscrit La Valière*, was a Conard.[86] Like his brother Guillaume, author of *Le Triomphe des Normands*, discussed in Chapter 4, Pierre was a member of the Puy de Palinod. Joseph Tasserie, the New World merchant and organizer of Henri II's entry festival, was his nephew. Another of Beck's suggestions is the lawyer Jacques Caillart.[87] Caillart wrote a number of farces, including a collection of local proverbs and sayings published in 1557 under the title *Fricassée crotestyllonnée*. That this book's dedication was signed "Caillart . . . abbé of Mocking (*Raillard*)," surely indicates that its author was a Conard.[88] Moreover, Caillart was a member of both the Puy de Palinod and one of the city's other major poetry societies, the Puy des Pauvres—a poetic brotherhood dedicated to helping Rouen's poor. This poetic concourse boasted some of Rouen's most illustrious citizens, including Louis Petremol, president of Normandy's parliament, Noël Boyvin, sieur de Tourville, échevin, and city councilor, Robert Le Roux, sieur de l'Esprevier, local notable, and counselor in parliament, Guillaume Le Seigneur des Croix, notaire et secrétaire du Roi, as well as Nicole Gallopin, Pierre du Couldray, Claude Chappuys, Michel Desarpens, and Nicole Malherbe who, as we have seen, were among the men charged by Rouen's city council with organizing Henri's entry.[89] It was none other than the "good Conard and guardian of communal laughter" himself, Jacques Sireulde, who in addition to publishing the account of the Conards' 1541 triumph, collected and introduced the poetry of the Puy des Pauvres under the title *Le Trésor immortel* in 1556.

The Carnivalesque: Classes, Hierarchies, and Questionable Identities

It has become clear in recent years that despite being associated with antiauthoritarian and antihierarchical values, the carnivalesque was neither a "letting off of steam" nor a revolutionary overturning of the powers that be. Heather Arden, for example, in her *Fool's Plays: A Study of Satire in the Sottie*, provides a much-needed corrective to our traditional notions of the carnivalesque. In her view, festive groups such as the Conards should be seen less in terms of the temporary revolt of the popular classes against the restrictive hierarchies and constraints of official culture, than as a conservative—indeed reactionary—backlash against those who were undermining the feudal tradition.[90] The Conards' satire, she argues, was directed less at the nobility and clergy than at those deemed responsible for destabilizing the traditional order—the gens nouveaux, les parvenus, les nouveaux riches: the new elites who, through their dishonest and dissimulating behavior, sought to attain social and political power that was not theirs by either birth or tradition.[91] Arden argues that the Conard's members were from the lower strata of the new middle classes.[92] Their resentment, she says, was directed not at the nobility, but at the upper echelons of their own class. The sottie, she continues, was not a transgressive but a conservative genre that aimed to undermine the corrupt present in the name of an idealized feudal past—a lost Golden Age that had been destroyed by the social ascension of the scheming gens nouveaux.

Though the Conards' members are typically thought to range from the sub-artisanal classes and small merchants to artisans and minor officials, our small sample contains a number of men who appear to have been part of what Arden describes as the "upper echelons" of the bourgeoisie. Given what one might surmise to be the general disinclination of the "haute bourgeoisie" to mingle with the *vulgum plebus*, and their desire to distance themselves from their own—or their families'—social origins, the question arises: Why would such men deign to involve themselves with the mixed social bag of Conards? Indeed, given their presence, how can one explain the Conards' anti-bourgeois satire at all? We ought, I think, to begin by jettisoning anachronistic notions of class based upon professional and economic criteria that had at best (as Arden herself admits) an ambiguous status in the sixteenth century.[93] Rather, like the members of the Puy de Palinod, the Conards were defined less by common economic status, occupational affiliation, the possession of mercantile wealth or land and title than by a shared commitment to, and interest in, the cultural life of their city. In this respect at least the Conards appear to have been part of the same civic-cultural elite discussed in previous chapters. This is not to say that membership in the Conards and/or the Puy can be subsumed into the more general category of a class or caste, but that their members were implicated in a form of life characterized by common patterns of behavior and attitude, cognitive skills, and cultural competencies. Though our sample of traceable, named Conards is relatively small, we can solidify their association with the sociocultural milieu of the Puy's Marian poets and with France's new civic cultural elites by shifting our attention to their prolific—and technically sophisticated—literary output.

Word Play and Identity

Barbara Bowen has shown that language itself was one of the essential themes of the sotties performed in Rouen.[94] This is nowhere more evident than in the Conards' intervention in the vitriolic dispute between two of Rouen's most notable poets, the renowned Clément Marot and the now obscure François Sagon.[95] In a pamphlet written in rhymed couplets in *dizaine* (ten syllables per line), entitled *Appologie faicte par le grant abbé des Conards sur les Invectives [de] Sagon [et] Marot . . . ,*" the Conards' abbé thrust himself into their poetic debate:

> My hand, you must intrude
> Take my pen, and we three [my pen, my hand and I]
>   will be joined together
> To say two words about that which we seem
> We three are but one. It is I, who will act
> So that by my hand my pen will write
> Why Brothers, if nothing untoward happens,
> I the Abbé [and we the Abbaye] fat and fattened
>   [as I—we—are]
> Will write to reform the vices
> Of these two madmen, our glorious novices.[96]

Madmen, poets, and Conards—Marot, Sagon, and their surrogates fought a vicious poetic war whose folly brought all into disrepute. The abbé had no choice but to intervene to make peace. By the trinity of his pen, his hand, and himself as abbé—and hence the unity of his redemptive word—the three (abbé, Marot, and Sagon) would thus be reconciled as one.

Another intervention by the Conards, entitled *Le Bancquet Dhonneur sur la Paix faicte entre Clement Marot, Francoys Sagon . . .* , describes a paradise of poets where all the gods, muses, and satyrs would assemble in *"paix et bon accord."* In this paradise "All true Poets of perfect eloquence/ All devotees of poetic science gathered."[97] Thus, the abbé implored Marot and Sagon ("two flowers of their [Conard] band") to put aside their differences, for here "all will find conviviality and conciliation."[98] "French Poets I bid you," he said, "To love one another like brothers and sons/ Of Minerva, and say to discord: Fie!"[99] Rouen's abbé seems to be addressing himself to—while at the same time articulating the boundaries of—an exclusive literary elite: a kind of Republic of Letters *avant la lettre.* Much like the final tableau vivant of Henri's entry, the Conards were to live in a kind of terrestrial paradise—the Elysian Fields—where all those enamored of arts and letters would find perfect peace and repose.

The 1541 chevauchée, held four years after the publication of these pamphlets, further demonstrates the importance of—and attachment to— the study and display of rhetoric, poetry, and linguistic virtuosity. This is evidenced, for example, in the back-and-forth negotiations conducted (most probably by Sireulde) in metered verse (!) with parliament. Even the parade of deformed noses in the chevauchée was a reference to the well-known poetic form known as the *blason anatomique.* There were several well-known poets who wrote *blasons* in honor of the nose.[100] Marot was the acknowledged master of the genre. Sagon also tried his hand at it; Claude Chappuys, one of the key organizers of the king's entry, wrote blasons to the hand, to the belly, and still another to the Virgin's c**.[101]

The Conards' parade, in this sense, was not simply a carnivalesque free-for-all that upturned and inverted the signs and signatures of elite identity, but was set to—and animated by—the rhythm of rhyming verse. Dizaines, huitains, ballades, rondeaux, and chants were read aloud and passed around to the crowds lining Rouen's streets. Literary skill and verbal dexterity intertwined with staging, costumes, and visual cues. Participants were identified by signs worn on their backs, by poems on placards, by *rébus* carried on banners—by rhetorical devices printed and words worn. Action was supplemented by verse and vice versa; indeed, words and symbols, figure and verse, visual tableaux and legible signs intermingled in ocular/aural displays that supplemented, played off, and undercut one another to form a multivalent (heteroglossic) mirror in which those with similar dispositions and cultural aptitudes could recognize themselves and each other; this is who we are: literate, culturally sophisticated elites—Conards.[102] The Conards' satire, in this sense, was neither an attack on the powers that be—the traditional social hierarchy—nor an artifact of the tensions between two differentiated class-positions within the bourgeoisie, but self-criticism born of the anxiety engendered by their own ambiguous social position.[103]

The Conards were *nouveaux gens*. As such, they were both the source (through their social mobility) and the sign of the world's fallen state. However, they also held out the possibility of a cure. Henri's entry presented this cure in terms of the qualities and dispositions that defined Rouen's new civic-cultural elite. Yet, the Socratic mirror they held up forced these nouveaux gens in Conard guise to recognize the inadequacies of this cure. Indeed, the topsy-turvy upside-down world of the sot, the sottie, and the chevauchée all revealed the precariousness of Rouen's new civic-cultural elite's claim to social authority. Language was ambiguous, culture was a mask, reason was folly—thus the Conards deconstructed the foundations upon which this new urban elite sought to justify its status. As the *Moral de tout le monde* reminds us: "Nobility comes from a noble heart/ And not from a villainous masquerade."[104]

The social ontology defining the relation between the sign and signified of elite status was thus becoming increasingly unstable. The ability to secure this status by linking the dispositions from which it derived (e.g., linguistic competency) to the longstanding Norman tradition of veneration for the Virgin (the Puys), was threatened by the unraveling of religious consensus. Criticism escalated: the new men had usurped traditional authority; overturned the well-ordered and organized feudal world and had risen by scheming pretension and dissimulating affectation to stations for which they had no right. "*Vous estes tous disimules*," said *Église* in one of *La Vallière's* plays.[105] The folly of conardie was not simply a mask worn on special occasions (e.g., *les jours gras*), but was perceived to be a fundamental aspect of the nouveaux gens' identity. Theirs was a kind of madness whose single-minded and relentless pursuit of social position led not only to the deception of others, but to an elemental confusion between interior and exterior, truth and dissimulation, reality and appearance.[106]

> The World by ambition
> Calls itself noble who hasn't any rents
> And by mad presumption
> Does not recognize kith or kin
> The world puts honor up for sale. . . .
> *Today All the World has gone mad.*[107]

Or, as *La Nouvelle sottie des trompeurs* puts it,

> If you would like to go by horse
> And be a man of importance,
> First you must feign
> To be wise and of good judgment,
> To say the worse and of the good to be silent
> And to be a most perfect liar,
> A guller of people, a charlatan and a con.
>
> .   .   .
>
> But, if you aren't a good flatterer,
> You won't be worth a halfpenny.
> Always say the worse, without fail
> Of someone when they are absent, . . .
> But in his presence
> Blandish him without moderation,
> Of good speech (*parole*) be a servant.[108]

The Conards' chevauchée was explicitly conceived as a mirror—a Socratic mirror wherein the Rouennais could see—"whether completely naked or clothed—if their natural bodies (*corps Nature*) had been corrupted or falsely decorated." The image reflected by this mirror was of a social and epistemological world in flux, a contingent world in which reason, truth, and faith were at the mercy of madmen and Conards.[109] Conardie, it seems, was everywhere. And indeed, the madness of the Conards was a measure of their detachment from a system of language rooted referentially in the world conceived as a mirror of nature. Cast adrift in a sea of particulars, theirs was a futile and sardonic search for authenticity across the seemingly unbridgeable gap between inner virtue and contingent outward appearance.[110] In exploring the ambiguities and uncertainties of their place in this New World that they had wrought, the Conards were acting not—*pace* Arden—as nostalgic defenders of a vanished feudal order, but as actors empowered to explore the boundaries between order and disorder, appearance and reality, truth and civility.[111]

New Worlds

The New World as it appeared in the farce and the sottie had little if anything to do with the recent geographical discoveries across the Atlantic, or with the promised return to an Age of Gold and a "port of grace of paradise" discussed in Chapter 5. Rather, it had to do with the new—and corrupt—world (the Age of Iron) brought into being by les nouveaux gens who precipitated humanity's descent into self-interest, pride, ambition, and violence.

In a certain sense, both different conceptions of the New World provoked the same kind of reaction—a new and increasingly intense perception of the problem of relativism. Typically, it is the geographic discovery of the New World, along with the Reformation, the humanist embrace of philology, and the advent of printing that take pride of place in this development.[112] The New World brought into being by the new men is rarely mentioned in this regard. Yet, the appearance of a new civic-cultural elite in France was not only symptomatic of a world that no longer made sense, it was perceived to be its principal cause. Whether we are speaking of the historicist revolution in legal thought, the Protestant Reformation(s), the print revolution, or the discovery of the New World, we cannot help but find the influence of these new men who had, through "force, favor and flattery," turned aside the accepted order of things.[113] Although their presence lurked behind the problem of relativism (and hence behind the eschatological surety that the end was at hand), they were imbued with the belief that they were also in possession of its cure, for the very intellectual and cultural dispositions that distinguished them as a new kind of elite were considered the best—and perhaps only—solution to the problems that their appearance presented. In other words, knowledge was not simply the distinctive feature by which the new men were to be identified, but was thought to be the means by which the Golden Age would be found anew. This, after all, was the oft-repeated message of Henri's entry: that a learned and eloquent king would reunite the world, conquer the barbarian, and lead all the world's people to the terrestrial paradise of the Elysian Fields. The instability of this solution is evident in the fact that its further elaboration—whether in natural history, biblical exegesis, legal thought, or philological practice—served only to intensify the problem. This was true both intellectually, insofar as humanist scholarship seemed only to widen the gulf existing between ancients and moderns, and socially, insofar as France's civic-cultural elite was increasingly successful in achieving—to the apparent detriment of traditional social order—the benefits of high office and noble status. For many, far from being a solution, the distinctive form of life of France's new civic-cultural elites was nothing less than a particularly pernicious form of conardie—the vanity of learning—and, as such, behind all the problems in the first place. It was, I believe, the growing perception of the problem and the uncertainty of the solution that was at the root of the anxiety responsible for the articulation of an auto-critique in which knowledge and culture were considered more veils that obscured than tools that redeemed. Thus, Jacques Lefèvre d'Etaples rails against the "*phantasie et presumption de noz intelligences et conceptions,*"[114] while the Conards stated simply that "All the men who count themselves wise/ Are nothing but fools."[115](See Plate 22.)

At the same time, however, another—extremely powerful—solution was being articulated across the discursive field opened up by this critique. Cast across the image of the New World and its peoples, it came to focus on the expression of a new sort of cultural ideal: men "without culture, without law and without religion"—men who could abandon accepted authority and turn instead, with a previously unthought openness, to experience itself.[116] This is nowhere more evident than in the verisimilar precision with which the Brazilian village was constructed for Henri's entry. As the entry's chronicler said: it "seemed to be true and not simulated." But the anonymous author of this account does not want the reader to simply take his word for this; he therefore calls upon the testimony of reliable witnesses who had "spent a great deal of time (*frequenté longuement*) in the land of Brazil and the Cannibals" to attest to the fact that Rouen's representation of Brazil was a "*certain simulacra de la verité.*"[117] Montaigne's essay "On Cannibals" is also relevant in this regard.[118] His praise for the simple, "primitive," and virtuous lives lived by the Brazilians (whom he met in Rouen in 1562) was effusive. The people of the New World, he said in another of his essays, lived as if in a younger age, one uncorrupted by the pernicious effects of science, art, and culture.[119] Though Montaigne ends his essay "On Cannibals" with a joke ("All this is not too bad—but what's the use? They don't wear breeches"), the narrative current of his text carries his readers back from the naked and honest truths spoken by the cannibals, across the *via moderna* of nominalistic skepticism, to the ignorant laborer who is his credible informant at its beginning. "This man who stayed with me," he says,

> was a plain, simple fellow, and men of this sort are likely to give true testimony. Men of intelligence notice more things and view them more carefully, but they comment on them; and to establish and substantiate their interpretation, they cannot refrain from altering the facts a little. They never present things just as they are but twist and disguise them to conform to the point of view from which they have seen them; and to gain credence for their opinion and make it attractive, they do not mind adding something of their own, or extending and amplifying. We need either a very truthful man, or one so ignorant that he has no material with which to construct false theories and make them credible: a man wedded to no idea. My man was like that.[120]

Montaigne's end thus returns his readers to his (and *the*) beginning, for his aim is to criticize the social, intellectual, and cultural hubris of the new men while valorizing the simplicity and (intellectual) nakedness of the men of the New World—which is to say, man as he once was and should be again.[121]

The Brazilians in Henri's entry—like the Conards' *farce des veaux*—were, in this sense, similar to the *exemplum* of the fool in the emperor's chariot: momento mori that challenged not simply the king's pretension to be a god, but the new men's social, cultural, and intellectual pretensions to be other than they are: "men who estimate themselves knowledgeable without knowledge,"—"nature's perfect *veaux*."[122]

This is nowhere better exemplified than in the not-for-royal-consumption account of the entry found in the records of the Hôtel de Ville. Midst the long list of honored sons of Rouen's richest and most notable citizens—the enfants d'honneur—who marched before the king, one entry stands out from all the rest: "*a poor man*."[123] That the Rouennais would include such a man in a procession of its most notable citizens speaks to the ambivalence that their worldly achievements held for them. By his presence, this poor man pointedly reminded the honored sons of the rich who surrounded him, and the king and his coterie who watched from their triumphal arch above, that their claims to power and authority were but vanity and wind.

This said, the savage and humble mirrors found in Henri's entry, and in the Conards' festivities a week later, surely referred to a common antecedent in the theological primitivism found, for example, in Erasmus' *Praise of Folly* where the "innocent folk of the Golden Age" are described as "living under the guidance of nothing but natural instinct."

> What need had they of grammar when all spoke the same language, and the sole purpose of speech was to make communication possible? They had no use for dialectic when there was no battle of conflicting opinions, no place for rhetoric where no one was out to make trouble for his neighbor, no demand for jurisprudence when there were no bad habits, which are the undoubted antecedents of good laws. They were also too pious in their beliefs to develop an irreverent curiosity for probing the secrets of nature, measuring the stars, calculating their movements and influence, and seeking the hidden causes of the universe. They thought it sacrilege for mortal man to attempt to acquire knowledge outside his allotted portion. The madness of inquiring into what is beyond the heavens never even entered their heads. But as the innocence of the Golden Age gradually fell away, the branches of learning were invented by those evil spirits, as I said. These were few at first and taken up by few, but later on the superstition of the Chaldeans and the idle frivolity of the Greeks adds hundreds more simply to torment the wits of man—indeed, it only takes a single system of grammar to provide continuous torture for life.[124]

Yet, like the Conards' poetic chevauchée, Erasmus' Folly, as Terence Cave has pointed out, was "a voice from a fallen world."[125] Indeed, the revolt against intellectualism, the distrust of reason, the critique of the arts and sciences, and the disdain for artifice in all its forms, were eloquently spoken in the condemned language of the new men.[126] This was less a contradiction, however, than a tension that was creatively exploited—an ambiguity that synergistically resonated with social experience to form the basis of a new mediation: that of the learned and pious fool. Here again the Conard's chevauchée mirrors rather than mocks elite culture. This is nowhere more apparent than in its comic parade where we once again meet the hybrid figure of Hercules. Dressed in animal fur and carrying the "most honored, worthy and precious *baston pastoral,* commonly called the Cross,"[127] Hercules' appearance sets the stage for the triumphal entry of the Conards' abbé himself. As we saw in Chapter 3, Hercules was a liminal figure who embodied and mediated competing notions of elite identity. Here, among the Conards, he once again acts the mediator; this time, however, he turns his reach inward to embrace the contradictions and ambivalences afflicting Rouen's civic-cultural elite to create a new synthesis: the personification of learned ignorance conjoined with piety, of comic seriousness and the folly of Christ, of the simple and naked savage and the well-spoken courtier, of the Conard and the new man.[128]

A Conard World

According to Bakhtin, "The feast was a temporary suspension of the entire official system with all its prohibitions and hierarchic barriers. For a short time life came out of its usual, legalized and consecrated furrows and entered the sphere of utopian freedom. The very brevity of this freedom increased its fantastic nature and utopian radicalism."[129] The fête was betwixt and between—a liminal parenthesis in the quotidian, a rupture in the ceaseless flow of the ordinary. The fête's anarchy was a whirlpool of contingent particulars, a welter of lascivious masks, a tumult of intertwined and laughing bodies dancing to the cacophonous beat of sexual frenzy. The fête was chaos incarnate bracketed by a sea of normalcy, order, and tradition. This is the view that still dominates our understanding of carnival. Perhaps it is right. But perhaps we too enthusiastically embrace the abandon that the carnivalesque is said to represent. Might the boundaries between the carnivalesque and the everyday be more permeable than previously thought? Might its topsy-turvy, upside-down and mocking world have spilled out into the everyday and vice versa? And might the instabilities that it represented *in situ* have reverberated beyond the frame said to enclose—and quarantine—its madness to just a few days of the calendar year?

In such a topsy-turvy world, Nature and man were no longer governed by knowable universals, but by God's indecipherable will. And indeed, the destabilization of identity concomitant with the transformation of the world inhabited by the new men, and more generally, France's new civic elites, was a reflection of—and gave animus to—a conception of a God who could, *de potentia absoluta,* do anything. From scholastic thought experiments regarding

God's unlimited and contingent power to an explanation for why the world no longer made sense, nominalism came to be infused with tremendous emotional and psychic significance—not as an intellectual movement, but as a visceral response to vertiginous social transformation. At the same time, as Michel de Certeau has argued, there was a "progressive separation that took place between an unknown absolute of the divine will and a technician's freedom, capable of manipulating words that [were] no longer anchored in being."[130] Born of this fallen world—where the correspondence between signs, the objects they were to signify, and the universal truths they were thought to express no longer held—was the authorial freedom to maneuver, play, and create, whether in the medium of written language or in social performance.[131] As du Bellay said, languages are not like plants, born of themselves, for "all their virtue is born in the world of human will and desire."[132]

The linguistic virtuosity of Rouen's civic-cultural elite was symptomatic of this contingent, topsy-turvy world; it was also an attempt to cure it by reinstating it to order. The encyclopedic distanciation and disciplining of language as found, for example, in the vernacular grammar by Pierre Fabri, ought to be seen in this light: as a means of recreating the bonds between lived reality and moral order, between language and truth. Perhaps this also explains something of the attraction that the doctrine of the Immaculate Conception of the Virgin Mary had for Normandy's new elites. The most outspoken and passionate defenders of Mary's special status were nominalists, or those influenced by nominalism—e.g., Scotus, Occam, Biel, Gerson, d'Ailly, the Franciscan Spirituals, and the Carmelites. Indeed, it was God's inscrutable and omnipotent power that preserved Mary from the stain of original sin.[133] At the same time, the very same power that granted her this unique status made sure knowledge of the world and man's place in it an impossibility; by definition, God's omnipotence was contingent and arbitrary. He does what he wants, bound only by the principle of noncontradiction. In nominalist theology, God's unrestrained and absolute will was subject only to laws he himself freely established in making his covenant with man. The immaculately conceived Virgin was, as a second Eve, the corporeal instantiation of this living promise. Thus, it is perhaps not a coincidence that Mary's eschatological role found a terrestrial analog, both in Henri's entry and in the dispositions of Rouen's new civic elites, for her task was not, as Oberman has pointed out, to "rule by power, but by influence; not to command, *imperare*, but to implore, *impetrare*."[134]

In a world where the correspondence between normative values and ontologically necessary universal structures could no longer be rationally deduced,[135] the problem of order was to have an overriding importance. In much the same way that God's *potentia absoluta* was restrained by his own will *de facto, de potentia ordinata*, the authorial freedom of the poet was to be constrained and channeled by the normatively established conventions, rules, and sensibilities that legislated the writing of poetry in honor of the Virgin.[136] The preoccupations of the new men with the writing of hypertechnical verse dedicated to the Virgin, with the study and elaboration of grammar (such as that explicitly written for them by Pierre Fabri), and with their literary performance (whether in the competitions of the Puys or the staging of royal entries), were all a measure of their concern with creating and maintaining order where it was found lacking.[137] At the same time, attempts to stabilize the apparently arbitrary nature of language (in grammars, rhetorics, and the like), seemed only to exacerbate the problem by making language's conventional status all the more apparent.[138] This paradox is, as I have tried to show, the essence of conardie, for the appearance of France's new civic-cultural elite was one of the contributing causes of the destabilization of social and epistemic order in the first place; and indeed, the self-same cultural/intellectual dispositions that distinguished them—and that were embraced as a solution to the problems their own appearance created—only exacerbated the problem, because they *were* the problem. Hence, the ongoing attempts to stabilize these conventions/dispositions/identities with reference to pious faith in the Virgin Mary—the mediatrix. Yet, the articulation of a rift between literary and spiritual spheres of life rooted in the coalescence of the sociocultural identity of France's new civic elites (see Chapter 4), as well as the Reformation's fracturing the appearance, if not the reality, of religious unity, undercut the legitimacy of this move, lending further impetus to attempts to build material/empiricist barriers to the threat of particularism—viz disorder—gone rampant.[139] Standing between the intellectual impulse to create order and the anti-intellectual desire to act as transparent mediums of experience, France's new elite was caught in an irresolvable contradiction. It was at this ironic fissure, where coherence itself seemed in danger of being overwhelmed, that nominalist theology came down to earth in the persona of an all-powerful king and in the ritual of the royal entry. Just as in the stopgap of an all-powerful God whose *potentia absoluta* is restrained *de facto, de potentia ordinata*, it devolved upon the power of the French monarch, as God's representative on earth, to stabilize—through his rule, through his example, and through his covenantal relationship with his subjects—the centrifugal forces threatening the continuity of political, social, and epistemological order.[140] It is to the entry's role in constructing—and restraining—just such a king that we turn next.

CHAPTER 7

Severed Heads, Relics, Savages, and Kings

RITES OF PASSAGE AND THE TRIUMPHAL ENTRY

Henri II's entry into Rouen was a ritual voyage. It actualized, if but for a few hours, the metaphorical journey from this world to the next, taking the king and the crowds that followed his progress from the sublunary streets of Rouen to the celestial city of the New Jerusalem. From the beginnings of his entry, when he passed through a triumphal arch and into the New World, until its end, when he entered the Cathedral of Notre Dame and ritually changed his clothes, Henri II's triumph was constructed as a rite of passage that transformed the king and his city and brought them both into close proximity with the divine.

Typically, millenarian and apocalyptic thought in the early modern period is traced to the enormous influence of Joachim of Fiore and his followers in the Order of the Franciscan Spirituals. Though the poetry and pageantry celebrating the king's triumphal apotheosis in sixteenth-century Rouen might be traced back to similar sources, I will here suggest a less traveled route, looking, as it were, beyond the streams running on the surface to a subterranean coursing of ideas and practices into which such tributaries as those articulated by Joachimites and Franciscans flowed. I will illuminate this current of mystical thought through an analysis of the secular and liturgical rituals historically associated with the entry festival itself. This will clarify not only the special position and Christ-like attributes that Henri II acquired upon his entry into Rouen, but it will also shed an entirely different light on the Brazilians who greeted him at the beginning of his journey.

The function of the Brazilians displayed in Rouen in 1550—despite their particularly local/temporal significance—was, I will argue, related to a repertoire of mythic and real beings and appurtenances that historically figured in entry rituals and/or their representations from their inception in antiquity: e.g., barbarians, wild men, triumphal arches, and chariots. Animated by age-old ritually embodied practices having to do with lending civic order and kingly authority divine sanction, Henri's entry utilized its New World savages in ways that, while perhaps not conscious of the debt, owed themselves to quite ancient ritual formulae for transforming mortal kings into gods. This chapter will situate the synchronic event of Henri II's triumph within this diachronic flow of ritual memory. Though the particular concerns of Rouen's new civic-cultural elite were grounded in the unique historical circumstances of their day, they were not thereby divorced from the past; rather, their interests were enacted with reference to a durable, though historically mutable, store of practices and traditions that traced the complex genealogy of the triumph from antiquity through the Renaissance. By examining the *longue durée* history of the triumphal entry as a rite of passage this chapter will demonstrate how, at specific moments, inherited ritual forms intersected with, were transformed by, and in turn inflected contingent "local" interests.

Hidden Passages and Invented Traditions

The chronicler of Henri's entry states that it surpassed all the expectations of the king and his court and greatly surpassed all other triumphs celebrated in France from time immemorial.[1] Though clearly a comparison calculated to impress, the allusion to an ongoing tradition of triumphal entries stretching back to times immemorial hints at a tantalizing possibility: that of a historical connection between sixteenth-century civic ritual and the ancient rites associated with the victories of generals, kings, and emperors.

The ancient triumph and the Renaissance royal entry ceremony shared many common characteristics. At first glance, the origin of these similarities can be located in the studied revival of Roman ritual practice by Italian humanists of the quattrocento.[2] The triumph was extremely popular in Renaissance Italy, not only in art and literature, but also in civic ceremony. When Charles VIII and Louis XII invaded Italy at the end of the fifteenth century, they were presented with elaborate recreations of these triumphs. According to Jean Marot, Louis XII's 1509 entry into Milan was among the most spectacular triumphs the world had ever seen; as he put it: "Never had Scipios, Pompey, or Caesar, entering Rome under triumphal arches, received such a beautiful display."[3] Robert de La Marck, seigneur de Fleuranges agreed, remarking that the Milanese entry was "the most grand entertainment and triumph that was ever made for a prince, for they gave him an entry according to the ancient custom of the Romans, and brought back to memory all the cities, and chateaux and battles that he had won, by paintings which they carried around the city."[4] In the wake of such spectacular receptions, it is little wonder that the themes and motifs of the triumph were quickly translated northward to France.

Given the history of this deliberate revival, any presumed connection between the Renaissance triumph and the ancient Roman triumph would appear to be altogether fanciful. This chapter will argue just the opposite, for though the Renaissance triumph was a deliberate accretion onto the medieval tradition of the joyeuse entrée, there were strong historical links connecting it to the triumphs of antiquity. In this sense, we should not let the obvious fact that the triumph was a relatively recent importation from Italy distract our attention from pursuing clues that are better hidden.

Contrary to abstract typologies that attempt to order the historical development of royal ceremonial along a series of discrete stages, the continuities existing between Renaissance triumphal entries and the ancient triumph are striking.[5] The lines of descent connecting these temporally and spatially distant rites were not in any simple sense linear. Following the insights of Wittgenstein, the hypothesized relationship between ancient and Renaissance rites can be characterized as a family resemblance. As pointed out in a particularly poignant passage from the *Philosophical Investigations*, a "family resemblance" consists in a "complicated network of similarities overlapping and crisscrossing: sometimes overall similarities, sometimes similarities of detail."[6] Such a resemblance, Wittgenstein continues, can be compared to spinning a thread, for "in spinning a thread we twist fibre on fibre. . . . [T]he strength of the thread does not reside in the fact that some one fibre runs through its whole length, but in the overlapping of many fibres."[7]

Thus, though there was not a continuous ritual tradition connecting the ancient to the Renaissance triumph, the approach suggested by Wittgenstein's remarks permits us to discern a common repertoire of related meanings and practices threading their way among them. As previously noted, ancient and Renaissance triumphs possessed numerous common features, like the chariot, the arch, the laurel, and the palm. In the case of the Renaissance triumph, these motifs were self-consciously revived as a means of replicating the glories of ancient Rome. Nevertheless, despite the studied character of their addition, they were situated within—and animated by—a ritual context that traced its origins directly back to the antique triumph. It is, I believe, by pursuing the metaphor of family resemblance that we will be able to ascertain the historical commonalties that—like the crisscrossing fibers found in Wittgenstein's description of a thread—composed the often ephemeral bonds connecting the Renaissance triumph to its ancient forebears. Moreover, by making explicit the ritual vocabulary that underwrote these temporally and geographically distant rites, we will also be able to see beyond the apparent novelty of the mise-en-scène of the New World scripted into Henri's 1550 triumphal entry to understand its relation to quite ancient suppositions about the mythic nature of divine kingship and royal power.

Rites of Passage

In antiquity the triumph was considered the highest honor that could be bestowed upon a mortal.[8] According to Versnel, the Greek word for triumph functioned as a ritual exclamation to evoke the epiphany of a god of the Dionysos-type from exile, sleep, or death.[9] The Latin word *triumphe* performed a similar function, for it was not associated directly with a victory in the sense of a cry of joy after a military success, but with the solemn return of a victorious general.[10]

No ordinary visitor, the Roman triumphator made his entry not through an existing gate, but through either a special breach made in a city's walls or a specially constructed gate or arch. Wearing the *ornatus Iovis* (a purple toga, an ivory staff surmounted by an eagle, a crown of laurel, and with his face painted with red lead), the triumphator would ride into the city on a chariot drawn by four horses. With a slave standing behind him holding a golden crown of oak leaves above his head, he would lead a procession to the temple of Jupiter.[11]

The Roman triumphal entry evinced what Van Gennep has labeled a rite of passage: a transition from "one phase of life to the next, from one social position to another."[12] The various formal attributes of the triumph—the chariot, the triumphal arch and/or breach—served to recapitulate this common theme: each signified a passage, the crossing of a threshold between earth and heaven, the material and the spiritual, the mortal and the divine. The shouts of triumph that greeted the return of the triumphator were a confirmation of this transformation. No longer a mere human, the triumphator was a god whose presence in a city was said to bring "prosperity, new life, [and] a new beginning."[13]

Messianic associations were woven deeply into the texture of the triumph. This was nowhere more apparent than in the case of Christ. Whether the epiphany of his birth, his entry into Jerusalem, or his Second Coming, his advent was understood with explicit reference to the Roman rite of triumph. Evidence for this can be found in the narratives of both Saint Paul and Saint John, each of whom refers to Christ's entry by using the precise technical terms that denoted the triumph.[14] Thus Christianized and seemingly severed from its pagan origins, the Roman triumph—recast as the Advent of Christ, the messiah—asserted its influence on the ceremonies associated with secular kingship.[15] Similarly, just as Christ's entry was incorporated into a pre-existing tradition of the pagan triumph, so too were the secular entries of kings in the Christian era assimilated to the form of Christ's exemplary Advent. As Kantorowicz notes: "Time and again it has been announced on these occasions that the comer is the Expected One and that accordingly the city whose gates have flung open to him, is another Zion. For whenever a king arrived at the gates of a city, celestial Jerusalem seemed to descend from heaven to earth."[16] This is not to say that the king became God upon his entry into a city. This would have been blasphemous; rather, the king was viewed as incarnating the figure and image of God. This is an important distinction. The *Norman Anonymous* of 1100 explicitly spelled it out:

> The king's power is the power of God, but it is God's by nature, the king's by grace. . . . Also the king is *Deus et Christus*, but by grace; and whatsoever he does, he does not simply as a man but as one who has been made *Deus et Christus* by grace; and even he who is *Deus et Christus* by nature [that is, God], does what he does through his vicar through whom vicariously he acts.[17]

Grace, in this context, was considered both an effect and an integral part of ecclesiastical ritual. A king, in this sense, was not divine, either by inheritance or mysterious inner virtue (i.e., by nature), but as the result of the role he played in carefully enacted rituals. It was through these rituals that a king came to be endowed with sacred and divine qualities. In other words, a king's God-like properties were not innate; they were made. According to the author of the *Norman Anonymous,*

> At the anointment . . . the spirit of the Lord and his deifying power "leap[s]" into the anointed changing [him] into [a] different [man]. In that moment, and from that moment on, [he] become[s] truly "figure and image" of God-man (*Christus figura fierent et imago*), inasmuch as the anointed on earth now becomes a *gemina persona*, that is, "one person by nature, the other by grace". . . . In view of one person he is, by nature, an individual man; in view of the other he is, by grace, a Christus, that is, a God-man.[18]

Like the rite of anointment, the entry festival was employed as a means of bestowing grace upon a king and thereby effecting a linkage between the political office of kingship and the soteriological premises of Christianity. This linkage was made possible through a reliance on the liturgical tradition associated with the celebration of Advent, as for example, in the liturgical triad invoking the image of Christ's Advent as the conquering God: *Christus vincit, Christus regnant, Christus imperat.* This formula was patterned after exclamations originally associated with the Roman triumph. Early on, it was also appropriated as the signature of secular kingship. This was especially true in France, where in the late Middle Ages the triad was invoked as the "sacred prerogative" of the French crown.[19] An allusion to this formula's origins, however, was preserved in the French usage, for though this litany was generally known by the name *laudes regiae,* in Paris it was designated simply *triumphus!*[20]

According to Kantorowicz, the entry of the exarch of Ravenna into Rome was the prototype for all subsequent Frankish and Germanic medieval entries. The exarch's arrival was marked by the exclamation of the faithful: *Benedictus qui venit in nomine Domini.* This greeting was originally used to welcome Christ upon his entry into Jerusalem on Palm Sunday.[21] It was thereafter closely associated with the liturgical and historical celebrations of Christ's Advent.[22] Its use during the exarch's entry, Kantorowicz argues, ". . . makes it quite evident that the Entry of Christ into Jerusalem on Palm Sunday was the prototype after which the reception of medieval princes was modeled."[23] Kantorowicz cites the use of the similar exclamation *Benedice, Benedice, Benedice* to welcome Charles the Bald during his entry into Metz as proof of the continuing influence of the liturgical tradition of the Advent on royal ceremonial in the Middle Ages.

Some five hundred years after Charles the Bald's entry, the first printed account of a royal entry appeared: that of the 1485 entry of Charles VIII into Rouen. In this account Charles was equated with the first Christian emperor, Constantine, who brought about the peace and unity of the world through his triumph over Maxence (Maxentius), the "cruel king of the barbarians."[24] Like his namesake, Charles the Bald, Charles VIII was described as a new Constantine whom "God had elected to rule the Nations." Both Charles VIII and Charles the Bald, though their respective entries were separated by close to half a millennium, were construed in similar messianic terms. Indeed, like his tenth-century counterpart, Charles VIII was greeted as God's chosen messenger with the exclamation: *Benedictus qui venit in nomine Domini.*[25]

That Charles was welcomed to Rouen with this liturgical chant can be seen to extend Kantorowicz' thesis, for it evidences the continuing influence of the Advent on entry rites in the early modern period. Indeed, if there were any doubt at all about the Christomimetic tenor of Charles VIII's entry, it is dispelled by the chant that immediately followed the *Benedictus,* for it explicitly praised the French king as it would Christ himself, as "*le chef du corps mystique.*"[26]

An Aura of Mysticism

Marc Bloch has suggested that in Pepin's day there was a "vague aura of mysticism" surrounding kingship that "was solely due to the influence upon the collective consciousness of obscure memories dating from pagan times."[27] Pepin's appropriation of the Hebrew rite of royal unction was, says Bloch, a means of consolidating his power by conferring upon it "a sort of religious prestige."[28] This manner of consecration, Bloch continues, was particularly apposite given the renewed interest in the Old Testament among Gaulish theologians.[29] However, we can with some justification give the articulation of an ideology of divine kingship a more determinant historical locus. The rituals associated with Episcopal Advent—which flourished in Gaul at the time of Pepin's adoption of the unction—provided a ready-made vocabulary that could be utilized to underwrite, and put into practice, the ritual sacralization of kingship.[30] As we shall see, the rites associated with Christ's Advent served to preserve across time and space a common core of ritual ideals originally derived from the ancient triumph.[31]

The reception/journey prescribed by the Advent was the prerogative of the anointed vicars of Christ on earth. The singularity of this right was given official sanction by the papal decree of Honorius III in 1221.[32] It was, like the unction, also the prerogative of the dying. In the *Rituale Romanum* there are a number of prayers known under the rubric of the *Office of the Dying*. Among these prayers is one that specifically treats the advent of the soul into heaven:

> May your soul, which is departing from the body, be met by the brilliant host of Angels, may it be received by the court of Apostles, welcomed by the triumphant army of resplendent Martyrs, surrounded by the lilied array of rubiate Confessors, greeted by the jubilant choir of Virgins, and embraced by the blessed peace in the bosom of the Patriarchs.[33]

Death was symbolically situated within the liturgical narrative of the Advent as a rite of passage. Departing from the anointed body, the soul embarked on its journey to the celestial Jerusalem where it was to be greeted with a joyeuse entrée by the heavenly host.[34] The formal structure of the funeral cortege reproduced precisely this imagery, transporting the dead in a triumphal procession.[35]

Death, Effigies, and Triumphs

One of the principal iconographic schemes of ancient representations of imperial divination upon death was the emperor's ascent to heaven on a chariot.[36] After Constantine this imagery was increasingly downplayed for its overtly pagan associations.[37] Yet despite the exclusion of such explicit formal referents, there remained a strong link between royal funeral ceremonial and the spiritual premises underlying both Advent and triumph.

Though it was not until the fifteenth century that such triumphal motifs as the use of chariots once again became an integral part of royal funeral ceremony, these were not simply neo-antique accretions of pomp and/or erudition, but were expressions of a faith animated by an ancient liturgical tradition that conceived of death in terms of Advent and triumph.[38] This can be seen by looking more closely at another, lesser known ritual attribute of triumph.

Two weeks prior to Henri's royal entry, a funeral ceremony was held for Georges II d'Amboise, archbishop of Rouen. It began, much as would the king's entry, with an elaborate procession of the city's political and ecclesiastic elite. After this procession, the anointed body of d'Amboise was transported to the abbaye of Saint-Ouen and then brought into the church through a "newly made door" (*la porte que l'on avoit fait fere de nouveau*) where it was placed before a cross of stone. The following day, after various rites had been observed, the corpse was once again transported, this time to the church of Saint-Amand where twelve chaplains from the Cathedral of Notre Dame carried it into the church through a door "which was not customarily opened" (*que l'on n'a point accoustumée de ouvrir*).[39]

These references to a "newly made door" and to a "door not normally used" recall an essential motif of the classical triumph. Predating and closely related to the triumphal arch, the practice of the triumphator entering a city through a gate or breach that was either made for the occasion or was not normally used suggests a relation between the obsequies of Georges II d'Amboise and the ancient imperial tradition of the triumph. Indeed, even explicitly revived motifs of triumph, such as the chariot, were animated by the web of significations structuring both the Advent ceremony and the imperial triumph. Thus, in the 1515 funeral of Louis XII, the king's body was transported on a *chariot d'armes*, and his funeral was described by the maréchal de Fleuranges as being "marvelously beautiful and triumphant." According to Guiffrey, it was not Louis' corpse but his effigy that was enthroned on the triumphal chariot.[40] The funeral of François I was similarly described. Though his body was carried on the chariot d'armes, his effigy— described by one commentator as entering the city in triumph—was the ceremonial center of a funeral fashioned after a triumphal Adventus.[41]

The use of an effigy representing the deceased king in the French Renaissance royal funeral ceremony is markedly similar to ancient rites associated with the *consecratio* of Roman emperors.[42] Here a wax effigy was made of the deceased emperor. This effigy was set aflame on a pyre several days after the burial of the body, symbolizing the emperor's ascent to heaven and his deification.[43] The rites associated with the effigy in Rome paralleled late-medieval/Renaissance usage. In both cases the effigy represented the transcendent values associated with legitimate political and spiritual authority: deification in the case of the emperor, and the juridical distinction between the king's mortal body and the immortal institution—the *dignitas*—of kingship, in the case of French royalty in the Middle Ages.[44]

According to Giesey, far from tracing its origins back to the consecratio of Roman emperors, the custom of the effigy in France had its beginnings in the practical necessity of displaying the dead king at a time when techniques of embalming were, at best, primitive—hence the substitution of an effigy of wax, wood, or leather for the dead king. Accordingly, Giesey argues, we should not be misled by attempts of sixteenth- and seventeenth-century commentators to situate the use of effigies within an historically continuous tradition extending back to Rome, for in actuality they were an independent invention clothed after the fact in neo-antique garb.

Yet, as Giesey himself points out, despite the lack of an historical connection, there were close philosophical parallels between the French funeral ceremonial and the Roman consecratio.[45] As he puts it:

> The apotheosis of the pagan Emperor's soul was not unlike the Christian king's throne-sharing with God. This principle was immanent in Christian thought during the dozen centuries between Constantine the Great and Francis I; does it, however, find expression in the funeral ritual during all those centuries, so that it could be argued that a direct historical tradition goes back . . . to the earliest Roman emperors?[46]

Ultimately, despite these obvious "philosophical parallels," Giesey responds to this question in the negative, and regards any imputed historical relationship between ancient and Renaissance funerary rites as being highly problematic.[47] He tells us, "I have avoided the temptation, so easy but (for the historian) so fruitless, to compare the peculiarities of funeral rites of remote cultures . . . ," like those of ancient Rome to those of Renaissance France. Thus, he concludes that Roman funerary practices were relevant only insofar as "the French believed that they were."

The narrowness of this approach, however, has the effect of a priori reinforcing Giesey's conclusion that the French royal funeral ceremony was an independent innovation. It does so by precluding the very possibility (as historically naive) of a connection between Renaissance rituals and those located in antiquity. As with any established tradition, the royal funeral ceremonial in France did not develop autonomously, but through a kind of cultural bricolage that made use of preexisting ritual vocabularies.[48] By extending our gaze to the larger context of royal and ecclesiastical rituals from which the French royal funeral ceremony was constructed, we will be able to discern what Giesey dismisses as altogether unlikely: the common historical thread that linked the antique ceremonies having to do with the consecratio of Roman emperors to the funeral rites staged for French kings during the Renaissance. This thread was the triumph, and its Christianized descendent was the Adventus.

The Relic, the Triumphator, and the Effigy

The initial rationale for the Roman custom of the funeral effigy was to circumvent taboos associated with the dead. The repugnance associated with the corpse in the Roman world translated into strict legislation forbidding the building of tombs and sepulchers within a city's walls. The use of an effigy as a substitute for the corpse was a means by which a deceased emperor could be brought to sanctified ground in the city. [49]

The effigy, however, was not an absolute requirement in this regard, for despite laws to the contrary, there was an important exception to this rule: that made for the bones of a triumphator. Cognizant of this apparent contradiction, Plutarch was moved to ask: "Why it was permitted to take a bone of a man who had at one time triumphed, afterwards dies and been cremated, and to bring it into the city and bury it there?"[50]

The answer to Plutarch's question ultimately lies in the divine status of the triumphator. Dead or alive, he represented the apotheosis and return of a god. The fact that the laws proscribing burial within a city did not apply to a triumphator calls into question the traditionally accepted view as to the symbolic raison d'être of the effigy. Yet in pointing out this sanctioned violation of a taboo, Plutarch also points to another possible interpretation: by discarding the over-determined opposition between purity and corruption, we can see that effigy and bones were rather more similar than not. In other words, they can be seen to tell different parts of the same story, both being closely related, indeed bound together, in the diachronic movement structuring the narrative of an emperor's ritual deification and return.

Sabine MacCormack has pointed out that "the funeral of the emperor was an occasion of triumph."[51] Hence, Dio Cassius' description of the wax effigy of Pertinax being dressed as if he were about to celebrate a triumph. Thus, though the effigy can still be interpreted as a substitute for the emperor's physical remains, its purpose was not to circumvent taboos proscribing contact with the dead, but rather to signify a triumphal passage from the

mortal world of men to the divine world of the gods. In other words, it signified the emperor's apotheosis, while the burial of his bones—*intra muros*—
signified his return and the beneficial effects that would follow from his incorporation within the living space of a city. It was in precisely these terms
that Ambrose described the entry of the "triumphal remains" of the emperor
Theodosius into Constantinople:

> Now Theodosius returns more powerful, . . . [and] more glorious, for the host
> of the angels leads him on, and the crowd of the saints follow him. Clearly you
> are blessed, you who receive the inhabitant of paradise, you who shall hold, in
> the revered dwelling place of his body when it is buried, him who lives in that
> city which is above.[52]

Ambrose here signals the correspondence between Theodosius' "triumphal
remains" and his actual presence in the city as both an emperor and a god.
His narrative is clearly that of the triumph, though in the Christianized form
of the Adventus.

The Mobility of Power

Closely paralleling the return and burial of the triumphator's remains
within a city, effigies and/or images also substituted for the living presence
of emperors in provincial triumphal entries.[53] This substitution symbolically
enabled an emperor to extend the reach of his power outside the realm of
his immediate personal control by duplicating hierarchies of political authority and social dominance across geographically disparate regions, thus
marking them as part of the unified space of the empire.[54] The capacity for
the image of the emperor to substitute for the emperor's actual presence was
attested to by the church father Saint Athanasius. As he put it, the image

> is the shape and form of the Emperor, and in the Emperor is that shape which
> is in the image. A person who looks at the image sees in it the Emperor, and he
> on the other hand who sees the Emperor recognises that it is he who is in the
> image. Whoever, therefore, adores the image, also adores therein the Emperor.[55]

The association of presence—and its literal incorporation within a city—
with good fortune, peace, and prosperity is morphologically similar to well-
known ritual practices associated with the translation of the relics of Christian saints and martyrs.

In what Jean Guyon has called a *"véritable mutation historique,"*[56] Christian millenarianism transformed the social and spiritual relations to the dead,
especially with regard to the bodies of saints and martyrs. What for Jew and
pagan alike had been considered impure and corrupt (the physical remains

of the dead), the Christian made into an object of veneration. Yet this inversion of the customary laws having to do with distance and proximity to the dead had clear precedent in the allowances made for the burial of the triumphator's bones. In this sense, the inhumation of a triumphator's remains intra muros prefigured the more general Christian reversal of ancient taboos concerning burial of the dead.[57]

The line of descent from the triumphator's bones to the relics of saints and martyrs is clear. In each case remains were viewed as instantiating the presence of (a) god on earth; their proximity and possession were thought— as with the entry of a living triumphator—to bring peace, prosperity, and good luck (as evidenced by the frequently ruthless efforts on the part of municipalities and/or individuals to obtain the right to possess sainted relics).[58] Moreover, just as the provincial triumphs of an emperor's effigy acted to replicate imperial power across the geographic expanse of the empire, so the translation of relics acted to mobilize, extend, and reproduce—from the Mediterranean to the North Atlantic coast—Christian doxa and the specific social relations of power and authority it implied.[59] These similarities were far from coincidental, for they had their provenance in the close intertwining of pagan and Christian ritual traditions.

Relics—like images, effigies, and the triumphator's bones—were explicitly situated within the narrative of the triumph in that they were greeted upon their arrival as the returning Christ triumphant.[60] Relics, after all, were not only identified with the saints of which they were fragments, but with Christ the Imperator himself.[61] As Saint Victricius of Rouen put it: "Saints are united with Christ. There is not any difference between them, . . . for by their sufferings they are forever associated with his cross."[62] How else, he asks, was one to celebrate their arrival other than with a triumph?

> If one of the princes of the age visits our city, all of a sudden garlands are placed everywhere, mothers appear joyfully upon the roofs, and people of all ages pour from the gates to . . . chant hymns of triumph. . . . And so my blessed sons, at the moment of the triumph of the Martyrs . . . why would we not similarly burst forth in joy?[63]

Thus, as with imperial images, relics were welcomed with triumphal entries. This translation from pagan to Christian ritual parallels the earlier linkage of the triumph with the Adventus. This time, however, the subject of the rite (the image or relic) was ritually transformed (transubstantiated) into the literal presence of Christ in a city. Or was it?

Presentia and Ritual Activation

Peter Brown has forcefully argued that in late antiquity and the early Middle Ages relics instantiated the real presence of saints and martyrs. He sees this identity as being metonymic as opposed to being merely metaphorical. Yet, as Brown points out:

> The precise events of the discovery of the relic and the ceremonies surrounding its arrival and installation counted for more than the mere fact of its presence in the city. *Many relics lapsed into obscurity after their arrival. What mattered was the arrival itself.*[64]

If it was the case that relics "lapsed into obscurity" once the rituals marking their arrival had ended, then Brown's strong claim for the metonymic status of the relic has to be modified. I would suggest that though relics might fade from significance outside the rituals associated with their entry, situated within the fanfare of these rituals, they were empowered to become that which we say they only represent. As Brown puts it, "the saint himself makes his presence felt all the more strongly [in the relic] by a ceremonial closely modeled on the *Adventus*, the 'arrival in state', of a Late Roman emperor."[65] In other words, what activated a relic's power to make present a saint, martyr, or Christ, was its emplotment in the narrative of a ritual of Adventus or triumph. It was, after all, during his triumphal entry that an emperor became a god, just as it was the funeral ritual—similarly modeled after the triumph—that activated the power of an effigy (or triumphator's bones) to become a god.

Representation: The Host and the King

From the eleventh century, the relics of saints were associated with the presence of Christ in the consecrated Eucharist, but by the thirteenth century, the Eucharist had achieved a singular status in Christian liturgy.[66] As a consequence relics became less significant. According to Patrick Geary, their diminishing power in comparison to the Eucharist corresponded to the crystallization of king-centered political authority. As he has pointed out in this regard:

> During periods of relatively weak central government . . . relics were prized . . . for their ability to substitute for public authority, protect and secure the community, determine the relative status of individuals and churches, and provide for the communities' economic prosperity. When new political, social, religious and economic systems began to develop in the twelfth century, the relative significance of relics in providing these services was weakened.[67]

Prior to the twelfth century, the multiplicity of relics corresponded to a political dynamic that was equally fragmentary. In this context, relics were able to confer status and authority upon diverse seats of local and regional power while at the same time uniting them in a larger unity, that of Christendom. With the crystallization of political authority around a relatively established monarchy, the power-conferring status of relics began to attenuate. Increasingly, the holy abandoned the multiplicity of saints' relics and gravitated instead toward the one true relic, the Eucharist (the real presence of Christ on earth).[68]

The bifocality of theological and political spheres that Kantorowicz noted for an earlier period was thus expressed in Carolingian times by the hallowing of the king in terms that precisely paralleled the rise of Christocentric devotion.[69] Hence the merging of these two lines of perspective into one focus: the political appropriation of the ancient Christological distinction between the two natures of Christ (i.e., the king's two bodies).[70] This interpenetration of the political and theological, however, only became possible insofar as religious forms of representation became increasingly abstract. The trajectory from images to relics and finally to the host was integral to the contemporaneous development of abstract notions and symbols of kingship. As Ginzburg has argued, the "victory for abstraction" associated with Eucharistic devotion permitted "the crystallization of the concrete symbol of the abstraction of the state, the effigy of the king."[71]

Ginzburg's argument can be summarized as follows: effigies and images from early in the Christian era were charged with ambiguity, for they implicitly posed the threat of idolatry. Similar fears were later associated with the veneration of the relics of saints, especially insofar as they were placed in reliquaries that figurally depicted a saint. The abstract, nonrepresentational character of the Eucharist was liberating in this regard, for it made possible the strongest sort of presence without raising the specter of idolatry. Obversely, the concentration of the holy in the host had as a consequence the desacralization of images. No longer the site of the actual presence of the divine on earth, images were freed from their associations with idolatry, thus setting out the conditions of possibility for the explosion of representational art in the thirteenth century.[72] In this sense the rise of Eucharistic devotion prepared the ground for the abstract representation of the immortal dignitas of kingship while making it possible for figural art—such as the effigy—to be its principal medium.

Ginzburg's argument, however, is somewhat different from the one I want to pursue here, for I believe we can directly link the morphological similarities of medieval kingship, its symbols, and the Eucharist to the common positions that each held in rituals modeled explicitly after the Adventus and the triumph.

As with previous examples of apotheosis (e.g., those involving emperors, Christ, images, effigies, and relics), the transubstantiation of the divine in the Eucharist was a transitory and momentous occasion closely associated with—and dependent upon—specific ritual practices, one of the most important being the celebrations associated with the festival of *corpus Christi*. The festival of corpus Christi was established in 1264. Closely related in both form and content to the processions associated with the translation of relics into a city, it was modeled after Christ's triumphant Adventus into Jerusalem.[73] Miri Rubin explains, "There was only one liturgical model for Eucharistic public processions, that on Palm Sunday, an Anglo-Norman usage which may have been introduced to England from Normandy in the Rouen rite."[74] As with the triumph of emperors, images, and relics, the ceremonial arrival of the consecrated host signified the immediate and real presence of God in a city. Indeed, the Eucharist's arrival was welcomed with the same liturgical chant used to greet the Advent of Christ: Benedictus qui venit in nomine Domini.[75]

Just as this liturgical chant was interwoven through the historical development of theological and political ceremonial, so too other elements of ecclesiastical ritual threaded their way into the ceremonial surrounding the French monarchy. The joyeuse entrée is a case in point: far from being an independent invention it was entirely reliant upon a preexisting liturgical vocabulary.[76] Recall, for example, that during Charles VIII's entry into Rouen, immediately after the chanting of the *Benedictus*, the king was greeted in terms that echoed those of Eucharistic devotion—that is, as the *chef du corps mystique*. Similarly, formal iconographic elements of corpus Christi day celebrations were assimilated to the entries of French kings. Thus, for example, the canopy that was held above the Eucharist as it was carried along its procession route was directly imported into the royal entry ceremony. In the entry, the king took the place of the host beneath the canopy; this was meant to signify the "majesty of kingship."[77] The structural equivalence between the Eucharist and kingship in these ceremonies was made absolutely clear by the contemporaneous case of the French royal funeral ceremony, for here the canopy was carried not over the dead king's body, but over the symbol of his dignitas—his effigy.[78]

Heaven and the Severed Head

Though the liturgy was extremely important in preserving across time and space a common core of ritual ideals and practices associated with the ancient triumph, it was not the only strand in the thread of this connection.[79] If we are to understand the significance of the mise-en-scène of Brazil in Henri's entry and more generally its historic relationship to royal ceremonial and power in France, we need to extend our analysis to another—less well-known—attribute of the ancient triumph: the gory practice of displaying barbarian heads.

The display of barbarian heads was one of the principal motifs of the Late Roman triumph. Carried on a pike, the head of a defeated enemy—usually a barbarian but sometimes a political/military rival—accompanied the triumphator into a city. This custom of displaying heads had a wide dispersion and was adopted by the early Christian emperors, Visigoths, Merovingians, Franks, and Burgundian kings. This bloody display was meant to represent both the triumphator's victory and, conversely, the futility of resistance.

According to Michael McCormick, victory was the principal criterion establishing the legitimacy of an emperor's political authority.[80] In this context, the display of a barbarian head was the relic of a victorious battle. As such, it was closely bound up with the identity of the triumphator. Indeed, the head of a vanquished barbarian was often used as a stand-in for the actual presence of an emperor. Thus, for example, a head might be dispatched to outlying provinces as a token of the emperor's ubiquitous presence. Perhaps not surprising, considering the series we have already assembled, these severed heads would be greeted upon their arrival with triumphal entries.[81] Heads displayed during these triumphs were demonstrable proof of an emperor's power and prestige.[82]

The arrival in state of the severed heads of defeated barbarians can be directly compared to ritual observances accompanying the arrival of a saint's relics: both occupied equivalent positions in ceremonies descended from the triumphal entry. First, they served a similar social/political function, for like the translation of relics, the dispatch of a barbarian head acted to establish and extend a particular regime of power and authority across politically divided territories. More important in the present context, however, is another parallel: namely, that the ceremonial triumph of a barbarian head represented the presence of an emperor in much the same way as the triumphal arrival of a relic instantiated the presence of a saint. Yet this is not quite accurate. Unlike relics and saints, the identity of an emperor with a barbarian's head was not metonymic, but associative; in other words, the significance of the severed head of a barbarian in a triumph was not to be found in its instantiation of the emperor, but in its representation of the abstract qualities that legitimized his rule—the ideal of eternal victory. In this manner, the severed head—though in some sense directly analogous to the image, the relic, and/or the

Eucharist (i.e., in so far as it constituted the ceremonial center of the triumphal entry)—had much more in common with such formal elements of the triumphal entry as the canopy, the breached wall, the arch, or the chariot. Each of these ritual elements of the triumph, including the head, recapitulated the common theme of the triumph: the transformation and apotheosis of the triumphator. A brief comparative example will illuminate this point.[83]

In his 1907 essay, "Contribution à l'étude sur la représentation collective de la mort," Robert Hertz explains that among Indonesian peoples funerals were characterized by an interval between death and final burial. During this interlude the soul of the dead—released from the body yet still tied to earth—was forced to wander without resting place until the time of its final burial; it would then be admitted to the land of the dead. The liberation of the dead from the material world at the time of the second burial was paralleled among the living by a liberation from the mourning taboo. Though the timing of the second burial was determined by the state of physical decomposition of the corpse, it was also closely associated with either a successful head-hunting mission or a human sacrifice by decapitation. Indeed, as Hertz says, the acquisition of a head, "a partly fortuitous event and in any case external to the state of the deceased, will be enough to assure the release of the survivors [from mourning]."[84] That the acquisition of a head was symbolically equivalent to the second burial can be seen by the several instances in which it came to supplant the final funerary rite. In either case, whether as an integral part of the final burial or as a substitute for it, the severed head of an enemy acted to mediate the movement of the soul from this world to the next.

Though the Olo Ngaju, the Olo Maanyan, and the Sea Dayak of Sarawak were not Romans, Merovingians, or Franks, their practices of burial throw an interesting comparative light on this obscure and bloody occidental tradition, for they enable us to see the functional similarities between the display of severed heads and such triumphal motifs as the breached wall, the arch, and the chariot. Each of these appurtenances of triumph, including the barbarian's head, was a representation of an emperor's immortal victory.[85] As an integral part of the triumphal entry ceremony, each mediated the relationship between an emperor's secular and spiritual authority by making it possible for him to cross the divide separating this world from the next. They thus operated to make actual the imaginary of an emperor's presence in a city as the center of both political and sacred power.

Victory, Barbarians, and Mediators

Judging from iconographic evidence preserved on Roman coins and statuary, the mediatory role that the severed head of barbarians played was paralleled by the display of barbarians atop triumphal arches. Generally recognizable by long hair, beards, and nudity, barbarians were characteristically depicted with hands tied behind their backs, and/or being trampled underfoot by the triumphator as a sign of submission.[86] Situated on an arch, they were typically juxtaposed with the conquering gods and goddess (for example, Victory) who derived their identities from the barbarian's defeat.[87] This perhaps explains the interchangeability of the barbarian slave for the goddess of victory in the Roman imperial triumph, with either one or the other accompanying the Imperator on his chariot ride to the temple of Jupiter holding a golden wreath over his head. It is significant, I think, that this role was also reserved for the fool. According to A. Caló Levi, "the barbarian attribute was the most economical way of depicting the emperor as *semper invictus* or of pointing out the association of the emperor and a divinity."[88] By a curious reversal, then, the defeated barbarian came to be construed positively, both as a symbol of victory and as the principal sign of a triumphator's power, authority and, indeed, of his very identity.

In his essay on the notion of the person, Marcel Mauss has noted that in Rome there existed a close and indissoluble connection between a *cognomen* (an additional personal name, a pseudonym) and an *imago* (a wax mask or statue of a dead ancestor).[89] In the present context it is of particular interest to note that the cognomen that an emperor took was derived from the names of barbarians he, or his line, had conquered.[90] Thus, along with the epithet "semper invictus," emperors also fashioned themselves triumphators by associating themselves with, for example, the triad of barbarian names by which Trajan was known: Germanicus, Dacicus, and Parthicus. The relation between imago and cognomen, then, can be directly translated to their specific historical/ritual referents in the triumphal entry: the effigies of emperors on the one hand and the display of conquered barbarians on the other. This is not to posit an identity among severed heads, effigies, barbarians, and emperors, but rather, to suggest a ritual equivalence in invoking a common third term—a triumphator's transformation into a god.[91]

Astride Two Worlds

The victory represented by the presence and display of a barbarian during the triumph alluded not simply to political/military victory, but to a victory of the human over the animal, of civilization over savagery. Yet the barbarian was not simply an anti-model serving as the negative pole of a positive assertion of a triumphator's self-identity, for he was a multivalent symbol who embodied many of the most esteemed values of Roman society. He not only represented the bestial and the inhuman; he also represented the heroic virtues of strength, virility, skill in warfare, simplicity, and constancy. The barbarian, in other words, was a commonplace representation of ideal man in his unreconstructed, natural state.[92] The barbarian's position in the world was nevertheless an ambiguous and ill-defined one. Somewhere between a human being and an animal, he was clearly both, yet at the same time, neither. Thus Seneca could praise him for his nobility, justice, and honesty, while at the same time describing him as being animated by something altogether inhuman: "something wild and intractable."[93]

Standing betwixt and between, neither here nor there, the barbarian seemed to slip fluidly from the mythological into the real and then back again; it was from this liminal position between worlds that he was endowed with the capacity to mediate an emperor's ritual transformation. The identification of the emperor with the defeated barbarian—whether decapitated, standing on the triumphal arch, being trampled beneath a triumphator's feet, or riding on his triumphal chariot—transcended the allegorical association of the barbarian with victory to point toward a mystic journey and a triumph over death itself.

Charivaris, Wild Men, and Crossing into the Other World

Wild men had a position analogous to the barbarian in the Christian successor to the triumph in the Middle Ages. Barbarous, naked, and covered with hair, wild men represented the tenuous divide between nature and culture, the animal and the human, the living and the dead. They also embodied many of the most esteemed and cherished values of the chivalrous knight (strength, courage, simplicity, and incorruptibility), while at the same time neatly encapsulating the arguments of their ecclesiastical critics, namely that the feudal nobility was ignorant, savage, and sexually profligate. As such, wild men fit nicely into the literary genre of the Mirror of Princes. Thus, the figure of the captured wild man finding eminence at court became something of a commonplace in medieval France, as, for example, Chrétien de Troyes' Perceval, Helias in the *Chevalier au Cygne*, or Tristan de Nanteuil.[94]

These wild men of courtly literature had festive counterparts in masquerades where noble men and women disguised themselves as hairy savages. The most famous example of this is the *Bal des Ardents* held in 1392, for which king Charles VI, "the Mad," at the suggestion of a Norman nobleman, donned the hairy guise of a wild man to help celebrate the marriage of a lady-in-waiting.[95] During the festivities three of the king's fellow revelers burned to death when their costumes caught on fire. The king was only just saved when the quick-thinking Duchess of Berry threw her cloak on him and smothered the flames. His madness was said to have its origins in this wild-man dance.[96] Such court festivities, in turn, were mirrored on the level of popular culture by the well-known practices of masquerade associated with the charivari.[97]

The oldest surviving account of a charivari is to be found in an interpolation to a manuscript copy of the *Roman de Fauvel* written in 1316 by a minor court official, Chaillou de Pesstain (probably Raoul Chaillou).[98] Chaillou describes an anonymous and noisy crowd (some nude, others covered with animal skins, with masks of lions, bulls, of grimacing human faces, and of *barboeres*)[99] following a club-wielding giant named Hellequin and two coffins "containing the heads of men and women set into niches recalling reliquaries."[100]

The leader of this motley crew, Hellequin, was commonly known in northern Europe as a demon of the underworld, and his followers as the Wild Horde (aka, the army of the dead). Among the earliest accounts of his exploits is one by the Norman historian Ordericus Vitalis in the twelfth century. In his *Ecclesiastical History* he recounts the case of a priest from Bonneval (near Chartres) who on January 1, 1091, chanced upon a *familia Herlechini*—a procession of dead souls comprised of men and women, clerics, soldiers, knights, and Ethiopians, led by the club-wielding giant Hellequin. The priest's description is of a theater of horrors—a procession of punishment for the sins committed by the dead while they were living. Knights, soldiers, and licentious women were singled out for especially harsh treatment. According to Jean-Claude Schmitt, this account is clearly related to the same Mirror of Princes literature as the triumphal entries of kings. As he put it, "we cannot define any better the ideological function that the church assigned to Hellequin's hunt [than to point to the] . . . moral mirror that it held up to those for whom violence was a trade."[101]

Mikhail Bakhtin, on the other hand, does not see Oderic's description of Hellequin and his family as a "mirror of the prince," but as a popular manifestation of carnival. Though little if anything in Oderic's description of horrific punishment is remotely carnivalesque, the individual participants of the march (the giant Hellequin, men wearing masks and the skins of wild animals while making an unholy din by banging on kitchen utensils), clearly belong to the world of carnival. Bakhtin argues that

> in spite of the distorting influence of the Christian presentation, the traits of the Saturnalia appear quite clearly. We find here the image of the giant which is characteristic of the grotesque body and is the constant protagonist of all such processions . . . [that is] *the image of Hercules and his mace* [who is closely] related [both] to the underworld [and to the popular traditions associated with carnival].[102]

There is, of course, no contradiction here, for symbols such Hellequin and his hunt could reside, and play an active role, in popular as well as elite culture. Moreover, the social power of Hellequin as either an exemplum of elite identity or as the embodiment of the popular tradition of the carnavalesque cannot be separated from his role as a mediator between the human and the animal, the living and the dead, the visible world of man and the invisible order of the cosmos.

Carlo Ginzburg has argued, in a context not entirely removed from the present one,[103] that the transformation into an animal or the cavalcade astride animals was integral to the soul's journey from the body to the world of the dead, where it would typically take part in battles to preserve the fertility of the coming year's crops.[104] The mediating capacity here attributed to the animal or animal-like can be compared to the function of defeated barbarians in the triumph (which, according to Versnel, had its roots in ancient fertility rites associated with Dionysious),[105] or to the presence of wild men in charivaris and court ceremonial. Ginzburg, for example, suggests that these Hellequin-led processions might refer to a widely diffused folkloric substratum having to do with the nocturnal processions of the dead and the mythical beings (e.g., Herlechinus) that led them.[106] Richard Bernheimer comes to a similar conclusion, though significantly, he also suggests a close historical connection between Hellequin and the wild man:

> the belief in the Wild Horde and its impersonation by masked revelers must antedate the introduction of the forest-dwelling . . . [wild man] into it. We must assume that the latter had been an independent mythological figure, when his affinity with the "human" participants in the Wild Hunt allowed him to take their place in the festivities; and that, consequently, the ritual figure of the wild man, as it existed toward the end of the Middle Ages, owes its existence to a mythological convergence.[107]

The affinity that Bernheimer suggests between wild men and Hellequin seems particularly relevant to northern Europe. For example, in Flanders, the wild man was depicted as a giant, covered with hair and armed with a club,

who kept watch on the fountain of life and "refused or allowed entry into paradise."[108] "Near the forest was the *Nobiskrug* where passports to the other
world could be obtained"; its insignia was a hairy giant.[109] The figure of the
wild man/Hellequin was particularly well known in Rouen where, in the
thirteenth century, he was said to have betrothed the evil witch Luque La
Maudite; the celebrations that accompanied their marriage were said to have
resulted in "an orgy of destruction . . . unique in the annals of Rouen."[110]
Moreover, in Rouen during the sixteenth century, the figure of Hellequin

> was placed above doors of houses, and appeared as a fireplace guardian against
> the underworld. [Similarly] he is found on the North portal of Rouen's Cathe-
> dral . . . [while] in his demonic aspect he appears on tombs, particularly in
> northern and central Europe, where [like barbarians in the ancient triumph, he
> is depicted as] being *trampled underfoot* by the commemorated figure."[111]

Whether in charivaris or courtly entertainments, the wild man clearly
summoned up an image of alterity and death.[112] The donning of his ritual
mask intimated a transformation and a metamorphosis—from the human to
the animal, from the living to the dead—and hence an initiation and a passage
to a world where the rules governing normal social behavior no longer applied. Though Hellequin, the wild man, and the barbarian each derived from
unique and quite distant historical circumstances, they co-existed on the same
plane of symbolic and ritual practices from which entry rituals took their animus. Indeed, wild men, in addition to their place in charivaris and courtly entertainments, also took part in the entry ceremonies held for French kings.

Wild Men, Gardens, and Triumphs

Even before Charles VI masqueraded as a wild man for the ladies and
knights of his court, he viewed them at stations in his royal entries. From 1389,
and subsequently throughout the fifteenth century, men and women would
cover themselves with hair and don animal skins in imitation of *les hommes
sauvages* as part of les entrées joyeuses held for French kings. Thus appareled
they would play, fight, and cavort on scaffolds, in gardens, and in fountains.[113]
Gardens and fountains were commonplace representations of paradise in the
medieval period.[114] The symbolism is unmistakable, and directly points to the
liminal status of wild men and women as mediators between material and
spiritual worlds.[115] Situated along the procession route of the royal entry, the
Edenic site occupied by wild men signified (like the Roman practice of situ-
ating barbarians on triumphal arches or accompanying a triumphal chariot)
the king's entry into paradise and/or his transformation into a god.

From the Garden Back to the Gate: The Return of the Native

In the early sixteenth century the historically distinct strands of the barbarian and the wild man converged not simply on the level of an underlying thematic affinity, but as interchangeable formal elements in a tradition of ritual practice. Thus, for Louis XII's entry into Milan in 1502 (about which Jean Marot and Jean d'Auton, both participants in Rouen's Puy de Palinod, wrote) a god, variously identified as Mars or Victory, riding a triumphal chariot, met the king just beyond the city's walls. S/he greeted the king as victor and paternal ruler and invited him to take his rightful place on the triumphal car.[116] Together with the gods Louis rode into Milan. The chariot, we are told, was escorted by a troop of wild men.

Five years later, for Louis XII's triumphal entry into Venice, wild men once again appeared, this time placed atop the city's southern gate next to figures representing France (Louis) and Brittany (Anne de Bretagne).[117] For François I's entry into Caen in 1532 not only was the king greeted by the rectors of the university wearing "triumphal" chapeaux, but by a chariot accompanied by six wild men.[118] That the figure of the savage/wildman had become a kind of stock trope of royal entries is given further support by an account of Henri II's 1548 triumph into Troyes. As its author states, "*According to the practice of the times . . .* the prince of fools and his supporters disguised (*travesti*) themselves as savages."[119] The account specifies that forty-eight men were costumed in hairy suits designed by the best local artists.[120] They carried shields and bows and arrows and were accompanied by a troop of satyrs.[121] This display was a huge success, much to the satisfaction of the city council that paid for it.[122]

In 1508 Thomas Auber took Jean Ango's ship *La Pensée* to the New World. He brought back seven "savages" to Rouen. They were among the first to be seen in France.[123] Despite having used his ship, Ango did not hire Auber; rather, he was in the employ of Rouen's archbishop and governor of Normandy, Cardinal Georges d'Amboise.[124] As we saw in Chapter 4, d'Amboise's château at Gaillon was among the first footholds of Renaissance humanism established in northern France. It was also the site of France's first triumphal arch, which the cardinal had built upon his return from Italy to commemorate his friend's, the king's, triumphs there. It is likely that the New World savages brought back by d'Amboise's agent were displayed for the king as part of the festivities surrounding his entry into Rouen in 1508. It is also, I think, probable that they figured in the king's visit to the cardinal's château. Perhaps they were even compelled to stand on scaffolds above the king as he passed beneath them and through the triumphal arch that d'Amboise specially commissioned to welcome him to Gaillon. Perhaps also it will come as no surprise that these Amerindians were described by eyewitnesses as *homines sylvestres*, that is, as wild men.[125]

Rereading Henri's Triumph

When Henri crossed the threshold of the triumphal arch leading from Sainte Catherine de Grandmont's priory to the Faubourg Saint-Sever, he stepped into another world. The king's pilgrimage into Rouen and his messianic transformation began there, at the first tableau vivant of the third movement of his entry: Brazil. It was through this intermediate world, this paradise inhabited by savage men who lived on the cusp of the animal, the human, and the divine, that his passage into Rouen as the Last World Emperor—the harbinger of, and ruler over, a renascent Golden Age—was made possible. Hence the recapitulation of this theme by the figure of Saturn as the king entered the city.[126] As the god himself promised, Henri's entry into Rouen augured the return of this Golden Age.[127] Standing on top of the arch and supporting the crescent upon which Saturn stood (which, as we have seen, was not only associated with the king's insignia but with the iconography of the Apocalyptic Woman) were two satyrs.[128] Like the savages from Brazil, wild men and barbarians, satyrs were liminal creatures situated ambiguously among the feral, the human, and the divine.[129] This is not to posit an identity between these different representations of alterity, but to point to the shared symbolic space they inhabited. Indeed, they formed part of a collective repertoire of resources that could be used in rites such as the entry.[130] Like Saturn above them, Brazil before them, and the triumphal arch upon which they stood, these satyrs reiterated the common theme of triumphal entries from the times of antiquity: the king's ritual transformation into a god as he passed beneath them, through the arch, and into Rouen.

As he crossed through the threshold of this arch and into Rouen, Henri was immediately placed beneath a canopy held aloft by four of the city's aldermen. The canopy, as we have seen, was a means of effecting a ritual equivalence between Henri and the Eucharist, as the *real* presence of Christ on earth, thus in a sense recapitulating in Christian terms the promise announced by Saturn moments before. Written upon the canopy was Henri's motto, *Donec totum impleat orbem*, which spelled out the dynastic appropriation of the theme of universal Christian empire.[131] This message was seconded by Hector, symbol of Henri's Trojan ancestry, who specified that it was heaven's judgment that the royal bloodline of France was to fill the world. Thus Hector's blood shot from the wounds he received from Achilles high into the sky, forming Henri's device, the triple crescent. Moreover, in the penultimate tableau, men of many nations gathered around the king to receive the sweet liqueur of *amyable confederation et obeisance* dripping from the fruited vine growing from the king's heart. The figural fusion of the monarch with Christ was made manifest with the consumption—as with the Holy Communion—of his blood. Standing balanced on a crescent, with the sun shimmering around his head, the king, in his left hand, held the flowering sword of justice; in his right, he held *the bloody severed head of a Gorgon*, symbolizing, the chronicler tells us, the king's "happy victory" over his enemies. This pageant ended with the winged Pegasus appearing above the stage. It was upon this strange and life-like animal breathing fire from its mouth, that the king was to ride, as did the ancient Roman triumphators, on his ascent to immortality, which would land him in the final tableau of the entry, the Elysian Fields. Here, Henri's journey came to an end, for he had come full circle, bringing the city of Rouen and France along with him to a new Golden Age. Like the Roman emperor arriving at the temple of Jupiter, when Henri entered the Cathedral of Notre Dame and ritually changed his clothes, his passage was finally complete, for his physical presence in Rouen had been fully transformed into the real presence of Christ in the New Jerusalem. (See Plate 23.)

CHAPTER 8

Fêtes and Cabinets

THE ORDER OF RITUAL
AND THE ORDER OF THINGS

At the outset of this work I remarked that one of the distinguishing features of the Brazilians presented to Henri II in Rouen was that they were not simply displayed, but that they were scripted into the larger narrative of the king's royal entry. At this point, we need to qualify this assertion, for the tableau vivant of Brazil was not only integrated into the specific story being told to Henri II in 1550, but was part of a very old narrative indeed—that of the triumphal entry. The narrative of a god's triumph and his bringing "prosperity, new life, and a new beginning" to a city formed the internal and overlapping filiation that extended from the antique to the Renaissance triumph. Like different strands crisscrossing and intertwining to form the thread of common connection, triumphal arches, chariots, effigies, barbarians, wild men, severed heads, relics, satyrs, *and* New World peoples all represented different means by which the sensible world and earthly authority could be brought into close proximity with the divine.

Henri II's entry into Rouen was a rite of passage that aimed to make the French king into the Christ-like avatar of a new, humanistically conceived, empire. Underlying the transformative power of the entry's sequence of tableaux vivants was a long-established ritual tradition associated with Adventus/triumph. This tradition, as we have seen, was intertwined with the textual tradition of the speculum principis. This, in turn was closely allied to practices and texts associated with spiritual meditation.

Like the speculum principis tradition to which the entry belonged, the aim of meditative texts was to teach one how to live. They did this by presenting readers with image-ideas to be contemplated, meditated upon, and emulated. The more striking—marvelous, strange, singular, and wondrous— the ideas and images to be contemplated were, the better they would be able to transport those who contemplated them into the ideal of reality to be imitated. By imprinting themselves on the imagination, and becoming part of the very material substance of a person's being, they would live on, not simply as pleasing images, but as fundamental and essential aspects of the self.[1] The living pictures—the tableaux vivants—of Henri's entry were thus explicitly designed to inscribe themselves upon the imagination of those who viewed them. As its chronicler put it, the entry was "imprinted on the brains of those who contemplated it" as an enduring and indelible image that "even the lapse of time could not efface from memory."[2]

A crucial part of late medieval and early modern meditative techniques was the way a meditator was urged to lose himself in his devotions as if acting out a role in a drama.[3] In the practice of meditation, however, the line separating the *dramatis personae* and the "real" person was to be blurred; indeed, this was the goal of meditation: total identification with the life of a saint or of Christ himself. In a similar way, the presence of the king in the entry was literally to be absorbed into the mirror of his various representations (Hercules, Saturn, Hector, François I), thus elliding (for both Henri and those observing him) the distance between real and mythical time, physical movement and ritual transformation.[4]

It is important to note that imagination in the early modern period had little to do with its modern meaning of fanciful/fictive creation, but was considered a passive cognitive capacity that could store experiences and make them available—through memory—to the understanding.[5] It was through this storehouse of the imagination that the intellect could recall to consciousness the experiences, images, thoughts, and feelings from which identity could be fashioned. The meditative scheme of tableaux vivants in the entry, like the Stations of the Cross, narrated scenes in which ideal models of the king were externalized and ritually choreographed into an allegorical pilgrimage that traced his physical movement through the city. Just as Christ's journey through life as recounted in the Gospels was to be the focal point for acts of spiritual meditation, so too was the king's journey through Rouen. As such, the entry was conceived as a mirror into which spectators were to gaze for a clear view of their soul's progress toward salvation. Blending the real time of his journey with the dreamlike or meditative allegorical system of sequential tableaux, the Rouen entry was organized as a pilgrimage whose aim was to dissolve the boundaries of normal time and space and take the king and those who followed him into a world where Henri was transformed into the "one who comes in the name of the Lord."

Similar to contemporary practices for composing compelling sermons, the entry's story was knit together by a carefully collected and choreographed series of memorable and striking examples—its tableaux vivants.[6] It perhaps goes without saying that secure recollective associations are forged of memorable things—things that stick out in one's mind. Memory retains best what is unusual and surprising. Yet, remarkable things are never simply "singular," for it is their very exteriority that gives shape and definition to the normal and everyday. Indeed, the identification of something as singular, rare, bizarre, or wonderful presupposes the articulation of the background against which it so strikingly stands out. Such examples are used not simply because they *stand out*, but because of their power to *stand for*, which is to say, they are noticed, chosen, made, and used for their ability to emblematically direct observers and auditors to larger social, cultural, and spiritual narratives. Thus, the account of Henri's entry into Paris tells us that the king "was not dazzled by the splendor of the magnificent delights that had been so amply prepared for him by his subjects: but always, having his eyes set to that end where honor, truth, sureness and the advancement of his estate lay, and with the happiness of his people truly winning his royal heart. . . . "[7]

As demonstrated by didactic and meditative techniques, one remembers by putting singular events and ideas within larger narrative contexts—by making them part of a story, a rhyming sequence, a song, etc., that moves sequentially from one item to be remembered to the next.[8] In this sense, the striking examples employed by a sermon to propel listeners along the course of its message are directly comparable to the entry's use of tableaux vivants. Like the auditors of a sermon, the viewers of the entry were led—along with the king—through a repetition of striking examples to seek the common thread linking the entry's different stations.[9]

More generally, for humanists, the goal of collecting was moral and spiritual edification. The more striking, singular, and marvelous an example, the more suitable it was as an object of contemplation and emulation.[10] One of the fundamental criteria for selection of items to be collected (objects, texts, exotic peoples, etc.) was their power to inspire curiosity and wonder. However, the ability to evoke an affective response was not valued in and of itself (indeed, it was frequently condemned),[11] but was considered as a particularly effective means of canalizing thoughts and emotions into appropriate moral and spiritual directions.[12] The entry's living display of Brazil, in this sense, was not simply an awe-inspiring wonder calculated to impress by its marvelous singularity, but part of a sequential narrative (of associated marvels/tableaux) that strategically aimed to redraw—through the king—the normative boundaries of elite identity in early modern France.

Royal rituals, in this sense, were not simply a means of displaying power, they were also a means of co-opting it—of rewriting it—so as to participate in it. Accordingly, the didactic/strategic function of royal ritual was directed at the prince as well as the watching public. This is significant on a number of levels, for it implies that the legitimacy of a prince's rule was in some measure dependent on his ability to learn from and conform to the mirror's presentation of ideal kingship. Falling short of this ideal, as it inevitably did, the mirror's didactic program nevertheless remained a powerful articulation of—and hence, a strategic attempt to stabilize and discipline—the sociocultural dispositions characterizing the new elites responsible for writing the entry's program. This strategic purpose, the same that we find structuring the entry's narrative as a civilizing journey toward a new humanistically inspired Golden Age, was thoroughly implicated in the discursive regimes that underwrote early modern practices of collecting.

Triumphal Entries and Collecting Power: Fêtes and Cabinets

Humanism in France steered philological-empiricist method toward the propaedeutic ends of mimesis. Whether we are speaking of ancient languages translated into the vernacular, the imitation of ancient rites, or the recreation of a Brazilian village, *imitatio* was the hand servant of virtue. It is here, I believe, that collecting practices came to intersect with meditative (devotional) practice, mnemotechniques, didactic literature (e.g., the Mirror of Princes), and royal rituals, for the architectonic foundations of all these spiritual-ethical-social practices were acts of collecting, of gathering *copia*, which could inspire and focus acts of imitatio.[13] Indeed, the social processes that defined the collection of *sententiae*, morally enlightening phrases, examples, and commonplaces from ancient texts also embraced the collecting of ancient inscriptions, medallions, coins, and curiosities.[14] The common goal of all these various forms of collecting was moral edification. As Krzysztof Pomian has put this: "It was believed that these examples and models would enable individuals to transcend time and attain glory, the secular equivalent of immortality."[15]

Singularities and wonders, such as those displayed before the king during his royal entry, were powerful mediums of exchange in early modern aristocratic culture. This was not simply because they were rarities that could be possessed by only a very special few, but because they "carried with them the sense of unmediated contact with another world."[16] Whereas Adventus rites activated the charismatic power of relics, images, and kings, wonder cabinets vested their collected objects with the capacity to metonymically stand for the macrocosm of the natural and spiritual order of things.[17] As such, both were essential elements in an aristocratic and intellectual culture where traffic in and knowledge of singularities and wonders was the currency of status and the identifying mark of authority. And indeed, from the moment he stepped through the triumphal arch into Rouen's representation of the New World, until the moment he stepped into the nave of the Cathedral of Notre Dame, Henri II was surrounded by a collection that would rival that of any cabinet of curiosities.[18] As the records of the Hôtel de Ville report, Henri saw "more singular things in his city of Rouen than in any other city of his realm."[19]

Wonder cabinets were, Pomian has argued, theaters of the world, microcosms "containing specimens of every category of things and helping to render visible the totality of the universe, which otherwise would remain hidden from human eyes."[20] Henri's entry was entirely consistent with this understanding of the cabinet's function.[21] The Brazilian mise-en-scène was but one exhibit among the many that were displayed in the encyclopedic spectacle presented to him over the course of his triumph. A brief list will suffice to demonstrate the range of the collection assembled: It included junipers, boxwood, and other trees from Brazil; grottoes encrusted with stones and minerals (both clear and of many colors); triumphal arches, Brazilian lodges, theaters, and gardens; monkeys, parakeets, elephants, hippopotami, unicorns, whales, and porpoises, as well as seven kinds of fish (*Aurades, Albachores, Thuns, Esturgeons, Haulsmoriens, Marsouyns,* and *Espardins*); maps made following the rules of perspective; Ionic, Persian, and Corinthian columns; and not only were there Brazilians, but also Turks, and Roman gladiators, gods, tritons, and muses. As this strange blend of natural and artificial, real and mythical, everyday and marvelously strange attests, the royal entry festival organized for Henri II in Rouen bore more than a passing resemblance to the early-modern phenomenon of the wonder cabinet.

Indeed, like a wonder cabinet, the entry aimed to spread out and unfold the entire universe before the king's eyes.[22] Here vision was tantamount to an act of possession.[23] This was especially the case with regard to a king, whose prerogative was to possess (as well as rule) all he surveyed.[24] That the objects collected in early cabinets were frequently compared to relics is not surprising, for their mediating capacity to present the world in its entirety places them in the category of objects that Pomian has labeled the *semiophore*—that is, objects that refer to "a realm of significance that is invisible and absent" (for example, the order of Nature), "and mediate the visitor's . . . access to this realm by making it metonymically visible and present."[25] Similar to the cabinet's collection, the entry offered up the universe in microcosm to the king's gaze; through it, he could mark not simply the geographical boundaries of his realm, but the entire expanse of the world as his territory. As his motto said: *Donec totum impleat orbem.* It was through such ritual acts of possession that the French monarch was told, in no uncertain terms, that he would bring unity to the world, and deliver mankind from the bloody Age of Iron to a new Age of Gold. The singularities contained in the collection, like those displayed in the entry, thus referred—at one and the same time—to God's infinite generative capacity to enact his will and to the king's analogous power to command, possess, and unify the natural and human worlds into a stable, perceptible, and rule-governed order.

The belief that a terrestrial monarch would be born who would lead the peoples of earth out of darkness and into a new Golden Age was a relatively common one in the sixteenth century.[26] There was an almost desperate urgency animating such a faith. At the time of Henri's entry, France was beset by constant war, intractable and violent religious controversy, innumerable plagues and famines, as well as the pangs of unprecedented social mobility. In addition, humanist and philological scholarship increasingly problematized the present's continuity with the past by elucidating the vast historical and cultural differences between Classical/pagan antiquity and the contemporary world.[27] In these circumstances, the discovery of the New World and its naked and barbarous peoples was taken as but another sign that the world was moving toward a predetermined and cataclysmic end. This gave impetus to a search for solutions that could restore the world to its original and uncorrupted state of harmony—to the terrestrial paradise, the Elysian Fields, the Golden Age. It was, I believe, this quest for lost unity, conjoined with the appearance of France's new civic-cultural elite and its longing for the stability of legitimate social position, that animated both the writing and enactment of Henri II's Rouen entry and the assembling of curiosity cabinets.[28]

Like the entry, the wonder cabinet was a response to a world that no longer made sense—a world composed of discrete and contingent particulars rather than knowable universals. Through it, the collector sought not only to win prestige, but to assemble the variegated and multifarious mosaic of existence into a more intimately comprehensible whole.[29] New plants, new animals, new peoples, new worlds, and the new men: the world of the sixteenth century had seemingly lost its coherence. This proliferation of novelty and singularity created a kind of cognitive charivari. In the cabinet, one could spin on one's heels, stretch out one's arms, and take in—and wonder at—all the world. At the same time, just as the charivari (as Natalie Zemon Davis has argued) enabled actors the possibility and the freedom to explore behavioral options not normally available to them, the apparent disorder of the cabinet's singular objects made possible a similar sort of experimentation on the cognitive level.[30] Seen from this perspective, the cabinet was nothing less than the physical embodiment of the nominalist/empiricist epistemology epitomized by Rouen's new civic-cultural elites. Here, however, it was the collector who stood in the position of the all-seeing—and potentially all-knowing—king.

The Renaissance collector's vision of natural order was closely allied to his vision of social order and his position within it. The cabinet reflected this symmetry between social and natural worlds. Not simply a microcosmic representation of the cosmos, it was an externalization of the collector's cognitive capacities and his social identity.[31] A Tupi war club, for example, could recall to mind—and conversation—not only descriptions found in travel narratives (such as those by Staden, Léry, and Thevet), but associations with the Germanic tribes described by Tacitus, or comparisons between Tupi *Morbicha* such as Quoniambec and Hercules (who was, of course, also armed with a club). From here, the way would be opened up to associations with the Gallic and Lybian Hercules, to the kings of France and Spain, and hence to such texts (and images) as those of Lefèvre, Lemaire de Belges, Dürer, Aneau, Tory, Erasmus, du Bellay, Cicero, Lucian, etc.[32] Like the tableaux vivants of the entry festival, a collection thus appealed to, signified, and advertised the collector's ability to creatively read and analyze the emblematic, associative, and sympathetic histories of its objects across a field of often arcane textual, material, and pictorial associations.[33] As with the tabula rasa of the New World, the decontextualized objects in a collection—uprooted and lifted from their original contexts of use and meaning—were (or could be) rewritten and reinscribed with new meanings and purposes by their collectors.[34] Accordingly, like the mise-en-scène of Brazil in Henri's entry, collections were less mirrors of nature than mirror reflections of their collectors. Enclosed and displayed in cabinets, singular objects became "archives"—repositories—that could act as disparate sites of embodied memory. A collection, like the entry, was thus a kind of memory theater, with its collected objects consisting in material incarnations of the projected dispositions and competencies of the collector. Moreover, as we saw earlier, these singularities served as meditative conduits that constrained, reinforced, disciplined, and refined these dispositions and skills.[35] The singularly wondrous objects in collections were, in this sense, nodal points through and around which a new intellectual cultural elite came into being.[36] If the cabinet/entry provided an epistemic "solution" to the problem of the world's disorder, it was a social one: its exhibition of singularities instantiated a social collectivity that was qualified by its specialized knowledge and skill to speak authoritatively about the nature of nature and the nature of truth.[37]

Words and Things, Social Order and Rhetoric

In Henri's entry, it was through the mediation of a reformed and perfected language as spoken by a learned and eloquent king that the unity of the world would be restored. According to the Imperial ambassador, Henri's entry praised François I "for having restored letters and saved [Rouen] from barbarism" while encouraging Henri to follow in his footsteps.[38] And who better to help him along the way than the local elites responsible for writing, organizing, and producing his entry? The entry's linkage of the Golden Age to the New Learning was clearly made with reference to humanist interests in linguistic propriety and the formal rules and protocols that governed it. Such rules and protocols, as articulated in books of grammar, rhetoric, and courtesy, were perceived to be the means by which the increasingly turbulent social world of the sixteenth century could be successfully navigated and the distinction of legitimate social status achieved and maintained. However, as we have also seen, the New Learning was viewed by many to be foremost among the causes for the world's fallen state. This ambivalence toward one—if not *the*—principal feature defining the identity of the new elite gave impetus to the development of empirical methods (e.g., antiquarianism and collecting) which could ground identity and virtue in the material substance of reality. This empiricist current marked an important transformation in the self-perception of France's civic-cultural elites.[39] It was the material artifacts of the world to which knowledge and virtue were to be tied, not simply the ephemeral and all-too-often duplicitous use of words. As Jean du Tillet said, introducing his archival investigation into history of French royal rituals,

> Today there are people who are so overly refined that they cannot countenance anything [in linguistic usage] which is not perfectly polished and smoothed, and they wish to frighten me into retreating [from this endeavor] because of the coarseness of my style. Such people consider *text rather than context, appearance rather than reality, a situation typical of the ignorant who treat [linguistic] eloquence as authoritative even if it is devoid of veracity.*[40]

Yet, despite such polemics, words and things were not so very far apart as they were *said* to be. Indeed, books of rhetoric, grammar, and courtesy were based upon principles closely intertwined with those operating in wonder cabinets. Inasmuch as it constituted a kind of repository where words were gathered together, set out, ordered, and displayed, the printed page closely resembled the physical site of a cabinet.[41] Moreover, as with the collection and exhibition of singular objects in a cabinet of curiosities, the skillful (or not so skillful) deployment of words, tropes, schemes, and affect in the context of courtly and civic discourse prompted the rigorous rehearsal of new empirical observational practices. Thus Antonio de Guevara was to describe life at court as a veritable fishbowl where "every word was noted; every pace measured; every possession registered; every fault tabulated, and every vile rumor published."[42] Notwithstanding statements to the contrary, the study—and systematization of—eloquence, grammar, and courtesy were deeply implicated in the development and articulation of collecting and display practices. This is nowhere better exemplified than in the grammar written by Pierre Fabri, *Le Grant et vray art de pleine rhetorique.*

There were six editions of Fabri's book between 1521 and 1544. Its stated purpose was to educate the members of the Puy de Palinod. In addition to laying out the proper rules for the writing of palinodic verse, Fabri's text was a catalogue of the figures, ornaments, and colors of eloquent speech.[43] For Fabri and his contemporaries, such linguistic embellishments were not merely formal rhetorical conventions, but were the foundations of truth, honor, and respectability. As he points out, for the orator, "the force of eloquence is not only about leading listeners to believe a thing is as it is, . . . but rather to lead listeners to believe that he himself is true."[44]

It is a commonplace of current scholarship that collecting in the early modern period was a tangible sign of—or a means of attaining—social status and authority. But it is important to note that collections were not simply casual conglomerations of wonderful and awe-inspiring singularities, but were constituted both in and by specific social and cultural narratives.[45] In books of grammar and rhetoric this narrative was contiguous with a social field in which status and legitimacy were established with reference to specific cultural capacities, disposition, and skills. The connection is eloquently expressed by Du Faur de Pibrac, a Parisian lawyer, in 1569 when he noted that:

> The mouth of the learned and educated man (*l'homme docte et sçavant*) has been compared to the door of a royal cabinet. For just as when the door of the cabinet opens, suddenly there appear, representing themselves before our very eyes, a thousand beautiful singularities . . . so many beautiful antique medals, so many exquisite things, sought out with curiosity and brought back from faraway and strange lands, and the whole thing structured and arranged therein with a marvelous order.[46]

Similarly, in books like Fabri's, words and texts were collected, ordered, and displayed on the printed page like so many singular wonders; as such, they could then be redeployed in diverse contexts (e.g., the Puy de Palinod's annual poetry competitions), not only as markers of social, cultural, and spiritual distinction, but as a "pathway to truth and salvation."[47] Indeed, it was by means of their specialized knowledge of grammar and rhetoric that the Puy's members presumed that they had—or could have—privileged access to the word of God.[48] It was thus no coincidence that the Puy restricted its membership to a maximum of seventy-two, for as their statutes stated: this was in memory to the "seventy-two disciples of our Lord Jesus Christ and to the seventy-two interpreters and translators of the holy and sacred scriptures."[49] This passage refers to the Septuagint: Brought to Alexandria by Ptolemy II Philadelphus, seventy-two translators were placed in separate cells with a Hebrew copy of the Old Testament. Miraculously, they all produced the exact same version of the Bible in Greek when they reappeared several days later.[50] This reference to the Septuagint, however, was less about God's miraculous intervention in the ability of translators to do their job than it was about the capacity of learned and pious men to decipher the one true language of God. As Saint Wandrille put it in his chant royal comparing the Virgin to a book of grammar:

> We have propagated (*semé*) an age-old error (*erreur primitif*)
> By which antique grammar was forfeited
> But by a verb [Jesus Christ] and a substantive noun [the Virgin]
> Everyone present returns . . .
> For we have true proof (*vray demonstratif*)
> The beautiful gift of perfect elegance.[51]

For Fabri and his fellow poets at the Puy (such as Wandrille), literary excellence, eloquence, and oratorical flair were the foundations upon which their claims to social status and spiritual authority were to be made. "*Rhetorique donc*," as Fabri said, "*est science politique.*"[52]

Henri's royal entry into Rouen also tells a tale of social differentiation and distinction. As we have seen, it aimed at setting out a version of social and political order that closely conformed to the interests of its organizers, many of whom were members of the Puy. This was demonstrated not only in the elaborate narrative told by the entry's tableaux vivants, but also in its opening moments when Henri was presented with a thorough taxonomy of the city's inhabitants in the form of a ceremonial procession. Processions, of course, were part of every royal entry festival in Rouen and elsewhere, but few before, at least in France, had ever been so elaborate, so carefully choreographed, or so detailed by ordering of rank, occupation, and social status.

This singular precision, as Philip Benedict has rightly pointed out, provides a marvelous window into the city's complex social structure.[53] Yet seen from a slightly different perspective, such precision points to the heightened and almost desperate compulsion of the city's civic leaders to establish a precise order by which to organize and display its populace.

At the end of the fifteenth century Raymond de Sebonde wrote that it was necessary to recognize the diversity of worldly estates and to reduce them all to an appropriate order; as he put it: "there is a perpetual diversity of estates between us, first there are laborers, who are the lowest (*le plus vil*), after them come the merchants and the bourgeoisie, then the nobles . . . , and then the king."[54] By the mid-sixteenth century, the estates mentioned by de Sebonde had become highly differentiated and vastly more complex. According to Jonathan Dewald, in Normandy, social categories "were becoming more sharply defined in the later sixteenth century, and rankings of more and less honorable positions were assuming new precision."[55] This new precision is evident as early as mid-century; thus, in Henri's entry, rankings were represented both by order of appearance and by the elaborate costumes distinguishing each group.[56] For example, the chronicler of the entry describes the twenty-four grain measurers as riding "on horseback wearing long coats of gray taffetas, with doublets of violet satin, caps of black velour decorated with white feathers, britches of violet velour and gray taffetas, with silver buckled white boots, and belts and scabbards of violet velour . . . , each carried a short standard which was sewn with gold *fleurs de lys* on fields of azure."[57] Following the grain measurers came the *courtiers de vin*; who were "dressed in large-cut gowns of black damask, with doublets of white satin, bonnets of black velour decorated with white feathers, wearing white Moroccan boots, and a belt and scabbard of white velour . . . , with long coats of black velour. . . . "[58] Such minute descriptions follow the order of the procession in tedious detail (amounting to fifty pages—almost half of *C'est la deduction*), recounting not simply the order and dress of the municipal and royal officials, the clergy and visiting dignitaries, but Rouen's tradesmen as well:

> 40 master weavers, 8 skinners, 2 nail-makers, 4 dyers, 14 tailors, 12 chandlers, 15 cordwainers, 15 shoemakers, 5 decorators of gilded swords, 5 bit- and spur-makers, 35 innkeepers, 2 furriers, 6 saddlers, 4 trunk-makers, 4 inkwell-makers, 8 comb-makers, 10 bakers, 2 hook-makers, 10 joiners, 6 sheath- and wallet-makers, 2 balance-makers, 10 hatters, 1 oar-maker . . . , 1 mirror-maker . . . [etc.].[59]

Clearly, the effort expended in establishing the correct order and social place of its citizens at its beginning resonated closely with the overall narrative structuring the entry as a whole. It thus might be possible to see that the collection, classification, and display of Rouen's social world was consistent with a range of practices associated with the ordering, classification, and display of language as found in books of grammar, rhetoric, and courtesy: both were recounting a similar tale of social distinction and the means by which it could be achieved and identified. As Fabri said, "all language . . . is composed of words or terms put in order, which [thus] assembled composes a proposition, [with] . . . several propositions, orderly disposed making an oration."[60] Taken in this sense, Rouen's citizenry—well-ordered, arranged, and disposed—formed a kind of social narrative (an oration) that foreshadowed that which would structure the king's journey from the barbarity of Brazil to the pious, eloquent, and learned prince represented by François I in the tableau vivant of the Elysian Fields. This narrative converged not only with the ritual self-representation of the civic elite responsible for the entry, but with such texts as Fabri's *Grant et vray art de pleine rhetorique*, Sebillet's *Art poétique françois*, Tory's *Champ fleury*, and du Bellay's *La Deffence et illustration de la langue Françoyse*, which sought to civilize the French language by collecting, ordering, and classifying it. Such classificatory acts underwrote and paralleled the performative deployment of civilized linguistic fashion as the means by which social distance could be asserted, maintained, and recognized.[61] Seen from this perspective, the social practices that made possible both the processional order of Rouen's inhabitants during the entry and the distanciation of language as an object to be collected in grammars and deployed in civil conversation, also embraced efforts to collect the natural world in cabinets of curiosity and in books of natural history—as, for example, those by Pierre Belon, François de Belleforest, Guillaume Rondelet, and André Thevet.[62]

Nature, of course, was the language of God, and all the earth's inhabitants—its fish, birds, animals, and plants—formed the alphabet in which it was written.[63] It was through the contemplative reading of these visible signs that one could gain access to the hidden order underlying the apparent incoherence (singularity) of everyday experience. The collection of these visible things (their names, their characteristics, their place and order in the world)—whether in manuscripts, books, and cabinets, or in gardens, menageries, and entry festivals—was the first step in the effort to decipher the mystical language of God in terms of its intelligible signatures. The study of natural history, in this sense, was not distinct from humanist attempts to reform and civilize language, for both were considered in essentially philological terms: that is, how to correct for the impurities and barbarisms that had infiltrated and corrupted postlapsarian language. One way to accomplish this was to begin the long and painstaking processes of collecting, setting out, and ordering the language of nature (natural history) and the nature of language (general grammar). In both cases, the restauration of divine knowledge was to be accomplished through similar efforts of decontextualization—that is, through the distanciation of words as objects to be collected, classified, and ordered on the printed page.[64]

The New Barbarians

Henri's entry into Rouen should be seen within the larger context of social and epistemic uncertainty that gave animus to, and intensified, efforts to solidify and legitimate social distinctions as the basis upon which order and truth could be established. Ironically, processes of social change and mobility—and their cultural expressions—were, in many ways, responsible for the perception of the problem in the first place. Rouen's new civic elite based its status not simply on its economic power, but on its cultural and intellectual skills.[65] Theirs, however, was not the overweening confidence that characterized the Enlightenment's faith in reason, for they were deeply marked by the cognizance of man's fallen nature and the precariousness of his attempts to impose human order upon God's world. This ambivalence lent momentum to empiricist undercurrents running through—and against—the belief in the powers of human reason. This problematized (or at least, reconfigured) attempts to legitimate social authority on the basis of etiquette, comportment, the arts of second rhetoric, etc., in favor of (putatively) more empirical/material registers of truth.[66]

We can see both of these crosscurrents operating in Henri's entry, for at the same time as its ritual narrative was championing the cause of eloquence and rhetorical virtuosity, its verisimilar presentation of Brazil (and of a Roman triumph) were gesturing toward the development of new forms of anti-rhetorical empiricism. These opposing currents met in the entry and intermingled in the ritual space occupied by the co-construction of this new elite's identity and the King's power. Thus for example, in the text of the entry, just prior to the appearance of the tableau vivant of Brazil, which began Henri's allegorical journey towards the humanist ideal of the perfect orator king, the anonymous chronicler proclaimed that he was so overwhelmed by the singular marvels he had witnessed that he was incapable of describing them. As he put it:

> I am forced to put a veil of silence over the magnificence, pomp, and excellence of this Triumph because its admirable success has so astonished me that I cannot promise more than to present a shadow of a description (*la peinture*). Taking upon myself to represent the image of this triumph to you would be

too bold an undertaking for me, seeing that even eloquence, in the progress of
the story, would find itself mute, or deprived of articulate voice. Following the
discourse that I have begun—from which we have by way of excuse and apol-
ogy somewhat strayed—let it be understood that (*fait à entendre que*). . . . [67]

And here the page, and the chronicler's thought, ends unfinished; it dangles
incomplete, to be followed by the figure of Brazil on the next page. Perhaps
this is simply a printer's error, but it could also be read as an allusion to a belief that words could never adequately express, no matter how well chosen
and arranged, more than a shadow of reality. Yet the very deictic gesture ("let
it be understood that . . . ") to the illustration and the circumstantially detailed descriptions following it indicate more than a simple repetition of the
trope of the inadequacy of language to communicate the experience of wonder, but points to the persuasive powers associated with the rhetoric of anti-
rhetoric—of evidence devoid of rhetorical dilation and eloquence—the illustration, the list, the table, and the painting with words of scenes with such
vivid clarity (*enargeia*) that the reader sees (witnesses) not words but reality itself as it jumps off the page.[68]

And indeed, though rhetoric and eloquence were championed in the
entry as the distinguishing characteristic of true and noble virtue, they were
also (through the presence of the mise-en-scène of Brazil and its naked inhabitants) being implicitly denounced as so much sleight of hand. The real
sleight of hand, however, was in the social construction of the distinction between truth (*res*) and rhetoric (*verba*) in the first place. What seems especially
bizarre, in this context, is the way in which this distinction came to collapse
upon itself, thus making the "prose of the world" quite literally a part of the
world, with words being collected, displayed, and classified as decontextualized linguistic artifacts on the printed pages of grammars, rhetorics, diction-
aries, and courtesy books.

In an interesting reversal, those who most inspired the rise of vernacular consciousness in France through their critiques of French cultural barbarism—namely, the Italians—were to become the most inviting targets in
polemics against the "rhetorical form of life" as it was lived in the courts of
the last Valois kings.[69] Though this might in part be due to the much-hated
queen mother and the putative power she had over her sons, it should also
be seen with reference to the commonplace view that power and culture
were in the process of fleeing the decadence of Rome to find a new home
north of the Alps. For many, the much-vaunted cultural superiority of the
Mediterranean world had been revealed to be little more than corruption,
effeminacy, and dissimulation. In this sense, once the barbarism of the
schools and the old nobles had been overcome, France's new elites (like their

king) were free to be barbarians again—but this time, they were to be barbarians in the manner of the simple eloquence of the savage Hercules from Brazil, Quoniambec. From this perspective, disdain for courtly acts of self-advertisement generated momentum toward naked—more humble—ways of knowing, speaking, and acting. Accordingly, the social instantiation of the dialectic between the valorization of rhetoric and anti-rhetorical empiricism manifested itself in the widening gap that came to separate the tropes of status from the accreditation of authority. Though courtly emblematics, the flowers of rhetoric, the ostentations of ancient learning were all integrally related to the rising social status of France's new civic-cultural elites, they were also increasingly viewed as pointing away from authenticity and toward the conardie of the parvenu.[70]

Paradoxically, we can also see the generation of this movement within the habitus of the court itself. Thus, the intense performative pressure weighing on the courtier was to contribute importantly to the development of new empirical observational practices. Indeed, acts of showing and display as a means of status distinction implied a parallel transformation in ways of seeing; the theater of correct manners, dress, and speech demanded not only that the actor be seen, but that he too observe—measure, dissect, and evaluate—the manners and motives of those around him. Perhaps all this helps explain what has come to be seen as a transition to the supposedly anti-rhetorical—stripped-down—natural history of the seventeenth and eighteenth centuries and the new, and increasingly voiced, emphasis on experience as the sole persuasive arbiter of truth. One of the first expressions of this tendency was to be found in the poetic arts; thus, for example, we see a movement away from the labored technical virtuosity of the *rhétoriqueur* school (with which Rouen's poets can be associated), to a notion of poetry as a divine gift that could not be learned. As du Bellay put this: "leave all these old French poesies . . . to the Puy of Rouen: the rondeaux, ballades, virelays, chants royaux, songs, and other such spices which corrupt the taste of our tongue, and serve for nothing beyond bearing witness to our ignorance."[71] Only a quarter century later we find a much more explicit statement of this view. Thus, while Jean de Léry describes his compatriots as having "such delicate ears and . . . [as being] so enamored of fine flowers of rhetoric that they will not approve or receive any writing without new-fangled and high-flown words,"[72] he goes on to assure those readers who "prefer the truth simply stated over the adorned and painted lie of fine language," that his history—though written in a "crude and ill polished" way[73]—was not only true, but "worthy of wonder."[74] Thus, he announces: "If someone finds it ill that hereafter, when I speak of savage customs, I often use this kind of expression—'I saw,' 'I found,' 'this happened to me,' and so on (as if I wanted to show myself off)—I reply that not only are these things within my own subject but also I am speaking out of my own knowledge, that is, from my own seeing and experience."[75] Perhaps not surprisingly, we find that this epistemic stance was extended to— and exemplified by—the Brazilian "savages" Léry's text describes: "They do not," he says, "pretend to be other than what they are."[76] Exemplary of a more simple, natural and unencumbered way of life, the naked Brazilians thus provide a corrective mirror to the ostentations and dissimulations (the conardie) of the French. As Jodelle put it in his dedicatory epistle to Thevet's *Les Singularités de la France antartique*:

> Ces barbares marchent tous nus,
> Et nous, nous marchons inconnus,
> Fardés, masqués. . . .[77]

Ritual and Normalization

Georges Canguilhem has suggested that the early-modern articulation of a systematized vernacular grammar was the seed crystal of normalization that spread to virtually every domain of human existence.[78] Such systemic processes of normalization derived much of their animus from processes of interclass competition and the ambiguities and tensions associated with elite identity formation; that is, from attempts to articulate and stabilize elite identity through the establishment of distinguishing norms and values. In the first instance, the ability to span the gulf between the sign and signified of elite status was built from the human material of embodied performance (speech, comportment, manners, etc.). Yet the power of these norms to persuade and convince did not simply derive from the referential link to the authority of the elites who embodied them, but to a prior claim: that they were linked to the invisible world of God and of nature. The stability of this linkage was undermined, however, by the progressive—and increasingly violent—unraveling of religious consensus and by the very pressures, resentments, and fears concomitant with the social mobility of the new elites who depended on it. Accordingly, the potential of these affected attributes and skills to translate into the presence of recognized authority was itself an effect of ongoing if evanescent attempts to ascribe a ritual equivalence—as for example, in Henri's entry—among the social, natural, and spiritual worlds.

The reformation of language by which the organizers of the Rouen festival sought to secure their newfound status was considered a potential mirror of reality. If embraced by the king, it was also considered the principal means by which the confusion of Babel could be overcome and the Golden Age restored. At the same time, such efforts were deemed vanity and wind—folly to be offset by the examination of the contingent material world and its peoples through unfettered and naked experience. The paradox here rests not so much in the tensions between these contrasting responses to uncertainty and disorder, but to their historical manifestations in similar sorts of dispositions and practices. The passion to collect, taken in this sense, whether in books of rhetoric or natural history, cabinets or court *fêtes*, was not simply a *prise-de-position* of an ascendant class, but an act of faith performed with the knowledge that the Last Days were imminent.

Between the spectral light emanating from the newly discovered world across the seas, and the nightfall of the impending apocalypse, a final stocktaking had begun. Henri's entry marked a point of conjuncture between this apocalyptic theology and its social roots in the liminality of an emerging elite. It was at this intersection, where the Old World met the New, where the old nobility met the new, and where the new men looked into a mirror image of their own savage souls, that the Brazilians made their appearance in Rouen's Faubourg Saint-Sever.

From Mobility to Ubiquity

According to Victor Turner, rituals place their participants "betwixt and between normal social roles, and close to some transcendent and sacred core of social and moral values."[1] Around this shifting center of sacred values, individuals and groups seek both to orient themselves and to mediate their relations with one another.[2] It is through such public manifestations of the divine that the nature of a community—and one's place within it—is defined and/or contested.[3] In the case of those rituals associated with Adventus and triumph, proximity to the numinous (whether the bones of a triumphator, the relics of a saint, an effigy, or a king) translated into social prestige and power. This perhaps explains the extension of triumphal rites to Christ's bishops and to kings, the frequently ruthless competition for a saint's relics, the jockeying for position for a place of honor near the king's effigy in a royal funeral ceremony, or the efforts expended by Rouen's civic elites to intermingle their interests—in both Rouen's New World trade and in the New Learning—with an established ritual tradition having at its core the mystical transformation of a king into the presence of a god. Accordingly, one might surmise that it was the marriage of the inherited ritual forms associated with the Adventus/triumph to the rise of France's new civic-cultural elites that spurred the articulation of absolutist notions of all-powerful kingship. However, the ephemeral nature of the entry as a context-bound ritual event clearly distinguishes it from seventeenth-century absolutism, based as it was on an ongoing machinery of state.[4] The grace that here turned a king into a god was a function of a ritual act. Like a relic that was considered the real presence of a saint during the ceremonies associated with its translation, the king's apotheosis lasted only so long as the rites that enacted it. Put somewhat differently, the singularity of the ritual event transforming the king into a god was a miracle made possible by the hard work, skill, and watching eyes of his dutiful subjects; which is to say, his *potentia absoluta* as a god-like being was contingent upon a ritual event that was created, enacted, collectively seen—and to an extent, controlled—by his subjects.

The question thus presents itself, how could the entry's formulation of divine kingship survive beyond the evanescence of its performance; that is, in what way did it contribute to the development of absolutism as an ideology? Indeed, how did the entry's ritual construction of absolutism detach itself from the specific confluence of interests that constructed it to become the seemingly immutable and ever-present foundation for monarchical rule in the seventeenth century? Moreover, how did it come to betray its social origins by making absolutely subservient those who were its architects—France's new civic-cultural elites? As we have seen, the Renaissance triumph in France was assembled from the intertwining myths, rites, and practices associated with the triumphs of Roman emperors and the Advent of Christ. There were, however, early modern accretions to these rites. It is to these that we ought to look if we are to see the line of historical development that created the conditions of possibility for absolutism.

Beyond the intricate tangle of (attenuated) continuities between the ancient triumph and its early modern counterpart, there were fundamental changes to the triumph in early modern France. Thus were the themes and motifs of the antique triumph (chariots, arches, equestrian statues, parades of prisoners, etc.) grafted onto the medieval joyeuse entrée tradition. It was the essence of antiquarianism to sift through ancient texts, inscriptions, and monuments so as to imitate and synergistically invent modern simulacra of the ancient world in writing and in deed. In this sense, the template upon which Henri II's entry was fashioned was part of a larger movement (*ad fontes*) calling for a return to original sources.[5] This becomes evident when one considers the precise and detailed scholarship arrayed by Mantegna in his *Triumphs of Caesar*, or perhaps more to the point, the binding of the themes and motifs of the ancient Roman triumph to medieval royal entry ceremonial. This involved intensive antiquarian and historical research.[6] The designer of Henri II's entry into Lyon, for example, was the poet and antiquarian Maurice Scève;[7] Jean Martin (an expert in ancient architecture and translator of Vitruvius' *De Architectura*) helped design Henri II's entry into

Paris. Indeed, the entry into Paris included actors dressed as Roman gladiators, triumphal arches, Ionic pillars with "architraves, friezes and cornices in well-observed proportion,"[8] while his Rouen entry too had gladiators, arches, and chariots constructed in "express imitation of the triumphant Romans."[9] Such details contributed to the illusion of a Roman triumph every bit as verisimilar as Rouen's reconstruction of the New World. As John Stewart said of the Paris entry of 1549: "I seem to see by a thousand sights and images, ancient Roman triumphs."[10] According to both Roy Strong and Margaret McGowan, the 1550 entry into Rouen was the "culmination of this development."[11]

The recreation of the classical past through such methods was not simply a display of intellectual virtuosity aiming at the production of marvelous spectacles that could impress potential patrons, however, but was directed toward the construction of mirrors that were to serve as models of, and spurs toward, virtuous action. The antiquarian scholarship from which entries were fashioned in the sixteenth century was integrally related to the *studia humanitatis* and its valorization of rhetoric and eloquence. Yet, the cultural dispositions that defined France's new elites were also perceived as a threat to social and epistemic order. The narrative of Henri's entry was an attempt to stabilize this threat—and thereby this new elite's place in the world—by linking their intellectual and cultural dispositions to the identity of the Most Christian king of France. But this was only one element of a solution.

Though very much part of what has been described as the "rhetorical form of life," philological/antiquarian acts of *translatio* were viewed by many as being its very opposite. As rhetoric came to be associated with the social success of—and the dangers presented by—France's new civic-cultural elites, it also came to be identified with duplicity, needless ostentation, superciliousness, and untruth. The privileging of naked experience as a method and its textual expression (e.g., antiquarianism, collecting, anti-rhetorical rhetoric, the list, the table, the footnote) were attempts to compensate for social, political, and spiritual uncertainty by securely binding knowledge (and virtue) to the inflexible materiality of things. In one sense, this was a revolt against the parvenu, but it was also a reflection of a deepening fissure in the new elite's identity. "Empiricist methodology" (as exemplified here by antiquarian practice) was viewed as a means of avoiding the pitfalls of dissimulation, the vanity of learning, and the sinfulness of pride (all thought to be hallmarks of an over-reliance on the arts of rhetoric). Yet this nominalist/empiricist solution presented its own problems, for the sheer copiousness of nature combined with the relativism implicit in so carefully distinguishing the antique past from the modern present, was considered no less a threat to social and epistemic order than the appearance of the new elites themselves.[12] Ultimately, both problem and putative solution had their origins in God's infinite and unrestrained power—a power that not only established the contingency of the created order, but, as Oberman has argued, freed "physics from the embrace of metaphysics so as to allow the investigation of the world by means of reason and experience."[13] God's absolute power could not, in this sense, be quarantined to the realm of theology alone; indeed, it was firmly rooted in the social ontology of new elite groups. Its inflection of juridical/political thought and practice had profound implications for notions of sovereignty and constitutionalism as they developed in early modern France. Thus, the belief in the divine right of kings was elaborated in terms that paralleled the conceptualization of God's *potentia absoluta*.[14] This went beyond the obvious associations with the translatio imperii and the vogue for associating French monarchs with their ancient "counterparts," the Caesars, for it was closely intertwined with the Gallican movement and associated attempts to historicize the nature and extent of royal power in France. The movement within nominalist theology that gave impetus to the empirical exploration of God's contingent creation—e.g., in antiquarian collecting practices—was, in this sense, mirrored by the articulation of royal ideology through philological and historicist methods, as exemplified by Budé, Charles Dumoulin, and Jean du Tillet, who sought the origins of the French monarchy in the archival record. Moving away from both essentialist justifications and classical precedents, these men located the source of the king's authority in France's exceptionalism—that is, in its unique (viz singular) feudal/Germanic history and its native traditions.

In his seminal book on the foundations of modern historical scholarship, Donald Kelley has shown the close intertwining of philological and legal/historicist thought with the growth of monarchical power.[15] Despite the close historical connection, however, there was a gradual disentangling of rhetoric from philology, antiquarianism, and juridical thought. We can see the symptoms of this unraveling in du Tillet's careful delineation between rhetoric and fact in his archival investigations into the history of royal rituals (such as the entry) and ancient constitutionalism.[16] Seen from this perspective, the triumphal form lent to Henri's entry into Rouen (like its verisimilar representation of the New World), was based upon epistemological assumptions seemingly at odds (at least at first glance) with the entry's narrative—that is, with the attempt to ritually transform the king into the embodiment of the virtues of eloquence and rhetoric. We thus see manifest in the entry the same conflicting forces and tensions as were operating in the identity of France's new elites. Put somewhat differently, Henri II's entry exemplified a historicist/empirical methodology no less than du Tillet's archival history of the same ritual. Whether one looks to the detailed array of antiquarian knowledge displayed in its reconstruction of a Roman triumph, its verisimilar representation of a Brazilian village, or the poignantly detailed elaboration of circumstantial detail in its chronicler's narrative reconstruction, all point to a preoccupation with an empirical methodology at odds with the entry's narrative, which cast the king in the role of an eloquent rhetorician who would lead the world's peoples to Christ's millennial kingdom through the power of his words.

Despite the apparent contradiction, both points of focus were mediated by the figuration of the king as the "one who comes in the name of the Lord." Just as the entry functioned to collapse the distinction between appearance and reality, performed persona and mortal king, so it aimed to mediate (through the king) the conflicting psycho-social tensions—and their epistemic expressions—of the new elites. The thaumaturgic qualities of the royal touch thus extended beyond healing the sick during his royal entry to healing the social and psychological wounds afflicting France's new elites. Standing at the juncture between earth and heaven, this world and the next, the king's charismatic presence as the incarnation of *potentia dei absoluta* (constructed in and by the entry ritual) formed the conduit between words and things, appearance (rhetoric) and reality (evidence), social order and the cosmos, thus ensuring—*de potentia ordinata* as *lex statuta*—the world's integrity, the continuity of social and political power, and the legitimacy of France's civic-cultural elites.[17]

✝

The other innovation associated with the entry rite in the early modern period was the debut of the printed entry. As we have seen, the very first printed account of an entry was that of Charles VIII into Rouen in 1485; soon afterwards, printed accounts were the norm for every important entry. There were even entries that existed only in print, as for example, the unpublished *Triumphal Procession* by Hans Burgkmair made for—and said to have been dictated by—Maximilian I.[18] What may have been a public relations ploy for the emperor,[19] was for the men who designed and wrote entry festivals—as for the municipalities that sponsored them—a powerful means of self-promotion. As such, printed accounts of entries were less about the normalization and extension of the entry rituals themselves, than about the articulation and advancement of the kinds of people who could write—or at least, understand—their arcane and technical vocabulary. In other words, they were less mirrors of kings than mirrors of France's new elites. But, as we have seen, this mirror reflected conflicting images.

More than simply commemorative gifts to kings and visiting dignitaries, such books had a dual purpose. On the one hand, they aimed—to borrow Steven Shapin's term—at the production of "virtual witnesses" to the rituals they so carefully described. Through their elaborate and circumstantial descriptions, their detailed engravings, and their exhaustive list making, published accounts of entries made spatially and temporally bounded rites live on in the minds of readers as if they were experienced firsthand.[20] Employing powerful anti-rhetorical–rhetorical methods, such as *enargeia* and *ekphrasis*, the writers of entry books aimed at making their texts glisten with the captivating evidentiary detail of the marvelous. By so doing, they aimed to attract—indeed, to create—readers who could literally see the entry through the words that "painted it" on the printed page.[21] On the other hand, they were also necessary to those who were present, for the intricacy of such rituals and their referents were not at all self-evident. Even viewers who were present were, in a certain sense, "absent" and could "see" only by reading—and following—the ritual in a book, such as Masselin's program of Henri's entry.[22] In either case, they constituted a particularly powerful form of symbolic address that appealed to, constituted, and expressed the culture of a particular community of readers. A reader such as Jean Miffant.

When Jean Miffant died in 1559 an inventory of his library was taken by the *sergent royal* of Rouen that indicates that he owned over three hundred books. These included Pliny's, *De l'Istoire du Monde*, a book entitled *Novus orbys*, two cosmographies by Apian, a book on *l'usaige de l'Astrolabe*, the *Cosmographie universelle de tout le monde* by Sébastien Munster, and an account of the king's entry into Rouen.[23] There were many Miffants (or Mynfants) in Normandy in the sixteenth century. It is clear by the size of his library—and by the fact that he married into the Croismare family, which as we've seen, was closely tied to the Puy, New World trade, and to the organization of Henri's entry—that he might have been the Jean Miffant who was a New World merchant as well as one of the Miffants who competed in the Puy's annual poetry competitions. Was he also related to David Miffant, counselor and governor of Dieppe and translator of Cicero (1502),[24] and his sons, Jacques, who translated Xenophon,[25] and Joachim, both of whom took part in the Puy? It is, I believe, likely.

Indeed, one might surmise that the increasing magnificence of both entries and their accompanying texts played an important role in orienting the social and cultural world of those who organized, watched, wrote, and read them. It is therefore not surprising that we find a gradual professionalization of those responsible for royal rites—from guilds and confraternities to representatives of civic municipalities to professional intellectuals in the royal employ. At the same time, there were pronounced efforts to centralize rituals of state—that is, to make them state rituals. Accordingly, the once-peripatetic king became less and less mobile while the representation of his majesty gained a new kind of ubiquity.[26] It was perhaps as an expression of this transformation that for his 1660 entry into Paris, Louis XIV not only chose a new route, but also tore down the walls of Paris, thus symbolically effacing the divide between the capital and the rest of his territories.[27] It was not long thereafter that he constructed a permanent triumphal arch at the Saint Denis Gate.[28] At the same time, there was a concerted—though unsuccessful—effort to eliminate popular and provincial fêtes.[29] According to Lawrence Bryant, the royal entry "flourished at a time when its ritual and art was inspired by a theory of juridical kingship and of shared authority."[30] In this sense, the king's power was bounded not only by the rite by which it was constructed, but by the men who constructed the rite. It was this double movement that proved the undoing of those who sought to augment their own power by building up that of the monarchy, for their success in creating a king as a reflection—and inflection—of their own creative (rhetorical) power, outstripped their capacity to control him. As a kind of a god, the king no longer needed them. Thus, though the entry's narrative was aligned with a notion of monarchy that was limited—that is, constitutional in the modern sense,[31] its empiricist/nominalist elements intimated the absolutist direction in which royal power was to be propelled.[32] And indeed, by the seventeenth century the constitutional elements of such rites had become, at least for those professional courtiers now in charge of court festivities, something of an anachronism.[33] Perhaps just too much could go wrong, or maybe more to the point, the royal dignitas was too precious to leave to the hands and minds of provincials who might inflect it according to their own interests and needs. Henceforth the king's power could not be seen to derive from man—that is, from the rhetorical power to persuade and memorialize—but from the incontrovertible materiality of history itself. [34]

Reference Matter

Notes

I have not modernized the orthography of sixteenth-century titles, here or in the bibliography. Many names have numerous alternative spellings as they appear in sixteenth-century documents and texts (e.g., Chappuis, Chappuys; Aubert, Auber; Wandrille, Wandrelle). I have standardized such spellings to avoid confusion.—M. W.

Introduction

1. The most extended analyses of the Brazilian scene represented at the entry are by Ferdinand Denis, *Une Fête Brésilienne célébrée à Rouen en 1550 suivie d'un fragment du XVIe siècle roulant sur la théogonie des anciens peuples du Brésil, et des poésies en langue tupique de Christovam Valente* (Paris, 1850); J. M. Massa, "Le Monde luso-brésilien dans la Joyeuse Entrée de Rouen," in J. Jacquot (ed.), *Les Fêtes de la Renaissance* (Paris, 1975), 3: 105–116; and Steven Mullaney's suggestive article, "Strange Things, Gross Terms, Curious Customs: The Rehearsal of Cultures in the Late Renaissance," in Stephen Greenblatt (ed.), *Representing the English Renaissance* (Berkeley and Los Angeles, 1988), 65–92. The scene is also discussed briefly in Gilbert Chinard, *L'Exotisme américain dans la littérature française au XVIe siècle* (Geneva 1970); Geoffroy Atkinson, *Les Nouveaux horizons de la Renaissance française* (Paris, 1935); J.-R. Béguin, "Présentation et réflexions sur quelques images," in A. Parent (ed.), *La Renaissance et le Nouveau Monde* (Quebec, 1984); and Margaret Hodgen, *Early Anthropology in the Sixteenth and Seventeenth Centuries* (Philadelphia, 1964). Readers of Hodgen's account should be wary of its many inaccuracies. The Brazilians are also mentioned in studies that focus more generally on the festival, meriting only passing reference as an indication

of the extent of Rouen's trade with the New World, or as exemplary of the lengths undertaken and difficulties surmounted in order to please the king. See, for example, Margaret M. McGowan's important work, "Forms and Themes in Henri II's Entry into Rouen," *Renaissance Drama* 1 (1968): 199–252; Josèphe Chartrou, *Les Entrées solennelles et triomphales à la Renaissance, 1484–1551* (Paris, 1928); and R. G. Schneider, "Le Thème du triomphe dans les entrées," in *Gazette des beaux-arts* 1 (1913): 85–106.

2. Anonymous, *Cest la deduction du Somptueux ordre, plaisantz spectacles et magnifiques theatres dresses et exhibes, par les citoiens de Rouen, ville metropolitaine du pays de Normandie, a la Sacree Majeste du tres Christien Roy de France Henry second leur soverain seigneur, et a tres illustre Dame, Ma Dame, Katherine de Medicis, La Royne son espouse, lors de leur triumphant, joyeulx et nouvel advenement en icelle ville, qui fut es jours de mercredy et jeudy premier et second jour d'octobre, Mil cinq cens cinquante,* fol. I ii (v°) (Rouen, 1551).

3. For an excellent general discussion of the royal entry, see the preface of Lawrence Bryant's *The King and the City in the Parisian Royal Entry Ceremony: Politics, Ritual, and Art in the Renaissance* (Geneva, 1986), 15–18; and Roy Strong's *Art and Power: Renaissance Festivals, 1450–1650* (Suffolk, 1984), 7–11.

4. M. Mauss, *The Gift: Forms and Functions of Exchange in Archaic Societies,* trans. I. Cunnison (New York and London, 1967). Perhaps even more to the point, they were, in Mauss's terms, *total social phenomena;* that is, phenomena in which religious, legal, moral, aesthetic, and economic institutions found simultaneous expression.

5. Strong, *Art and Power,* 8.

6. Royal entries, in this sense, bear more than a passing relationship to Mauss's description of potlatch; the economic burdens required to produce such elaborate spectacles would force a city into extreme debt, as amply documented in the case of Henri's entry into Lyon. See Maurice Scève, *Entry of Henri II into Lyon, September 1548,* facsimile edition with an introduction by Richard Cooper (Tempe, Arizona, 1997), 27–30. In the case of the Rouen entry, the expenditures the city council required were such that many of the city's wealthier citizens were compelled—by threat of imprisonment—to pay for the honor of participating in the entry. See *Bibliothèque Municipale de Rouen* (hereafter BMR), *délibérations* A. 16, fol. 92 (r°).

7. There are several contemporaneous accounts of Henri's entry; these include *Cest la deduction du Somptueux ordre;* Margaret McGowan has introduced a facsimile edition of this anonymous text, *L'Entrée de Henri II à Rouen 1550* (Amsterdam, 1977). See also the text published by Robert Masselin, *L'Entrée du Roy nostre sire faict en sa ville de Rouen ce mercredy premier de ce moys d'octobre pareillement celle de la Royne qui fut le jour ensuivant* (Paris, 1550); this text was also reproduced by A. Beaucousin (Rouen, 1882). A third account can be found in an anonymous manuscript, *L'Entrée du très Magnanime très Puissant et victorieux Roy de France Henry deuxism de ce nom en sa noble cité de Rouen . . . ,* BMR, Ms. 1268 (Y. 28); there is a nineteenth-century edition of this text introduced by S. Merval (Rouen, 1868). An account also exists in the deliberations of the *Hôtel de Ville* (BMR, Registre A. 16, *délibérations,* fols. 110–115). There is compilation of BMR, Ms. Y. 28 and the woodcuts from the *Cest la deduction* titled *Les Poutres et figures du sumptueux ordre plaisantz spectacles, et magnifiques the-*

atres dressée et exhibés par les citoiens de Rouen [. . .] Faictz à l'entrée de la sacrée Maiesté du très chretien Roy de France, Henry second . . . (Rouen, 1557). Another text, one not cited in any other accounts of the entry, is *Epithome en rithme Francoyse sur L'entrée, du trespuissant, & tresvictorieux Roy de France, Henry second de ce nom, en sa ville & cité de Rouen, le premier iour d'Octobre, mil cinq cens cinquante, & presentée audict Seigneur* (Rouen, 1552), which is a printed version of BMR, Ms. Y. 28. My aim here is neither to reconstruct the "real" entry "behind" these contemporary accounts, nor, in eschewing such a naively positivistic approach, to yield to an equally naive relativist one where reality itself disappears in the oscillating shadow-play of representation. Rather, the admittedly elusive ground upon which this history will stand will be demarcated by the question "who represents?" Accordingly, my aim will be to interpret the textual accounts of the entry as situated performative acts. In other words, my focus will be the groups who designed, paid for, enacted, and *then* wrote about the entry, albeit as a carefully choreographed ideal. Of the secondary works that discuss this festival, the most complete can be found in André Pottier, "Entrée de Henri II à Rouen," in *Revue de Rouen, Nouvelle série* 5 (1835): 29–43, 85–108; Chartrou, *Entrées solennelles*, especially 130–140; McGowan, "Forms and Themes"; Victor E. Graham, "The Entry of Henry II into Rouen in 1550: A Petrarchan Triumph," in K. Eisenbichler and A. Iannucci (eds.), *Petrarch's Triumphs: Allegory and Spectacle*, University of Toronto Italian Studies 4 (Ottawa, 1990): 403–413; Lawrence Bryant, "Politics, Ceremonies, and Embodiments of Majesty in Henry II's France," in H. Duchhardt, R. A. Jackson, D. J. Sturdy (eds.), *European Monarchy: Its Evolution and Practice from Roman Antiquity to Modern Times* (Stuttgart, 1992), 274–294; and Ivan Cloulas, *Henri II* (Paris, 1985).

8. There is a clear connection between the specification, definition, and display of Others and acts of self-definition, promotion, and distinction. Though such acts might well be based on relations of difference—i.e., the essentialized other as a negative anti-model pointing to and affirming the status, solidarity, and identity of a more positively construed self—they are not solely oppositional in character. Indeed, it is all too easy to theorize the Other—Woman, Jew, Leper, Oriental, Savage—in terms of opposition. Relations with Others, however, are interanimated not merely by hate, fear, loathing, and the corresponding imperative to destroy, confine, or exile, but by the much more ambivalent emotions of desire and longing for that which is forbidden, impure, or low. This should be seen not merely as the repressed desire that fetishizes the forbidden, as, for example, exotic, marvelous, or new, but as the expression of broader sociocultural processes of distinction and distancing. In this sense, whether embraced or shunned, the Other circulates as capital in a symbolic nexus of values and meanings that encode systems of hierarchically distanced relations. Whether instantiated as knowledge, artifact, or ornament, the Other, thus collected, represented, or displayed, becomes a mark of distinction and a site of authenticity in the contested territory of the self.

9. See, for example, Elie Konigson, *L'Espace théâtral médiéval* (Paris, 1975), 57.

10. Edmund Leach, *Political Systems of Highland Burma: A Study of Kachin Social Structure* (Boston, 1965), 15, 16, 17. As he puts this, "Ritual is a language of signs in

terms of which claims to rights and status are expressed, but it is a language of argument, not a chorus of harmony." Ibid., 278.

11. See especially Clifford Geertz, "Centers, Kings, and Charisma: Reflections on the Symbolics of Power," in *Local Knowledge: Further Essays in Interpretative Anthropology* (New York, 1983), 121–146; and idem, *Negara: The Theatre State in Nineteenth-Century Bali* (Princeton, 1980). Geertz is absolutely right in wanting to stress ritual's fusion of the social and celestial orders; my point, however, is somewhat different, for I want to draw our attention to the agonistic, contested, and highly strategic character of ritual as a means of gaining and/or legitimating power through specific articulations of the relations between this world and the next. See, for example, David Cannadine's introduction to D. Cannadine and S. Price (eds.), *Rituals of Royalty: Power and Ceremonial in Traditional Societies* (Cambridge, 1987), 1–19.

12. See Eugene F. Rice, "The Patrons of French Humanism," in A. Molho and John Tedeschi (eds.), *Renaissance Studies in Honor of Hans Baron* (De Kalb, 1971), 689–702.

13. See especially Gilbert Gadoffre, *La Révolution culturelle dans la France des humanistes: Guillaume Budé et François I*er (Geneva, 1997); and George Huppert, *Les Bourgeois Gentilshommes: An Essay on the Definition of Elites in Renaissance France* (Chicago, 1977). See also James Wood, *The Nobility of the Election of Bayeux, 1463–1666: Continuity Through Change* (Princeton, 1980); Jonathan Dewald, *The Formation of a Provincial Nobility: The Magistrates of the Parlement of Rouen, 1499–1610* (Princeton, 1980); J. H. M. Salmon, *Society in Crisis: France in the Sixteenth Century* (New York, 1975), and idem, "Storm over the Noblesse," *Journal of Modern History* 53 (1981): 242–257; E. Schalk, *From Valor to Pedigree: Ideas of Nobility in France in the Sixteenth and Seventeenth Centuries* (Princeton, 1986); and Donna Bohanan, *Old and New Nobility in Aix-en-Provence 1600–1695: Portrait of an Urban Elite* (Baton Rouge, 1992).

14. See Gadoffre, passim; and Huppert, *Les Bourgeois Gentilshommes*, especially, 59–83. See also Nancy Lyman Roelker, *One King, One Faith: The Parlement of Paris and the Religious Reformations of the Sixteenth Century* (Berkeley and Los Angeles, 1996), 129–130. That words and manners increasingly fulfilled the symbolic function previously met by force of arms is characteristic of what Norbert Elias has called the "civilizing process"—see especially volume 1 of *The Civilizing Process, The History of Manners* (New York, 1978), for example, at 271 and 280. Also see Ullrich Langer's "A Courtier's Problematic Defense: Ronsard's 'Responce aux injures'," in *Bibliothèque d'Humanisme et Renaissance* 46, 2 (1984): 343–355.

15. See especially, Dewald's *Formation of a Provincial Nobility*.

16. This view stands in contrast to Tzvetan Todorov's well-known thesis that there was a radical difference between European and New World "symbolic economies"— the former being based upon a "technology of writing," the latter being purely oral. See Tzvetan Todorov, *The Conquest of America: The Question of the Other*, trans. R. Howard (New York, 1984). According to Todorov the conquest can ultimately be explained only by reference to the superior capacity of Europeans to manipulate written signs, which allowed for the privileging of context over code, improvisation

over reaction, present over past. The Indians, he believes, could only understand the European by assimilating him into a never-ending cycle of ritual, myth, and prophecy. Hence, the fatal error of mistaking Cortés for the returning Quetzalcoatl, an error that Cortés—an "improvisational virtuoso"—consummately exploited. In the pages that follow, I will show that Europeans understood and classified the New World in precisely the same terms that Todorov uses to describe the "Indians" who inhabited it; that is, in terms of the cognitive and conceptual categories supplied by myth, ritual, and prophecy. Moreover, not only was the New World understood in these terms, but so was the New Learning—and thus the very "symbolic technology of writing"—by which Rouen's urban elites sought to distinguish themselves as a new kind of nobility and by which Todorov seeks to distinguish Europeans from America's indigenous peoples. Paradoxically, Todorov here uncritically recapitulates the sixteenth-century assumption that though speech was adequate to the task of maintaining social cohesion and the survival of a community, it was only writing that made possible the understanding and control of nature. See Anthony Pagden, *The Fall of Natural Man: The American Indian and the Origins of Comparative Ethnology* (Cambridge, 1982), 130. From a different perspective, Kristen Neuschel's analysis of warrior-nobles in sixteenth-century France is also relevant, insofar as she shows that despite varying levels of literacy the manner in which French nobles "perceived and expressed knowledge about their world was still largely an oral one." Kristen B. Neuschel, *Word of Honor. Interpreting Noble Culture in Sixteenth-Century France* (Ithaca and London, 1989), 103, 113–114. Conversely, Todorov greatly minimizes Aztec and Mayan literary technology. See Deborah Root, "The Imperial Signifier: Todorov and the Conquest of Mexico," in *Cultural Critique* 9 (Spring, 1988): 197–219.

17. Though the word *civilisation* was an eighteenth-century invention, the adjective *civilité* and the verb *civiliser* both existed in the sixteenth. Devoid of the later associations with ideas of progress, the idea of civilization—as cultural/spiritual superiority of the civil, urbane, and courteous—certainly predated the invention of the word. See Lucian Febvre, "Civilisation: évolution d'un mot et d'un groupe d'idées," in *Pour une histoire à part entière* (Paris, 1962), 481–528; and George Huppert, "The Idea of Civilization in the Sixteenth Century," in Molho and Tedeschi, *Renaissance Studies*, 761–762.

18. See Pauline Smith, *The Anti-Courtier Trend in Sixteenth-Century French Literature* (Geneva, 1966).

19. Michel de Montaigne, *The Complete Essays of Montaigne*, trans. Donald M. Frame (Stanford, 1992), 152; for the original, see Montaigne, *Essais, Reproduction photographique de l'édition originale de 1580 . . .* (Geneva, 1976), 1: 318.

20. On the historicization of our representational practices see, for example, Lorraine Daston, "Baconian Facts, Academic Civility, and the Prehistory of Objectivity," in A. Megill (ed.), *Rethinking Objectivity* (Durham, 1994), 37–63; and Bruno Latour, *We Have Never Been Modern* (Cambridge, MA, 1993).

21. *C'est la deduction*, fol. I ii (v°).

Chapter 1

All citations are from *Cest la deduction,* unless otherwise indicated.

1. Fol. M ii (r°).

2. Fol. D iii (r°).

3. Ibid.

4. Fol. D ii (r°).

5. Fol. K iii (iv°)–K iv (r°).

6. The inclusion of women as well as men is indicated by the "program" account by Masselin, *L'Entrée du Roy,* fol. B iii (v°).

7. Fol. K iv (r°).

8. Fol. L i (r°).

9. Ibid.

10. Fol. L ii (v°).

11. Fol. M i (r°).

12. Fol. M ii (v°).

13. Fol. Miii (v°).

14. Fol. N I (r°).

15. Fol. N ii (r°).

16. Fol. N iii (v°).

17. Fol. O I (r°), the description of this pageant as a terrestrial paradise can be found in Masselin, fol. C i (v°).

18. Fol. O ii.

19. Fol. O ii (v°).

20. Ibid.

21. Fol. O iii (v°).

22. Ibid. Masselin's program mistakenly attributes the oration to Cardinal de Vendôme, who was not in Rouen at the time of the entry, *L'Entrée du Roy,* fol. C ii (r°).

23. Fol. O iv (v°).

Chapter 2

1. J.-A.-S. Desmarquets, *Mémoires chronologiques pour servir à l'histoire de Dieppe et à celle de navigation française* (Paris, 1785), 1: 91–98.

2. There are no contemporary sources for the legend of Jean Cousin's discovery of America. The English bombardment of Dieppe and the destruction of the *Archive de l'école royale hydrographique* obliterated any such records, assuming they ever existed. See, for example, Louis Estancelin, *Dissertation sur les découvertes faites par les navigateurs Dieppois* (Abbeville, nd), 17–19; L'Abbé A. Anthiaume, *Cartes marines, constructions navales, voyages de découverte chez les Normands, 1500–1650* (Paris, 1916), 2: 183; C.-M. de La Roncière, *Histoire de la marine française* (Paris, 1914), 2: 401–404.

3. Henri Lancelot-Voisin, Sieur de la Popellinière, *Les trois mondes* (Paris, 1582), 20–21.

4. See "Relation du voyage du capitaine Gonneville et ses compagnons aux Indes, et remarques faites sur le dit voyage fournies en justice par le capitaine et ses dits compagnons . . . ," in Ch.-A. Julien, R. Herval, and Th. Beauchesne (eds.), *Voyages au Canada, avec les relations des voyages en Amérique de Gonneville, Verrazano et Roberval* (Paris, 1989), 49–69.

5. Julien et al., 53

6. Ibid., 55.

7. Ibid., 57.

8. Ibid.

9. Gonneville's observation is confirmed by an anonymous Jesuit chronicler who mentions that during the course of 1504 four French ships landed at the Port of

Bahia and traded with the natives there; *l'Enformaçao do Brasil e de suas capitanias*, cited in Paul Gaffarel, *Histoire du Brésil français au seizième siècle* (Paris, 1878), 57.

10. Julien et al., 63. Nothing was heard of Binot again until almost two centuries later when his descendants petitioned the king, arguing that the author of their family line, Binot Paulmier, had been brought to France with the promise that he be returned to his native land, and that insofar as this promise had been broken, they were under no obligation to pay taxes. See Charles Bréard, *Note sur la famille du Capitaine Gonneville* (Rouen, 1885); and Julien et al., 65 n. 1.

11. Robert Gaguin, *La Mer des chroniques et mirouer hystorial de France* (Paris, 1536), ccxxxii–ccxxxiii; this account, attributed to Pierre Desrey, is identical to the 1514 edition of *La mer des chroniques*; see also *Eusebius Caesariensis episcopi chronicon* (1512), fol. 172, cited in Julien et al., 25.

12. Lucien Febvre and Henri-Jean Martin, *The Coming of the Book: The Impact of Printing, 1450–1800* (London, 1976), 278–281. Also see, for example, John H. Elliott, "Renaissance Europe and America: A Blunted Impact?" in F. Chiappelli, M. J. B. Allen, and R. L. Benson (eds.), *First Images of America: The Impact of the New World on the Old* (Berkeley and Los Angeles, 1976), 1:11: "The impact on the Old World of the discovery of the New was in many respects both disappointingly muted and slow in materializing."

13. Sculptural representations of native Americans abound in Normandy's churches and towns. See Yves Bottineau-Fuchs, "Les piles figurées de l'église Saint-Martin de Veules-les-Roses," in *Annales de Normandie* 2 (juin, 1980): 103–138; and idem, "Indiens et Normands au début du XVIe siècle," *Les Normands et la Mer*, XXVe Congrès des Sociétés Savantes 4–7 oct. 1990 (Saint-Vaast-la Hougue, 1995), 150–159.

14. Michel Mollat, *Histoire de Rouen* (Toulouse, 1979), 154. Also see his "Anciens voyages Normands au Brésil," in *Bulletin de la Société de l'Histoire de Normandie* 5 (Rouen, 1887–1890): 236–239; and idem, *Le Commerce maritime Normand à la fin du Moyen Age: Étude d'histoire économique et sociale* (Paris, 1952), 249–267; E. Gosselin (ed.), *Documents authentiques et inédits pour servir à l'histoire de la marine normande et du commerce rouennais pendant les xvie et xviie siècles* (Rouen, 1876), 142–171; M. Desmont's "Le Port de Rouen et son commerce avec l'Amérique," in *Société normande de géographie* 33 (1911): 403–419, see especially 404–410.

15. For example, in 1531, the Norman ship, *La Pélerine*, was captured. The inventory taken of its cargo noted 15,000 *quintaux* (one quintal equals 100 kilograms, or about 200 pounds) of Brazilwood; 300 quintaux of cotton, 600 parakeets, which already knew a few words of French, 3,000 "leopard" skins and those of other animals, 300 monkeys, about 3,000 ducats of gold, and about 1,000 ducats' worth of medicinal oils, all of which was worth about 602,300 ducats. See Gaffarel, *Histoire*, 77; E. Guénin, *Ango et ses pilotes d'après des documents inédits, tirés des archives de France, de Portugal et d'Espagne* (Paris, 1901), 43–44; also see Maurice Pianzola, *Les Français à la conquête du Brésil (XVIIe siècle), Les Perroquets jaunes* (Paris and Geneva, 1991), 40.

16. According to Delumeau the word for Brazil is derived from the Dutch term *Hy Bressail* or *O Brazil*, meaning Happy Isle. Jean Delumeau, *History of Paradise: The*

Garden of Eden in Myth and Tradition, trans. M. O'Connell (New York, 1995), 104. However, trees coming from the Orient that were used for red dyes had been known from antiquity as *Braxillium* or *Brasilium*. In the Middle Ages such trees were called *kerka bersil*; one finds mention of them, for example, in the *Droitures, coustumes et appartenances* of the Viscomte de l'Eau of Rouen in the thirteenth century and the *Coutume de Dieppe* in 1396 (e.g., "la carche du brésil 8 deniers, la balle 3 deniers"). See Jean-Marc Montaigne, *Le Trafiq du Brésil. Navigateurs Normands, Bois-Rouge et Cannibales pendant la Renaissance* (Rouen, 2000), 38.

17. This trade was typically organized by men known as *facteurs*, usually said to be Norman, who had supposedly "gone native"—living among the Indians, speaking their language, and adopting their customs (some even boasted of becoming cannibals). These *facteurs* acted as intermediaries between arriving ships and local peoples. This contrasted starkly with the Portuguese methods of trade organized through permanent settlements/fortresses set up along the coast. See Alexander Marchant, *From Barter to Slavery: The Economic Relations of Portuguese and Indians in the Settlement of Brazil, 1500–1580* (Gloucester, MA, 1966). Regarding Norman *facteurs* see Jean de Léry, *History of a Voyage to the Land of Brazil, otherwise called America . . .* , trans. Janet Whatley (Berkeley and Los Angeles, 1990).

18. See John Hemming, *Red Gold: The Conquest of the Brazilian Indians* (Cambridge, MA, 1978), 8.

19. Rouen was among the most important linen manufacturing centers in all of France. See Philip Benedict, *Rouen During the Wars of Religion* (Cambridge, 1981), 18–20; also see Mollat, *Commerce;* and Frank Lestringant, *Le Huguenot et le sauvage. L'Amérique et la controverse coloniale en France, au temps des guerres de religion (1555–1589)* (Paris, 1990), 29.

20. BN, Ms. fr. 379 fol. 24 (v°).

21. BMR, Ms. Ac, Rouen, Fonds de l'Académie G1, fol. 67–68 (r°).

22. Ernest de Fréville, *Mémoire sur le commerce maritime de Rouen, depuis les temps les plus reculés jusqu'à la fin du XVIe siècle* (Paris, 1857), 2: 430–431.

23. See, for example, Gosselin, 142.   24. Guénin, 190.

25. Ibid.   26. Ibid., 192.

27. M. Mollat and J. Habert, *Giovanni et Girolamo Verrazano, navigateurs de François Ier* (Paris, 1982), 78.

28. Guénin, 191.

29. Mollat and Habert, 80.

30. Further evidence of these preparations is to be found in the Archives départmentales, Seine-Maritime, hereafter ADSM, *tabellionage série* 2E 1, *meubles*, 3/26/1523; see Mollat and Habert, 82.

31. See Mollat and Habert, 88.

32. Mollat, *Commerce*, 501.

33. See, for example, D. Seward, *Prince of the Renaissance: The Life of François I* (London, 1974), 114–136.

34. Mollat, *Commerce*, 502.

35. See the contract reprinted in Pierre Margry, *Les Navigations françaises et la révolution maritime du XIVe au XVIe siècles d'après les documents inédits tirés de France, d'Angleterre, d'Espagne et d'Italie* (Paris, 1867), 194–196.

36. See Gaffarel, *Histoire*, 93; also see Marchant, 30.

37. Mollat and Habert, 117.   38. Ibid., 118.

39. See Mollat, *Commerce*, 255–256.   40. Ibid., 257

41. 2 million gold écus, of which 1.2 million was to be paid in one lump sum; François was also obliged to pay an additional 290,000 écus, settling Charles' debt to Henry VIII.

42. See Guénin, 194–195, 249; Julien et al., 98–99, and Gaffarel, *Histoire*, 105–106.

43. See Guénin, 93–102.

44. For example, at La Rochelle Ango had the goods of five Portuguese merchants sequestered, while simultaneously arming ten ships for expeditions to Brazil against the Portuguese. See La Roncière, 283–284; and Guénin, 102–103.

45. See Mollat, *Commerce*, 504; Julien et al., 106–107; Guénin, 103–104.

46. BMR, *déliberations*, A. 13, fol. 153 (v°), August 26, 1531.

47. Ibid.; also see Mollat, *Commerce*, 261.

48. Anthiaume, 2: 193.   49. Quoted in ibid., 194.

50. Quoted in ibid.   51. See La Roncière, 286.

52. See, for example, Benedict, *Rouen*, 31.

53. According to local legend, in response to the pleas of the Portuguese ambassador, François replied, "It is not me who makes war with you, but Ango. . . . " See La Roncière, 283–284.

54. There is some evidence that Chabot was not entirely scrupulous in his dealing with his Portuguese masters. See La Roncière, 291.

55. Julien et al., 112; also see La Roncière, 286; and Guénin, 149.

56. Quoted in Margry, 220–221.

57. Julien et al., 113–114; Guénin, 156.

58. Quoted in Julien et al., 114.

59. See ibid., 116; and R. J. Knecht, *Francis I* (Cambridge, 1982), 333.

60. Julien et al., 114; Guénin, 199–200; La Roncière, 3: 291.

61. Anthiaume, 196.

62. Guénin, 200–202.

63. *Catalogue des actes de François Ier*, published by the Académie des Sciences Morales et Politiques (Paris, 1889), 8: 657 (32696).

64. Ibid., 661 (32716).

65. Ibid., 3: 666 (10562), and renewed again, at the request of the Portuguese king, in January of 1538; Ibid., 8: 681 (32829).

66. BMR, *délibérations*, A. 14, fol. 283; see Guénin, 203–205.

67. Ibid., fol. 285 (v°).

68. See Leon Guérin, *Histoire maritime de France depuis la fondation de Marseille, 600 ans avant J.-C., jusqu'à l'année 1850* (Paris, 1851), 189.

69. See *Catalogues des actes*, 3: 704 (10731); also see Guénin, 167, 203–204.

70. *Catalogues des actes*, 3: 723 (10817).

71. See, for example, Guérin, 193–194; La Roncière, 297.

72. *Catalogue des actes*, 8: 698 (32929).

73. Despite the fact that with Mme. d'Etampes' support, François was persuaded to excuse Chabot only a month later, giving him new estates and offices in June of '41 and absolving him of lèse-majesté in March of '42.

74. See Mollat, *Histoire*, 154. Also see Gosselin, 142–171.

75. In a letter from Charles to the cardinal of Toledo, cited in La Roncière, 300.

76. Cited in ibid., letter from the cardinal of Toledo to the emperor, dated January 27, 1541.

77. BMR, *délibérations*, A. 14, fol. 337 (v°).

78. See Gaffarel, *Histoire*, 110.

79. Quoted in La Roncière, 305.

80. Anthiaume, 195.

81. François Rabelais, *Bringuenarilles, cousin germain de Fessepinte* (Rouen, 1545).

82. Letter cited by Julien et al., 172 n. 3.

83. Ibid., 173 n. 2.

84. See La Roncière, 303–304.

85. See Note 75 of Chapter 3.

86. On May 12, 1548; see Guénin, 233–234; also Margry, 314.

87. Guénin, 234.

88. See *Catalogue des actes de Henri II* (Paris, 1986), 2: 78 (2309).

89. *Catalogue des actes de Henri II* (Paris, 1990), 3: 343 (5385); also see La Roncière, 304; Anthiaume, 2: 198. This proved all but fatal to Ango whose business was centered in the port of Dieppe. Having lost the patronage of François I and having alienated most of his other associates with his arrogance, he died in 1551 leaving his family burdened with law suits and debts; see Gaffarel, *Histoire*, 110–111.

90. *Catalogue des actes de Henri II*, 3: 404 (5648).

91. Ibid., 434 (5783); also see Margry, 314; Guénin, 233–234; and Anthiaume, 198.

92. BMR, *délibérations* A. 16, fol. 78 (r°). Despite the fact that this was a negotiated—not a military—victory.

93. BMR, *délibérations* A. 16, fol. 96 (v°).

94. Patrick Fraser Tytler, Esq., *England Under the Reigns of Edward VI, and Mary* (London, 1839), 1: 326.

95. *Cest la deduction*, fol. L (v°).

96. The formulation is Michel de Montaigne's, cited in Huppert, *Les Bourgeois Gentilshommes*, 46.

97. See Chapter 3 of this book for more details regarding this point.

98. Godefroy, 1: 303, cited in McGowan, "L'Entrée de Henri II," 24.

99. *La Magnificence de la superbe et triumphante entree de la noble & antique Cité de Lyon faicte au Treschrestien Roy de France Henry deuxiesme de ce Nom, et la Royne Catherine son Espouse le XXIII de Septembre M. D. XLVIII* (Lyon, 1549), 75–85.

100. Ibid., 81.

101. In describing the event, held for a second time for the queen, *Cest la deduction's* chronicler says that there were so many ships on the Seine that day that "les Poissons se pouvoient bien dire couvertz, comme souz l'umbrage d'une crote de glace, contenant uniement tout le planice de leau." *Cest la deduction*, fol. P iv (r°). This is lifted word-for-word from *La Magnificence de la superbe et triumphante entree*, 85.

102. Masselin, fol. B iv (v°).

103. Letter of October 6, 1550 to the privy council; see Tytler, 326.

104. *Cest la deduction*, fol. K iv (r°).

105. Hans Staden, *Nus féroces et anthropophages* (Paris, 1979), 104.

106. Quoted in Anthiaume, 197.   107. See Hemming, 75, 164.

108. de Léry, 25–26.   109. BMR Ms. 1268 (Y. 28), fol. 17.

110. BMR, *délibérations*, A. 14, fol. 337 (v°).

111. On Tasserie being named one of the entry's organizers, see BMR *délibérations*, A. 16, fol. 78. Regarding his involvement in New World trade see, for example, ADSM, *tabellionage, série* 2E 1 *meubles* 01/05/1549.

112. BMR, *délibérations* A. 16, fol. 96 (v°); regarding his involvement in New World trade, see, for example, ADSM, *tabellionage, série* 2E 1 *meubles* 07/11/1522.

113. See *Catalogue des actes de Henri II* (Paris, 1994), 4: 217 (7351). See also Brunelle, *The New World Merchants of Rouen, 1559–1630* (Kirksville, 1991), 33.

Chapter 3

1. *Cest la deduction*, fol. M i (v°).

2. Ibid., L i (r°).

3. Pierre de Bourdeille, Seigneur de Brantôme, *Œuvres Complètes du Seigneur de Brantôme. Vies des hommes illustres et capitaines Français* (Paris, 1822), 2: 330.

4. Cited in F. Baumgartner, *Henry II, King of France, 1547–1559* (Durham, 1988), 40.

5. See Brantôme, 103–104; and E. Bourciez, who describes the *Amadis de Gaule* as a "bréviaire, où la Cour de Henri II apprit à penser et à exprimer ses sentiments . . . ," in his *Les Mœurs polies et la littérature de cour sous Henri II* (Geneva, 1967), 63. Arlette Jouanna cites a poem by Michel Sévin in which he treats the *Amadis de Gaule* as a manual teaching the nobility its proper social role; see her *Ordre social. Mythes et hiérarchies dans la France du XVIᵉ siècle* (Poitiers, 1977), 130; also see A. Tilley, *The Literature of the French Renaissance* (New York, 1959), 162.

6. *Cest la deduction*, fol. K iii (v°).

7. See, for example, Randolph Starn, "Seeing Culture in a Room for a Renaissance Prince," in Lynn Hunt (ed.), *The New Cultural History* (Berkeley and Los Angeles, 1989), 226, 230–231; Paolo Rossi, "Society, Culture, and the Dissemination of Learning," in S. Pumfrey, P. Rossi, and M. Slawinski (eds.), *Science, Culture and Popular Belief in Renaissance Europe* (Manchester, 1991), 161; David Freedberg, *The Power of Images: Studies in the History and Theory of Response* (Chicago, 1989), 162; and Roy Strong, *Art and Power*, 22–23.

8. See Lawrence Bryant, "Politics, Ceremonies, and Embodiments of Majesty in Henry II's France," in H. Duchhardt, R. A. Jackson, D. J. Sturdy (eds.), *European*

Monarchy: Its Evolution and Practice From Roman Antiquity to Modern Times (Stuttgart, 1992), 132. Bryant's article wonderfully shows how the humanist valorization of eloquence over and above the chivalrous idealization of force was integrated into the imagery (the nude Hercules) and narrative of Henri II's 1547 entry into Paris.

9. See Joachim du Bellay, *La Deffence et illustration de la langue Françoyse* (Paris, 1549), chapter 2, "concerning the meaning of this word barbarous: in ancient times they were called barbarous who spoke Greek incorrectly. . . . Afterwards, the Greeks transported the name to brutal and cruel manners, calling all nations outside Greece, Barbarians." Also see Denys Hay, "Italy and Barbarian Europe," in E. F. Jacob (ed.), *Italian Renaissance Studies* (London, 1960), 48–68; and Anthony Pagden, *The Fall of Natural Man: The American Indian and the Origins of Comparative Ethnology* (Cambridge, 1982), especially chapter 2.

10. BMR, Ms. 1268 (Y. 28) describes the French as being "tout belliqueux and martiaulx," see fol. 14; also see James J. Supple, *Arms Versus Letters: The Military and Literary Ideals in the 'Essais' of Montaigne* (Oxford, 1984), 7–8. Among the French, the Normans were regarded as being especially savage; see Pagden, *Fall of Natural Man*, 15, 24, 50; with regard to their reputation as warriors, see G. A. Austin's Ph.D. dissertation, "Concepts of Secular Greatness in Normandy: ca. 1000–1150" (Los Angeles, 1977), especially 66–97. Regarding the barbarity of native Americans see, for example, Anthony Pagden, *European Encounters with the New World: From Renaissance to Romanticism* (New Haven and London, 1993), chapter 4, "The Savage Decomposed," 117–140. Also, see Olive Dickason, "The Concept of *l'homme sauvage* and early French colonialism in the Americas," in *Revue française d'histoire d'outre-mer* 64 (1977): 5–32. Similar charges were leveled at the Scots, see Arthur H. Williamson, "Scots, Indians and Empire: The Scottish Politics of Civilization 1519–1609," in *Past & Present* 150 (1996): 46–83.

11. Still the best statement of the power of the "powerless" can be found in Nietzsche's seminal work *The Genealogy of Morals* (New York, 1969).

12. According to Anne Denis, in Italy of the early sixteenth century, the horror of the French surpassed even that of the Turks. See her *Charles VIII et les Italiens: Histoire et mythe* (Geneva, 1979), 138. Also see Hay, passim; G. Gadoffre, *La Révolution culturelle dans la France des humanistes: Guillaume Budé et François Ier* (Geneva, 1997); and Samuel Kinser, "Temporal Change and Cultural Process in France," in Molho and Tedeschi (eds.), *Renaissance Studies in Honor of Hans Baron* (De Kalb, 1971), 736; and the important series of articles by Robert W. Scheller, "Imperial Themes in Art and Literature of the Early French Renaissance: The Period of Charles VIII," in *Simiolus* 12 (1981–1982): 5–69; *idem*, "Ensigns of Authority: French Royal Symbolism in the Age of Louis XII," in *Simiolus* 13 (1983): 75–141; and *idem*, "Gallia cisalpina: Louis XII and Italy 1499–1508," in *Simiolus* 15 (1985): 5–60.

13. My emphasis. In this context, du Bellay was clearly using the appellation "Roman" to refer to his contemporaries on the Italian peninsula (as opposed to "ancient Romans").

14. The title of du Bellay's second chapter, "That the French Language should not be called barbarous" makes the connection clear.

15. In 1509 Claude de Seyssel stated in blunt terms that "the French [were] reputed by the Italians to be barbarians, both in regard to their morals as well as their language." Cited in Ferdinand Brunot, "Un Project d' 'enrichir, magnifier et publier' la langue Française en 1509," in *Revue d'histoire littéraire de la France* 1 (Paris, 1894): 31, 27–37.

16. Castiglione, *The Book of the Courtier*, trans. Charles Singleton (New York, 1959), 67. Also see André Chastel's *Culture et demeures en France au XVIᵉ siècle* (Paris, 1989), 19–20, and Denis, 110.

17. In response to charges of barbarism, a concerted effort was made by French men of letters (as Jean Lemaire de Belges puts it) to honor the history and language of France "in the French language, which the Italians, *par leur mesprisance accoustumée,* call barbaric, though it is not." Quoted in Marc-René Jung, *Hercule dans la littérature française du XVIᵉ siècle: De l'Hercule courtois à l'Hercule baroque* (Geneva, 1966), 54.

18. Erasmus, *A Declaration on the Subject of Early Liberal Education for Children*, in Erika Rummel (ed.), *The Erasmus Reader* (Toronto, 1990), 86, my emphasis.

19. From *Sommaire ou epitome de livre De Asse* (Paris, 1522), fol. 12(rᵒ), quoted in Kinser, 748. Jacques de Beaune takes a similar stand in his *Discours comme une langue vulgaire se peult perpetuer* (Lyon, 1548), fol. B iv; as does Pierre-Robert Olivétan, who in the preface to his vernacular translation of the Bible, remarks that the French language was little more than a barbarous jargon next to the eloquence of Greek and Hebrew, *La Bible . . . le Nouveau translatez en Françoys . . .* (Neufchatel, 1535). Also, see Gadoffre, 16; and Joseph Trapp, *Essays on the Renaissance and Classical Tradition* (Vermont, 1990), especially 8–21. On the attempt to model speech and manners along lines exemplified by the Italians, see Bourciez, 268–299. On the cultural competition between France and Italy, see Franco Simone, *The French Renaissance: Medieval Tradition and Italian Influence in Shaping the Renaissance in France*, trans. H. G. Hall (London, 1969), especially 79–104.

20. See Cynthia Jane Brown, *The Shaping of History and Poetry in Late Medieval France: Propaganda and Artistic Expression in the Works of the Rhétoriqueurs* (Birmingham, 1985), 153.

21. Étienne Dolet, *La Manière de bien traduire d'une langue en aultre . . .* (Lyon, 1540), 4–5 (my emphasis). For the expression of similar views also see, in addition to du Bellay, Thomas Sebillet, *Art poétique françois* (Paris, 1910), 16; Pierre du Val, *Le Printemps de Madame Poësie chanté par les vrays amantz au Theatre de magnificense* (Lyon, 1551), fol. Dv-Dvi; Geoffroy Tory, *Champ fleury* (Paris, 1529), 3; Claude de Seyssel (trans.), *Les Histoires universelles de Trogue Pompée, abbrégées par Justin, historien . . .* (Paris, 1559), aaij-aaiiij.

22. *Cest la deduction,* fol. O i (rᵒ).

23. Ibid., fol. O ii (vᵒ).

24. He is also praised for having given thirty thousand *livres tournoys de rent* a year as a stipend to a number of royal doctors. Ibid.

25. Ibid.

26. This is also supported by what we know about appointments to the *Collège.* François I made approximately sixteen appointments between 1530 and 1545, while from 1547 to 1551 there were approximately seven appointments. See Abel Lefranc's

Histoire du Collège de France depuis ses origines jusqu'à la fin du premier empire (Paris, 1893), 381.

27. Thus, before a solemn assembly held in 1534, Guillaume Budé, the principal architect of the royal college, forcefully argued that to neglect the study of philology would make all efforts at interpreting God's word utterly sterile. See Abel Lefranc, "Les Commencements du Collège de France (1529–1544)," in H. V. Lindan and F. L. Ganshof (eds.), *Mélanges d'histoire offerts à Henri Pirenne* (Brussels, 1926), 1: 10. Also, see Erika Rummel, *The Humanist-Scholastic Debate in the Renaissance and Reformation,* Harvard Historical Studies 120 (Cambridge and London, 1995), for example, 2, 83–84, and 91–95.

28. On the resistance of the university to the *Collège* see Bulaeus (César Égasse) du Boulay, *Historia Universitatis Parisiensis* (Frankfurt, 1966), 6: 239–242. Also see James Farge, *Orthodoxy and Reform in Early Reformation France: The Faculty of Theology of Paris, 1500–1543* (Leiden, 1985), 170; and Gadoffre, 59. The view that the vulgate was too vile and barbarous to meddle with such "high matters" as philosophy and theology was a common one; it was one of the main targets of the royal readers and the members of the academies, who vigorously defended French as a vehicle for philosophy. See du Bellay, *La Deffence,* 89, 94; or Pontus de Tyard, who opened his book, *L'Univers, ou discours des parties et de la nature du monde* (Lyon, 1557), with a defense of the suitability of the French language for philosophy. See Robert J. Sealy, *The Palace Academy of Henry III* (Geneva, 1981), 91; and Francis Yates, *The French Academies of the Sixteenth Century* (New York, 1988), 77.

29. See Du Boulay, 6: 239, and Francis M. Higman, *Censorship and the Sorbonne: A Bibliographical Study of Books in French Censured by the Faculty of Theology of the University of Paris, 1520–1551* (Geneva, 1979), 50, and 52 n. 18. The battle between the two institutions was fierce, as illustrated by the controversy that ensued when it was proposed that a rhetorician, rather than a theologian, be given the honor of haranguing the king during his entry into Paris. See I. D. McFarlane (ed.), *The Entry of Henri II into Paris, 16 juin 1549* (Binghamton, 1982), 20.

30. On the charge of Lutheranism and heresy see LeFranc, *Histoire,* 122–123; and Rummel, *Humanist,* 8 and 71–72.

31. As, for example, Beza: "who would have imagined that a single individual [Jacques Lefèvre] . . . would have succeeded in chasing barbarism from the world's most famous university where over a period of many years it had been firmly entrenched?" Quoted in Philip Edgcumbe Hughes, *Lefèvre: Pioneer of Ecclesiastical Renewal in France* (Grand Rapids, Michigan, 1984), xi.

32. Lefranc, *Histoire,* 61.

33. Desiderius Erasmus, in Craig R. Thompson (ed.), *Literary and Educational Writings* (Toronto, 1978), Volume 23 of *The Collected Works of Erasmus,* 35, and note 15. Also see James D. Tracy, "Against the 'Barbarians': The Young Erasmus and His Humanist Contemporaries," in the *Sixteenth Century Journal* 11:1 (1980): 3–22.

34. As Baumgartner points out, Montmorency believed that learning was conducive to heresy, and that he "little esteemed savants and their books." Baumgartner, 47; similarly, the association between scholasticism and barbarism was a commonplace in humanist polemics. See for example, Rummel, *Humanist,* 1, 8, 48, and 79.

35. See Jung, 8.

36. See *Mémoires d'Olivier de La Marche, maître d'hôtel et capitaine des gardes de Charles Le Téméraire*, (Paris, 1883–1888), 1: 43. Also see William Caxton's translation (c. 1474) of Raoul Lefèvre's text, *The Recuyell of the Historyes of Troye*, published with an introduction by H. O. Sommer (London, 1894). Here Hercules is portrayed as a knight as he goes about his twelve labors. The same chivalrous narrative is followed by the festival enacted in celebration of the marriage of Margaret of York to Charles the Bold, see *Mémoires d'Olivier de La Marche*, 3: 101–201.

37. See C. A. Marsden, "Entrées et fêtes espagnoles au XVIe siècle," in Jacquot, 2: 407 n. 77. Also see R. Hallowell, "Ronsard and the 'Gallic Hercules Myth'," *Studies in the Renaissance* 9 (1962): 242–255, 250 n. 28.

38. See P. Du Colombier, "Les triomphes en images de l'empereur Maximilien Ier," in Jacquot, 2: 99–112, 112 n. 33.

39. "Réception organisée par les habitants de Vienne à l'occasion de la joyeuse entrée dans cette ville de notre sire, le roi dauphin Charles VIII, l'an 1490 décembre," in B. Guenée and F. Lehoux (eds.), *Les Entrées royales françaises de 1328 à 1515* (Paris, 1968), 295–306.

40. See Jean Lemaire de Belges, *Œuvres*, ed. Stecher (Louvain, 1882–1885), 1: 12, 59, and book 3, and also 2: 261. Also see Hallowell, 244; and L. Bryant, *The King and the City in the Parisian Royal Entry Ceremony: Politics, Ritual, and Art in the Renaissance* (Geneva, 1986), 130.

41. On the importance of figural topoi such as Hercules, see, for example, Ernst Cassirer, *The Individual and the Cosmos in Renaissance Philosophy*, trans. Mario Domandi (New York, 1963), 73–75. Roger Chartier's discussion of images and symbols and their strategic role in demarcating the "positions and interests of social agents" is relevant here; see his *Cultural History: Between Practices and Representations*, trans. L. G. Cochrane (Ithaca, 1990), 6. See also my "Civilizing the Savage and Making a King: The Royal Entry Festival of Henri II (Rouen, 1550)," the *Sixteenth Century Journal* 29: 2 (1998): 467–496.

42. Cited in E. Wind, "'Hercules' and 'Orpheus': Two Mock-Heroic Designs by Dürer," *Journal of the Warburg and Courtauld Institutes* 2:2 (1938): 206–218, 209.

43. See Jean Lefevre, *Livret des emblemes de maistre André Alciat, mis en rime françoyse . . .* (Paris, 1536); Gilles Corrozet, *Hecatomgraphie* (Paris, 1540); and Barthélemy Aneau, *Emblemes d'Alciat, de nouveau translatez en François, vers pour vers . . .* (Lyon, 1549). It even became the fashion at François' court to wear golden earrings to symbolize the courtier's allegiance to their eloquent king; see Jung, 80–81; also see Hallowell, 251. On the Gallic Hercules as a symbol of kingship, see Strong, *Art and Power*, 24; Jean-René Béguin, "Présentation et réflexions sur quelques images," in Alain Parent (ed.), *La Renaissance et le Nouveau Monde* (Quebec, 1984), 271; and Francis Yates, *Astrea: The Imperial Theme in the Sixteenth Century* (London, 1975), 208–214. Also see Christiane Lauvergnat-Gagnière, *Lucien de Samosate et le lucianisme en France au XVIe Siècle. Athéisme et polémique* (Geneva, 1988), for example, 86, 89, 104.

44. According to Wind's important essay, Holbein's depiction of Luther as the Hercules Germanicus was guided by Erasmus' knowledge of Lucian's description.

He goes on to argue that the print was meant to satirically depict the Lutherans' violent destruction of the culture of humanism. As he puts it: the "monsters slain by the fury of this Hercules are the most venerable figures of classical and Christian learning." However, as Ginzburg points out, the print is not satiric, but an attempt to portray Luther in terms sympathetic to Erasmus' project. The men slain were not representatives of humanism, but were the founding fathers of scholasticism, Aristotle, Saint Thomas, Ockham, Duns Scotus, etc. See Wind, 217–218; also see Hallowell, 249. Hallowell follows Wind's argument with regard to Holbein's print. The relevant passages in Ginzburg can be found on 33–34, 179–180 n. 73 of his essay, "From Aby Warburg to E. H. Gombrich: a Problem of Method," in *Clues, Myths, and the Historical Method*, trans. John and Anne Tedeschi (Baltimore and London, 1989). The opposition, however, was more polemical than real; as numerous scholars have shown, humanism was thoroughly embedded in the scholastic tradition.

45. *Registres des délibérations du bureau de la ville de Paris* (Paris, 1886), 3: 170. This entry was greatly influenced by du Bellay's *Deffence et illustration* and was drafted—at least in part—by Thomas Sebillet, author of the *Art poétique françois*. See François Gébelin, "Un Manifeste de l'école néo-classique en 1549: l'Entrée de Henri II à Paris," in *Bulletin de la Société d'Histoire de Paris* 51 (1924): 35–45; V. L. Saulnier, "L'Entrée de Henri II à Paris et la révolution poétique de 1550," in Jacquot, 1: 31–59; also see Bryant, *King*, 65, 130, 133.

46. BMR, *délibérations* A. 16, fol. 78. Among C. Chappuys' other books one can find such explicitly didactic works on courtesy as the *Discours de la court, présenté au Roy par Chappuys son libraire et varlet de chambre ordinaire* (Paris, 1543).

47. See Hay, 66.

48. See A.-M. Best, "Additionnal (sic) Documents on the Life of Claude Chappuys" in *Bibliothèque d'humanisme et renaissance. Travaux et documents* 28 (1966): 134–140.

49. Claude Chappuys, *S'ensuivent les triumphantes et honorables entrées faictes par le commandement du Roy tres-Christien Françoys premier de ce nom, à la sacrée Majesté Impériale, Charles V. Item la complaincte de Mars, dieu des bataylles sur la venue de l'empereur en France* (Lille, 1539). Chappuys' nephew, Gabriel, was an even more prolific translator and writer of courtesy literature; his books include *Le Misaule ou haineux de court, lequel, par un dialogisme et confabulation fort agréable et plaisante, démontre sérieusement l'estat des courtisans et autres suivans la court des Princes. Avec la manière, coustumes et moeurs des courtisans . . .* (Tours, 1585); a translation of Castiglione's *Book of the Courtier* titled *Le Parfait courtisan* (Paris, 1585); as well as translations of S. Guazzo, *La Civile conversation . . .* (Lyon, 1579); J. de Urrea, *Dialogues du vray honneur militaire* (Paris, 1585), and *Le quinziesme (Vingtuniesme et dernier) livre d'Amadis de Gaule* (Lyon, 1577–1581).

50. Claude Chappuys, *Le sacre et couronnement du tres auguste, tres puissant & treschrestien Roy Henry deuxiesme de ce nom . . .* (Paris, nd). See Louis P. Roche, *Claude Chappuys (?-1575), Poète de la cour de François Ier* (Paris, 1929), 54.

51. Similarly, another of Claude Chappuys' works, his 1538 *Panegyric* to François, directly foreshadowed the message of Henri's Rouen entry through his explicit

praise of François as having no equal either among kings, poets, or orators in his knowledge of letters and of arms. According to Chappuys, the king even surpassed the virtues of Caesar through his patronage of languages and his revival of the seven liberal arts, as witnessed by his creation of the Collège de France. See Claude Chappuys, *Panégyrique récité au très illustre, très magnanime, très vertueulx, et très chrestien Roy Françoys premier de ce nom, à son retour de Provence, l'an mil cinq cens trente huit, au mois de Septembre . . .* (Paris, nd), fol. 5(v°).

52. See Françoise Joukovsky, *Orphée et ses disciples dans la poésie française et néo-latine du XVIᵉ siècle* (Geneva, 1970), 25–26.

53. See P. E. Hughes, 5.

54. *Cest la deduction*, fol. L i (r°).

55. BMR, Ms. 1268 (Y. 28), fol. 19, and *Cest la deduction*, ibid. The word *Mars* in the third line of *Cest la deduction* reads as *maintes* in the manuscript, otherwise the verses are the same.

56. See Benedict, *Rouen*, 41 n. 1.

57. Tracy and Jung point to the appropriation of Plato's joke of the hydra as she-sophist (*Euthydemus*, 297c) by Boccaccio—see *De Genealogia Deorum*, ed. V. Romano (Bari, 1951), volume 2: book xiii, chapter i, 640; relevant passages in Tracy can be found at 18–19, and 19 n. 85; and in Jung at 29 n. 30, and 178 n. 83. Rabelais' characterization of the doctors at the University of Paris can be found in *Gargantua and Pantagruel*, trans. J. M. Cohen (New York, 1978), book 1, chapters 17–21. His support for the program of the *Collège de France* can be found in Gargantua's letter to Pantagruel, book 2, chapter 8. The letter from Glareanus is cited in Abel Lefranc, *Histoire*, 58.

58. Cited in P. Bietenholz and T. Deutscher (eds.), *Contemporaries of Erasmus: A Biographical Register of the Renaissance and Reformation* (Toronto, 1985), 1: 105.

59. Cited in Lefranc, *Histoire*, 118; also see Gadoffre, 45–46.

60. Aneau, 168–169.

61. *Cest la deduction*, fol. M iii (r°).

62. Ibid., fol. M iii (v°).

63. Ibid.

64. See, for example, Gadoffre, 286; Trapp, 10; and George Huppert, "The Trojan Franks and Their Critics," in *Studies in the Renaissance* 12 (1965): 227–241. Indeed, according to one widely dispersed myth, the Trojans founded Rome. See Castiglione, 231.

65. *Cest la deduction*, fol. N iii (r°).

66. Ibid., fol. R iii (r°).

67. Ibid., fol. O iii (v°): "Hercules fut des monstres odieulx,/Par ses effortz en fin victorieux,/Les Roys scavans sont par Bonnememoire,/En seur repotz translatez iusque aux cieulx. . . . " Comparisons of the New World with the terrestrial paradise was a common trope in literature of the "discovery"; see for example Columbus's letter (1498) recounting his third voyage in *Journals and Other Documents on the Life and Voyages of Christopher Columbus*, trans. and ed. S. E. Morison (New York, 1963). A good account can be found in Valerie I. J. Flint's important book, *The Imaginative Landscape of Christopher Columbus* (Princeton, 1992), especially chapter 5, "The Terrestrial Paradise," 149–181; in Djelal Kadir, *Columbus and the Ends of the Earth: Europe's*

Prophetic Rhetoric as Conquering Ideology (Berkeley and Los Angeles, 1992), especially chapter 6, "Divine Primitives," 137–192; Harry Levin, *The Myth of the Golden Age in the Renaissance* (Bloomington, 1969); and Geoffroy Atkinson's essential work, *Les Nouveaux horizons de la Renaissance française* (Paris, 1935), 139–146.

68. *Calendar of State Papers* (Spanish), 1550–1552, X, 182; also see S. Mullaney, "Strange Things, Gross Terms, Curious Customs: The Rehearsal of Cultures in the Late Renaissance," in S. Greenblatt (ed.), *Representing the English Renaissance* (Berkeley and Los Angeles, 1988), 71 and 90 n. 14.

69. It is no coincidence that the frescoes at the Gallery at Fontainebleau were meant to represent the humanist ideal of the political assimilation of the barbarian by the force of civilization. See F. Joukovsky, "L'Empire et les barbares dans la galerie François Ier," in *Bibliothèque d'Humanisme et Renaissance* 50 (1988): 6–27, 18. On the relationship between the Gallery and the *Collège de France*, see Chastel, 25–30.

70. See for example, Barbara C. Bowen, *Words and the Man in French Renaissance Literature* (Lexington, 1983), 21.

71. To French commentators the reigns of Charles V and his son, Philip II, were closely associated with the rule of the sword, as opposed to the Ciceronian political theory of eloquence that was championed at the French courts; see Bryant, "Politics," 144.

72. Indeed, as a mark of his commitment to chivalric values, Henri took to wearing his battle armor everywhere; see ibid., 132–133. According to Baumgartner, in the years following his death, the old nobility looked back upon Henri's reign with "unabashed nostalgia"—his wars having "provided numerous opportunities for the nobility to exercise its God-given right to fight and win glory; for many nobles," he continues, "the monarchy's only purpose was to provide wars." See Baumgartner, 75.

73. Bryant, "Politics," 132–133. Gadoffre has pointed out that Henri's patronage of nobles might say more about changes in the nobility than about his attitudes toward the New Learning. He argues that if Henri gave posts to nobles once reserved for robins, this was because the nobles of his reign were far different than those of François'—which is to say, they now embraced the same intellectual and moral ideals as their "social inferiors" in the *robe*. Gadoffre, 165. Also see Henri Weber, *La Création poétique au XVIe siècle en France: de Maurice Scève à Agrippa d'Aubigné* (Paris, 1956), 68.

74. The expedition to save Mary was led by none other than Nicolas Durand de Villegagnon, the man who was to lead the French attempt to establish a colony in Brazil (1555–1560).

75. According to the account of Maréchal de Vieilleville, *Mémoires* (Paris, 1757), I: 437, Montmorency had "executé plus de sept vingt personnes à mort en diverses sortes de supplices, comme de pendus, decapitez, rouez, empellez, desmembrez à 4 chevaux, et bruslez." Persecution of heresy was on the increase during the early years of Henri's reign, as exemplified by the establishment of the *Chambre ardente* (1547) which passed—from 1548–1550—some 450 sentences, 60 of them being capital; see N. Weiss, *La Chambre ardente* (Geneva, 1970). Bryant fruitfully compares François' treatment of the revolt of La Rochelle in 1544 to Henri's treatment of Bordeaux.

Henri's father, rather than resorting to violence, had—according to Bodin—by "the maiestie of his speech terrified them" back to obedience; cited in Bryant, "Politics," 142–143.

76. *Registres des délibérations du bureau de la ville de Paris* (Paris, 1886), 3: 169 (my emphasis); also see Jung, 90.

77. On the increasing interdependence of cultural elites and the feudal nobility see Gadoffre, especially chapters 4 and 5, 115–166; and J. Dewald, *The Formation of a Provincial Nobility: The Magistrates of the Parliament of Rouen, 1499–1610* (Princeton, 1980), passim.

78. See, for example, M. Bakhtin, *Speech Genres and Other Late Essays*, eds. C. Emerson and M. Holquist, trans. V. W. McGee (Austin, 1986), especially 132–172; and also Peter Stallybrass' and Alan White's use of Bakhtin's notion of social/linguistic hybridization in analyzing inter-class identity formation in *The Politics and Poetics of Transgression* (London, 1986). Also see Michel de Certeau, who describes Jean de Léry's voyage to the New World as a journey "from the self to the self, through the mediation of the other;" in *The Writing of History* (New York, 1988), 209–243; and Anthony Pagden, *European Encounters with the New World: From Renaissance to Romanticism* (New Haven and London, 1993), 47.

79. Denise Gluck, "Les Entrées provinciales de Henry II," in *L'information d'histoire de l'art* 10 (1965): 191–218.

80. Claude-Gilbert Dubois, *Celtes et gaulois au XVIᵉ siècle. Le développement littéraire d'un mythe nationaliste. . . . Avec l'édition critique d'un traité inédit de Guillaume Postel: De ce qui est premier pour reformer le monde* (Paris, 1972), 37. On Hercules as Christ in the sixteenth century, see G. Karl Galinsky, *The Herakles Theme: The Adaptations of the Hero in Literature from Homer to the Twentieth Century* (Oxford, 1972), 202–205.

81. *Cest la deduction*, fol. K iii (v°).

82. Michel de Montaigne, *The Complete Essays*, 156; *Essais* 1: 318.

83. Montaigne, *Complete Essays*, 154; *Essais*, 312–313. Also see Michel de Certeau, *Heterologies: Discourse on the Other* (Minneapolis, 1986), 67–79.

84. See David Bitton, *The French Nobility in Crisis, 1560–1640* (Stanford, 1969), 89, and 145 n. 42. Also see Bourciez, especially 17–36.

85. Montaigne, *Complete Essays*, 694; *Essais* 3: 399.

86. Montaigne, *Complete Essays*, 158; *Essais*, 1: 262. William Brandon argues that Tupi poetry became quite fashionable in Henri's court as a result of this festival. I have not been able to verify this assertion by any other source. See *New Worlds for Old: Reports from the New World and Their Effect on the Development of Social Thought in Europe, 1500–1800* (Athens, Ohio, 1986), 15.

87. Montaigne, *Complete Essays,* 158; *Essais* 1: 325.

88. Montaigne, *Complete Essays,* and *Essais*. On Anacreon see, Tilley, 330–336; and C.-A. Sainte-Beuve, *Tableau de la poésie Française au XVIᵉ siècle* (Paris, 1876), 1: 289–316.

89. Jean de Léry, *History of a Voyage to the Land of Brazil, otherwise called America,* trans. Janet Whatley (Berkeley and Los Angeles, 1990) 178–195.

90. A number of scholars have pointed to the ways in which ancient Greek and Roman myths gave animus to interpretations of the New World and its peoples. For example, see Sabine MacCormack, *Religion in the Andes: Vision and Imagination in Early Colonial Peru* (Princeton, 1991); and more recently "Limits of Understanding: Perceptions of Greco-Roman and Amerindian Paganism in Early Modern Europe," in Karen Ordahl Kupperman (ed.), *America in European Consciousness, 1493–1750* (Chapel Hill and London, 1995), 79–129; Anthony Grafton, with April Shelford and Nancy Siraisi, *New Worlds, Ancient Texts: The Power of Tradition and the Shock of Discovery* (Cambridge, MA, 1992); and John Elliott, *The Old World and the New, 1492–1650* (Cambridge, 1970).

91. Lawrence Bryant argues that the figure of the nude Hercules was a radical departure from traditional imagery of kingship; it was meant, he says, to communicate a humanist ideal in which the king derived his authority from nature rather than from divine grace or from extra-royal ecclesiastical and juridical sources. Bryant interprets the Rouen display of the nude Brazilian king as a possible parody of this ideal of the orator king. He argues that the Brazilian king, rather than leading his people through learning and eloquence toward civilization, leaves them in a state of warfare, barbarism, and savagery ("Politics," 150). While not discounting this possibility, I would suggest that by reincorporating the mise-en-scène of Brazil into the larger narrative structure of the entry, we can add further support to Bryant's overall thesis by firming up the connections (e.g., through the mediation of New World "savages") between Hercules' nudity, his eloquence, and his natural virtue. Thus, for example, in addition to praising the Brazilians for their poetic eloquence, Montaigne also comments that they were endowed by nature herself with "the true, most useful, and natural virtues and properties." See Montaigne *Essais* 1: 254.

92. Marc Lescarbot, *The History of New France*, trans. W. L. Grant (Toronto, 1907–1914), 3: 132–134, as cited in M. Hodgen, *Early Anthropology in the Sixteenth and Seventeenth Centuries* (Philadelphia, 1964), 314 (my emphasis).

93. André Thevet, *La Cosmographie universelle . . .* (Paris, 1575), fol. 952 (v°); and the superb studies by Frank Lestringant, *L'Atelier du cosmographe, ou l'image du monde à la Renaissance* (Paris, 1991), 105–107, 130–136; and also his *Le Huguenot et le sauvage. L'Amérique et la controverse coloniale en France, au temps des guerres de religion (1555–1589)* (Paris, 1990), 43–44.

94. André Thevet, *Portraits et vies des hommes illustres* (New York, 1973), 2: 662.

Chapter 4

1. R. C. Strong, *Art and Power: Renaissance Festivals, 1450–1650* (Suffolk, 1984), 8.

2. Ibid., 40; also see Clifford Geertz's essay "Centers, Kings and Charisma," which makes much the same point, in *Local Knowledge: Further Essays in Interpretive Anthropology* (New York, 1983), 121–146.

3. Émile Mâle, "L'Art symbolique à la fin du moyen âge," in *La Revue de l'art ancien et moderne* 107/19, 10ᵉ année (février, 1906): 112.

4. The first triumph in France was said to have been enacted by students at the Université de Caen in 1513. In 1532, for the entry of Éléonore d'Autriche into Rouen, the identifying feature of the triumphal entry, the chariot, made its first appearance in French civic ritual. See Josèphe Chartrou, *Les Entrées solennelles et triomphales à la Renaissance, 1484–1551* (Paris, 1928), 87. Also see F. Joukovsky, *Orphée et ses disciples dans la poésie française et néo-latine du XVIe siècle* (Geneva, 1970), 423.

5. This is revealed in a receipt made by Nicolas Fagot, *tapissier ordinaire* of the king, on December 24, 1495 in BN, n.a. fr. 7644, fol., 195–196; see the communication of Pierre Lesueur, "Les Italiens à Amboise au début de la Renaissance," in the *Bulletin de la Société de l'Histoire de l'Art Français* 8 (1929–1930): 7–11.

6. Ibid., 11. Also see "Heures et malheurs du château de Gaillon," by Elisabeth Chirol in *Précis analytique des travaux de l'Académie des Sciences, Belles-Lettres, et Arts de Rouen* (1982–1983), 67.

7. Roberto Weiss, "The Castle of Gaillon in 1509–10," *Journal of the Warburg and Courtauld Institutes* 16: 1 (1953): 1.

8. As Gilbert Gadoffre has eloquently put it: "La culture n'est pas innocent. Elle se dévore, et confère un surcroît de puissance en même temps que l'humanitas." See G. Gadoffre, *La Révolution culturelle dans la France des humanistes: Guillaume Budé et François Ier* (Geneva, 1997), 53.

9. Not, as Chartrou claimed, the arch built for the 1515 entry of François I into Lyon. See M. le Chanoine Jouen (ed.), *Comptes, devis et inventaires du manoir archiépiscopal de Rouen*, with an historical introduction by Monsignor Fuzet, Archevêque de Rouen (Paris and Rouen, 1908), clx.

10. Achille Deville (ed.), *Comptes de dépenses de la construction du château de Gaillon, publiés d'après les registres manuscrits des trésoriers du Cardinal d'Amboise* (Paris, 1850), 434.

11. This was sculpted by Antoine Juste (Antonio di Giusto Betti), the same man responsible for carving the still extant bas-reliefs of Louis' triumph over Milan on the king's tomb in the Cathedral of St. Denis. See Anatole de Montaiglon, "La Sculpture française à la Renaissance: la famille des Juste en France," in *Gazette des Beaux-Arts* 12 (November and December, 1875): 385–404 and 515–526. This *bas-relief* is mentioned in Deville, *Les Comptes*, lxi, lxxix. See also R. Weiss, 6. On the triumph over the Genoese, see Bonner Mitchell, *The Majesty of the State: Triumphal Progresses of Foreign Sovereigns in Renaissance Italy (1494–1600)* (Florence, 1986), 90–93. On the arch see E. Chirol, "Heures," 73. This entry was designed both by the cardinal's nephew, Charles Chaumont d'Amboise, viceroy of Milan, and Leonardo da Vinci. See G. Souchal, "Le Mécénat de Charles d'Amboise," in *Les Informations d'histoire de l'art* (May-June, 1972): 176–181; E. Chirol, "Heures," 68.

12. R. Weiss, 7. Also see Elisabeth Chirol, "L'Influence de Mantegna sur la Renaissance en Normandie," in *Actes du XIXe Congrès International d'histoire de l'art* (1968): 240–247, 240; and idem, *Un premier foyer de la Renaissance en France: Le Château de Gaillon* (Rouen and Paris, 1952), 57, 99. An admirer of Mantegna, the Cardinal possessed a number of his paintings. Nevertheless, Chirol gives Mantegna's work too much credit for influencing the iconographic and ceremonial forms that triumphs

employed in France. R. Scheller makes a similar point, see his "Gallia cisalpina: Louis XII and Italy 1499–1508," in *Simiolus* 15 (1985): 42–43.

13. See Elaine Yu-Ling Liou, "Cardinal Georges d'Amboise and the Château de Gaillon at the Dawn of the French Renaissance." Ph.D. diss., Pennsylvania State University, 1997, 259.

14. Thus foreshadowing the publication of Longueil's panegyric to Louis XII in 1510. Christophe de Longueil, *Oratorio de laudibus divi Ludovici, atque Francorum* . . . (Paris, 1510). See Margaret M. McGowan, *Ideal Forms in the Age of Ronsard* (Los Angeles and Berkeley, 1985), 18.

15. J. Marot, BN, Ms. fr. 5091 and Ms. n.a. fr. 11679; a modern critical edition has been published by Giovanni Trisolini, *Le voyage de Gênes* (Geneva, 1974), 85, fol. 3; compare Marot's assessment of the Genoese, for example, to Thevet's characterization of the Brazilians as "sans foi, sans loi, sans religion, sans civilité aucune, mais vivant comme bêtes irraisonnables," in André Thevet, *Les Singularités de la France antarctique*, ed. F. Lestringant (Paris, 1983, first published in 1557), 49.

16. J. Marot, 95, fol. 11.

17. Quoted in S. Anglo, *Chivalry in the Renaissance* (London, 1990), 18.

18. See Franco Simone, *The French Renaissance: Medieval Tradition and Italian Influence in Shaping the Renaissance in France*, trans. H. G. Hall (London, 1969), especially chapter 5, "The Fortune of Petrarch in France in the First Half of the Sixteenth Century," 179–268.

19. Ibid., 257, 266.

20. Ibid., 258, my emphasis.

21. Ibid., 229.

22. These are Mazarin Ms. fr. 1581, and BN, Mss. fr. 54, 223, 224, 225, 594, 595, 596, 2502, 2678, 2679, and 22541.

23. BN, fonds Ital., 552 (7773) and 553 (7772); BN, fonds Ital., 1024 and 1026; BN, fonds Ital., 1016 and 1025; see Elisabeth Pellegrin, *Manuscrits de Pétrarque dans les bibliothèques de France* (Padua, 1966), 336–338, 350–353, 432–323, respectively. One of the earliest manuscripts of Petrarch's *I Trionfi* to fall into French hands was made for Lorenzo de Medici. According to Delisle, the manuscript stands as one of the masterpieces of fifteenth century Florentine art. It was given to Charles VIII when he passed through Florence in 1494. BN, fonds Ital., 548, see E. Pellegrin, *Manuscrits de Pétrarque dans les bibliothèques de France* (Padua, 1966), 328–331; L. Delisle, "Note sur un manuscrit des poésies de Pétrarch rapporté d'Italie en 1494 par Charles VIII," in *Bibliothèque de l'École de Chartes* 61 (1900): 450–458, 450, and Myra Orth, "The Triumphs of Petrarch Illuminated by Godefroy Le Batave (Arsenal, Ms. 6480)," *Gazette des beaux-arts*, vi^e période, 104 (December, 1989): 197–206, 205, note 13.

24. BN, Ms. fr. 1119. That the manuscript was made at the behest of d'Amboise cannot be stated definitively, but its inclusion in a collection along with the *chroniques de Normandie* and the *chroniques* of the Amboise family makes this attribution likely. See Élie Golenistcheff-Koutouzoff, "La Première traduction des «Triomphes» de Pétrarque en France," in *Mélanges de philologie, d'histoire et de littérature offerts à Henri Hauvette* (Paris, 1934).

25. V. E. Graham, "Entry of Henry II," 406.

26. "Les triomphes du poethe messire Françoys Petrarche translatez à Rouen de vulgaire Ytalien en Françoys . . . ," fol. 1, BN, Ms. fr. 594 (7079), and BN, Ms. fr. 225. Also see Pellegrin, 406–409, and 437–439; and George Ritter and Jean Lafond, *Manuscrits à peintures de l'école de Rouen: Livres d'heures normands* (Rouen, 1913), 15, 17, which also contains copies and descriptions of the miniatures illustrating BN, Ms. fr. 594. According to Delisle, these miniatures are masterpieces of the Rouen school.

27. The word *puy* derives from the Latin for podium, while *palinod* derives from two Greek words, *palin* and *odè,* and refers to the recurring final verse, the refrain, at the end of each stanza in a *chant royal.* For more details regarding this see Gérard Gros, *Le Poète, La Vierge et le prince du Puy: étude sur la poésie mariale en milieu de cour aux XIVe et XVIe siècles* (Paris, 1992), 25–29. For a wonderfully detailed literary-historical study of Rouen's *puys,* I refer the reader to Denis Hüe's magisterial *La Poésie palinodique à Rouen (1486–1550)* (Paris, 2002); I regret that this appeared after the present work was completed so that it does not receive the attention it deserves here.

28. See, for example, François Farin, *Histoire de la ville de Rouen, divisée en trois parties* (Paris, 1668) 3: 168; and Eugène de Robillard de Beaurepaire, *Les Puys de Palinod de Rouen et de Caen* (Caen, 1907), 40–41.

29. See Louis Delaruelle, *Guillaume Budé: Les origines, les débuts, les idées maîtresses* (Geneva, 1970), 84. Budé was also related to another of the Puy's most celebrated poets, the merchant, noble, and writer, Nicolas de La Chesnaye. See Sylvie Charton-Le-Clech, *Chancellerie et culture au XVIe siècle: les notaires et secrétaires du roi de 1515 à 1547* (Toulouse, 1993), 60, 190–192, 305, 324; also see 15–34, 121–146. On the relationship between the Collège de France and Henri's entry, see Chapter 3 above, as well as Gadoffre, passim.

30. He was responsible for commissioning a number of elaborate manuscripts, including at least two collections of the Puy's poetry. The manuscripts of palinodic poetry are BN, Ms. fr. 1715 and BN, Ms. fr. 379. Other titles include *Heures de l'Immaculée Conception,* BN collection Rothchild, I, N. 31; the *Histoire d'Esther,* BN, Ms. n.a. fr., 1816; the *Oraison de Madame sainte Barbe,* BN *Catalogue de la collection Yemeniz,* n. 150; and a collection of religious poetry by Norman poets, BMR, 1064 (Y 226a). See, for example, Emile Picot, *Notice sur Jacques Le Lieur, échevin de Rouen, et sur ses heures manuscrites* (Rouen, 1913).

31. Jean Bouchet, *Epistres morales et familières du traverseur,* facsimile of the edition published in Poiters, 1545 (Yorkshire and New York, 1969), 98. Also see, for example, Jennifer Britnell, *Jean Bouchet* (Edinburgh, 1986), 23–24; and Auguste Hamon, *Jean Bouchet* (Paris, 1901), 103.

32. BMR, 1063 (Y. 16), fols. 1(v°)–2(r°).

33. Pierre Fabri, *Le Grant et vray art de pleine rethorique . . .* (Rouen, 1534), 2: 2. It is possible that Fabri himself was responsible for the 1516 announcement. In his treatment of the complex structure of the *chant royal,* 97–111, Fabri uses similar wording in the stricture that one ought "eviter les couppes feminines, s'ilz ne sont synalimphées ... ," 101.

34. BN, Ms. fr. 1715, fol. 1(v°)–2(r°).

35. On confraternities as social groups defined by adherence to common norms and values, see Catherine Vincent, "La confrérie comme structure d'intéraction: l'exemple de la Normandie," in *Le mouvement confraternel au Moyen Age. France, Italie, Suisse*. Actes de la Table Ronde organisée par l'Université de Lausanne avec le concours de l'École Française de Rome et de l'unité associée du CNRS École Française de Rome . . . (Geneva, 1987), 111–131, especially 112.

36. See David Scobey, "Anatomy of the Promenade: The Politics of Bourgeois Sociability in Nineteenth-Century New York," in *Social History* 17/2 (May, 1992): 204. Regarding status distinction based upon specific cultural and intellectual dispositions and practices, see P. Bourdieu, *Distinction: A Social Critique of the Judgement of Taste*, trans. R. Nice (Cambridge, MA, 1984); idem, "Social Space and the Genesis of Groups," in *Theory and Society* 14 (November, 1985): 723–744; idem, "Social Space and Symbolic Power," in *Sociological Theory* 7 (1989): 14–25; and Jean-Marie Apostolidès, *Le roi-machine. Spectacle et politique au temps de Louis XIV* (Paris, 1981), especially 39–40.

37. E. de Robillard de Beaurepaire, 107.

38. Ibid., 106.

39. This concern is manifested in the literary quarrel between Jehan Munier, a vanquished participant in Dieppe's Puy of the Assumption (whose early history and membership were closely intertwined with Rouen's Puy de Palinod), and the victor of its competition, Arnoul Jacquemin. Émile Picot has published the poetic debate between Munier and Jacquemin in "Une querelle littéraire aux pallinods (sic) de Dieppe au XVe siècle," in *Mélanges de philologie romane et d'histoire littéraire offerts à Maurice Wilmotte* (Geneva, 1972). Also see Pierre Dufay's article "Ronsard par Henri Longnon," in *Revue de la Renaissance* 5 (Paris, 1913): 51–52. Jehan Munier was a priest born in Rouen and living in Paris. Clearly disturbed at having lost the Puy's competition, he wrote a poetic diatribe ridiculing the skill and judgment of Dieppe's poets. In his *Ballad against Dieppe* he argued that while he faithfully served Ladies Rhetoric and Poetry, the "poets" of Dieppe—represented by their laureate, Jacquemin—dishonored them (Picot, *Querelle*, 462); Munier characterized Dieppe's provincial poets as "a group of shit-begotten knaves" (*merdaille*) who preferred "*soloé (solécisme)* and *cacephaton* and their like, to either *rimes équivoque* or *léonine*" (463). Despite Munier's disparagement, the winner of the Puy's competition, Arnoul Jacquemin, *chapelain, curé de Cistern and notaire de la cour espirituelle*, was clearly conversant with the theory and structure underlying palinodic verse. For example, in his response to Munier, titled *Ballad for Dieppe*, he frequently employed both the *rime léonine* (e.g., 472 (vi: 36–38), "cestui, plain de *presumpcion*, [. . .] Au beau pui de *l'Assompcion*,), and the *rime équivoque* (e.g., 467 (ix: 60–61), "Pour noz pourceaulx *enmoutarder*, Encor vous di sans *moult tarder*"). As to the charge of having mutilated the language with such barbaric usages as *cacephaton* and *soloé*, Jacquemin responded by turning the tables on his accuser, arguing that "On the contrary, I propose to him/ That his chant had an ugly sound/ Which wasn't worth a pock" (473 [x: 64–70]). Not content at having challenged Munier's self-proclaimed superiority, Jacquemin shifted the ground of their quarrel

away from stylistic concerns and toward Munier's overweening arrogance in elevating the profane science of rhetoric over that of theology, berating Munier for his reliance on such pagan authorities as Plato, Cicero, and Virgil, rather than either the scriptures or the sainted doctors (473 (xii: 78–81)). According to Jacquemin, Munier was "a dreaming fellow who completely erred in his understanding." And indeed, he posited that Munier was not alone in this regard, but was following the current fashion among the Parisian clergy, which—in Jacquemin's words—was "completely vain and childish in putting its trust in pagans . . . [such as] dames Rhetoric and Poetry" (471 [i: 1–5 and 8–11]). Yet—and this is the crucial point—despite the acerbity of their exchange, both poets shared a common understanding of the structural complexities and grammar of palinodic verse. Indeed, both poets shared in a culture within which the skills and virtues attached to the reading, writing, and display of poetry were highly prized and sought after.

40. BN, Ms. fr., 1715, fol. 2.

41. Most of the documentation having to do with the founding, organization, and operation of the Puy was lost during the religious wars. A copy of some of these documents, including the Puy's statutes, can be found in a booklet entitled *Approbation et confirmation par le pape Léon X des statuts et privilèges de la confrérie de l'Immaculée Conception dite Académie des Palinods, instituée à Rouen*. This was published and extended in the early seventeenth century (1615) by Alphonse de Bretteville as part of the effort to revive the Puy's waning fortunes. This was published again under the same title by Édouard Frère (Rouen, 1864). See E. de Robillard de Beaurepaire, *Puys de Palinod*, 76; also see Chas. B. Newcomer, "The Puy at Rouen," in *Publications of the Modern Language Association of America* 31, 1; ns, 24, 1 (March, 1916): 211–231.

42. BN, Ms. fr., 379, fols 7 (v°)–8 (r°). Wandrille might have been Jacques des Hommetz, the abbé of Saint Wandrille.

43. In 1530 Bucer was to write to Luther that Protestantism had become so widespread in Normandy that its enemies called it a "petite Allemagne." Cited in Jonathan Beck, *Théâtre et propagande aux débuts de la Réforme* (Geneva and Paris, 1986), 45–46. See also David Nicholls, "Social Change and Early Protestantism in France: Normandy, 1520–62," in *European Studies Review* 10 (1980): 279–308; P. Benedict, *Rouen During the Wars of Religion* (Cambridge, 1981); H. Prentout, "La Réforme en Normandie et les débuts de la Réforme à l'Université de Caen," in *Revue historique* 114 (1913); M. Oursel, *Notes pour servir à l'histoire de la Réforme en Normandie au temps de François Ier* (Caen, 1913); N. Weiss, "Note sommaire sur les débuts de la Réforme en Normandie (1523–1547)," in *Congrès du millénaire normand* 1 (Rouen, 1911); V. Madelaine, *Le Protestanisme dans le pays de Caux* (Paris, 1906); G. Le Hardy, *De L'Histoire du protestantisme en Normandie depuis son origine jusqu'à la publication de l'Édicte de Nantes* (Caen, 1869).

44. See François Farin, *Histoire de la ville de Rouen, divisée en six parties* (Rouen, 1731), 182; also see N. Weiss, "Note sommaire," 8.

45. As for example, the seigneur de Bobaistre, Jean Cossart, who was a lawyer in Normandy's provincial parliament; the seigneur de Sydetot, Germain du Couldray, who was the *contrôleur du domaine du roi*; and Pierre Le Vasseur, who was a *greffier* at

parliament and an active member of Dieppe's municipal government. Members of the Puy are singled out for suspicion of heresy in ADSM G. 232 and 405.

46. See especially, Lucien Febvre's "Une question mal posée: les origines de la réforme française et le problème des causes de la réforme," in *Revue historique* 161 (1929): 1–73.

47. In an *épître* written to Jean Bouchet entitled *Praise of Eloquence and the Abuses to which it is Presently Employed* in Bouchet, fols. lxx (v°)–lxxi (v°).

48. See Émile Picot's *Querelle de Marot et Sagon* (Geneva, 1969); also Paul Bonnefon, "Le différend de Marot et de Sagon" in *Revue d'histoire littéraire de la France* 1 (1894): 103–138, 259–285; and Richmond Laurin Hawkins, *Maistre Charles Fontaine, Parisien* (Cambridge, MA, 1916), 15–40. Regarding Marot's admiration of Petrarch, Hauvette remarked: "N'exagérons rien. Clément Marot fut un fidèle disciple de Pétrarch: il s'en vantait et il a traduit de son maître." Cited in Simone, 308 n. 5.

49. *Le Coup d'essay de Francoys de Sagon, Secretaire de l'abbé de sainct Ebvroul. Contenant la responce a deux epistres de Clement Marot . . .* (nd, sl), fol. C iiii, reprinted in Picot's *Querelle de Marot*.

50. Ibid.

51. Marot's defense of the "noble Academy of three languages" can be found in C. A. Mayer (ed.), *Œuvres Complètes de Clément Marot* (London, 1958), 1; and *Les Epîtres*, in Mayer, *Œuvres de Marot*, 36: 40–47.

52. *Le Coup d'essay*, fol. A iii.

53. Ibid.

54. See M. Mollat, *Le Commerce maritime normand à la fin du Moyen Age: Étude d'histoire économique et sociale* (Paris, 1952), 510.

55. Sagon brags about this lineage in one of his attacks, titled *Pour les disciples de Marot. Le page de Sagon parle a eux* (nd, sl), fol. n, reprinted by Picot in *Querelle de Marot*, "Cognoistre de son parentage,/ Il est a Rouen bien congnu: /Demande dont il est venu,/ Il est d'une race autentique,/ Bien renommee & fort antique:/ Qui portois Ango en surnom."

56. Jean Quintanadoine, for example, acquired the seigneuries of Brétigny-sur-Brionne, Saint-Denys, and Bosguerard, and he frequently took part in the deliberations of the Hôtel de Ville of Rouen. Charles de Saldaigne bought the seigneurie of Incarville as well as a number of important offices, including *notaire* and *secrétaire* to the king and controller general of royal finances in Normandy. Jean Puchot, sieur de Gerponville, became an *échevin* in Rouen's city council and a representative at the *Etats généraux* of Normandy. The son of Albaro de la Tour became the sieur de Sequeville. For further details on Rouen's Iberian merchant community, see Mollat, *Commerce*, especially 509–522; Christiane Douyère, "Les Marchands étrangers à Rouen au XVIᵉ siècle," in *Revue des sociétés savantes d'Haute-Normandie* 76 (1974): 27–61; Gayle Brunell's "Immigration, Assimilation and Success: Three Families of Spanish Origin in Sixteenth Century Rouen," the *Sixteenth Century Journal* 20: 2 (Summer, 1989): 203–219, as well as her *New World Merchants of Rouen, 1559–1630* (Kirksville, MO, 1991).

57. Douyère, 30.

58. As were several others, such as Gaille Antoine de Salamangue, Ferdinand Zaratte, Jean Savalle, Vincent Puchot, and, of course, François Sagon.

59. *Le Valet de Marot contre Sagon* (Paris, 1537), reprinted in Picot, *Querelle de Marot,* fol. A iii.

60. *Le rabais du caquet de Fripelippes de Marot dict Rat pele adictione avec le comment. Faict par Mathieu de Boutigni page de maistre Francoys de Sagon . . .* (sl, nd), fol., C i, reprinted in ibid.

61. Ibid., fol. C ii.

62. For example, Bonnefon, Hawkins and Picot, all make this argument.

63. See Sagon's *Le rabais du caquet de Fripelippes et de Marot . . .* (nd, sl), fol. B iiii, as reprinted in Picot, *Querelle de Marot;* regarding the origins of the Quintanadoine family, see Brunell, "Immigration," 205. In this regard I would like to thank Professor Brunell for pointing out the Jewish origins of many of the Iberian merchants who came to Rouen in the late fifteenth and early sixteenth centuries.

64. These letters are included in an appendix to Louis Roche's *Claude Chappuys (?-1575), Poète de la cour de François Ier* (Paris, 1929); also see Aline Mary Best's introduction to her critical edition of Chappuys' *Poésies Intimes* (Geneva, 1967).

65. *Le Valet de Marot contre Sagon* (Paris, 1537), fol. A ii, reprinted in Picot *Querelle de Marot.*

66. V. L. Saulnier, "Sebillet, du Bellay, Ronsard: L'Entrée de Henri II à Paris et la révolution poétique de 1550," in Jacquot 1: 32, 31–59.

67. See Chapter 3.

68. Just as in the relation between France and Italy, so too with Normandy and the capital: the charge of provincialism produced grandiose efforts to compensate for perceived inferiority. The relationship between Normandy's poetry societies and the poets of Paris, however, was not one of unilateral dependence. Far from being a provincial backwater, Normandy's poets often took the lead in arbitrating the boundaries of acceptable literary composition. Through its example, as well as its explicit acts of rule making, the Puy not only incorporated, but extended, elaborated upon, and influenced the style adopted by such fashionable court poets as Jean Marot, André de La Vigne, Jean Boucher, Mellin de Saint-Gelays, etc. This can be seen, for example, in the widespread adoption of rules condemning the epic and lyric caesura, rules that were first articulated in relation to the Puy's annual competitions—in the 1516 notice (cited in Note 32) and in Fabri's *Le Grant et vray art de pleine rhetorique.* See Britnell, *Jean Bouchet,* 27–28; and also L. E. Kastner's "Les Grands rhétoriqueurs et l'abolition de la coupe féminine," in *Revue des langues romanes* 45 (1903): 289–297.

69. Du Bellay, *La Deffence et illustration de la langue Françoyse* (Paris, 1549), 108–109.

70. According to Chartrou it was the fullest and most elaborate expression of French Renaissance pageantry; as she put it: "L'entrée de Henri II à Rouen . . . est de toutes les cérémonies du même ordre qui se sont déroulées pendant le siècle et la première moitié du XVIe, la plus somptueuse et la plus originale, la plus antiquisante aussi." Chartrou, 130.

71. *Le Trésor Immortel*, facsimile presented by Ch. de Robillard de Beaurepaire (Rouen, 1899; originally 1556), xxxij.

72. See, for example, ADSM, *tabellionage*, série 2E 1, *meubles* 7/11/1522.

73. As to the other unnamed "priests and orators" assigned the task of creating something special for the king's entry, we can only speculate. Many, without a doubt, had tested their literary and oratorical talents by composing poetry in honor of the Virgin at the Puy's annual competitions; such men, as we have seen, composed the bulk of the Puy's membership.

74. It is also possible that Joseph himself was a member, for numerous works are signed only with a family name, thus making a precise identification impossible.

75. Joseph Tasserie was both a member of the delegation sent before François I to lobby for continued free trade with Brazil as well as one of the men named in the deliberations of the city council to help organize Henri's entry. As such, it is safe to assume his involvement with the *tableau vivant* of Brazil constructed as part of the entry. See Chapter 2. His father's *mystère* was presented by the Puy in 1499; on this see J.-E.-A. Gosselin, *Recherches sur les origines et l'histoire du théâtre à Rouen avant Pierre Corneille* in (Rouen, 1868), 27–32.

76. BN, Ms. fr. 24315, fol. 114 (v°). This has been published by P. Le Verdier, *Le Triomphe des Normands. Suivi de La Dame à l'agneau, par G. Thibault* (Rouen, 1908). The words on the shield, *tota pulcra*, are an abbreviation of the phrase taken from the *Canticle of Canticles* (4:7): *Tota pulchra es, amica mea, et macula non est in te*. "Thou art all fair, my love, and there is no stain in thee." See E. D. O'Connor (ed.), *The Dogma of the Immaculate Conception, History and Significance* (Notre Dame, 1958), 476.

77. BN, Ms. fr. 24315 and Le Verdier, *Triomphe*, fol. 115(r°), 134(r°), and 140(r°).

78. Ibid., fol. 139(v°)–140(r°).

79. After 1515, with the introduction of new forms of poetry to the Puy's competition—the epigram, the ballade, and the rondeau—triumphal themes were intermixed with signs and tokens associated with the Immaculate Conception of the Virgin, such as the lily and the rose.

80. Frère, fol. 6 (v°); see also Eugène de Robillard de Beaurepaire's posthumous work, *Les Puys*, 74–75 (my emphasis).

81. Ibid., 170–173.

82. These are to be found on fols. 2 (v°)–3 (r°), 3 (r°)–(v°), 11 (r°)–(v°), 13 (r°)–(v°), 23 (r°), 26 (r°)–(v°), 26 (v°)–27 (r°), 27 (v°)–28 (r°), 28 (v°), 29 (r°), 30 (r°), 30 (v°), 31 (v°)–32 (r°). For example, the palinodic line on fols. 11 (r°)–(v°) by Maillard reads: "Le Lys croissant en triumphe et victoire"; on fol. 23 (r°) by Jehan Lis: "Pour vivre en paix en triumphe de gloire"; by Nicole Du Puys on fols. 26 (r°)–(v°): "Passa les montz en triumphe & gloire."

83. See Note 82, above. Also see Anne-Marie Lecoq's superb book, *François Ier imaginaire. Symbolique & politique à l'aube de la Renaissance française* (Paris, 1987), 341–353.

84. The fourth stanza reads: "Il fut mene en arroy magnificque/Dune licorne et dung fort elephant/Suyvant le pas et lourdeur pacificque/De la panthere a tirer

sechauffant/Victoire en palme en laurier triumphant/Avec trophee et pompe le convoye/Triumphe y porte ung estandard de soye/Enluy rendant lhonneur cesarien/Et issue suyt ce charroy honneste/Que tient david fidele hystorien/Le chariot du fort geant celeste."This poem appears in BN, Ms. fr. 379, fols. 2 (v°)–3 (r°) and BN, Ms. fr. 1537, fols. 33 (v°)–34 (r°) and BN, Ms. fr. 2205, fol. 59 (r°)–60 (r°).

85. The miniature accompanying this poem, in BN, Ms. fr. 1537, depicts a joust between an evil king called Pharaon, dressed in black and riding upon a black chariot, and the *fort geant celeste* riding on a chariot drawn by a unicorn, an elephant, and a panther.

86. This representation closely resembles the chariots in Henri II's entry. Though the similarity extends to the chariot of Fame, it is most particularly apt for the case of the chariot of Religion. According to the prose account, this chariot was drawn by unicorns while upon the chariot sat a number of figures: Victory, Vespa, Royal Majesty, Reverence, and Fear, *Cest la Deduction*, fol. F iiii. The verse account, however, gives this chariot a different appellation—the chariot of Victory. BMR, Ms. 1268 (Y. 28). See, for example, Plates 7 and 10.

87. See BN, Ms. fr. 379, fol. 41 (v°)–42 (r°). "Rondeau en form de triumphe/A lhumble vierge qui triumphe/Avril/En triumphant sur le serpent pervers/La Vierge est quicte, en passant le travers/Dhumain acquit on vit peche renverse/Quand en son car de vertu qui ne verse/Tous les tresors de grace a recouvers./Hault sur son car tient palme et rameaux verds/Bas enchaynes sont prisonnyers divers/Parce que Force avec elle converse./En triumphant./Les biens de paix longtemps tenus couvers/Sont aux humains par elle descouvers/ Aprez avoir mis guerre a la reverse/Dont Saint Esprit loing de fortunee adverse/Le rejouyt chantant hymnes et vers./En triumphant."

88. BN, Ms. fr. 379, fol. 11.

89. See Gadoffre, 52.

90. Dewald, *Formation*, 56. He goes on to note that despite the importance of the Puy's competitions in the city's social life, members of *noblesse de robe* were, for the most part, only marginally involved with its activities. Between 1544 and 1554, he continues, only six can be found to have been associated with the Puy. Though certainly correct in claiming that much of the Puy's membership was of bourgeois origin, Dewald's assertion that there was little association between the bourgeois belonging to the Puy and those belonging to the courts must be reassessed in the light of a more complete membership list than that upon which he relied, mainly, BMR, Ms. 1060 (Y. 186).

91. Many of the titles held by the Puy's members were of recent acquisition; in fact, of all the men ennobled during the reign of François I, approximately one-fifth came from Normandy, and among these almost all were either themselves members of the Puy, or had family names identical to those who were members, and thus might well have been sons, fathers, uncles, brothers, cousins, and in-laws of the Puy's competitors. See J. Richard Bloch, *L'Anoblissement en France au temps de François Ier* (Paris, 1978), especially 153–190. The *confrérie* of the Puy of Notre Dame of Amiens

had a similar composition. According to BN, Ms. fr. 145 (c. 1517), which lists the occupations of Amiens' palinodic poets, 34 percent were robe officials, 22 percent were ecclesiastical officials and notables, 13 percent were listed only as *sieur* or *seigneur*. The rest were, for the most part, merchants. Given their economic power and their association with the Puy, there is a high probability that these men were either related directly or through marriage to Amiens' elite. For more on Amiens' Puy, see Gros, who devotes the first half of his book to this society.

92. Some, of course, held multiple offices. A.-G. Ballin, *Notice historique et bibliographique sur L'Académie des Palinods* (Rouen, 1834), 62–64.

93. The Puy's membership for the sixteenth century has been reconstructed using a variety of texts and manuscripts; first, BMR Ms. 1060 (Y. 186), *Registre des membres de la Confrérie de l'Immaculée Conception de la Vierge, à Rouen, 1548–1657;* I also consulted BMR, Ms. 1062 (Y. 18), *Table chronologique des princes ou présidens, des juges . . . 1486–1789* (which forms the basis of the tables found in *Le Poète, la Vierge et le Prince du Puy* by Gérard Gros). The information found through these sources was supplemented by J.-A. André Guiot's *Les Trois siècles palinodiques ou histoire générale des palinods de Rouen, Dieppe, etc.* (Rouen and Paris, 1898). The manuscript Ms. 2677 (anc. Y. 50) of this work at the BMR was also consulted, as was Guiot's *Histoire de l'Académie de l'Immaculée Conception*, Ms. 2678 (Y. 48). The names of other poets involved with Rouen's Puys were found by examining the manuscript collections of the Puy's poetry at both the BN and the BMR. Other Norman poets were identified using the following printed sources: Pierre Du Val's collection, *Le Puy du souverain amour*, reprinted by Le Verdier (Paris, 1920); Jacques Sireulde's collection of the *Puy des pauvres'* poetry; and Pierre Vidoue, *Palinodz, chants royaulx, ballades . . .* (Paris, 1525), reprinted in facsimile and introduced by E. de Robillard de Beaurepaire, *Palinods présentés au Puys de Rouen. Recueil de Pierre Vidoue* (Rouen, 1897).

94. Guiot and Ballin were helpful sources in the determination of the social position of the Puy's poets. Additionally, titles and occupations were determined through the examination of the deliberations of Rouen's city council, BMR *Série* A. 9 through A. 18, and the *Journal des échevins*, BMR, *Série* B. Henri de Frondeville's *Les Conseillers du parlement de Normandie au seizième siècle (1499–1594), Recueil généalogique . . .* (Rouen, 1960); and *Les Présidents du parlement de Normandie (1499–1790), Recueil généalogique . . .* (Rouen, 1953); and Farin, *Histoire . . . en trois parties* were also consulted.

95. The composition of the council was determined through records of the deliberations of the Hôtel de Ville, BMR, A. 16. For details regarding the administrative structure of Rouen, see Benedict, *Rouen*, 31–37.

96. Thus, in 1548, of the 46 named members, 7 were ecclesiastics, one of whom was a bishop. See Ballin, 62–64.

97. Indeed, the earliest and most important patrons of the humanist program were lay and ecclesiastical officials. See E. Rice, Jr., "The Patrons of French Humanism," in A. Molho and J. Tedeschi (eds.), *Renaissance Studies in Honor of Hans Baron* (De Kalb, 1971), 689–702, passim, but especially 697 and 701.

98. Catherine Vincent, *Des Charités bien ordonnées. Les confréries normandes de la fin du XIIIe siècle au début du XVIe siècle* (Paris, 1988), 218, 253. Right of entry cost 100 *sous*, plus another 70 to be paid annually. Cost of entry in Rouen's other confraternities varied from 5 to 20 *deniers* (12 deniers = 1 sou), with an annual fee of around 4 *sous* 4 *deniers*. See BMR, Ms. 1060 (Y. 186), fol. 6.

99. Regarding these privileges, see Frère, passim. The value of one livre tournois was 16 sous (and not to be confused with the *livre parisis*, valued at 20 sous).

100. See Mollat, *Commerce*; Brunelle, *New World Merchants*, and Douyère. Bonshons, for example, was one of Verrazano's key backers on his 1529 trip to Brazil, ADSM, *tabellionage*, *Série* 2E 1, *meubles* 9/22/1529 and 9/27/1529; see Mollat, *Commerce*, 244. Charles de Saldaigne also played an active role in organizing trade with the New World, helping to finance voyages to Brazil and to North America, ADSM, *tabellionage*, 2E 1, *meubles*, 1/30/1570 and 2E 1, 1/14/1576. With regard to Le Seigneur, see *ibid.*, 3/31/1543, 1/26/1549, 1/31/1549, 1/22/1555, 11/3/1558, 12/3/1558, 12/21/1560.

101. Ibid., 2/13/1560.

102. See, for example, ADSM, *tabellionage*, 2EP 1/335: 8/11/1567, 1/336: 5/6/1568, 5/26/1568, 1/337: 11/30/1568. Others associated with the Puy involved in overseas trade included: Jehan Puchot (ADSM *tabellionage*, 2E1 *meubles* 2/24/1547 and 3/1/1549); Jean Cossart (ibid., 2/19/1549 and 2/16/1549, 3/18/1549); Albaro de la Tour (2/14/1549); (Nicolas?) Boyvin (2/28/1549).

103. Du Four's son, Robert, married the daughter of another member of the Puy, the New World merchant Jean Voisin, seigneur de la Haye-des-Mares. In turn, Voisin's daughters married, respectively, the merchant Jean du Moncel, whose brother Robert was a member of the Puy, and Guillaume Le Prevost, also a merchant member of the Puy.

104. To carry the genealogy further, the mother of Pierre's cousin, Jacques Croismare, was Ango's sister, Perrette. Jacques Croismare went on to marry the niece of another of the Puy's prominent members, Guillaume Chalenge, whose brother Jean Chalenge married the daughter of the *sieur* de Brametot, Jacques Le Lieur.

105. BMR, *délibérations*, A. 14, fol. 337 (v°).

106. For example, BN, Ms. fr. 379, fol. 7(v°)–8(r°).

107. For example, BN, Ms. fr. 2206, fol. 17.

108. For example, BN, Ms. fr. 379, fols. 5 and 16 (r°)–(v°).

109. For example, BN, Ms. fr. 379, fol. 10 ; BMR, Ms. Ac, Rouen, *Fonds de l'Académie* G1, fol. 67–68; BN, Ms. fr. 1537 fol. 36–37; BMR, Ms. 1063 (Y. 16), fol. 22.

110. For an extended discussion of a *chant royal* on the astrolabe see Chapter 5; also see the poem by Parmentier, "Les hault secret des mouvemens celestes" in BN, Ms. fr. 19369, fol. 10 (v°).

111. Guillaume Dubois, *Les Œuvres de G. Dubois natif de la paroisse de Putot-enBesin et ouvrier du métier de maçon maistre tailleur de pierres à la ville de Caen, où il lui a eté donné le don d'écrire en poesie française, par un ordre alphabétique, pour opposer au fantastique, comme on pourra voir en ce petit livre* (Paris, 1606).

112. This was made explicit in an anonymous *chant royal* written in praise of Jean Donnest. Donnest was one of the "luminaries of the college of Saint-Cande," a city councilor and a writer of a book of grammar; he was also one of the many prominent members of the city's cultural elite to be a member of the Puy. "Le principal de grammaire est le maistre;/ Voyant icelle estre en destruction,/ Feist un Donnest excellent pour remestre/ Ses escolliers à vraye instruction./ Un quel il mist, pour sa construction,/ Toutes les parts propres à ceste affaire./ Pour mieulx apprendre à parler, à bien faire,/ Tant l'exorna par son impératif/ Qu'il ne reçut jamais comparatif./ Car il ny eust oncques chose imparfaite/ Dont fut nommé par digne vocativ/ Le beau Donnest d'élégance parfaite." See BMR, Ms. 2677 (Y. 50) and Guiot, *Trois siècles palinodiques*, 1: 246.

113. Avril's ballade can be found in Vidoue's printed collection of palinodic poetry, fol. lxix: "Les orgueilleux logicians/ Ny veullent adiouster credence/ Mais les vrays rhetoriciens/ Inspirez par bonne credence/ Voyant divine prouidence/ Que leur faict reuelation/ Quelle est et fut par euidence/ Vraye prognostication." On the relationship between those who championed the New Learning and the doctors at the University see Chapter 3.

114. See Antoinette Lang-Verte, "Quelques triomphes figurés dans l'art Normand, du XVe au XVIe siècle," in *Bulletin des amis des monuments Rouennais* (Rouen, 1935–1938); also see "La Renaissance à Rouen" by Elisabeth Chirol, in *Connaître Rouen* (Rouen, 1970); and idem, "L'Hôtel de Bourgtheroulde" and "Le Gros Horloge" in the same collection.

115. Translated by O'Connor, 479–480 n. 48. The full text of the poem can be found in the BMR, Ms. 1062 (Y. 18), fol. 8 and BN, Ms. fr. 19184, fol. 105; see also P. Le Verdier, *Triomphe*, 71–73. For a more detailed description of the windows see Abbé Bouillet, "L'Église Saint-Foy de Conches et ses vitraux," in *Bulletin monumental* 54 (1888): 289–293.

116. For example, Caradas du Heron, Raoulin, Langlois, Rousselin, Maignard, and Cavelier; see Farin's *Histoire . . . en trois parties*, 2: 108–112.

117. See Benedict, *Rouen*, 28.

118. See Pierre Le Verdier (ed.), *Documents relatifs à la confrérie de la Passion de Rouen* (sl, 1891).

119. The proximity of the triumph of the Virgin to that of Christ is played out not just in the overlapping membership of the confraternities of the Passion and the Immaculate Conception, but in the church of Saint-Foy, where windows of the triumph of the Virgin are found next to windows, also donated by Pierre du Couldray, known as the *Triumph of the Eucharist*.

120. On Saint-Patrice see Benedict, *Rouen*, 29. The main difference between these windows and those of Saint-Vincent is that the chariot of redemption carries both Christ on the cross as well as the Virgin (who sits at the head of the chariot), while the final chariot at Saint-Vincent carries only Mary.

121. The social mobility of France's bourgeois merchant class was extremely rapid in the early modern period. As Claude de Seyssel wrote, "La facilité y est telle

que l'on voit tous les jours aucuns de l'estat populaire monter par degrés jusqu'à celuy de noblesse, et au moyen estat sans nombre." See Claude de Seyssel, *La Monarchie de France*, ed. J. Poujol (Paris, 1961), 125. See Gadoffre, 75.

122. See Brunelle, *New World Merchants*, 58. Of approximately thirty-one confreres who were counselors at Normandy's parliament, three-fourths matriculated to office after the second decade of the century.

123. The triumphal windows of the parish of Saint-Nicolas were destroyed; drawings made in the eighteenth century indicate that they were copies of those at Saint-Vincent. Though little demographic data exists regarding Saint-Nicolas, its proximity both to the law courts and to the parish of Saint-Lô—which was heavily populated by office holders, lawyers, and merchants—suggests that its parishioners were actively involved in the Puy.

124. On the relationship among art, religion, civic pride, and individual identity, see Michael Baxandall, *Painting and Experience in Fifteenth Century Italy: A Primer in the Social History of Pictorial Style* (Oxford, 1972), 2.

125. These were located at 13 rue de l'Écureuil. The first panel depicted Adam and Eve, bound as prisoners, being led by a chariot out of paradise. The second represented the victory of death, sin, and the devil. The third, isolated by a pillar, portrayed redemption, taking the now-familiar form of the Virgin making her triumphal entry on a chariot. These bas-reliefs no longer exist. For detailed descriptions see E. de la Quérière, *Notice sur diverses antiquités de la ville de Rouen* (Rouen, 1825), 6–8; and Pierre Chirol, *Un siècle de vandalisme. Rouen disparu* (Rouen and Paris, 1929), Pl. XCIII; and especially Lang-Verte, 179–180. Verte dates these reliefs to the reign of Louis XII.

126. The hôtel was located between the rue Ganterie des Hermites and rue Saint-Laurent. See Lang-Verte, 183. There were several members of the Duval family involved with the Puy over the course of the sixteenth century. I have yet to determine whether any of them was from the branch known as de Coupeauville.

127. Located at 16 rue des Maillots, ibid., 185.

128. The house was located at 115 rue du Gros Horloge. "Le bon helye en esprit prophetique/ Au chariot plain de feu reluysant/ Jadis ravy est figure autentique/ De cestuy cy salut nous produysant/ Phaeton le fol le sien mal conduysant/ Monstrre celuy de ce roy qui forvoye/ Que le geant en tenebres renvoye/ Pour demourer infernal cytoyen/ Car il na peu en sentier des honneste/ Faire verser par sinistre moyen/ Le chariot du fort geant celeste." See Note 84, above.

129. See E. Chirol, "L'Hôtel du Bourgtheroulde," 9–13; and Albert Lafon and Alexandre Marcel, *L'Hôtel du Bourgtheroulde à Rouen* (Paris, 1888). Additionally, there were other representations of triumphs in and around Rouen, including those decorating the Cour Daneri as well as those that can still be seen on the Gros Horloge—which depict the triumph of the seasons and the hours utilizing astrological figures. See E. Chirol, "Le Gros Horloge," 15–17. Triumphs were also popular motifs in the villages and cities surrounding Rouen, as for example, the triumphs depicted at the Hôtel Duval in Caen, at the manor of the Nollents in Dieppe, at Beumont-le-Roger

in Gisors, and at Saint-Foy at Conches. They were also depicted in the elaborate wood carvings decorating La Pensée, the manor of the overseas merchant, Jean Ango. Triumphal themes also appeared in books widely circulated in Normandy, such as Simon Vostre's *Heures à l'usage de Rouen*, Geoffroy Tory's *Heures de la Vierge*, and Francesco Colonna's *Le songe de Poliphile*, which was translated and published (Paris, 1547) by Jean Martin, one of the principal designers of Henri II's entry into Paris in 1549.

130. Lang-Verte, 180–182. The first panel at Le Roux's *château* represented the creation of man and the world; the second depicted the naked figures of Adam and Eve riding triumphantly into paradise on a chariot; the third consisted of the triumph of sin, represented by a woman with the body of a snake driving Adam and Eve out of Eden; and fourthly, the triumph of the Virgin, whose chariot is depicted crushing the head of a dragon beneath its wheels. The two remaining panels depict, according to Verte, the triumphs of Esther and Judith.

131. du Val, *Le Puy*, fol. B (r°).

132. The list also includes such well-known figures as Arnoul Gréban, Alain Chartier, Jean de Meun and Meschinot, as well as others—de Loris; Georges (Chastelain?), ladvanturier; and Jehan le Maire (Lemaire de Belges?)—whom I have not been able to identify. See du Val, *Le Puy*, fol. A iv (v°). See also, Fabri, 1: 11 for a similar list of great orators/poets. It is perhaps not surprising that years later, when Ronsard dreamed in verse of going to "Les Isles Fortunées" (which he identified in his *Discours contre Fortune* with Villegagnon's *colony sous le Pole Antartique*), he did so in the company of Belleau, du Parc, du Bellay, Dorat, Baïf, and Jodelle. See "Les Isles Fortunées," verses 60–69, Pierre de Ronsard, *Œuvres complètes* (Paris, 1994), 2: 780–785.

133. BMR, Ms. 1063 (Y. 16), fol. 184 (v°).

134. *Cest la deduction*, fol. I (v°). Indeed, Rouen's civic leaders made participation in this procession mandatory for Rouen's wealthiest bourgeoisie. Thus the records of the Hôtel de Ville for July 17 bluntly state that "Les bourgeois notoirement riches seront [punis], en cas de refus de á lad. entrée. . . . " See BMR, A. 16, fol. 92(r°).

135. BMR, A. 16, fol. 113–114.

Chapter 5

1. Pontus de Tyard, *Œuvres poétiques*, ed. Charles Marty-Laveaux (Paris, 1875), 123; also see Zoé Samaras, *Le Règne de Cronos dans la littérature française du XVIᵉ siècle* (Paris, 1983), 32.

2. *Cest la deduction*, fol. O iii (v°). Interestingly, in his *Disputationes Camaldulenses* (Paris, 1511), Cristoforo Landino argues that the *Aeneid* is "a eulogy of the contemplative life: Aeneas stands for wisdom; Troy for sensuality; Juno for ambition; Dido for the active life; and the journey from Carthage to Italy for the transition from the active to the contemplative life." In this sense, it precisely mirrors the trajectory of Henri's entry into Rouen. See Paolo Rossi, *Francis Bacon: From Magic to Science* (Chicago, 1968), 75.

3. The story of Helsin is recounted in most every account of the Puy. It finds a prominent place in such foundational texts as Tasserie's, *Le Triomphe des Normands*, reproduced by P. Le Verdier (Rouen, 1908), fol. 115. Regarding Wace, and the Puy, see Bretteville (ed.), Anon., *Approbation . . .*, 1. Accounts also appear in Farin's *Histoire de la ville de Rouen* (Rouen, 1731), 56; A.-G. Ballin, *Notice historique et bibliographique sur l'Académie des Palinods* (Rouen, 1834), 6; and G. Gros, *Le Poète, la Vierge et le prince du Puy: étude sur la poésie mariale en milieu de cour aux XIVe et XVIe siècles* (Paris, 1992), 109–110. The poem can be found in *L'Établissement de la fête de la Conception Notre-Dame dite la fête aux Normands*, published by M. Mancel and G.-S. Trébutien (Caen, 1842). See also, Mirella Levi D'Ancona, "The Iconography of the Immaculate Conception in the Middle Ages and Early Renaissance," in *Monographs on Archaeology and Fine Arts* 7 (New York, 1957), 12.

4. BN, Ms. fr. 2205, fols. 6–7.

5. There is a modern critical edition of Parmentier's poetry, *Œuvres Poétiques*, ed. F. Ferrand (Paris and Geneva, 1971); this poem can be found on 17–20. The manuscript sources consulted are as follows: BN, Ms. fr. 2205, fol. 42; BN, Ms. fr. 19184 fol. 44–46; BN, Ms. fr. 2206, fol. 73; and in BMR, Ms. 1062 (Y. 18).

6. Ibid., 27–29. Parmentier was not alone in making this comparison; for example, in an anonymous ballad included in Taillepied's history of Rouen, the Virgin was described as having a "good mast, anchor and keel." See Noel Taillepied, *Antiquitez et singularitez de la ville de Rouen* (Rouen, 1610), 141.

7. Cited in Eugène de Robillard de Beaurepaire, *Les Puys de Palinod de Rouen et de Caen* (Caen, 1907), 66.

8. See Farin (1731), *Histoire*, 56. The Virgin was of special importance to the Rouennais. As Farin put it: "There is no gate of the city, no street, no corner, and virtually no noteworthy house which is not adorned with the figure of that divine intercessor . . . " (60); he adds, Rouen ought to be known as the "Ville de la Vierge since its inhabitants seem to have more zeal and devotion towards this empress of the heavens than all the other peoples of France" (164).

9. BN, Ms. fr. 2205, fol. 7.

10. BN, Ms. fr. 379, fol. 20.

11. Parmentier, *Œuvres*, 40; BN, Ms. fr. 379, fol. 18–19.

12. Parmentier, 62–65; also see BN, Ms. fr. 1739, fol. 99; for a contemporary account of the astrolabe see Jacques Focard, *Paraphrase de l'astrolabe* (Lyon, 1544). On the attribution to Crignon, rather than to Parmentier, see Denis Hüe, "Un nouveau manuscrit palinodique, Carpentras, Bibliothèque Inguimbertine n° 385," *Le Moyen Français* 35–36 (1995):175–230.

13. In a similar *chant*, written earlier in the sixteenth century, Nicolas Osmont also compares the Virgin to a "sphere showing all the secrets of the heavens." This "instrument," says Osmont, was the Virgin Mary by whose eternal grace the heavens were revealed to human eyes. At its zenith was the star of the Arctic pole by which men navigated the seas; at its nadir was the pole [star] of the Antarctic, "giving clarity to barbaric people, showing that it was from this young girl that all fruit, good,

grace, and clarity flowed." Pierre Vidoue, *Palinods, chantz royaulx, ballades, rondeaulx et epigrammes, à l'honneur de l'Immaculee conception de la toute belle mère de Dieu Marie (Patronne de Normands)* ... (Paris, 1525). Reprinted in facsimile and introduced by E. de Robillard de Beaurepaire, *Palinods présentés au Puys de Rouen. Recueil de Pierre Vidoue* (Rouen, 1897), fols. xxiv–xxv.

14. The astrolabe mimicked the heavens. It was composed of a complex series of circles, both engraved and attached as overlaid plates; as such it was meant to duplicate the rational harmony imprinted upon the cosmos. It was used for didactic purposes— in teaching astronomy and geometry—and as a kind of astronomical computer.

15. Parmentier, 92.

16. The mariner's astrolabe (which was introduced in the late fifteenth century) was among the most important tools available in the sixteenth century for oceanic navigation. See J. A. Bennett, *The Divided Circle: A History of Instruments for Astronomy, Navigation and Surveying* (Oxford, 1987), 33–34; Anthony Turner, *Early Scientific Instruments. Europe 1400–1800* (London, 1987), 65–68; G. Beaujouan and E. Poulle, "Les Origines de la navigation astronomique au XIVᵉ et XVᵉ siècles," in *Le Navire et l'économie maritime du XVᵉ aux XVIIIᵉ siècles, travaux du Colloque d'histoire maritime tenu le 17 mai 1956, à l'Académie de marine* presented by Michel Mollat and O. de Prat (Paris, 1957), 112–113; and D. Howse, "Navigation and Astronomy," in *Renaissance and Modern Studies* 30 (1986): 62–63. However, the instrument described by Crignon, with its gold tympan, its rete, and its variety of parts, was clearly a planispheric or a universal astrolabe, not the scaled-down mariner's astrolabe used as a position-finder at sea. On the planispheric astrolabe, see J. A. Bennett, 14–16, and A. Turner, 11–16; for an in-depth discussion of the planispheric astrolabe and its workings, see H. S. Saunders, *All the Astrolabes* (Oxford, 1984); and W. Hartner, "The Principle and Use of the Astrolabe" in *Oriens–Occidens* (Hildesheim, 1968), 287–311, reprinted from A. U. Pope, (ed.), *Survey of Persian Art* (Oxford, 1939), 3: 2530–2554.

17. See Parmentier, 64; BN, Ms. fr. 1739, fol. 99. Similar views are expressed by Crignon's captain, Jean Parmentier, for example, in the *chant royal* with the palinodic line: "l'isle où la terre est plus halt que les cieulx," Parmentier, 59–61, verse 49, BN, Ms. fr. 379, fol. 29; or the *chant*: "la mappemonde aux humains salutaires," ibid., 24–26; BN, Ms. fr. 1537, fol. 95, where Parmentier refers to the inability of the astrolabe to sight the pole star properly in the southern hemisphere.

18. Parmentier, 65, BN, Ms. fr., 1739, fol. 99.

19. See C. A. Bouman, "The Immaculate Conception in Liturgy," in E. D. O'-Connor (ed.), *The Dogma of the Immaculate Conception* (Notre Dame, 1958), 118. These themes are frequently reflected in the Puy's poetry.

20. Ibid., 53.

21. Vidoue, fols. xii–xiii.

22. Parmentier, 61, BN, Ms. fr. 379, fol. 29.

23. This association was not exclusive to the Puy's members, but was commonly made from as early as the fifth century. Patrick M. de Winter, however, places this identification much later—in the ninth century. See his "Vision of the Apocalypse

in Medieval England and France," *Bulletin of the Cleveland Museum of Art* (September, 1983): 396–417, 406.

24. Revelations, chapter 12:1.

25. See for example, Laurie Bergamini's "From Narrative to Icon: The Virgin Mary and the Woman of the Apocalypse in Thirteenth-Century English Art and Devotion," in *Studies in Iconography* 13 (1989–1990): 80–112.

26. ADSM, *tabellionage, Série E 1 meubles,* 12/31/48, cited in *Bulletin de la commission de la Seine Inférieure* xviii (Rouen, 1930): 46–51.

27. Regarding Albaro de La Tour, see Chapter 4.

28. In O'Connor, 471.

29. Ibid.

30. See Fr. Pommeraye, *Histoire de l'église cathédrale de Rouen* (Rouen, 1686), 684–685.

31. Mirella Levi D'Ancona, 24. Also see Jean Fournée, "Les Thèmes iconographiques de l'Immaculée Conception en Normandie au moyen-âge de la Renaissance," in *Virgo Immaculata, Acta Congressus Mariologici-Mariani Romae anno MCMLIV celebrati,* Volume 15, *De Immaculata Conceptione in litteratura et in arte Christiana* (Rome, 1957). See also, the representation of the Virgin trampling a dragon in the manuscript of palinodic verse, BN, Ms. fr. 19369.

32. See Annalina Caló Levi, *Barbarians on Roman Imperial Coins and Sculpture* (New York, 1952); and Michael McCormick, *Eternal Victory: Triumphal Rulership in Late Antiquity, Byzantium, and the Early Medieval West* (Cambridge and Paris, 1990).

33. On the trampling of barbarians as a common part of the Roman triumph, see McCormack. Also see the admirable article by Robert Baldwin, "'I slaughter barbarians': Triumph as a Mode in Medieval Christian Art," *Konsthistorisk Tidskrift* 59: 4 (1990): 225–242, 233; and Chapter 7 of the present work for a much more detailed analysis of the significance of the imperial triumph for Renaissance entry ceremonial.

34. See, of course, L. Febvre, *The Problem of Unbelief in the Sixteenth Century: The Religion of Rabelais,* trans. B. Gottlieb (Cambridge, MA; London, 1982). However, I follow Carlo Ginzburg's more nuanced approach here in eschewing Febvre's notion of religiosity as a collective mentality, to focus instead on that of a specific group. See Ginzburg's comments in *The Cheese and the Worms: The Cosmos of a Sixteenth-Century Miller* trans. J. and A. C. Tedeschi (New York, 1982), xxiii–xxiv.

35. See Marjorie Reeves, "The Development of Apocalyptic Thought: Medieval Attitudes," in C. A. Patrides and J. Wittreich (eds.), *The Apocalypse in English Renaissance Thought and Literature: Patterns, Antecedents and Repercussions* (Ithaca, 1984), 41. As Reeves puts this, "the Middle Ages lived in the consciousness of being in the end of time." I would add that much the same point can be made with regard to sixteenth-century France. Regarding apocalyptic thought and its "omnipresence in the system of representation of the first part of the sixteenth century," see Denis Crouzet, *Les Guerriers de Dieu. La Violence au temps des troubles de religion (vers 1525–vers 1610)* (Seysell, 1990), 1: 182.

36. See Guy Bois, *The Crisis of Feudalism: Economy and Society in Eastern Normandy c. 1300–1500* (Cambridge, 1984), especially 369–390. As he aptly comments (369), the

period between 1500 and 1550 is when the "Norman peasantry emerged from its Golden Age and plunged without transition into an Iron Age." Regarding the economic and social conditions in the first half of the sixteenth-century in Normandy, also see David Nicholls, "Social Change and Early Protestantism in France: Normandy, 1520–62," in *European Studies Review* 10 (1980): 279–308.

37. See Farin (1731), 174–178.

38. Pauperism, begging, and crime grew. The repressive measures meted out by the city's various governing bodies became more draconian. For example, see G. Panel (ed.), *Documents concernant les pauvres de Rouen, 1224–1634* (Paris and Rouen, 1917), 20–21.

39. Robert Le Rocquez, *Le Miroir d'éternité comprenant les sept aages du monde, les quatre monarchies et diversité des règnes d'iceluy en la fin duquel sont contenus le general Jugement de Dieu . . .* (Caen, 1589), 116–117.

40. See, for example, Jean Calvin, *Contre les libertins* (Geneva, 1545); and his *Épistre contre un certain cordelier suppost de la secte des libertins lequel est prisonnier a Roan* (Geneva, 1547), in which he attacks the apocalyptic/millenarian beliefs of a sect of "libertins" operating in Northern France and Rouen. While this heretical sect believed it was living in the Last Days, Calvin opined that theirs was precisely the sort of *"coq à l'asne"* that would be responsible for unleashing the Apocalypse. On the influence of these ideas in Rouen, see E. Picot, (ed.), *Théâtre mystique de Pierre du Val et des libertins spirituels de Rouen au XVIe siècle* (Paris, 1882).

41. P. Le Verdier, *Le Triomphe des Normands*, fol. 130 (r°).

42. Vidoue, fol. l iii.

43. See, for example, BN, Ms. fr. 379, fol. 15; and BN, Ms. fr. 19184, fol. 226.

44. See, for example, Parmentier, 24–26.

45. In 1534, for example, after the Affair of the Placards, the city's monastic orders led a procession composed of groups of citizens representing Rouen's four quarters, members of its confraternities, and 673 children dressed in white and carrying candles. They were followed by the Archbishop of Tours carrying the Eucharist, the Cathedral's *chanoine* carrying the holy water, chaplains and canons carrying candles and relics. The entire body of Parlement came next, and behind them, a huge crowd of men and women carrying candles followed. Such processions were repeated time and time again. See Farin (1731), 1: 44–51.

46. With regard to the widespread circulation of ideas associated with the apocalypse, see M. Bloomfield and M. Reeves, "The Penetration of Joachimism into Northern Europe," *Speculum* 29 (1954): 772–793; N. Cohn, *The Pursuit of the Millennium: Revolutionary Millenarians and Mystical Anarchists of the Middle Ages* (New York, 1970); M. Reeves, *The Influence of Prophecy in the Later Middle Ages: A Study in Joachimism* (Oxford, 1969). With particular regard to the French case, I refer the reader to Jennifer Britnell, "Jean Lemaire de Belges and Prophecy," in the *Journal of the Warburg and Courtauld Institutes* 42 (1979): 144–166; and Crouzet, especially chapters 2 and 3 of the first volume.

47. Regarding the discovery of the New World and its associations with Joachimist and Franciscan eschatology, see M. Bataillon, "Évangélisme et millénar-

isme au Nouveau Monde," in *Courants religieux et humanisme à la fin du XV et au début du XVI siècle, Colloque de Strasbourg* (Paris, 1957), 25–36; J. Phelan, *The Millennial Kingdom of the Franciscans in the New World* (Berkeley and Los Angeles, 1970); Delno West, "Medieval Ideas of Apocalyptic Mission and the Early Franciscans in Mexico," in *The Americas* 45: 3 (January, 1989): 293–313; Pauline Moffitt Watts, "Prophecy and Discovery: On the Spiritual Origins of Christopher Columbus's 'Enterprise of the Indies'," *The American Historical Review* 90:1 (February, 1985): 73–102; Christopher Columbus, *The Libro de la profecías*, eds. Delno West and August Kling (Gainesville, 1991); and also see Chapter 3 Note 67.

48. Columbus, *Libro de las profecías*, 71, cited in D. Kadir, *Columbus and the Ends of the Earth: Europe's Prophetic Rhetoric as Conquering Ideology* (Berkeley and Los Angeles, 1992), 221.

49. See Parmentier, 64, BN, Ms. fr., 1739, fol. 99.

50. Parmentier, 27, BN, Ms. fr. 379, fol. 24.

51. Ibid., 40–42, BN, Ms. fr. 379, fol. 18.

52. BN, Ms. fr. 2206, fol. 82; and BN, Ms. fr. fol. 87–88.

53. BN, Ms. fr. 19184, fol. 78.

54. Parmentier, 46, BN, Ms. fr. 379, fol. 20.

55. Quoted in Jean de Léry, *History of a Voyage to the Land of Brazil, otherwise called America,* . . . trans. Janet Whatley (Berkeley, 1990), xlix.

56. André Thevet, *Les Singularités de la France antarctique*, ed. F. Lestringant (Paris, 1983, first published 1557), 49.

57. Pero de Magalhaes de Gandavo, *The Histories of Brazil* (New York, 1922), 85.

58. C. Beaune, *Naissance de la nation France* (Paris, 1985); Anne-Marie Lecoq, *François Ier imaginaire. Symbolique et politique à l'aube de la Renaissance française* (Paris, 1987); Francis Yates, *Astraea: The Imperial Theme in the Sixteenth Century* (London, 1975), especially 121–126; Joseph Strayer, "France: The Holy Land, the Chosen People, and the Most Christian King," in T. Rabb and J. Seigel (eds.), *Action and Conviction in Early Modern Europe* (Princeton, 1969), 3–16; and W. J. Bouwsma, *Concordia Mundi: The Career and Thought of Guillaume Postel (1510–1581)* (Cambridge, MA, 1957).

59. Quoted in P. E. Hughes, *Lefèvre: Pioneer of Ecclesiastical Renewal in France* (Grand Rapids, MI, 1984), 66.

60. Quoted in R. Scheller, "Imperial Themes in Art and Literature of the Early French Renaissance: The Period of Charles VIII," in *Simiolus* 12 (1981–1982): 36.

61. Ibid., 8.

62. Ibid., 7–8, and 5.

63. Ibid., 34; also see, for example, Donald Weinstein, "Millenarianism in a Civic Setting: The Savonarola Movement in Florence," in Sylvia Thrupp (ed.), *Millennial Dreams in Action* (The Hague, 1962), 187–203.

64. See Yates, *Astraea*, 122.

65. Quoted in P. E. Hughes, 66 (my emphasis).

66. Jean Thenaud, Bibliothèque de L'Arsenal Ms. 5061 (1520), fol. C (v°)–D (r°), cited in Lecoq, 305.

67. *Epistre envoiée de Paradis au très chrestien roy de France Fransçoys, premier de ce nom, de par les empereurs Pepin et Charlemaigne* . . . (1515), in M. Anatole de Montaiglon (ed.), *Recueil de poésies de François des XVe et XVIe siècles* . . . (Paris, 1856), 4: 189; also see Lecoq, 273.

68. Strayer, 8; Kantorowicz also addressed this: "In France the 'holy soil' of the *Terra Sancta* overseas and the 'holy soil' of *la dulce France* were not at all incompatible and incomparable notions, and . . . both were equally filled with emotional values. The kingdom of France, *Francia*, whose very name suggested to her children that she was the Land of the Free (*franci*), was considered the home of a new chosen people." Kantorowicz, *The King's Two Bodies: A Study in Medieval Political Theology* (Princeton, 1957), 237.

69. See for example Guillaume Thibault, "La Dame à l'aigneau et la dame à l'aspic," BMR, Ms. 1062 (Y. 18), fol. 101. This was published by P. Le Verdier.

70. Guillaume Postel, of course, was one of the most ardent champions of this millenarian role for the kings of France. In his epistle to the *Loy salique*, he describes Henri II as "him whom God has chosen to establish the foundation of His eternal kingdom. . . . " Quoted in Bouwsma, *Concordia*, 226.

71. Quoted in J.-F. Maillard, "Postel et ses disciples Normands," in *Guillaume Postel, 1581–1981, Actes du Colloque International d'Avranches, 1981* (Paris, 1985), 80.

72. Quoted in Maillard, 80.

73. Bouwsma, 55–56.

74. According to Georges Weill, Postel helped to organize Queen Éléonore's entry into Rouen in 1532; see his *Vie et caractère de Guillaume Postel*, trans. François Secret (Milan, 1987), 31.

75. Bernard Guenée and François Lehoux(eds.), *Les Entrées royales françaises de 1328 à 1515* (Paris, 1968), 250; the account that follows can be found on 251–253. The manuscript of this entry, authored by Robert Pinel, was reproduced in facsimile and introduced by Ch. de Robillard de Beaurepaire, *Entrée de Charles VIII à Rouen en 1485* (Rouen, 1902).

76. Revelations, 5:12–13.

77. Scheller, "Imperial Themes," 16–17.

78. Guenée and Lehoux, 256.

79. Ibid., 247.

80. Ibid., 259.

81. See Chapter 2; it is perhaps of interest to note that a ship with the same name was used by Jean Parmentier on his final voyage to the Indies. The connection between Ango and Louis' entry was certainly the Cardinal Georges d'Amboise; additionally, a possible connection exists through Guillaume Ango, who represented the Cauchoise quarter of Rouen in the city's government and was one of those given the honor of helping to carry the canopy over the king during his entry.

82. *L'Entrée du treschrestien et tresvictorieux Roy de France Françoys premier de ce nom faicte en sa bonne ville et cité de Rouen le second jour d'aoust. En l'an de la redemption humaine Mil cinq cent dix sept* (Rouen, nd). There is a published version of this intro-

duced by Ch. de Robillard de Beaurepaire, *L'Entrée de François Ier roi de France dans la ville de Rouen au mois d'août* (Rouen, 1867); also see Anne-Marie Lecoq, 113–114 and 361–362; and Penny Richard's "Rouen and the Golden Age: The Entry of Francis I, 2 August 1517," in C. Allmand (ed.), *Power, Culture and Religion in France* (Woodbridge, 1989).

83. *L'Entrée du treschrestien*, fol. C.

84. Ibid., fol. C iv, emphasis added. The following year, this pageant was duplicated for François' entry into Angers, see *L'Entrée du trescrestien et chevalereux roy de France . . . en Angiers . . . le vi jour de juing l'an mil v cens xviii* (sl, nd).

85. This would not have been without precedent as Louis XII also entered Rouen on September 28. *Cest la deduction*, fol. B ii. The 1550 entry was delayed several days because of inclement weather. According to the prose account, the king made his entry on Wednesday, October 1. Masselin's text, though it confirms this date, indicates that the Queen's entry took place on the second day of October—on "le lundy second iour de ce present moys d'octobre." Masselin's account, called the "program," was produced before the entry; though redacted to say that the king made his entry on Wednesday (October 1) and to indicate that the queen made hers on the following day. See Fol. C v (r°). The detail of the day was overlooked with the text indicating that it took place on Monday rather than being replaced by the Thursday when her entry took place. Monday was September 29. The error strongly suggests that the original date on which the king's entry was planned was Sunday, September 28.

86. See C. Beaune, 188–206.

87. Regarding this manuscript (BN, Ms. fr. 5748) and Saint Michel's role as guardian angel of the French monarchy and of France, see Lecoq, 445; regarding images of Saint Michel that employed the visages of François I and Henri II, see ibid., 446 and 526 n. 39, and C. Beaune, 198.

88. See Exodus, chapter 23: 20–23.

89. See Lecoq, 445.

90. See McGowan, *Ideal Forms in the Age of Ronsard* (Los Angeles and Berkeley, 1985), 26–27.

91. "Ce Roy a sur la test/ Un soeil radieulx. . . . /Ses pieds sur un croissant . . . /Dessoubz sa main senestre/Iustice est florissant, /Et dessoubz sa main dextre /Discord est impuissant . . . ," *Cest la deduction*, fol. N iv (r°).

92. Ibid., fol. N iii (r°).

93. Charles Paradin, *Devises héroïques et emblêmes de M. Claude Paradin* (Paris, 1621), 19.

94. Many authorities have remarked upon the crescent's ambiguity in signifying both the king's wife, Catherine de Medici, and his mistress, Diane de Poitiers. The goddess Diana is closely associated with the moon. The verse account of the entry makes explicit mention of this: "O Diane!/ A louer la majesté/ Du Roy, qui ton croissant porte. . . . " BMR, Ms. 1268 (Y. 28), fol. xviii. Also see, for example, Cloulas, *Henri II*, 110–111.

95. Cited in McGowan, *Ideal Forms*, 25.

96. *Cest la deduction*, fol. M iii (v°).

97. In this sense it can perhaps be compared to the equally ubiquitous lily, which, according to the Joachimist tradition, was the "floral symbol of the Last Age." See Bouwsma, 77.

98. *Cest la deduction*, fol. Q iv (r°).

99. Ibid., emphasis added.

100. "Roy triomphant au monde sur tous Roys." Ibid., fol. Q iii (r°).

101. Ibid., fol. Q iv (r°).

102. As M.-R. Jung points out, the Hercules Musagète was to become an emblem of noble patronage of the arts for the Pléiade, see *Hercule dans la littérature française du XVIᵉ siècle. De l'Hercule courtois à l'Hercule baroque* (Geneva, 1966), 131.

103. Michel de Certeau, *Heterologies: Discourse on the Other* (Minneapolis, 1986), 87.

104. *Cest la deduction*, fol. O ii (v°).

105. Joachim du Bellay, *Œuvres poétiques*, ed. H. Chamard (Paris, 1908), 3: 70. Imagery such as this was common throughout the 1540s and 1550s, and was oft-repeated by the likes of du Bellay, Ronsard, Tyard, Marot, and many others. See Samaras, especially 75–108.

Chapter 6

1. On the Conards, see Dylan Reid, "The Triumph of the Abbey of the Conards: Spectacle and Sophistication in a Rouen Carnival," in Joëlle Rollo-Koster, *Medieval and Early Modern Ritual: Formalized Behavior in Europe, China and Japan* (Leiden, Boston, Köln, 2002), 147–173; and idem, "Carnival in Rouen: A History of the Abbaye des Conards" in *The Sixteenth Century Journal* 32 (2001): 1027–1055; Charles Mazouer, "Spectacle et théâtre dans la chevauchée des Conards de Rouen au XVIᵉ siècle," in *Fifteenth Century Studies* 13 (1988): 387–399; M. Rousse, *Le Théâtre des farces en France au Moyen Age*, volume 5, *Textes de farces, documents d'archives*, typescript thesis (Reims, 1983); Hertha Schulz, *A Study of the Moralités in the La Vallière Manuscript, Bibliothèque Nationale, Ms. Fr. 24341*, typescript thesis (Toronto, 1982), 37–45; R. Lebègue, "La Vie dramatique à Rouen de François I à Louis XIII," *Etudes sur le théâtre français* (Paris, 1978), 2: 85–112; André Corvisier, "Une Société ludique au XVIᵉ siècle: L'Abbaye des Conards de Rouen," in *Annales de Normandie* 2 (1977): 179–193; Natalie Zemon Davis, "The Reasons of Misrule," in *Society and Culture in Early Modern France* (Stanford, 1975), 97–123; Howard Mayer Brown, *Music in the French Secular Theater, 1400–1550* (Cambridge., MA, 1963), 27–29; L. Petit de Julleville, *Histoire du théâtre en France, Les comédiens en France au moyen age* (Paris, 1885); J. E. A. Gosselin, *Recherches sur les origines et l'histoire du théâtre à Rouen avant Pierre Corneille* (Rouen, 1868): 34–43; J.-X. C. Du Busserolle, *Notice sur l'abbaye des Conards, Confrérie célèbre qui a existé à Rouen du quatorzième au dix-septième siècle, à Évreux, de 1345 à 1420* (Rouen and Paris, 1859); and A. Floquet, "Histoire des Conards de Rouen," in *Bibliothèque de l'école des Chartes* 1 (1839): 105–123.

2. See Jonathan Beck, *Théâtre et propagande aux débuts de la Réforme* (Geneva and Paris, 1986), 52.

3. The organizers of Henri's festival forbade the setting up of any independent displays—the Conards were the one exception. See BMR, A. 16 *délibérations*, fol. 92(r°).

4. *Cest la deduction*, fol. R (v°).

5. Natalie Zemon Davis has given a somewhat different translation of these names, see *Society and Culture*, 99. The names are in most cases puns, Davis is of course correct in translating *Platte Bourse* as "flat purse," and *Maucomble* as "bad measure," but I thought I would offer different translations to give the reader an idea of some of the other associations these names might have evoked.

6. We do not have any information about the Conards' *chevauchée* of 1550 other than an account of the farce they performed, but—as indicated by *Cest la deduction*, fol. R (v°)—this was but one part of a larger program. There is a detailed account of the Conards' celebrations of 1540 (1541 new style); see Note 7. The "farce des veaux" can be found in La Vallière manuscript (BN, Ms. fr. 24341)—a collection of farces and moralités performed by the Conards and Rouen's Puys. There is a facsimile edition of this manuscript edited by Le Roux de Lincy, *Manuscrit La Valière (Recueil de farces, moralités et sermons joyeux)*, intro. Werner Helmich (Geneva, 1972).

7. The following account derives from *Les Triomphes de l'abbaye des Conards, sous le resveur en decimes Fagot, Abbé des Conards, contenant les criées et proclamations faites, depuis son advenement jusques à l'An présent [1587]; Plus l'ingénieuse Lessive qu'ils ont Conardement monstrée aux jours gras de l'an MDXL; plus le Testament D'Ouinet de nouveau augmenté par le commandement dudit Abbé, non encores veu. Plus la Letanie, l'Ancienne et l'Oraison faite en ladite maison Abbatiale en l'an 1580* (Rouen, 1587); also see the nineteenth-century reedition of this text by M. De Montifaud, *Les triomphes de l'Abbaye des Conards avec une notice sur la fête des fous* (Paris, 1874); Rousse, 30–50; and Mazouer.

8. Rousse, 31.

9. Ibid., 30–31.

10. Ibid., 31.

11. Ibid., 32.

12. Ibid.

13. Ibid., 38.

14. Regarding the possible significance of this, see Chapter 7.

15. *Les Triomphes*, fol. B vii (r°–v°).

16. Ibid., fol. D iii (v°).

17. Rousse, 30–31.

18. *Les Triomphes*, fol. B vii (v°).

19. Beside them were the "Maistres D'Hostel" representing the Nobility, the Church, Labor, Money Thrown Away, Credit, and Trade. The pensioners of Marchandise (dressed in *babelou*) came next; they could be identified by signs hung across their shoulders: Solicitude, Envy, Profit, Chance, Hardiness, Dissimulation, Fear, Boredom, Melancholy, False-Seeming, Invention, Infidelity, Abjection, Anxiety, Hopelessness, Robbery, Ruin, Peril, Enterprise, Defiance, Assurance, and Deception. Ibid., fol. C (r°–v°).

20. Ibid., fol. C ii (r°).

21. Ibid., fol. D (v°).

22. Ibid., fol. D ii (v°).

23. These included, I Don't Know Who, Authority, Time, Folly, Old Fathers, Hypocrisy, Business, Good Faith, Money, Goods, Ambition, Public Good, Madness, Law, Up-and-Comers, and Who You Want. Ibid., fol. D iii (r°).

24. Ibid., fol. D iv (r°).

25. Ibid., fol. E (v°).

26. See ibid., fols. E ii (r°)–F (v°); also see Schulz, 185–193. This farce is also to be found in BN, Ms. fr. 24341, fol. 81(v°).

27. Cited in Schulz, 249.

28. See "Le Monde et abuz," in Émile Picot, *Recueil général des sotties* (Paris, 1904), 2: 27, 126–131; cited in Heather Arden, *Fool's Plays. A Study of Satire in the Sottie* (Cambridge, 1980), 97. Though Picot identifies this sottie's provenance as Toulouse, its author, André De la Vigne, was one of the Puy de Palinod's most illustrious confreres.

29. Cited in Arden, 100.

30. *Farce nouvelle moralisée des gens nouveaulx*, in Picot, *Recueil* 1: 128; cited in Arden 89.

31. *Les Triomphes*, fol. C ii (r°).
32. Ibid., fol. F (r°).
33. Ibid., fol. F ii (v°).
34. Ibid., fol. F iii (r°).
35. Ibid.
36. Ibid., fol. F iv (v°).
37. Ibid., fol. G (r°)–G iv (v°).
38. Ibid., fol. H iii (r°).
39. Ibid., fol. G iii (v°)–G iv (r°).

40. *Les Menus propos* in Picot, *Recueil* 1: 73, see also Arden, 115.

41. *Sottie du Monde* in Picot, *Recueil* 2: 335.

42. The poet Maximien c. 1500, cited in Mollat, *Le Commerce maritime normand à la fin du Moyen Age: Étude d'histoire économique et sociale* (Paris, 1952), 528. Also see Benedict, *Rouen*, 2–3.

43. See Brunelle, *The New World Merchants of Rouen, 1559–1630* (Kirksville, MO, 1991), 8; and Mollat, *Commerce*, 119 ff.

44. *Les Troys pelerins et malice* in Picot, 2: 311, and 302; this farce alludes, in particular, to the famine of 1521. Also G. Bois, *The Crisis of Feudalism: Economy and Society in Eastern Normandy c.1300–1550* (Cambridge, 1984), 375; and François Farin *Histoire de la ville de Rouen, Divisée en six parties* (Rouen, 1731), 176–177.

45. According to Salmon, the purchasing power of the *livre tournois* fell by slightly more than half between 1461 and 1559. Grain prices doubled in the first six decades of the sixteenth century and the cost of agricultural produce generally increased by 25 percent in the first quarter of the century, and by 37 percent in the second. See J. H. M. Salmon, *Society in Crisis: France in the Sixteenth Century* (New York, 1975), 38.

46. D. Nicholls, "Social Change and Early Protestantism in France: Normandy, 1520–62," in *European Studies Review* 10 (1980): 281.

47. Cited in Michel Mollat, "Mue d'une ville Médiévale (environ 1475–milieu du XVIᵉ siècle)," in M. Mollat (ed.), *Histoire de Rouen* (Toulouse, 1979), 145–178, 164.

48. See especially Natalie Zemon Davis's seminal article, "Poor Relief, Humanism, and Heresy," in *Society and Culture*, 17–16.

49. See G. Panel, *Documents concernant les pauvres de Rouen, 1224–1634* (Paris and Rouen, 1917), 1: 20–21.

50. René Herval, *Histoire de Rouen* (Rouen, 1949), 2: 63.

51. *Cest la deduction*, fol. N iii (r°).

52. Henri Fouquet, *Histoire civile, politique et commerciale de Rouen* (Rouen, 1875), 368.

53. In the years leading up to the entry, there had been a constant stream of representatives flowing from Rouen to the court to try to persuade the king to forgo, or at least reduce, what they felt to be the exorbitantly high taxes levied on its citizens. See, J. Félix (ed.), *Comptes-Rendus des échevins de Rouen* (Rouen, 1890), 1:39; and BMR, A. 16, fol. 80 ff.

54. Its fairs, for example, were famous throughout Europe, as in the case of the *foire de la Chandeleur* in 1548, where over seventy ships arrived in Rouen's port. See Mollat, "Mue d'une ville Médiévale," 148.

55. The severe inflation that left so many destitute and starving also had the effect of stimulating the economic growth of Rouen's "international" merchant-trade industries, and also of further exacerbating an already skewed distribution of wealth. Salmon, 37.

56. G. Huppert, *Les Bourgeois Gentilshommes: An Essay on the Definition of Elites in Renaissance France* (Chicago, 1977), 4.

57. The impulse to bury Marchandise and to direct newfound mercantile wealth down the well-trodden path toward traditional means of assuring social status— property rather than mobile wealth—had the effect of contributing to the already marked decrease in agricultural productivity and the rise of the rural poor, hence exacerbating the divide between rich and poor even more. See Salmon, *Society,* 46.

58. *Les Triomphes,* fol. D iv (r°).

59. *Moral de tout le monde,* in Picot, *Recueil* 3: 36.

60. Ibid.

61. On this process see Huppert, *Bourgeois Gentilshommes,* 34–37.

62. *Moral de tout le monde,* 39.

63. See Stuart Carroll, *Noble Power During the French Wars of Religion: The Guise Affinity and the Catholic Cause in Normandy* (Cambridge, 1998); Gayle Brunelle's *New World Merchants,* and idem, "Immigration, Assimilation and Success: Three Families of Spanish Origin in Sixteenth-Century Rouen," in the *Sixteenth Century Journal* 20: 2 (Summer, 1989); and Mollat, *Commerce,* especially 483–541.

64. See M. C. Oursel, *Notes pour servir à l'histoire de la Réforme en Normandie au temps de François Ier* (Caen, 1913), 23.

65. *Les Triomphes,* fol. D iv (v°).

66. Ibid.

67. Le Roux de Lincy, 1: 16.

68. Ibid. This charge was echoed by Montaigne some forty years later in his essay, "On Coaches." He laments: "Biens crains-je que nous aurons bien fort hasté sa [the New World's] declinaison et sa ruyne par nostre contagion, et que nous luy aurons bien cher vendu nos opinions et nos arts." Montaigne, *Essais,* 3: 123.

69. *Le Monde abuz*, 39. See also Montaigne's oft-quoted abhorrence of innovation in his essay "On Custom," Frame 86. Montaigne's view was not an exceptional one; humanists, as Rummel notes in *The Humanist-Scholastic Debate* (15 and 98), were "frequently confronted with the charge that they were 'keen on new things', that is, that they were revolutionaries." Thus, for example, on April 5, 1543, Rouen's municipal government was debating the king's desire to create a new *Chambre des Comptes*. Citing a history of Demosthenes, Claude Chappuys exclaimed that innovations were both "pernicious and dangerous"; someone who creates something new, he said, is like a man who "has a rope around his neck."

70. See, in particular, *Les Quatres Ages* in Le Roux de Lincy.

71. Cited by Kipling, *Enter the King: Theatre, Liturgy, and Ritual in the Medieval Civic Triumph* (Oxford, 1998), 185.

72. Ibid., also see 201.

73. See, for example, Philippe Deschamps, "Un épisode de l'entrée de Henri II à Rouen. La Chevauchée des Conards et la 'Farce des Veaulx'," in *Précis analytique des travaux de l'Académie de Rouen, 1970* (Fecamp, 1971): 23–33; Jean-Claude Aubailly, *Le Monologue, le dialogue et la sottie* (Paris, 1976); Gustave Cohen, "La Farce des Veaux," in *Mélanges de linguistique et de littérature romanes à la mémoire d'István Frank* (Saarbrucken, 1957); and Schulz, *A Study of the Moralités*, 43–45.

74. "La Farce des Veaulx," in *Recueil de farces, moralités et sermons joyeux* (Paris, 1837), 2 (no pagination).

75. Ibid.   76. Ibid.

77. Ibid.   78. Ibid.

79. Bakhtin's formulation is the common reference point for this interpretation.

80. BMR, A. 15, fol. 29 (r°-v°); Rousse, 53–54; and A. Héron, *Deux chroniques de Rouen* (Rouen, 1900), 1:165, who offers a somewhat different account (for example, twelve heralds divided into two groups of six, and a procession of seventy following them) describing the Conards' escutcheon as a golden sun in which IHS.M was embroidered. Regarding the Conards' participation in other processions, see Rousse, 5: 27; Héron, 151.

81. See, for example, Howard Graham Harvey, *The Theatre of the Basoche: The Contribution of Law Societies to French Medieval Comedy* (Cambridge, MA, 1941), 11.

82. See E. Gosselin, *Recherches*, 37.

83. ADSM, Registres du Parlement, 1 BP 19, Registre d'audience, février–mars 1541, cited in Gosselin, *Recherches*, 38; and Rousse, 63–64.

84. BMR, A. 16, fol. 96 (r°).

85. Ibid., fol. 113 (v°).

86. Beck, 52.

87. Others identified by Beck as being associated with the Conards included Pierre Du Val, who was also a member of the Puy, Cardinot, Coquin, Pierre le Carpentier, Martainville, Le Boursier (Nicolas Coquevent).

88. See Schulz, 19–20 and Emmanuel Philipot, "Les 'sieurs d'ais' confrérie dramatique rouennais des XVᵉ et XVIᵉ siècles," in *Romania* 39 (1910): 93–95.

89. See Chapter 4.

90. Arden's analysis is directed at the genre of works known as the *sottie*; I believe that my focus here on the Conards is consistent with her view, for as she herself states, the plays in *La Vallière* manuscript were written in Rouen and performed by the Conards. See Arden 24.

91. Ellery Schalk argues that "in the first half of the sixteenth century France was a society in which at least the upper classes and the literate people assumed they had no major or overriding social problems." (*From Valor to Pedigree: Ideas of Nobility in France in the Sixteenth and Seventeenth Centuries* (Princeton, 1986), 61. Many historians of this period embrace a similar chronology (albeit, not stated quite so starkly). Such views are difficult to reconcile with the evidence here presented. Perhaps Paul Zumthor was right when he remarked that theater is the art that is "the most receptive to changes in the social structure, and the most revelatory of those changes." Cited in Enders, *Rhetoric and the Origins of Medieval Drama* (Ithaca, 1992), 11.

92. "The Bourgeoisie," she argues, "was in the process of dividing into the wealthy, influential members at the higher levels, and the poor, economically insecure craftsmen and merchants at the lower levels." Arden, 75. "The lower bourgeoisie," she continues, "tried to maintain the status quo, thus becoming more and more the guardian of tradition, while the higher bourgeoisie attempted to acquire new and greater social, economic, and political powers. The result was a pronounced class tension." Ibid., 133; also see 137 ff.

93. This is exemplified by the case of Guillaume Auber. Auber was a major player in Rouen's civic affairs in the 1540s and 1550s; he was a member of the city's ruling council and a participant in the Puy de Palinod. In the records of the Hôtel de Ville he is referred to either by his name alone, as the Sieur de la Hay, or as a merchant draper. Draper, noble, city official, and poet: Auber is but one example of many. How are we to classify him?

94. Barbara Bowen, "Théâtre du Cliché," in *Cahiers de l'Association internationale des Etudes françaises*, 26 (1974): 33–47; and idem, "La Revanche verbale dans la farce Française de la Renaissance," in *Kwartalnik Neofilogiczny*, 23 (1–2/1976): 57–64.

95. See Chapter 4.

96. *Apologies*, in Picot, *Querelle de Marot*, fol. A ii (r°).

97. Ibid., *Le bancquet*, fol. A iii (r°).

98. Ibid.

99. Ibid., A iv (v°).

100. Such as *Le Blason du Nez*, d'Eustorg de Beaulieu, or that of J. N. d'Arles. See Aline Mary Best, *Claude Chappuys: Poésies intimes* (Geneva, 1967), 174 n. 114.

101. Ibid., 170–178.

102. It is significant to note, in this regard, the *chant royal* by Jo. James that lists the comic poets who competed in the Puy: Pignollet, Bullin, Caudebec, and Maistre Gueffin Cambrette . . . , BMR, 1063 (Y. 16), fol. 174 (v°). Moreover, many of the "serious" poems read before the Puy had a strong sexual/comic undercurrent, as for example, *Le chariot du fort geant celeste*. One need only point to the name of one of

the Puy's sister societies—the *Puy d'Amour*—to see how intimate were the relations between piety and lasciviousness among Normandy's poets. Indeed, one finds, decorating a manuscript commissioned by Jacques Le Lieur, BMR, 1064 (Y. 226a), illustrations of charivari-like scenes that would, at least to modern eyes, seem far more appropriate to the pages of Rabelais than to the margins of solemn religious verse dedicated to the Virgin.

103. Even the poets of the Puy des Pauvres, which, as we have seen, included some of Normandy's richest and most esteemed citizens, virulently attacked the rich and worldly men who abandoned their responsibilities to the poor. See J. Sireulde *Le Tresor immortel* (Rouen, 1556), for example, fol. L iii (r°)–L iv(r°). Several of the Conards (Cotton, Fouquet, Delacroix, Baillart) were integrally involved in the city's efforts to help the poor. See Panel, 58, 62, 95–96.

104. *Moral de tout le monde*, 37.

105. Cited in Schulz, 200.

106. See Arden, 146–147.

107. *Moral de tout le monde*, 43 (my emphasis).

108. *Sottie nouvelle des trompeurs*, in Picot, *Recueil* 3: 19.

109. On the relationship between nominalistic theology and the sottie, see Olga Ann Dull, *Folie et rhétorique dans la sottie* (Geneva, 1994).

110. The Conards' critique is thus closely allied to contemporary criticisms of the court; see for example, *Le mepris de la court & de la louange de la vie Rusticque*, A. M. (Lyon, 1542), 100–101.

111. See, of course, Natalie Zemon Davis' classic formulation in her "The Reasons of Misrule," in *Society and Culture*, 123.

112. See Zachary S. Schiffman, *On the Threshold of Modernity: Relativism in the French Renaissance* (Baltimore and London, 1991), 5. The marvels and wonders discovered in the New World have been seen by some as the principal cause behind the "conceptual overload" that—putatively—led to the development and elaboration of a new and radically empiricist solution to this problem. See, for example, William Ashworth, "Natural History and the Emblematic World View," in D. Lindberg and R. Westman (eds.), *Reappraisals of the Scientific Revolution* (Cambridge, 1990), 302–332; and Lorraine Daston and Katharine Park, *Wonders and the Order of Nature 1150–1750* (New York, 1998), 136.

113. *La Triomphe*, fol. D iii (r°).

114. Cited in Ulrich Langer, *Divine and Poetic Freedom in the Renaissance* (Princeton, 1990), 14.

115. *Les Sobres sotz*, in Picot, *Recueil* 3: 73.

116. See, for example, Hiram Haydn's brilliant—though too often overlooked—*The Counter Renaissance* (New York, 1950), 117. Jacques Lefèvre d'Etaples' extreme sort of skepticism was perhaps not unrelated to the Ciceronian suspicion of elaborate metaphysical and natural philosophical systems; indeed the humanist practice, exemplified by Valla and Agricola, of presenting arguments *in utramque partem* surely contributed to the critique of systems, and a reorientation of knowledge claims toward both probabilism and the experiential world. See Nicolas Jardine, "The Forg-

ing of Modern Realism: Clavius and Kepler Against the Sceptics," in *Studies in History and Philosophy of Science* 10 (1979): 141–173, 146.

117. *Cest la deduction*, fol. K iv (r°).

118. See especially the important article by Michel de Certeau, "Montaigne's 'Of Cannibals': The Savage 'I'," in *Heterologies: Discourse on the Other* (Minneapolis, 1986), 67–79.

119. Montaigne, *Essais* 3: 123.

120. Donald M. Frame (trans.), *The Complete Essays of Montaigne* (Stanford, 1992), 108; Montaigne, *Essais*, 1: 253. Similar statements were made by, for example, Jacques Cartier and Jean de Léry. Thus, according to Cartier: "les simples marins d'à présent . . . ont connu le contraire de cette opinion des philosophes par la vraie expérience." Quoted in G. Atkinson, *Les Nouveaux horizons de la Renaissance française* (Paris, 1935), 256. Or as Jean de Léry put it: "One of our pilots, called Jean de Meun, of Harfleur, although he didn't know A from B, had nevertheless by long experience with his maps, astrolabes, and Jacob's staff become so expert in the art of navigation that often, and especially during storms, I would see him silence a learned personage . . . who in calm weather would pride himself on teaching the theory of it. Not, however, that I condemn or wish in any way to disparage the sciences that are acquired and learned in schools, and by the study of books; such is far from my intention. But I must ask that you not so settle on a mere opinion, whosoever's it may be, that you cite me reason against the experience of a thing." See his *History of a Voyage to the Land of Brazil, otherwise called America . . .* , trans. Janet Whatley (Berkeley, 1990), 22.

121. As de Léry was to say: "They do not pretend to be other than what they are." See ibid., lx. On the relationship between the savage and the *Idiotus*, see de Certeau, *Heterologies*, 73–74. For a different reading of Montaigne's joke, see François Rigolot, "Montaigne: European Reader of America," in *Diogenes* 164, 41/4 (1993): 1–12.

122. "La Farce des Veaulx," 13.

123. BMR, A. 16, fol. 113 (my emphasis).

124. Erasmus, *Praise of Folly and Letter to Maarten Van Dorp*, trans. B. Radice (London and New York, 1993), 51–52.

125. T. Cave, *The Cornucopian Text: Problems of Writing in the French Renaissance* (Oxford, 1979), 166.

126. Haydn, 84–85 ff.

127. Sireulde, *Les Triomphes*, fol D(v°).

128. On Christ's folly see, for example, M. A. Screech, *Ecstasy and The Praise of Folly* (London: 1980), and *idem, Laughter at the Foot of the Cross* (London and New York, 1997).

129. Mikhail Bakhtin, *Rabelais and his World*, trans. H. Iswolsky (Bloomington, 1984), 89.

130. Michel de Certeau, *The Mystic Fable* (Chicago, 1992), 29–30.

131. See, for example, Nancy Struever's important *The Language of History in the Renaissance* (Princeton, 1970), 44. Struever cites Nicholas of Cusa's analogy of God's creative power in the realm of natural forms and real entities and Man's power in the

realm of artificial forms and rational entities to demonstrate the belief that "man's similitude to God lies precisely in his *creative* use of symbol" (45). The telos of this power she says is to be found not simply in erudition, but in its attempts to promulgate virtue through the eloquent display of morally appropriate *exemplum*. Nevertheless, it seems to me one needs to balance this understanding of humanism with the deep ambivalence that permeated its intellectual and moral ambitions—e.g., the vanity of learning. See Haydn, 76–130.

132. Cited in Langer, 152.

133. See, for example, Heiko Oberman, *The Harvest of Medieval Theology: Gabriel Biel and Late Medieval Nominalism* (Grand Rapids, 2000), 295.

134. Ibid., 311.

135. See Heiko A. Oberman, "The Shape of Late Medieval Thought: The Birth Pangs of the Modern Era," in Charles Trinkaus and Heiko Oberman (eds.), *The Pursuit of Holiness in Late Medieval and Renaissance Religion* (Leiden, 1974), 67–92.

136. On the conjunction between the search for order in language and the search for social order (e.g., *raison d'état*) see de Certeau, *Heterologies*, 87.

137. See, for example, Steven Ozment, "Mysticism, Nominalism and Dissent," in Trinkaus and Oberman, 67–92, at 80.

138. As Montaigne, for example, was all too aware: "There is the name and the thing. The name is a sound which designates and signifies the thing; the name is not a part of the thing or of the substance, it is an extraneous piece attached to the thing, and outside of it." See "Of Glory," in Frame, 468. Pretensions to a science of language that could reinstate the prelapsarian unicity between words and things was nothing less than *conardie* by his way of thinking. See J. J. Supple, *Arms Versus Letters: The Military and Literary Ideals in the 'Essais' of Montaigne* (Oxford, 1984), 148.

139. See Hans Blumenberg, *The Legitimacy of the Modern Age*, trans. Robert M. Wallace (Cambridge, MA, 1983), 328 as cited by Langer, 8.

140. Regarding the relationship between nominalistic theology and theories of monarchical rule see, for example, Francis Oakley, *Omnipotence, Covenant and Order* (Ithaca, 1984), 93–122.

Chapter 7

1. See *Cest la deduction*, fol. K ii (r°). This assessment was seconded by the English ambassador, John Mason; see P. F. Tytler, *England Under the Reigns of Edward VI, and Mary* (London, 1839), 1: 326.

2. Ancient texts, such as those by Pliny, Suetonius, Appian, and Plutarch, provided descriptions upon which Renaissance triumphs were modeled. To these texts, the bas-reliefs found on the columns of Trajan and Marcus Aurelius, and the triumphal arches of Titus and Constantine gave a visual dimension. See J. Chartrou, *Les Entrées solennelles et triomphales à la Renaissance, 1484–1551* (Paris, 1928), 57; and R. Scheller, "Gallia cisalpina: Louis XII and Italy 1499–1508," in *Simiolus* 15 (1985): 7.

3. Quoted in B. Mitchell, *The Majesty of the State: Triumphal Progresses of Foreign Sovereigns in Renaissance Italy (1494–1600)* (Florence, 1986), 103.

4. Robert de La Marck, seigneur de Fleuranges, "Histoire des choses mémorables advenues des règnes de Louis XII et de François Ier (1499–1521)," in Michaud et al. (eds.), *Nouvelle collection des mémoires relatifs à l'histoire de France* (Paris, 1854), 5: 16.

5. Giesey, for example, characterizes the development of the entry festival in terms of a fourfold scheme of the distinct stages of kingship: sacral, juristic, historic, and humanistic; see "Models of Rulership in French Royal Ceremonial," in S. Wilentz (ed.), *Rites of Power: Symbolism, Ritual, and Politics since the Middle Ages* (Philadelphia, 1985). This seems a modification of his earlier position that recognized the substantial continuities between medieval and renaissance entries. As he put it: "The basic form of the French *entrée* remained constant despite the substitution of pagan mythologies for Christian moralities in the tableaux and props." Ralph Giesey, *The Royal Funeral Ceremony in Renaissance France* (Geneva, 1960), 118 n. 59. As a corrective to this view, see Robert Baldwin, "'I slaughter barbarians': Triumph as a Mode in Medieval Christian Art," *Konsthistorisk Tidskrift* 59: 4 (1990): 225–242; and Gordon Kipling, *Enter the King: Theatre, Liturgy, and Ritual in the Medieval Civic Triumph* (Oxford, 1998), passim.

6. Ludwig Wittgenstein, *Philosophical Investigations*, trans. G. E. M. Anscombe (New York, 1968), § 66. Also see Rodney Needham's *Against the Tranquility of Axioms* (Berkeley and Los Angeles, 1983), chapter 3, "Polythetic Classification: Convergence and Consequences," 44. According to Needham, a group K is defined in terms of a set G of properties *f1, f2 . . . , fn*. In a given aggregate of individuals each will possess various properties of G; and though each of these properties will be shared by many, there is no one property in G that is common to all. Nevertheless, he says, "All the members of K will resemble one another, though they will not resemble one another in respect to a given *f.*"

7. Ibid., 32 § 67.

8. H. S. Versnel, *Triumphus: An Inquiry into the Origin, Development and Meaning of the Roman Triumph* (Leiden, 1970), 304.

9. Ibid., 36–37.

10. Ibid., 47.

11. Ibid., 56–57. Also see J. G. Frazer, *The Golden Bough: A Study in Magic and Religion* (New York, 1950), 171.

12. Versnel, 145–146.

13. Ibid., 92. Also see S. MacCormack, "Change and Continuity in Late Antiquity: The Ceremony of *Adventus*," in *Historia* 21, 4 (1972): 722.

14. Saint John uses the term *Hypantesis* and Saint Paul uses its synonym, *Apantesis*, to describe Christ's entry into Jerusalem, and his Second Coming. See Ernst Kantorowicz, "The 'King's Advent' and the Enigmatic Panels in the Doors of Santa Sabina," *Arts Bulletin* 26/4 (December, 1944): 211, 216; and idem, *Laudes Regiae: A Study in Liturgical Acclamation and Mediaeval Ruler Worship* (Berkeley and Los Angeles, 1946), 71; also see MacCormack, "Change and Continuity," 724–725; and Kipling, 21. Despite associations with pagan idolatry, imperial ceremonial was of central importance in the articulation and elaboration of early Christian ritual; as Alain Guéry puts

this: "Ce n'est pas la liturgie ecclésiastique qui a inspiré le cérémonial monarchique, mais très précisément l'inverse . . . les gestes, les manières d'invocation, d'imploration, les cortèges, qui sont ceux des cérémonies religieuses, ont été d'abord ceux des cérémonies impériales dans ce qu'elles avaient de religieux." See his "Le Roi est Dieu, le Roi et Dieu," in N. Bulst, R. Descimon, and A. Guerreau, *L'État ou le roi. Les fondations de la modernité monarchique en France (XIVe–XVIIe siècles)* (Paris, 1992), 27–47, 38. It is equally important to note that once Christianized imperial ceremonial played an integral role in the subsequent development of secular monarchic ideology and ritual.

15. Kantorowicz, *Laudes*, 211 and 216. Also see, for example, Strong, 8; and Scheller, "Imperial Themes," 6–7, 15, and 17; and Kipling, passim.

16. Quoted in Kantorowicz, " 'King's Advent'," 210.

17. Quoted in Kantorowicz, "*Deus Per Naturam, Deus Per Gratiam*: A Note on Mediaeval Political Theology," *The Harvard Theological Review* 45 (1952): 253–277, 254.

18. Quoted in Ibid., 255. Also see Guéry, 32–33.

19. Kantorowicz, *Laudes,* 3.

20. Ibid., 31.

21. Kantorowicz, " 'King's Advent'," 210.

22. Ibid., 211.

23. Ibid., 210.

24. See B. Guenée and F. Lehoux (eds.), *Les Entrées royales françaises de 1328 à 1515* (Paris, 1968), 259.

25. Kantorowicz, " 'King's Advent'," 209.

26. See Guenée and Lehoux, 247; also see Kantorowicz, *The King's Two Bodies: A Study in Mediaeval Political Theology* (Princeton, 1957), 193–272.

27. Marc Bloch, *The Royal Touch: Sacred Monarchy and Scrofula in England and France* (London, 1973), 56–57.

28. Ibid.

29. Ibid.

30. See MacCormack, "Change and Continuity."

31. Kantorowicz, *Laudes*, 3, 30–31, and n. 60.

32. Kantorowicz, " 'King's Advent'," 208.

33. Quoted in ibid., 207. According to Kipling, "Just as the liturgy of Advent repeatedly imagines the coming of Christ in terms of an emperor's ceremonial civic reception, so the liturgy of the funeral office imagines the solemn adventus of the soul into the celestial Jerusalem." See *Enter the King*, 202–205.

34. Ibid. In the twelfth century the administration of unction was associated with the last rights of the dying. Prior to this time it was also thought to have curative powers and was administered to the sick as well.

35. See F. Paxton, *Christianizing Death: The Creation of a Ritual Process in Early Medieval Europe* (Ithaca, 1990), 42.

36. S. MacCormack, *Art and Ceremony in Late Antiquity* (Berkeley and Los Angeles, 1981).

37. Changed practices, such as burial rather than cremation, would seem to have structurally lent themselves to the continuation of this triumphant iconography in the form of chariots as a means of physically transporting the dead. Yet, the chariot was closely associated with pagan rites—i.e., the chariot as the means by which an emperor's soul, freed from the constraints of physical existence, could ascend to the heavens. On this imagery see MacCormack, ibid., 102; on its disappearance also see ibid., 125.

38. Chariots were reintegrated in funeral ceremonies in France as early as 1400. They made their first appearance in a royal French funeral ceremony in 1461 for Charles VII. Subsequently, they were used in the royal funerals of Louis XII, François I, and Henri II. Regarding the chariot, see Leopold Ettlinger, "The Duke of Wellington's Funeral Car," in *Journal of the Warburg and Courtauld Institute* 3 (1939–1940): 254–259, 255. Representations of these triumphs—those over Genoa and Milan—were subsequently carved onto the base of Louis' tomb at Saint-Denis.

39. This account, found in the *Archive de la Seine-Inférieure, H, fonds de Saint-Ouen, layette 3, liasse, pièce cotée J*, was transcribed and published by Paul Le Cacheux in *Bulletin de la société de l'histoire de Normandie* 14 (1925–1930): 203–209.

40. Quoted in Giesey, *Royal Funeral*, 117.

41. Thus Herald Guyenne said of the funeral: "Ayant esté toutes lesdites choses faictes et accomplies, et toutes autres choses utiles et necessaires pour l'antree dudit triumphe en ladite ville, et principallement aux effiges tant dudit feu seigneur que desdits seigneurs ses enfans . . . ," cited in Giesey, ibid., 14 n. 54. On the effigy as the center of the triumph while the mournful elements of the funeral were attached to the corpse (which was transported separately), see Kantorowicz, *King's Two Bodies*, 430.

42. On the *consecratio* of Roman emperors, see Florence Dupont, "The Emperor-God's Other Body," in M. Feher, R. Naddaff, and N. Tazi (eds.), *Fragments for a History of the Human Body* (Zone, 1989), 396–419.

43. See, for example, Giesey, *Royal Funeral*, 152.

44. Giesey, ibid. The artistic representation of the king's two bodies can also be seen in the double figuration of the *gisants* decorating the tombs of France's Renaissance kings. See Anatole de Montaiglon, "La Sculpture française à la Renaissance: La Famille des Juste en France," in *Gazette des Beaux-Arts* 12 (November and December, 1875); also see Pierre Pradel, *Michel Colombe, le dernier imagier gothique* (Paris, 1953); Erwin Panofsky, *Tomb Sculpture: Four Lectures on its Changing Aspects from Ancient Egypt to Bernini* (New York, 1964); and Jean-Marie Jenn, Françoise Jenn, Jean-Pierre Babelon, and Alain Erlande-Bradenbourg (eds.), *Le Roi, la sculpture et la mort: Gisants et tombeaux de la basilique de Saint Denis*, in *Archives departmentales de la Seine-Saint-Denis . . . , Bulletin* 3 (June, 1975).

45. Giesey, *Royal Funeral*, 152.

46. Ibid., 154.

47. Ibid., 157.

48. See Eric Hobsbawm and Terence Ranger (eds.), *The Invention of Tradition* (Cambridge, 1993), 1–14. Though Hobsbawm specifically refers to the "invented tradition"

as belonging to the nineteenth century, the concept is also relevant for understanding Renaissance court pageantry, which self-consciously sought to model itself after antiquity.

49. F. Dupont, "L'autre corps de l'empereur-dieu," in *Le temps de la réflexion* 7 (1986): 234–235, 237, cited in C. Ginzburg, "Représentation: le mot, l'idée, la chose," in *Annales* 46: 6 (November–December, 1991): 1226.

50. *The Roman Questions of Plutarch*, trans. H. J. Rose (Oxford, 1924), question LXXIX, 153; also see F. Hartog, *The Mirror of Herodotus: An Essay on the Representation of the Other*, trans. J. Lloyd (Berkeley and Los Angeles, 1988), 134–137, with regard to the hero being the exception to the rule; and Jack Goody, *Representations and Contradictions: Ambivalence Towards Images, Theatre, Fiction, Relics and Sexuality* (Oxford, 1997), 82–83.

51. MacCormack, *Art and Ceremony*, 154; also see Versnel, 123.

52. Quoted in MacCormack, *Art and Ceremony*, 145–146.

53. Kantorowicz, "'King's Advent'," 212 n. 28; MacCormack, "Change and Continuity," 747; and K. Setton, *Christian Attitude Towards the Emperor in the Fourth Century* (New York, 1941), especially 196–211.

54. See MacCormack, "Change and Continuity," 722.

55. Setton, 199.

56. J. Guyon, "La Vente des tombes à travers l'épigraphie de la Rome Chrétienne," in *Mélanges d'archéologie et d'histoire: Antiquité* 86 (1974), 594, cited in Peter Brown, *The Cult of the Saints: Its Rise and Function in Latin Christianity* (Chicago, 1981), 133 n. 16.

57. Patrick Geary makes a related point in his *Furta Sacra: Thefts of Relics in the Central Middle Ages* (Princeton, 1978), 30.

58. Ibid., passim.

59. See Peter Brown, *Cult of the Saints*, 96; see also his collection of essays, *Society and the Holy in Late Antiquity* (Los Angeles and Oxford, 1989), 189; and Patrick Geary, *Furta*, 19–20, 37.

60. Kantorwicz points out the early transference of triumphal rites from the effigy or image to relics, "'King's Advent'," 212 n. 28; as does MacCormack, "Change and Continuity," 747–748. As Versnel concisely states: "The relics, as the bearers of good fortune to the city, form a good illustration of what ancient man expected of a man vested with magic power, as was the triumphator . . . ," 384.

61. Saint Victrice, *De laude sanctorum, d'après les variantes tirées des mss de s.-Gal par le Chanoine Sauvage, publié et annoté par l'abbé A. Tougard* (Paris, 1895), 76.

62. Ibid., 57.

63. Ibid., 69; also see Brown, *Cult of the Saints*, 98: "The *De laude sanctorum* of Victricius of Rouen, and later evidence, make plain that such ceremonies were consciously modeled on the ceremonial of the emperor's *adventus*, or 'arrival in state' at a city." On the triumphal reception of relics, also see the entry under "reliques et reliquaires" by H. Leclercq in F. Cabrol and H. Leclercq (eds.), *Dictionnaire d'archéologie chrétienne et de liturgie*, 15 volumes (Paris, 1907–1932), 14: 2304, 2311, 2314–2315.

64. Brown, *Cult of the Saints*, 93 (my emphasis).

65. Brown, *Society and the Holy*, 7; also see his "The Saint as Exemplar in Late Antiquity," in *Representations* 1:2 (Spring, 1983): "It was possible for an adaptation of the Imperial ceremonials of a state arrival to make the tiny relic-jar of the bones of the prophet Zachariah seem 'as if living and present' to the populations through which the *cortège* passed on its way from Jerusalem to Constantinople," 18.

66. See Geary, *Furta*, 24–26; C. Ginzburg, "Représentation," 1229.

67. Patrick Geary, "Sacred Commodities: The Circulation of Medieval Relics," in Arjun Appadurai (ed.), *The Social Life of Things: Commodities in Cultural Perspective* (Cambridge, 1986), 179.

68. See, for example, Miri Rubin, *Corpus Christi: The Eucharist in Late Medieval Culture* (Cambridge, 1991), 12–14.

69. See Kantorowicz, *Laudes*, 56.

70. Kantorowicz, *King's Two Bodies*, 199.

71. Ginzburg, "Représentation," 1230.

72. Thus, it is probably not a coincidence that the first portrait of a king was made at precisely this time in France. See R. Starn and L. Partridge, *A Renaissance Likeness: Art and Culture in Raphael's Julius II* (Berkeley and Los Angeles, 1980), 13.

73. See Brown, *Society and the Holy*, 183; and Rubin, 244.

74. Rubin, ibid.

75. Geoffrey Wainwright, *Eucharist and Eschatology* (London, 1971), 70–71. Corpus Christi processions were sometimes also accompanied by hymns taken from the Palm Sunday liturgy, such as *Rex venit*. See Rubin, 246.

76. This is best demonstrated by Gordon Kipling's *Enter the King*.

77. Rubin, 259; also see Guenée and Lehoux, 5–8; and, for example, Sarah Hanley, *The Lit De Justice of the Kings of France: Constitutional Ideology in Legend, Ritual, and Discourse* (Princeton, 1983), 41.

78. See Kantorowicz, *King's Two Bodies*, 430. At this juncture, one might speculate as to the origins of the thaumaturgic qualities associated with the French monarchy. Could it be that the analogous positions of kings, relics, and Eucharist within a family of contiguous rituals associated with the "real presence" of the holy betokened the direct transposition and correlation of the attributes associated with divine power to those charged with secular authority? If this were the case, we could more clearly ascertain the origin of those thaumaturgic qualities most commonly displayed by French kings at the time of their joyous entries by noting the similar powers that relics manifested at the time of their translations. Similarly, one could also perhaps link the tradition of the royal freeing/pardoning of prisoners at the time of a king's royal entry to a similar custom practiced at the arrival of relics and the host, for as prefigurations of the second coming, their arrival announced a kind of general amnesty and pardon—a reintegration of all the disparate elements of a city into an ideal community, symbolically manifested by the inclusion of freed prisoners in the entry processions. With regard to the pardoning of prisoners at the time of royal entry festivals see Natalie Zemon Davis, *Fiction in the Archives: Pardon Tales and their Tellers in Sixteenth-Century France* (Cambridge, 1987), and Lawrence Bryant, *The King*

and the City in the Parisian Royal Entry Ceremony: Politics, Ritual, and Art in the Renais-sance (Geneva, 1986), 25; with regard to freeing prisoners for the arrival of relics see Brown, *Cult of the Saints*, 100. On Henri II's pardon of criminals at the time of his Rouen entry, see M.-N. Baudouin-Matuszek (ed.), *Catalogue des actes de Henri II, année 1550* (Paris, 1994), 4: 192 (7173).

79. See Kantorowicz, "'King's Advent'," 211.

80. Michael McCormick, *Eternal Victory: Triumphal Rulership in Late Antiquity, Byzantium, and the Early Medieval West* (Cambridge and Paris, 1990), 182.

81. Ibid., for example, 40, 45–46, 60–63, 73, 189–191.

82. It is interesting to note an apparently distinct indigenous tradition among the Gauls that considered the severed heads of defeated enemies as sacred booty. These heads, along with other "relics" of victorious battle, including weapons, shields, etc., would be taken to a special place and dedicated to the gods. Entirely removed from the human exchange system, they became sacrosanct property; contact with them was forbidden under the threat of painful death.

83. On the use of comparative anthropological evidence, see Marc Bloch, *Royal Touch*, 29–30.

84. Robert Hertz, *Death and the Right Hand*, trans. R. and C. Needham, intro. E. E. Evans-Pritchard (London, 1960), 40.

85. Likewise, relics were thought to have special powers in this regard. They were displayed in ritual processions before going to battle, and incorporated into weapons, armor, and standards. Constantine, for example, had relics built into his war helmet and into his horse's harness. See McCormick, 357.

86. Annalina Caló Levi, *Barbarians on Roman Imperial Coins and Sculpture* (New York, 1952), 7.

87. Ibid., 38.

88. Ibid., 40.

89. M. Mauss, "A Category of the Human Mind: The Notion of the Person, the Notion of Self," in M. Carrithers, S. Collins, S. Lukes (eds.), *The Category of the Person: Anthropology, Philosophy, History*, trans. W. D. Halls (Cambridge, 1985), 16; also see Ginzburg, "Répresentation," 1224.

90. McCormick, *Eternal Victory*, 21–22.

91. Regarding the notion of ritual equivalence and the positing of an absent—or desired—third term, see A. M. Hocart, *Kings and Councilors: An Essay in the Comparative Anatomy of Human Society* (Chicago and London, 1970), 46–47.

92. Take for example the deeply ambivalent comments of Seneca on the Germans (354–367). On the one hand, he describes them "after the manner of lions and wolves . . . free by reason of their wildness. . . . Just as they cannot submit themselves to governance, so they are incapable of governing; for the force that they possess is not that of a human being, but of something wild and intractable" (*De ira*, II, xv). On the other hand, he describes them in terms of a happy self-sufficiency (*De providentia*, IV, 14–15), or idealizes them as a true and natural nobility. Thus he describes the Chauci as "the noblest people among the Germans, a people which prefers that

its greatness be sustained by justice. Without greed . . . peaceful and reserved, they never provoke war, nor are they busied with rapine and pillage. The most conspicuous proof of their courage and their strength is that in order to be victors they do not employ wrongful means. Yet their arms are always ready and, if affairs demand it, their armies as well, with a large number of men and horses. And their renown is undiminished when they are at peace" (XXXV). Cited in A. Lovejoy and G. Boas, *Primitivism and Related Ideas in Antiquity* (New York, 1935), 287–367. See also Mircea Éliade, "Le Myth du bon sauvage," *Nouvelle revue française* 32 (August, 1955): 229–249, 231.

93. Ibid.

94. As Bernheimer puts this: "The existence in literature of figures such as these, whose wildness in their formative years is the cause or condition of their later eminence, affords us a first glimpse of an evaluation of wild-man life, not in terms of its imperfections as compared with civilized practice, but of superiority" (19). Like Hercules (discussed in Chapter 3), the figure of the wild man demarcated a discursive field in which the normative values of elites could be negotiated and/or contested. It is thus perhaps not surprising that Hercules, carrying a club and clad in the skin of a lion, was also associated with the wild man, as for example in the fourteenth-century miniature accompanying Seneca's *Hercules Furens*, where he is shown "as a beast with tail and claws on his feet, yet standing upright and endowed with human hands." See R. Bernheimer, *Wild Men in the Middle Ages: A Study in Art, Sentiment, and Demonology* (Cambridge, MA, 1952), 101–102; also see O. Dickason, "The Concept of *l'homme sauvage* and early French colonialism in the Americas," in *Revue française d'histoire d'outre-mer* 64/234 (1977): 16. Moreover, it should be noted that the figure of Hercules, as God-man-savage, was not simply a model of kingship in the sixteenth century but was of central importance to the entire Graeco-Roman tradition of rulership, "down to the divinization of the Roman emperor on the pyre whence he rises to the Gods, *Herculis ritu.*" See Walter Burkert, *Structure and History in Greek Mythology and Ritual* (Berkeley and Los Angeles, 1979), especially his chapter, "Heracles and the Master of Animals," 78–98, quotation at 98.

95. Jean Froissart, *Chronicles of England, France and Spain and the Adjoining Countries,* trans. J. Bourchier (London, 1924), part 2, 419. Also see Timothy Husband, *The Wild Man: Medieval Myth and Symbolism* (New York, 1980), 148–149; and Bernheimer, 67.

96. The origins of Charles' insanity in his experience as a wild man conform to commonplace narratives having to do with mortals who visit the world of the dead; for a (perhaps) related example see Jean-Claude Schmitt, *Ghosts in the Middle Ages: The Living and the Dead in Medieval Society,* trans. T. L. Fagan (Chicago, 1998), 111–112; regarding the relationship between madness and death for a slightly later period see Claude Blum, *La Représentation de la mort dans la littérature française de la Renaissance* (Paris, 1989), 85–186; on the relationship between wild men and insanity see Husband, 7–8.

97. On the *charivari*, also see Natalie Zemon Davis, "The Reasons of Misrule," in *Society and Early Modern Culture in Early Modern France: Eight Essays* (Stanford, 1975), 97–124.

98. Gervais du Bus, *Le Roman de Fauvel* (Paris, 1914–1919), 164–167; also see Carlo Ginzburg, "Charivari, associations juvéniles, chasses sauvages," in J. Le Goff and J.-C. Schmitt (eds.), *Le Charivari* (Paris and New York, 1981), 133; Schmitt, 164–169; Anonymous, "The Evolution of Harlequin," *Quarterly Review* 196 (1902): 462–482, 467–468.

99. Bernheimer, 66; Schmitt, 165; and Ginzburg, "Charivari," 135. *Barboeres* is translated by Schmitt as "savages."

100. *Le Roman de Fauvel*, quoted in Schmitt, 164.

101. Schmitt, 120. It is perhaps significant, given Schmitt's argument regarding Hellequin's place in the *speculum principis* tradition, and my own regarding the significance of the eloquent savage Hercules as a model of kingship in the sixteenth century, to note that whilst many scholars trace Hellequin's name to the Graeco-Roman demon Orcus, to the storm God Wodan, or to the Scandinavian Elf-king, Erlkönig, Allardyce Nicoll has suggested that the medieval Herlechinus was a corruption of the name Herculinus, a suggestion which derives added force from Hellequin's physical stature and from his ever-present club. Also significant in this regard is the frequent association of Hellequin's name with Charles VI's father, Charles Quint. See Allardyce Nicoll, *Masks, Mimes and Miracles: Studies in the Popular Theatre* (New York, 1963), 268–269; Anonymous, "The Evolution of Harlequin"; and Schmitt, 114.

102. M. Bakhtin, *Rabelais and His World*, trans. H. Iswolsky (Bloomington, 1984), 392 (my emphasis).

103. That is, insofar as the triumph was a ritual of renewal and rebirth integrally related, in its most ancient form, with agricultural fertility rites.

104. Carlo Ginzburg, *Ecstasies: Deciphering the Witches' Sabbath*, trans. R. Rosenthal (London, 1990); on the deep roots of the abilities ascribed to animals to ritually "establish communication between the visible and the invisible . . . ," see 260–263.

105. This was also clearly linked to festivals of renewal, new years' festivals, and the like (indeed, the date that Oderic's informant met the *familia Herlechini* was New Year's Day 1091); as Jacques de Voragine said regarding the ancient Roman celebrations of the new year, people take "des formes monstrueuses; les uns se revêtaient de peaux d'animaux, d'autres mettaient des têtes de bêtes, et ils prouvaient par là qu'ils n'avaient pas seulement l'apparence de bêtes, mais qu'ils en avaient le fond." See Jacques de Voragine, *La Légende Dorée*, trans. B. Roze (Paris, 1967), 1: 113, cited in Marie-Christine Pouchelle, "Des peaux de bêtes et des fourrures. Histoire médiévale d'une fascination," in *Le temps de la réflexion* 2 (1981): 403–438, 411.

106. Ginzburg, "Charivari," 134, and *Ecstasies*, 191.

107. Bernheimer, 73; regarding the relationship between the Hellequin and Orcus, the Italic god of death and the underworld, see ibid., 64.

108. Dickason, 24.

109. Ibid.

110. Ibid., and Bernheimer, 65–66.

111. Dickason, my emphasis; on the imagery of trampling and its relationship to the triumph, see Chapter 5.

112. See Schmitt, 175.

113. See Guenée and Lehoux, 66, 145, 239, and 289; and Bernheimer, 69–70.

114. T. Comito, "Renaissance Gardens and the Discovery of Paradise," *Journal of the History of Ideas* 32:4 (1971): 483–506. See also Kipling, 235–236.

115. See Elie Konigson, "Le Masque du démon, phantasme et metamorphoses sur la scène médiévale," in O. Aslan and D. Babet, eds., *Le Masque du rite au théâtre* (Paris, 1985), 103–117, especially, 112–113.

116. Scheller, "Gallia cisalpina," 45.

117. Mitchell, *Majesty*, 86.

118. Charles de Bourgueville, *Les Recherches et antiquitez de la province de Neustrie, à present duché de Normandie, comme des villes remarquables d'icelle, mais plus speciallement de la ville et Université de Caen* (Caen, 1588), fol. 03.

119. Albert Babeau, *Les Rois de France à Troyes au XVIe siècle* (Troyes, 1880), 48 (my emphasis).

120. Ibid., 57.

121. Ibid.

122. Ibid. Clearly this was not a spontaneous addition by Troyes' Conards, but an official part of the entry's program.

123. See Chapter 2 for details regarding Auber and the people from the New World he brought to Rouen.

124. Louis Le Gendre, *Vie du Cardinal d'Amboise premier ministre de Louis XII . . .* (Amsterdam, 1726), 371.

125. On the merging of the categories of the wild man and the New World "savage," see Dickason, especially 17–22; François Ganon, "Le thème médiéval de l'homme sauvage dans les premières représentations des Indiens d'Amérique," in G.-H. Allard (ed.), *Aspects de la marginalité au Moyen Age* (Montreal, 1975), 83–99; Susi Colin, "The Wild Man and the Indian in Early 16th Century Book Illustration," in C. Feest (ed.), *Indians and Europe: An Interdisciplinary Collection of Essays* (Aachen, 1987), 5–36.

126. According to Dickason, Titus Saturn, who reigned over a Golden Age of innocence and purity, but who was also a cannibal who ate all but three of his own children, was closely associated with the wild man in Roman mythology. See Dickason, 15.

127. "The age of gold, which flourished before the silver, the iron and the bronze, by the virtues of a king will rise into the world and begin to live again." *Cest la deduction*, fol. M iii (v°).

128. Masselin, fol. C; according to *Cest la deduction*, fol. M iii (r°), they were sibyls.

129. On the close relationship between satyrs and wild men, see Lynn Frier Kaufmann, *The Noble Savage: Satyrs and Satyr Families in Renaissance Art* (Ann Arbor, 1984).

130. Thus, for example, for the entry of Henry II into Lyon in 1548, at the Gate of Bourgneuf, just before the king was placed under the sacred canopy carried by the city's oldest and most respected councilors (and thus, just before he was put in

the same ritual role as that occupied by the entering Eucharist), he was met by a group of satyrs—magical beings: half man, half animal, covered with hair and with the feet and horns of goats. *La Magnificence de la superbe et triumphante entree de la noble & antique Cité de Lyon* . . . , 37.

131. On the king's device see *Devises heroiques et emblemes de M. Claude Paradin* (Paris, 1621, originally 1557), 18–20. Robert Scheller makes a similar point in regard to Charles VIII's entry into Rouen, see "Imperial themes," 17.

Chapter 8

1. Michel Jeanneret, "The Vagaries of Exemplarity: Distortion or Dismissal?" *Journal of the History of Ideas* 59:4 (October 1998): 565–579, 578.

2. *Cest la deduction*, fol. I ii (v°).

3. See Denise Despres, *Ghostly Sights: Visual Meditation in Late-Medieval Literature* (Norman, 1989), 29–30. Perhaps worth noting here is that a king's (Christ's) entry in state was one of the images that Loyola set out in his *Spiritual Exercises* as a means of focusing the contemplative mind's eye.

4. Ibid., 32. On the transformation of consciousness during and after a performance see Richard Schechner, *Between Theater & Anthropology* (Philadelphia, 1985), 9, and especially 117–150.

5. Ibid., 28.

6. On the place of the *exemplum* in early modern culture, see John D. Lyons, *Exemplum: The Rhetoric of Example in Early Modern France and Italy* (Princeton, 1989), especially his introduction, 3–34.

7. *Cest la deduction*, fol. A ii (r°).

8. See Mary Carruthers, *The Book of Memory: A Study of Memory in Medieval Culture* (Cambridge, 1990), 245.

9. Lyons, 26–7.

10. On the role of singular wonders in mediating universal truths as seen through Renaissance interpretations of Aristotelian poetics, see Baxter Hathaway, *Marvels and Commonplaces: Renaissance Literary Criticism* (Ithaca, 1968), 57–87.

11. See Carlo Ginzburg "High and Low: The Theme of Forbidden Knowledge in the Sixteenth and Seventeenth Centuries," in *Clues, Myths, and the Historical Method*, trans. J. Tedeschi and A. C. Tedeschi (Baltimore and London, 1989); and L. Daston and K. Park, *Wonders and the Order of Nature 1150–1750* (New York, 1998), for example, 110–133.

12. Singularities were charged with mysterious and troubling ambiguity. As expressions of Nature's irregularity, they were considered problems to be shunned, solved, or ignored. For scholastic Aristotelians true knowledge could only be based upon unchanging regularity, not on the shifting world of particular phenomena. Empiricism, for them, rested on the desire to normalize the contingent (singular aspects of experience) relative to universals. Similarly, Neo-Platonic and Hermetic philosophy aimed to discover the hidden—occult—bonds connecting the world's disparate phenomena into a coherent order. Yet, there were also alternative ways of

looking at the world that reserved an important role for the singular, marvelous, and wondrous. This was particularly the case for the designers of court *fêtes*, who were, in general, not only antiquarians but also poets (e.g., Chappuys, Scève, Dorat, Ronsard, to name only a few). Indeed, according to Aristotle's *Poetics* "Poetry is more philosophical and more serious than history. Poetry tends to express universals, and history particulars." Whereas history was thought to focus on singularities—i.e., particular events and personages—poetry, by contrast, was considered a means of expressing universals through the eloquent arrangement of particulars. On the role of singularities and Aristotelian poetics see Hathaway, 55; and Stephen Greenblatt, *Marvelous Possessions: The Wonder of the New World* (Chicago, 1991), 79.

13. On collecting *copia* see Lyons, 17–18; also see Terrence Cave, *The Cornucopian Text: Problems of Writing in the French Renaissance* (Oxford, 1979), especially 5–6.

14. See, for example, Anthony Grafton, *Bring Out Your Dead: The Past as Revelation* (Cambridge, MA, 2001), "The New Science and the Traditions of Humanism," 97–117.

15. K. Pomian, *Collectors and Curiosities: Paris and Venice, 1500–1800*, trans. E. Wiles-Portier (Cambridge 1990), 84.

16. P. Mason, "From Presentation to Representation: Americana in Europe," in *Journal of the History of Collections* 6 (1994): 1–20, 6; and Pomian, *Collectors*, especially chapter 1.

17. It is interesting to note, in this context, that the first "collections" belonged not to men, but to the dead or to the gods. The connection is even more direct insofar as the collections—in the form of captured booty, the heads of enemies, etc.—were associated with military victories and displayed during triumphal entries. Such objects were considered the sacred possessions of the gods and referred directly to the triumphator's status as their representative on earth. See Pomian, *Collectors*, 14–15. Also see A. Reinach, "Les Têtes coupées et les trophées en Gaule," *Revue celtique* (1913): 38–60, 253–286.

18. Michel de Certeau makes a similar argument with regard to *The Garden of Delights* by Hieronymous Bosch, see *The Mystic Fable*, trans. Michael B. Smith (Chicago, 1992), 55.

19. BMR, A. 16, *délibération*, fol. 93 (r°).

20. Pomian, *Collectors*, 69. On early modern collecting also see P. Findlen, *Possessing Nature: Museums, Collecting, and Scientific Culture in Early Modern Italy* (Berkeley and Los Angeles, 1994); G. Olmi, "Science-Honor-Metaphor: Italian Cabinets of the 16th and 17th Centuries," in O. Impey and A. MacGregor (eds.), *The Origin of Museums: The Cabinet of Curiosities in Sixteenth- and Seventeenth-Century Europe* (Oxford, 1985).

21. It is perhaps not a coincidence that Francis Bacon employed the triumph to express the social, economic, and political power of his great instauration. Accordingly, when his weary travelers landed on the isle of Bensalem and were taken to Solomon's House, they there witnessed a grand triumphal entry (a "coming in state"), not of kings or emperors, but of art, science, and industry, as represented by

one of the Fathers of Solomon's House riding on his chariot accompanied by all the "officers and principals of the Companies of the City." See the *Works of Francis Bacon*, eds. J. Spedding, R. L. Ellis and D. D. Heath (London, 1857), 3:154–155.

22. See, for example, Stephen Orgel, *The Illusion of Power: Political Theater in the English Renaissance* (Berkeley and Los Angeles, 1975), 1–36.

23. F. Lestringant, "Fictions de l'espace brésilien à la Renaissance: L'exemple de Guanabara," in F. Lestringant and J. Christian (eds.), *Arts et légendes d'espaces: figures du voyage et rhétoriques du monde* (Paris, 1981), 205–256: 207.

24. See Olmi, 5.

25. See Tony Bennett, *The Birth of the Museum* (London, 1995), 35.

26. C. Beaune, *Naissance de la nation France* (Paris, 1985); W. J. Bouwsma, *Concordia Mundi: The Career and Thought of Guillaume Postel (1510–1581)* (Cambridge, MA, 1957); A.-M. Lecoq, *François Ier imaginaire. Symbolique et politique à l'aube de la Renaissance française* (Paris, 1987); J. Strayer, "France: The Holy Land, the Chosen People, and the Most Christian King," in T. Rabb and J. Seigel (eds.), *Action and Conviction in Early Modern Europe: Essays in Memory of E. H. Harbison* (Princeton, 1969), 3–16; and F. Yates, *Astrea: The Imperial Theme in the Sixteenth Century* (London, 1975), especially 121–126.

27. That this distance was mediated by medieval and humanist learning does nothing to diminish the relativistic shock that it engendered. On "historical perspective," see the classic article by Erwin Panofsky and Fritz Saxl, "Classical Mythology in Mediaeval Art," *Metropolitan Museum Studies* 4 (1933): 228–280, especially, 274–278.

28. Insofar as possession (of the actual objects or of the kinds of knowledge that pertained to them) redounded to the power of those who came into contact with them, the dangers they presented—i.e., that the world was composed of discrete singularities detached from binding universal laws—could be dispelled; that is, they could be anchored to seemingly "fixed" points in the constellation of early modern social relations, the apex of which was, of course, the king.

29. See P. Rossi, "Society, Culture, and the Dissemination of Learning," in S. Pumfrey, P. Rossi, and M. Slawinski (eds), *Science, Culture and Popular Belief in Renaissance Europe* (Manchester, 1991), especially 162–164; on pansophism see R. J. W. Evans, *Rudolph II and his World: A Study in Intellectual History, 1576–1612* (Oxford, 1973); and also A. Jouanna, *Ordre social: mythes et hiérarchies dans la France du XVIe siècle* (Poitiers, 1977), 440–451.

30. Natalie Zemon Davis, *Society and Culture in Early Modern France: Eight Essays* (Stanford, 1975), 129.

31. On the distribution of identity and cognitive competencies see Hélène Mialet, "Do Angels Have Bodies: The Cases of William X and Mr. Hawking," *Social Studies of Science* 29:4 (1999): 551–582.

32. See Chapter 3.

33. It is worth noting, in the light of Foucault's argument in *The Order of Things: An Archaeology of the Human Sciences* (London, 1970), that the objects collected in cabinets were defined less by any systematic regulating principle—the prose of the

world, to use his well-known phrase—than by a heteroglossic interaction of competing, complementary, and contingently available discourses. See, for example, Anthony Grafton's *Cardano's Cosmos: The Worlds and Works of a Renaissance Astrologer* (Cambridge, MA, 2000), 176–177; and Ian Maclean, "Foucault's Renaissance Episteme Reassessed: An Aristotelian Counterblast" in *Journal of the History of Ideas* 59 (1998): 149–166; also see S. Hanley, *The Lit De Justice of the Kings of France: Constitutional Ideology in Legend, Ritual and Discourse* (Princeton, 1983), 143. Alasdair MacIntyre put it well: "In any given social situation it is frequently the case that many different transactions are taking place at one and the same time between members of the same group. Not one game is being played, but several, and, if the game metaphor may be stretched further, the problem about real life is that moving one's knight to QB3 may always be replied to with a lob across the net." *After Virtue: A Study in Moral Theory* (Notre Dame, 1981), 93–94.

34. This decontextualization is a common feature of objects in collections; see, for example, Philip Fisher, *Making and Effacing Art: Modern American Art in a Culture of Museums* (Oxford, 1991).

35. On the relation of collections to identity formation, see S. Stewart, *On Longing: Narratives of the Miniature, the Gigantic, the Souvenir, the Collection* (Baltimore, 1984), 162; and also J. Tribby "Body/Building: Living the Museum Life in Early Modern Europe," *Rhetorica* 10 (1992): 139–163.

36. With specific regard to natural philosophy, see L. Daston, "Curiosity in Early Modern Science," in *Word & Image* 2/4 (October–December, 1995): 391–404: 402; and Daston and Park, 153, 170, passim.

37. Though addressing a different context, i.e., England during the Restoration, see Steven Shapin and Simon Schaffer, *Leviathan and the Air-pump: Hobbes, Boyle, and the Experimental Life* (Princeton, 1985).

38. *Calendar of State Papers* (Spanish), 1550–1552, 10, 182, quoted in Mullaney, "Strange Things," in S. Greenblatt (ed.), *Representing the English Renaissance* (Berkeley and Los Angeles, 1988), 71 and 90 n. 14.

39. It is important to note that in a certain very specific sense Western "science" has always been dominated by empiricism—not as historically situated discrete events (i.e., singularities/experiments), but as established—agreed upon—observations about the way nature usually behaves. See Peter Dear, *Discipline and Experience: The Mathematical Way in the Scientific Revolution* (Chicago, 1995), 20–21.

40. My emphasis. Cited in Hanley, 105–106. William Bouwsma, for example, has pointed out the pervasiveness of such attitudes amongst those trained in law. See his "Lawyers in Early Modern Culture," in *The American Historical Review* 78:2 (April, 1973): 303–327.

41. Thus, for example, Ong describes the "typographic culture" of the Renaissance as a "silent maneuvering of objects [e.g., words] in a spatial field. . . . " See W. J. Ong, "From Allegory to Diagram in the Renaissance Mind: A Study in the Significance of the Allegorical Tableau," in *The Journal of Aesthetics & Art Criticism* 17/4 (1959): 424–440, passim.

42. Antonio de Guevara, *Le favori de court, contenant plusieurs advertissemens et bonnes doctrines pour les favoris des princes, et autres Seigneurs et Gentilshommes qui hantent la Court*, trans. Iaques de Rochemore (Anvers, 1557), 135.

43. Pierre Fabri, *Le Grant et vray art de pleine rethorique*, for example, 2: 2.

44. Fabri, 1: 21.

45. See, for example, Stewart, 155.

46. Cited and translated in Jody Enders's *Rhetoric and the Origins of Medieval Drama* (Ithaca, 1992), 48. Enders translates *cabinet royal* as royal office. The context indicates that de Pibrac was speaking here of a cabinet of curiosities. The emphasis is mine.

47. See Anthony Grafton and Lisa Jardine, *From Humanism to the Humanities: Education and the Liberal Arts in Fifteenth- and Sixteenth-Century Europe* (Cambridge, MA, 1986), 136, and especially, 122–157. On the decontextualization of language and its epistemic significance, see W. Ong, *The Presence of the Word: Some Prolegomena for Cultural and Religious History* (New Haven, 1967), 17–92; J. Goody, *The Domestication of the Savage Mind* (Cambridge, 1977), 37–73; M. Slaughter, *Universal Languages and Scientific Taxonomy in the Seventeenth Century* (Cambridge, 1982), 38–48; Bruno Latour, "Visualization and Cognition," in *Knowledge and Society* 6 (1986): 1–40; Z. S. Schiffman, *On the Threshold of Modernity: Relativism in the French Renaissance* (Baltimore and London, 1991), 1–24; and A. Blair, *The Theater of Nature: Jean Bodin and Renaissance Science* (Princeton, 1997), 65–82.

48. See, for example, Timothy J. Reiss, *Knowledge, Discovery and Imagination in Early Modern Europe: The Rise of Aesthetic Rationalism* (Cambridge, 1997), 31; and A. L. Gordon, "The Ascendancy of Rhetoric and the Struggle for Poetic in Sixteenth-Century France," in J. J. Murphy (ed.), *Renaissance Eloquence: Studies in the Theory and Practice of Renaissance Rhetoric* (Berkeley and Los Angeles, 1983), 376–384.

49. *Approbacion et confirmacion*, x. See also, Ch. Ouin-Lacroix, *Histoire des anciennes corporations d'arts et métiers et des confréries Religieuses de la capitale de la Normandie* (Rouen, 1850), 463. Each of the 72 was required to pay 70 *sols tournois* a year, and another 100 on the day of his inauguration.

50. See G. P. Norton, *The Ideology and Language of Translation in Renaissance France and their Humanist Antecedents* (Geneva, 1984), 9.

51. BN, Ms. fr. 379, fol. 8 (r°).

52. Fabri, 1:15; see also Reiss, 56.

53. See the prologue of P. Benedict, *Rouen During the Wars*. More generally, on the importance of processions, see Edward Muir, *Civic Ritual in Renaissance Venice* (Princeton, 1981), 185–211; Robert Schneider, *The Ceremonial City: Toulouse Observed 1738–1780* (Princeton, 1995), 113–147; and Richard C. Trexler, *Public Life in Renaissance Florence* (Ithaca, 1980), passim.

54. Quoted in M. T. Hodgen, *Early Anthropology in the Sixteenth and Seventeenth Centuries* (Philadelphia, 1964), 399–400.

55. J. Dewald, *The Formation of a Provincial Nobility: The Magistrates of the Parliament of Rouen, 1499–1610* (Princeton, 1980), 100–101.

56. This procession was described as following "a solemn order." Whereas today the word solemn is defined as pertaining to serious and dignified, in the sixteenth-

century it referred to assemblies or processions where "rank and order [were] observed and assigned to each" participating group. The words are du Tillet's and are quoted in Hanley, 107–108.

57. *Cest la deduction*, fol. B iii (v°)–B iv (r°).

58. Ibid., fol. B iv (r°).

59. BMR, A. 16, *délibérations*, fol. 111 (r°); the parade of occupations continues on fol. 111 (v°); I have, for the most part, employed Benedict's excellent English translation of these often obscure occupations though I have reordered them to conform to their order of appearance in the entry.

60. Fabri, 1:17.

61. There is a clear relationship between linguistic fashionability and other outward markers of social distinction. On the importance of clothing in this regard see D. O. Hughes, "Regulating Women's Fashion," in George Duby and Michelle Perrot (eds.), *A History of Women in the West*, volume 2, Christine Klapisch-Zuber (ed.), *Silences of the Middle Ages* (Cambridge, MA, 1992), 136–158; Jouanna, 89 and 93. Regarding speech and social performativity see M. Bakhtin, *The Dialogic Imagination*, trans. M. Holquist and C. Emerson (Austin, 1981); and idem, *Speech Genres and Other Late Essays,* ed. C. Emerson and M. Holquist, trans. V. W. McGee (Austin, 1986), especially 132–172. Also see, for example, Henri Estienne's biting satire of courtly affectations, *Deux dialogues du nouveau langage françois* (Geneva, 1578), 43–61 and 231–232.

62. For a more detailed exposition regarding the extension of this argument to natural history, see Wintroub, "Taking Stock at the End of the World: Rites of Distinction and Practices of Collecting in Early Modern Europe," *Studies in History and Philosophy of Science*, 30: 3 (September 1999), especially 412–416. This is also suggested by Schiffman, 10; Jouanna, 108; and by Hodgen, 124–125, who notes that a "linkage appears to have existed . . . between the study of flora and fauna and the study of language or folklore." She cites the example of Conrad Gesner, who wrote the most widely read of all natural histories in the early modern period and who was also a linguist and author of a *Universal dictionary* (1545); see W. B. Ashworth, "Emblematic Natural History of the Renaissance," in N. Jardine, J. Secord, and E. Spary (eds.), *Cultures of Natural History* (Cambridge, 1996), 17–37: 17.

63. W. B. Ashworth, "Natural History and the Emblematic World View," in D. Lindberg and R. Westman (eds.), *Reappraisals of the Scientific Revolution* (Cambridge, 1990), 302–332: 309; also see Blair, 154.

64. Though one pole of this response, as I argue here, encompassed new forms of empiricism—i.e., collecting practices, antiquarianism, etc.,—the other led to the seventeenth-century embrace—and reform—of mathematics. In this regard, see Reiss, especially parts 2 and 3. Also see, for example, Amir Alexander, "The Imperialist Space of Elizabethan Mathematics," *Studies in History and Philosophy of Science* 26 (1995): 559–591; Mario Biagioli, "The Social Status of Italian Mathematicians, 1450–1600," *History of Science* 27 (1989): 41–95 and idem, *Galileo, Courtier: The Practice of Science in the Culture of Absolutism* (Chicago, 1993); and Robert Westman, "Proof, Poetics, and Patronage: Copernicus's Preface to *De revolutionibus*," in Westman and

Lindberg (eds.) *Reappraisals of the Scientific Revolution* (Cambridge, 1990), 167–205 and idem, "The Astronomer's Role in the Sixteenth Century: A Preliminary Study," *History of Science* 18 (1980): 105–147.

65. See Reiss, for example, 48.

66. See Chapter 6; also see Jouanna, 133–134.

67. *Cest la deduction*, fol. K ii (r°).

68. On the rhetoric of anti-rhetoric, and in particular, on the trope of enargeia, see Wintroub, "The Looking Glass of Facts: Collecting, Rhetoric and Citing the Self in the Experimental Natural Philosophy of Robert Boyle," in *History of Science* 35 (1997): 189–217. Also see Thomas M. Greene, "Ritual and Text in the Renaissance," in the *Canadian Review of Comparative Literature* (June/September, 1991): 179–197, 182.

69. See especially Pauline Smith's *The Anti-Courtier Trend in Sixteenth-Century French Literature* (Geneva, 1966), passim.

70. See J. Céard, *La nature et les prodiges. L'insolite au XVIᵉ siècle* (Geneva 1996), 196. In a similar vein, Daston and Park note (202) that by the seventeenth century, "monsters inspired repugnance because they violated the standards of regularity and decorum not only in nature, but also in society and the arts." The parvenu was just such a monster. The new men, it seems, had closed their ranks.

71. See Joachim du Bellay, *La Deffence et illustration de la langue Françoyse* (Paris, 1549), 108–109.

72. Jean de Léry, *History of a Voyage to the Land of Brazil, otherwise called America . . .*, trans. Janet Whatley (Berkeley, 1990), lxi.

73. Ibid., xliii.   74. Ibid., lxii.

75. Ibid., lxi.   76. Ibid., lx.

77. Cited in H. Haydn, *The Counter Renaissance* (New York, 1950), 483. In this sense, the symmetry pointed out earlier (Chapter 6) between the simple laborer who serves as Montaigne's informant at the beginning of his essay "The Cannibals" and the Indian's capacity for pointing out French barbarity and hypocrisy at the essay's end, is no coincidence. His joke, but they have no clothes, is less a joke than a quite serious point about the nature and capacity for truth-telling.

78. G. Canguilhem, *The Normal and the Pathological*, trans. C. Fawcett and R. Cohen (New York, 1989), 244.

Coda

1. Victor Turner, *The Ritual Process: Structure and Anti-Structure* (Chicago, 1969), 65.

2. See C. Geertz, "Kings, Centers and Charisma," in *Local Knowledge: Further Essays in Interpretive Anthropology* (New York, 1983).

3. Edmund Leach, *Political Systems of Highland Burma: A Study of Kachin Social Structure* (Boston, 1965), 15.

4. See, in particular, Norbert Elias, *The Court Society* (New York, 1975); J.-M. Apostolidès, *Le Roi-machine: spectacle et politique au temps de Louis XIV* (Paris, 1981); Louis Marin, *Portrait of the King* (Minneapolis, 1988); and Peter Burke, *The Fabrication of Louis XIV* (New Haven, 1992). Also see Alan Boureau, "Ritualité politique et

modernité monarchique," in N. Bulst, R. Descimon, and A. Guerreau (eds), *L'État ou le roi. Les fondations de la modernité monarchique en France (XIVe-XVIIe siècles)* (Paris, 1992), 9–25.

5. D. R. Kelley, *Foundations of Modern Historical Scholarship. Language, Law, and History in the French Renaissance* (New York and London, 1979), 23.

6. See, for example, B. Mitchell, *The Majesty of the State: Triumphal Progresses of Foreign Sovereigns in Renaissance Italy (1494–1600)* (Florence, 1986); V. E. Graham, "The Triumphal Entry in Sixteenth Century France," in *Renaissance and Reformation* 10: 3 ns (1986): 237–257; R. Scheller, "Imperial Themes in Art and Literature of the Early French Renaissance: The Period of Charles VIII," *Simiolus* 12 (1981–1982): 5–69. Henri's 1549 entry, for example, was greatly influenced by Joachim du Bellay's *Deffence et illustration*, and was drafted—at least in part—by the theorist of the French language, and author of the *Art poétique françois*, Thomas Sebillet. Jean Martin, one of the most famed antiquarians of his day, was also involved in the entry—especially with regard to its use of ancient architectural forms, such as the triumphal arches that marked the king's itinerary. See F. Gébelin, "Un Manifeste de l'école néo-classique en 1549: l'Entrée de Henri II à Paris," in *Bulletin de la Société d'histoire de Paris* 51 (1924): 35–45; also V. L. Saulnier, "Sebillet, du Bellay, Ronsard: L'Entrée de Henry II à Paris et la révolution poétique de 1550," in Jacquot, 1: 31–59; also see L. M. Bryant, *The King and the City in the Parisian Royal Entry Ceremony: Politics, Ritual, and Art in the Renaissance* (Geneva, 1986), 65, 130, 133.

7. Along with the antiquary, Guillaume du Choul, author of *Discours de la religion des anciens Romains* (Lyons, 1556).

8. Anonymous, *C'est l'ordre qui a esté tenu à la nouvelle et joyeuse entrée que le Roy tres chrestien Henry deuxiesme de ce nom a faicte en sa bonne ville et cité de Paris* . . . (Paris, 1549), fol. G iii (v°); cited in M. M. McGowan, *Ideal Forms in the Age of Ronsard* (Los Angeles and Berkeley, 1985), 144.

9. *C'est la deduction*, fol. D iii (r°).

10. Cited in McGowan, *Ideal Forms*, 144.

11. See ibid., 144; and R. C. Strong, *Art and Power*, 81–82. Also see J. Chartrou, *Les Entrées solennelles et triomphales à la Renaissance, 1484–1551* (Paris, 1928), 130. Whether or not this was the case, the Rouen entry clearly pointed toward the antique flavor of later entries, for example, Charles IX's entry into Paris in 1571, designed by Ronsard and his teacher, the most eminent classicist of his day, Jean Dorat; see F. A. Yates, *Astrea: The Imperial Theme in the Sixteenth Century* (London, 1975), 127–148.

12. See Kelley, 24.

13. Oberman, *The Impact of the Reformation: Essays* (Grand Rapids, 1994), 11.

14. Ibid., 10; and also Francis Oakley, *Omnipotence, Covenant and Order* (Ithaca, 1984), 93–118.

15. D. R. Kelley, *Foundations*, 199 and passim.

16. On du Tillet's commission to write a history of royal entries for François I (c. 1530), see Bryant, *King*, 63 n. 47; on Du Tillet's method, see S. Hanley, *The Lit De Justice of the Kings of France.: Constitutional Ideology in Legend, Ritual and Discourse* (Princeton, 1983), for example, 120, 343. See especially du Tillet's comments quoted in Chapter 8.

17. See Oberman, *Impact*, 20.

18. See, for example, Pierre du Colombier, "Les Triomphes en images de l'empereur Maximilien Ier," in Jacquot, 2: 99–112.

19. See Larry Silver, "Paper Pageants: The Triumphs of Emperor Maximilian I," in B. Wisch and S. Scott Munshower (eds.), *"All the world's a stage . . . " Art and Pageantry in the Renaissance and Baroque* (University Park, 1990), 292–332.

20. S. Shapin, "Pump and Circumstance: Robert Boyle's Literary Technology," in *Social Studies of Science* 14 (1984): 481–520.

21. On these rhetorical methods of "painting" with words, see M. Wintroub, "The Looking Glass of Facts: Collecting, Rhetoric and Citing the Self in the Experimental Natural Philosophy of Robert Boyle," *History of Science* 35 (1997). Similar rhetorical tropes, of course, were, employed in travel literature; see, for example, Anthony Pagden, *European Encounters with the New World: From Renaissance to Romanticism* (New Haven and London, 1993), 51–87; and François Hartog, *The Mirror of Herodotus: An Essay on the Representation of the Other*, trans. J. Lloyd (Berkeley, 1988), 260–288. Interestingly, these detailed circumstantial narratives of entries were, despite their implied claims to verisimilitude, representations of an ideal. In other words, they were beautified, redacted, and disciplined representations of the authorial intentions implicit in the scripting of entries that were often lost in their actual performance. Regardless of denials, which in themselves were one of the chief tropes employed in the rhetoric of anti-rhetoric (i.e., "this present text (*escript*) is not sufficiently furnished with proper terms and adorned language to give witness to the entry," *Cest la deduction*, fol I ii [v°]), chroniclers of entries aspired to the rhetorical production of presence. In this sense, a printed account of an entry was a performative act every bit as much as the actual enactment of the entry. However, the metonymic intent of these accounts was mediated by the artist's need to be extolled as author. In other words, there had to be a carefully maintained disjuncture between representation and event if a text was to be *persuasively* verisimilar. The same holds true for the production of such verisimilar tableaux vivants as the living display of Brazil constructed for Henri's entry (or as the attempt to create an entry with the appearance of an antique triumphal victory celebration). To create such "perfect" representations required that one had the requisite skills and authority—e.g., an intimate familiarity with rhetorical techniques, with antiquarian practice, etc., and the groups that gave them sanction. All of which is to say that to be effective as representation, the distinction between presence and text, reality and tableau vivant, had to be recognized and at the same time denied, for it was upon this carefully maintained ambiguity that the author's status depended.

22. I would like to thank Professor Biagioli for pointing this out to me.

23. *Société de l'Histoire de Normandie. Mélanges,* Treizième Série, ed. A. Lestringant and A. Picard (Rouen and Paris, 1937), 7–55; unfortunately, which king and what account we are not told.

24. David Miffant (trans.), Cicero, *S'ensuyt le livre Tulles des Offices, c'est à dire des opérations humaines, vertueuses et honnestes, familiarement, clèrement et selon la vraye sentence*

et intencion de facteur translaté en françoys par honnorable et prudent homme David Miffant,
conseillier et gouverneur de la ville de Dieppe . . . (Paris, 1502).

25. *Le Dialogue de Xenophon . . . nommé le Tyrannicque ou bien Hieron, tourné de grec*
en françoys par Jacques Miffant, de Dieppe . . . , trans. Jacques Miffant (Paris, 1550).

26. As René Demoris has pointed out, the obsession of classical discourse was to
never "utter the place where the king is not." Quoted in Marin, *Portrait,* 10.

27. Bryant, *King,* 205.

28. Ibid.

29. See especially, R. Chartier, *The Cultural Uses of Print in Early Modern France,*
trans. L. Cochrane (Princeton, 1987), 13–31.

30. Bryant, *King,* 204.

31. Sarah Hanley, for example, has argued that those who championed the use of
rhetoric as a methodology in the Parlement of Paris were arguing for a constitutional form of government that bound the king up in an institutional context that
limited his power. The nominalist/empiricist method employed by du Tillet, by contrast, envisaged the king's power as historically unique and not bound by any but
those of his own making. See for example Hanley, 142–143.

32. See the suggestive comments of Oberman, *Impact,* 20.

33. Bryant, *King,* 216.

34. Insofar as there was an implicit teleology leading inexorably from civic ritual
to absolutism, it was as an unintended consequence of cities—and individuals—aiming (in the most general terms) at just the opposite ends, that is, to maintain and
augment the local and municipal power(s) guaranteed by France's "ancient" consti-
tution. But perhaps more important, in the present context, is to note the parallel
between power and knowledge; for in similar fashion, we see here the beginnings of
the distinctions between rhetoric and knowledge, words and things, vain and idle
speech, and the incontrovertibility of material evidence.

Bibliography

Please note that I have not modernized the orthography of sixteenth-century titles, here or in the notes.—M. W.

Manuscript Sources Cited

ARCHIVES COMMUNALES DE ROUEN, BIBLIOTHÈQUE
MUNICIPALE DE ROUEN (BMR)

Série A, *Régistre des délibérations*, A. 13–18.
Ms. Ac, Fonds de l'Académie G1.
Ms. 1060 (Y. 186).
Ms. 1062 (Y. 18).
Ms. 1063 (Y. 16).
Ms. 1064 (Y. 226a).
Ms. 1268 (Y. 28).
Ms. 2677 (Y. 50).
Ms. 2678 (Y. 48).

ARCHIVES DÉPARTEMENTALES DE LA SEINE MARITIME (ADSM), ROUEN

G. 232.
G. 239.
G. 405.
Tabellionage, Série 2E 1, meubles: 3/26/1523.
Tabellionage, Série 2E 1, meubles: 9/22/1529.

Tabellionage, Série 2E 1 meubles: 9/27/1529.
Tabellionage, Série 2E 1 meubles: 12/31/1548.
Tabellionage, Série 2E 1 meubles, 1/22/1555.
Tabellionage, Série 2E 1 meubles: 11/3/1558.
Tabellionage, Série 2E 1 meubles: 12/3/1558.
Tabellionage, Série 2E 1 meubles: 2/13/1560.
Tabellionage, Série 2E 1 meubles: 12/21/1560.
Tabellionage, Série 2E 1 meubles: 1/30/1570.
Tabellionage, Série 2E 2 meubles: 1/14/1576.
Tabellionage, Série 2E 1 meubles: 7/11/1522.
Tabellionage, 2EP 1/335: 8/11/1567.
Tabellionage, 2EP 1/336: 5/6/1568.
Tabellionage, 2EP 1/336: 5/26/1568.
Tabellionage, 2EP 1/337: 11/30/1568.

BIBLIOTHÈQUE DE L'ARSENAL, PARIS

Ms. 6480.
Ms. 5061.

BIBLIOTHÈQUE NATIONALE DE FRANCE (BN), PARIS

Ms. fr. 54.
Ms. fr. 223.
Ms. fr. 224.
Ms. fr. 225.
Ms. fr. 379.
Ms. fr. 594.
Ms. fr. 595.
Ms. fr. 596.
Ms. fr. 1119.
Ms. fr. 1537.
Ms. fr. 1581.
Ms. fr. 1715.
Ms. fr. 1739.
Ms. fr. 2205.
Ms. fr. 2206.
Ms. fr. 2502.
Ms. fr. 2678.
Ms. fr. 2679.
Ms. fr. 5091.
Ms. fr. 19184.
Ms. fr. 19369.
Ms. fr. 22541.
Ms. fr. 24315.

Ms. n.a. fr. 7644.
Ms. n.a. fr. 11679.
Ms. fonds Ital., 548.
Ms. fonds Ital., 552.
Ms. fonds Ital., 553.
Ms. fonds Ital., 1016.
Ms. fonds Ital., 1024.
Ms. fonds Ital., 1025.
Ms. fonds Ital., 1026.

Primary Sources

Aneau, Barthélemy, *Emblèmes d'Alciat* (Lyon, 1549).

Anonymous, *C'est l'ordre qui a esté tenu à la nouvelle et joyeuse entrée que le Roy tres chrestien Henry deuxiesme de ce nom a faicte en sa bonne ville et cité de Paris . . .* (Paris, 1549).

Anonymous, *La Magnificence de la superbe et triumphante entree de la noble & antique cité de Lyon faicte au Treschrestien Roy de France Henry deuxiesme de ce nom, et la Royne Catherine son Espouse le XXIII de septembre M. D. XLVIII* (Lyon, 1549). There is also a facsimile of this text published by Georges Guigue (Lyon, 1927).

Anonymous, *L'Entrée du Roy nostre sire faicte en sa ville de Rouen ce mercredy premier de ce moys d'octobre pareillement celle de la Royne qui fut le jour ensuivant ...* (Paris, 1550). This text was also reproduced with an introduction by A. Beaucousin (Rouen, 1882). It is identified here by the name of its original publisher, Robert Masselin.

Anonymous, *Cest la deduction du Somptueux ordre, plaisantz spectacles et magnifiques theatres dresses et exhibes, par les citoiens de Rouen, ville metropolitaine du pays de Normandie, a la Sacree Majeste du tres Christien Roy de France Henry second leur soverain seigneur, et a tres illustre Dame, Ma Dame, Katherine de Medicis, La Royne son espouse, lors de leur triumphant, joyeulx et nouvel advenement en icelle ville, qui fut es jours de mercredy et jeudy premier et second jour d'octobre, Mil cinq cens cinquante* (Rouen, 1551). There is also a facsimile of this text, introduced by Margaret McGowan, *L'entrée de Henri II à Rouen 1550* (Amsterdam and New York, 1970).

Anonymous, *Les Poutres et figures du sumptueux ordre plaisantz spectacles, et magnifiques theatres dressés et exhibés par les citoiens de Rouen ville metropolitaine du pais de Normandie. Faictz à l'entrée de la sacrée Maiesté du très chretien Roy de France, Henry second, leur souverain Seigneur. Et à tres illustre Dame, ma Dame Katherine de Medicis la Royne, son espouse. Qui fut ès iours de mercredi et ieudi, premier et second iour d'octobre. Mil cinq cens cinquant* (Rouen, 1557).

Anonymous, *Approbation et confirmation par le pape Léon X des statuts et privilèges de la confrérie de l'Immaculée Conception dite Académie des Palinods, instituée à Rouen.* Edited by A. de Bretteville (Rouen, 1615). There is also a nineteenth-century copy of this text introduced by Edouard Frère (Rouen, 1864).

Anonymous, *Epistre envoiée de Paradis au très chrestien roy de France Françoys, premier de ce nom, de par les empereurs Pepin et Charlemaigne . . . 1515,* in *Recueil de poésies françaises des XVe et XVIe siècles* . . . , in Anatole de Montaiglon (ed.), *Recueil de poésies de François des XVe et XVIe siècles* . . . 4 (Paris, 1856).

Anonymous, *L'Entrée du treschrestien et tresvictorieux Roy de France Françoys premier de ce nom faicte en sa bonne ville et cité de Rouen le second jour d'aoust. En l'an de la rédemption humaine Mil cinq cent dix sept* (Rouen, nd). There is a facsimile of this text, introduced by Ch. de Robillard de Beaurepaire, *L'entrée de François Ier roi de France dans la ville de Rouen au mois d'août* (Rouen, 1867).

Anonymous, *L'Entrée du trescrestien et chevaleureux Roy de France . . . en Angiers . . . le vi iour de juing l'an mil v cens xviii* (sl, nd).

Anonymous, *Le Jardin de plaisance et fleur de réthorique* (Paris, 1909).

Bacon, Francis, *Works of Francis Bacon*. Edited by J. Spedding, R. L. Ellis, and D. D. Heath. 3 volumes (London, 1857).

Beaune, Jacques de, *Discours comme une langue vulgaire se peult perpetuer* (Lyon, 1548).

Boccaccio, Giovanni, *De Genealogia Deorum*. Edited by V. Romano (Bari, 1951).

Bouchet, Jean, *Epîtres morales et familières du traverseur*, facsimile of the edition published in Poiters, 1545 (Yorkshire and New York, 1969).

Bourgueville, Charles de, *Les Recherches et antiquitez de la province de Neustrie, à present duché de Normandie, comme des villes remarquables d'icelle, mais plus speciallement de la ville et Université de Caen* (Caen, 1588).

Brantôme, Pierre de Bourdeilles, seigneur de, *Œuvres Complètes du Seigneur de Brantôme. Vies des hommes illustres et capitaines français*. 2 volumes (Paris, 1822).

Bréard, C., and P. Barrey, "Documents relatifs à la marine normande au XVe et XVIe siècles," in *Mélanges Sociales et historiques de Normandie* 6e série (1906): 203–291.

Budé, Guillaume, *De Asse* (Paris, 1532).

Calvin, Jean, *Contre les libertins* (Geneva, 1545).

———, *Épistre contre un certain cordelier suppost de le sect des libertins lequel est prisonnier a Roan* (Geneva, 1547).

Castiglione, Baldesar, *The Book of the Courtier*. Translated by Charles Singleton (New York, 1959).

Catalogue des actes de François Ier (Paris, 1889).

Catalogue des actes de Henri II 2: 1 janvier–31 décembre 1548 (Paris, 1986).

Catalogue des actes de Henri II 3: 1 janvier–31 décembre (Paris, 1990).

Catalogue des actes de Henri II 4: année 1550 (Paris, 1994).

Chappuys, Claude, *Panégyrique récité au très illustre, très magnanime, très vertueulx, et très chrestien roy françoys premier de ce nom, à son retour de provence, l'an mil cinq cens trent huit, au mois de septembre* (Paris, nd).

———, *La complaincte de Mars sur la venue de l'empereur en France* (Paris, 1539).

———, *S'ensuivent les triomphantes et honorables entrées faictes par le commandement du Roy très-Christien Françoys premier de ce nom, à la sacrée Majesté Impériale, Charles. Item la complaincte de Mars, dieu des batayllés sur la venue de l'empereur en France* (Lille, 1539).

———, *Discours de la Court, présenté au Roy par Chappuys son libraire et varlet de chambre ordinaire* (Paris, 1543).

———, *L'Aigle qui a faict la poulle devant le coq à Landrecy* (Paris, 1544).

————, *Le Sacre et couronnement du très auguste, très puissant et trèschrestien Roy Henry deuxiesme de ce nom* … (Paris, nd).

————, *Poésies Intimes*. Edited and introduced by Aline Mary Best (Geneva, 1967).

Chappuys, Gabriel (trans.), *Le Quinziesme-Vingtuniesme et dernier livre d'Amadis de Gaule* . . . (Lyon, 1577–1581).

————(trans.), *Le Parfait courtisan* (Paris, 1585).

————(trans.), *Le Misaule ou haineux de court, lequel, par un dialogisme et confabulation fort agréable et plaisante, démonstre sérieusement l'estat des courtisans et autres suivans la court des Princes. Avec la manière, coustumes et moeurs des courtisans* (Tours, 1585).

Colin, Jacques (trans), *Le Courtisan, nouvellement traduict de langue Ytalicque en françoys* (Paris, 1537).

Colonna, Francesco, *Le songe de Poliphile*. Translated by Jean Martin (Paris, 1547).

Columbus, Christopher, *Journals and Other Documents on the Life and Voyages of Christopher Columbus*. Edited and translated by S. E. Morison (New York, 1963).

————, *The Libro de la profecías*. Edited by D. West and A. Kling (Gainesville, 1991).

Corrozet, Gilles, *Hécatomgraphie* (Paris, 1540).

Cotgrave, Randle, *A dictionarie of the French and English tongues*. Reproduced from the 1st. ed., London, 1611, with introduction by William S. Woods (Columbia, SC, 1950).

de Longueil, Christophe, *Oratio de laudibus divi Ludovici, atque Francorum* . . . (Paris, 1510).

Desmarquets, Jean-Antoine-Samson, *Mémoires chronologiques pour servir à l'histoire de Dieppe et à celle de navigation française*. 2 volumes (Paris, 1785).

Deville, Achille (ed), *Comptes de dépenses de la construction du château de Gaillon, publiés d'après les registres manuscrits des trésoriers du Cardinal d'Amboise* (Paris, 1850).

Dolet, Etienne, *La Maniere de bien traduire d'une langue en aultre* (Lyon, 1540).

du Bellay, Joachim, *La Deffence et illustration de la langue Françoyse* (Paris, 1549).

————, *Œuvres poétiques*. Edited by H. Chamard. 8 volumes (Paris, 1908–1923).

Dubois, Guillaume, *Les Œuvres de G. Dubois natif de la paroisse de Putot-en-Besin et ouvrier du métier de maçon maistre tailleur de pierres à la ville de Caen, où il lui a été donné le don d'écrire en poesie française, par un ordre alphabétique, pour opposer au fantastique, comme on pourra voir en ce petit livre* (Paris, 1606).

du Boulay, César Egasse, *Historia Universitatis Parisiensis*. 6 volumes (Frankfurt, 1966).

du Bus, Gervais, *Le Roman de Fauvel* (Paris, 1914–1919).

du Mans, Jacques Peletier, *Dialogue de l'ortografe et prononciation françoese, departi an deus liures* . . . (Poitier, 1550).

————, *L'Art poetique: departi an deus livres* (Lyon, 1555).

Durand, Georges, *Tableaux et chants royaux de la Confrérie du Puy de Notre Dame d'Amiens, reproduits en 1517 pour Louise de Savoie, Duchesse D'Angoulême* (Paris, 1911).

du Val, Pierre, *Le Puy du souverain amour*, facsimile edition. Introduced by P. Le Verdier (Rouen, 1920; originally 1543).

————, *Le Printemps de Madame Poësie chanté par les vrays amantz au Theatre de magnificense* (Lyon, 1551).

Erasmus, Desiderius, *Literary and Educational Writings*. Edited by Craig R. Thompson, translated by Margaret Mann Phillips (Toronto, 1978).

———, *The Erasmus Reader*. Edited by Erika Rummel (Toronto, 1990).

———, *Praise of Folly and Letter to Martin Van Dorp*. Translated by B. Radice (London and New York, 1993).

Estienne, Henri, *La precellance du langage francois. Traicté de la conformité du langage françoys auec le grec ...* (1569).

———, *Deux dialogues du nouveau langage francois italiznizé et autrement desguizé, principalement entre les courtisans de ce temps: de plusieurs nouveautez qui ont accompagné ceste nouveaute de langage: de quelques courtisanismes modernes, et de quelques singularitez courtisanesques* (Geneva, 1578).

Estienne, Robert, *Traicte de la grammaire francoise* (1557).

Fabri, Pierre, *Le Grant et vray art de pleine rethorique...* (Rouen, 1534). Also published in facsimile with an introduction by A. Héron, 2 volumes (Rouen, 1890).

Farin, François, *Histoire de la ville de Rouen, divisée en trois parties* (Paris, 1668).

———, *Histoire de la ville de Rouen, Divisée en six parties* (Rouen, 1731).

Félix, Julien (ed.), *Comptes-Rendus des échevins de Rouen* (Rouen, 1890).

Focard, Jacques, *Paraphrase de l'astrolabe* (Lyon, 1544).

Froissart, Jean, *Chronicles of England, France and Spain and the Adjoining Countries*. Translated by J. Bourchier (London, 1924).

Furetière, Antoine, *Dictionnaire universel ....* 2 volumes (La Haye and Rotterdam, 1691).

Gaguin, Robert, *La Mer des Chroniques et mirouer hystorial de France . . . par Robert Gaguin, . . . nouvellement traduict de latin en vulgaire françoys* [par Pierre Desrey] *et augmenté de nouveau* [par Pierre Desrey] (Paris, 1536).

Godefroy, Théodore, *Le Cérémonial François*. 2 volumes (Paris, 1649).

Gosselin, Edouard, *Documents authentiques et inédits pour servir à l'histoire de la marine normande et du commerce rouennais pendant les xvie et xviie siècles* (Rouen, 1876).

Gregory of Tours, *The History of the Franks* (New York, 1986).

Guenée, Bernard, and Françoise Lehoux (eds.), *Les Entrées royales françaises de 1328 à 1515* (Paris, 1968).

Guevara, Antonio de, *Du Mepris de court ...* (Lyon, 1542 and Paris, 1551).

———, *Le Favori de court, contenant plusieures advertissemens & bonnes doctrines pour les Favoris des Princes, & autres Seigneurs & Gentilshommes qui hantent la Court*. Translated by Iaques de Rochemore (Anvers, 1557).

Jouen, M. Le Chanoine, *Comptes, devis et inventaires du manoir archiépiscopal de Rouen*. Introduced by Mgr. Fuzet, Archevêque de Rouen (Paris and Rouen, 1908).

Julien, Charles-André, R. Herval, and T. Beauchesne (eds.), *Voyages au Canada, avec les relations des voyages en Amérique de Gonneville, Verrazano et Roberval* (Paris, 1989).

La Marche, Olivier de, *Mémoires d'Olivier de La Marche, maître d'hôtel et capitaine des gardes de Charles Le Téméraire*. 4 volumes (Paris, 1883–1888).

La Marck, Robert de, seigneur de Fleuranges, "Histoire des choses mémorables advenues des règnes de Louis XII et de François Ier 1499–1521," in *Nouvelle collection des mémoires relatifs à l'histoire de France*. Edited by Michaud, Poujoulat, Bazil, Champollion et al. (Paris, 1851).

La Perière, Guillaume de, *Theatre des bons engins* (Paris, 1539).

Lebas, G., *Les Palinods et les poètes dieppois* (Dieppe, 1904).

Lefèvre, Jean, *Livret des emblemes de maistre André Alciat, mis en rime françoyse* . . . Paris, (1536).

———, *Les Emblemes . . . mis en rime francoyse* . . . (Paris, 1540).

Lefèvre, Raoul, *The Recuyell of the Historyes of Troye*. Translated by William Caxton c. 1474 (London, 1894).

Le Gendre, Louis, *Vie du Cardinal d'Amboise premier ministre de Louis XII* ... (Amsterdam, 1726).

Lemaire de Belges, Jean, *Œuvres*. Edited by Stecher. 3 volumes (Louvain, 1882–1885).

Le Rocquez, Robert, *Le Miroir d'éternité comprenant les sept ages du monde, les quatre monarchies et diversité des règnes d'iceluy en la fin duquel sont contenus le general Jugement de Dieu* . . . (Caen, 1589).

Léry, Jean de, *History of a Voyage to the Land of Brazil, otherwise called America* . . . Translated by Janet Whatley (Berkeley and Los Angeles, 1990).

Lescarbot, Marc, *The History of New France*. Translated by W. L. Grant (Toronto, 1907–1914).

Le Verdier, Pierre (ed.), *Documents relatifs à la confrérie de la Passion de Rouen* (sl, 1891).

———, *Le Triomphe des Normands. Suivi de la Dame à l'agneau, par G. Thibault* (Rouen, 1908).

Lincy, Le Roux de (ed.), *Manuscrit La Valière (Recueil de farces, moralités et sermons joyeux)*. Introduced by Werner Helmich (Geneva, 1972).

Magalhaes de Gandavo, Pero de, *The Histories of Brazil* (New York, 1922).

Margry, P., *Les Navigations françaises et la révolution maritime du XIVe au XVIe siècles d'après les documents inédits tirés de France, d'Angleterre, d'Espagne et d'Italie* (Paris, 1867).

Marot, Clément, *Œuvres complètes de Clément Marot*. Edited by C. A. Mayer. 6 volumes (London, 1958).

Marot, Jehan, *Le Voyage de Gênes*. Edited by G. Trisolini (Geneva, 1974).

McFarlane, I. D. (ed.), *The Entry of Henri II into Paris, 16 juin 1549* (Binghamton, 1982).

Meigret, Louis, *Traité touchant le commun usage de l'escriture françoise* (Paris, 1542).

Montaigne, Michel de, *Essais, reproduction photographique de l'édition originale de 1580* . . . 3 volumes (Geneva, 1976).

———, *The Complete Essays of Montaigne*. Translated by D. M. Frame (Stanford, 1992).

Olivétan, Pierre-Robert, *La Bible qui et toute la sainte Escripture en laquelle sont contenus le Vieil Testament et le Nouveau translatez en Françoys, le Vieil de l'[h]ébrrieu, et le Nouveau de grec* . . . (Neufchâtel, 1535).

Panel, Gustave (ed), *Documents concernant les pauvres de Rouen, 1224–1634* (Paris and Rouen, 1917).

Paradin, Claude, *Devises héroïques et emblêmes de M. Claude Paradin* (Paris, 1621; originally 1557).

Parmentier, Jean, *Œuvres Poétiques*. Edited by F. Ferrand (Paris and Geneva, 1971).

Picot, Emile (ed.), *Théâtre mystique de Pierre du Val et des libertins spirituels de Rouen au XVIe siècle* (Paris, 1882).

————, *Recueil général des sotties*. 3 volumes (Paris, 1904).

————, *Querelle de Marot et Sagon*, É. Picot and P. Lacombe (eds.). Introduction by Georges Dubosc (Geneva, 1969).

————, "Une Querelle littéraire aux pallinods de Dieppe au XVe siècle," *Mélanges de philologie romane et d'histoire littéraire offerts à Maurice Wilmotte* (Geneva, 1972).

Pinel, Robinet, *L'Entrée de Charles VIII à Rouen en 1485*. Facsimile, introduced by Ch. de Robillard de Beaurepaire (Rouen, 1902).

Plutarch, *The Roman Questions of Plutarch*. Translated by H. J. Rose (Oxford, 1924).

Pommeraye, Fr. Jean-François, *Histoire de l'église cathédrale de Rouen* (Rouen, 1686).

Popellinière, Henri Lancelot-Voisin, Sieur de la, *Les trois Mondes par le Seigneur de la Popellinière* (Paris, 1582).

Rabelais, François, *Bringuenarilles, cousin germain de Fessepinte* (Rouen, 1545).

————, *Gargantua and Pantagruel*. Translated by J. M. Cohen (New York, 1978).

Registres des délibérations du bureau de la ville de Paris (Paris, 1886).

Robillard de Beaurepaire, Charles de (ed.), *Inventaire-Sommaire des Archives Départementales antérieures à 1790, Seine-Inférieure, Archives Civiles* (Rouen, 1903).

Ronsard, Pierre de, *Œuvres complètes*. Edited by J. Céard, D. Ménager, and M. Simonin. 2 volumes (Paris, 1993–1994).

Sainte-Beuve, Charles-Augustin, *Tableau de la poésie française au XVIe siècle*. 2 volumes (Paris, 1876).

Scève, Maurice, *The Entry of Henri II into Lyon, September 1548*. Facsimile with an introduction by Richard Cooper (Tempe, AZ, 1997).

Sebillet, Thomas, *Art poétique françois* (Paris, 1910).

Seyssel, Claude de, *La Monarchie de France*. Edited by J. Poujol (Paris, 1961).

————, *Les Histoires universelles de Trogue Pompée, abbrégées par Justin, historien, translatée de latin en françois par messire Claude de Seyssel* (Paris, 1559).

Sireulde, Jacques, *Le Tresor immortel . . .* (Rouen, 1556). A modern version can be found edited by Charles de Robillard de Beaurepaire (Rouen, 1899).

————, *Les Triomphes de l'abbaye des Conards, sous le resveur en decimes Fagot, Abbé des Conards, contenant les criées et proclamations faites, depuis son advenement jusques à l'An présent [1587]; Plus l'ingénieuse Lessive qu'ils ont Conardement monstrée aux jours gras de l'an MDXL; plus le Testament D'Ouinet de nouveau augmenté par le commandement dudit Abbé, non encores veu; Plus la Letanie, l'Ancienne et l'Oraison faite en ladite maison Abbatiale en l'an 1580* (Rouen, 1587).

Staden, Hans, *Nus féroces et anthropophages* (Paris, 1979; first published Marburg, 1557).

Taillepied, Noel, *Antiquitez et singularitez de la ville de Rouen* (Rouen, 1610).

Thevet, André, *Les Singularités de la France antarctique*. Edited by F. Lestringant (Paris, 1983, first published in 1557).

————, *La Cosmographie universelle …* (Paris, 1575).

————, *Portraits et vies des hommes illustres*. 2 volumes (New York, 1973; first published Paris, 1584).

Tory, Geoffroy, *Champ fleury. Au quel est contenu L'art et Science de la deue et vraye proportion des lettres attiques, quon dit autrement lettres antiques, et vulgairement lettres romaines proportionnees selon le corps et visage humain* (Paris, 1529).

Tyard, Pontus de, *L'Univers, ou discours des parties et de la nature du monde* (Lyon, 1557).

———, *Œuvres poétiques*. Edited by Charles Marty-Laveaux (Paris, 1875).

Tytler, Patrick Fraser, Esq., *England Under the Reigns of Edward VI, and Mary*, Volume 1 (London, 1839).

St. Victrice, *De laude sanctorum, d'après les variantes tirées des mss de s.-Gal par le Chanoine Sauvage, publié et annoté par l'abbée A. Tougard* (Paris, 1895).

Vidoue, Pierre, *Palinods, chantz royaulx, ballades, rondeaulx et epigrammes, à l'honneur de l'Immaculee conception de la toute belle mère de Dieu Marie (Patronne de Normands)* … . (1525). Reprinted in facsimile and introduced by E. de Robillard de Beaurepaire, *Palinods présentés au Puys de Rouen. Recueil de Pierre Vidoue* (Rouen, 1897).

Vieilleville, François de Scépeaux, compte de Durtal, sire de, *Mémoires de la vie de François de Scépeaux*. 5 volumes (Paris, 1757).

Vienne, Philibert de, *Le Philosophe de court* (Paris, 1547).

Wace, Robert, *L'Établissement de la fête de la Conception Notre-Dame dite la fête aux Normands* (Caen, 1842).

Secondary Sources

Alexander, A. "The Imperialist Space of Elizabethan Mathematics," *Studies in History and Philosophy of Science* 26 (1995): 559–591.

Allard, G.-H. (ed), *Aspects de la marginalité au Moyen Age* (Montreal, 1975).

Anglo, S., *Chivalry in the Renaissance* (London, 1990).

Anonymous, "The Evolution of Harlequin," *Quarterly Review* 196 (1902): 462–482.

Anthiaume, A., *Cartes marines, constructions navales, voyages de découverte chez les Normands, 1500–1650*. 2 volumes (Paris, 1916).

Apostolidès, J.-M., *Le Roi-machine: spectacle et politique au temps de Louis XIV* (Paris, 1981).

Arden, H., *Fool's Plays: A Study of Satire in the Sottie* (Cambridge, 1980).

Ashworth, W. B., "Natural History and the Emblematic World View," in D. Lindberg and R. Westman (eds.), *Reappraisals of the Scientific Revolution* (Cambridge, 1990), 302–332.

———, "Emblematic Natural History of the Renaissance," in N. Jardine, J. Secord, and E. Spary (eds), *Cultures of Natural History* (Cambridge, 1996), 17–37.

Aslan, O., and D. Babet (eds), *Le Masque du rite au théâtre* (Paris, 1985).

Atkinson, G., *Les Nouveaux horizons de la Renaissance française* (Paris, 1935).

Aubailly, J.-C., *Le Monologue, le dialogue et la sottie* (Paris, 1976).

Austin, G. A., "Concepts of Secular Greatness in Normandy, ca. 1000–1150" (Ph.D. Dissertation, Los Angeles, 1977).

Babeau, A., *Les Rois de France à Troyes au seizième siècle* (Troyes, 1880).

Bakhtin, M., *The Dialogic Imagination*. Translated by M. Holquist and C. Emerson (Austin, 1981).

———, *Rabelais and His World*. Translated by H. Iswolsky (Bloomington, 1984).

———, *Speech Genres and Other Late Essays*. Edited by C. Emerson and M. Holquist, translated by V. W. McGee (Austin, 1986).

Baldwin, R., "'I slaughter barbarians': Triumph as a Mode in Medieval Christian Art," *Konsthistorisk Tidskrift* 59 (1990): 225–242.

Ballin, A. G., *Notice historique et bibliographique sur l'Académie des Palinods* (Rouen, 1834).

Barasch, M., *Imago Hominis: Studies in the Language of Art* (Vienna, 1991).

Bataillon, M., "Évangélisme et millénarisme au Nouveau Monde," in *Courants religieux et humanisme à la fin du XV et au début du XVI siècles, Colloque de Strasbourg* (Paris, 1957), 25–36.

Batra, R., *Wild Men in the Looking Glass: The Mythic Origins of European Otherness.* Translated by C. T. Berrisford (Ann Arbor, 1994).

Baumgartner, F. J., *Henry II, King of France, 1547–1559* (Durham, 1988).

Baxandall, M., *Painting and Experience in Fifteenth Century Italy: A Primer in the Social History of Pictorial Style* (Oxford, 1972).

Beaujouan, G., and E. Poulle, "Les Origines de la navigation astronomique au XIVᵉ et XVᵉ siècles," in M. Mollat and O. de Prat (eds.), *Le Navire et l'économie maritime du XVᵉ au XVIIIᵉ siècles* (Paris, 1957), 103–117.

Beaune, C., *Naissance de la nation France* (Paris, 1985).

Beck, J., *Théâtre et propagande aux débuts de la Réforme* (Geneva and Paris, 1986).

Béguin, J.-R., "Présentation et réflexions sur quelques images," in A. Parent (ed.), *La Renaissance et le Nouveau Monde* (Quebec, 1984).

Benedict, P., *Rouen During the Wars of Religion* (Cambridge, 1981).

Bennett, J. A., *The Divided Circle: A History of Instruments for Astronomy, Navigation and Surveying* (Oxford, 1987).

Bennett, T., *The Birth of the Museum* (London, 1995).

Bergamini, L. J., "From Narrative to Icon: The Virgin Mary and the Woman of the Apocalypse in Thirteenth Century English Art and Devotion," in *Studies in Iconography* 13 (1989–1990): 80–112.

Bergot, F. (ed.), *La Renaissance à Rouen.* Catalogue of the exposition held at the Musée des Beaux-Arts de Rouen, 28 novembre 1980–28 février 1981 (Rouen, 1980).

Bernheimer, R., *Wild Men in the Middle Ages: A Study in Art, Sentiment, and Demonology* (Cambridge, MA, 1952).

Best, A.-M., "Additionnal (sic) Documents on the Life of Claude Chappuys," in *Bibliothèque d'humanisme et Renaissance. Travaux et documents* 28 (1966): 134–140.

Biagioli, M., "The Social Status of Italian Mathematicians, 1450–1600," *History of Science* 27 (1989): 41–95.

———, *Galileo, Courtier: The Practice of Science in the Culture of Absolutism* (Chicago, 1993).

Bietenholz, P. G., and T. B. Deutscher (eds), *Contemporaries of Erasmus: A Biographical Register of the Renaissance and Reformation.* 3 volumes (London, 1985–1987).

Bitton, D., *The French Nobility in Crisis, 1560–1640* (Stanford, 1969).

Blair, A., *The Theater of Nature: Jean Bodin and Renaissance Science* (Princeton, 1997).

Bloch, J. R., *L'Anoblissement en France au temps de François Iᵉʳ* (Paris, 1978).

Bloch, M., "The Ritual of the Royal Bath in Madagascar," in D. Cannadine and S. R. F. Price (eds.), *Rituals of Royalty: Power and Ceremonial in Traditional Societies* (Cambridge, 1987), 271–297.

Bloch, M. L. B., *French Rural History: An Essay on its Basic Characteristics*. Translated by J. Sondhe (Berkeley, 1966).

———, *The Royal Touch: Sacred Monarchy and Scrofula in England and France* (London, 1973).

Bloomfield, M., and M. Reeves, "The Penetration of Joachimism into Northern Europe," in *Speculum* 29 (1954): 772–793.

Blum, C., *La Représentation de la mort dans la littérature française de la Renaissance* (Paris, 1989).

Bohanan, D., *Old and New Nobility in Aix-en-Provence, 1600–1695: Portrait of an Urban Elite* (Baton Rouge, 1992).

Bois, G., *The Crisis of Feudalism: Economy and Society in Eastern Normandy c.1300–1550* (Cambridge, 1984).

Bonnefon, P., "Le différend de Marot et de Sagon," in *Revue d'histoire littéraire de la France* 1 (1894): 103–138, 259–285.

Bottineau-Fuchs, Y., "Les piles figurées de l'église Saint-Martin de Veules-les-Roses," in *Annales de Normandie* 2 (juin, 1980): 103–138.

———, "Indiens et Normands au début du XVIe siècle," *Les Normands et la Mer*, XXVe Congrès des Sociétés Savantes 4–7 oct. 1990 (Saint-Vaast-la Hougue, 1995), 150–159.

Bouillet, A., "L'Eglise Saint-Foy de Conches et ses vitraux," in *Bulletin monumental* 54 (1888): 289–293.

Bouman, C. A., "The Immaculate Conception in Liturgy," in E. D. O'Connor (ed.), *The Dogma of the Immaculate Conception* (Notre Dame, 1958).

Bourciez, É., *Les Mœurs polies et la littérature de cour sous Henri II* (Geneva, 1967).

Bourdieu, P., "Le Langage autorisé: note sur les conditions sociales de l'efficacité du discours rituel," in *Actes de la recherche en sciences sociales*, 1: 5/6 (1975): 183–190.

———, *Distinction: A Social Critique of the Judgement of Taste*. Translated by R. Nice (Cambridge, MA, 1984).

———, "Social Space and the Genesis of Groups," in *Theory and Society* 14 (November, 1985): 723–744.

———, "Social Space and Symbolic Power," in *Sociological Theory* 7 (1989): 14–25.

Boureau, A., "Ritualité politique et modernité monarchique," in N. Bulst, R. Descimon, and A. Guerreau (eds.), *L'État ou le roi. Les fondations de la modernité monarchique en France (XIVe-XVIIe siècles)* (Paris, 1992), 9–25.

Bouwsma, W. J., *Concordia Mundi: The Career and Thought of Guillaume Postel (1510–1581)* (Cambridge, MA, 1957).

———, "Lawyers in Early Modern Culture," *The American Historical Review* 78: 2 (April, 1973): 303–327.

Bowen, B. C., "Théâtre du Cliché," in *Cahiers de l'Association internationale des études françaises* 26 (1974): 33–47.

———, "La Revanche verbale dans la farce Française de la Renaissance," in *Kwartalnik Neofilologiczny* 23 (1976): 57–64.

———, *Words and the Man in French Renaissance Literature* (Lexington, 1983).

Brandon, W., *New Worlds for Old: Reports from the New World and Their Effect on the Development of Social Thought in Europe, 1500–1800* (Athens, OH, 1986).

Bréard, C., *Note sur la famille du Capitaine Gonneville* (Rouen, 1885).

Britnell, J., "Jean Lemaire de Belges and Prophecy," in *The Journal of the Warburg and Courtauld Institutes* 42 (1979): 144–166.

———, *Jean Bouchet* (Edinburgh, 1986).

Brown, C. J., *The Shaping of History and Poetry in Late Medieval France: Propaganda and Artistic Expression in the Works of the Rhétoriqueurs* (Birmingham, 1985).

Brown, H. M., *Music in the French Secular Theater, 1400–1550* (Cambridge, MA, 1963).

Brown, P., *The Cult of the Saints: Its Rise and Function in Latin Christianity* (Chicago, 1981).

———, "The Saint as Exemplar in Late Antiquity," in *Representations* 1 (Spring, 1983): 1–25.

———, *Society and the Holy in Late Antiquity* (Los Angeles and Oxford, 1989).

Brunelle, G., "Immigration, Assimilation and Success: Three Families of Spanish Origin in Sixteenth-Century Rouen," in the *Sixteenth Century Journal* 20 (Summer, 1989): 203–219.

———, *The New World Merchants of Rouen, 1559–1630* (Kirksville, MO, 1991).

Brunot, B., "Un Project 'd'enrichir, magnifier et publier' la langue Française en 1509," in *Revue d'histoire littéraire de la France* 1 (Paris, 1894): 27–37.

Bryant, L. M., *The King and the City in the Parisian Royal Entry Ceremony: Politics, Ritual, and Art in the Renaissance* (Geneva, 1986).

———, "Politics, Ceremonies, and Embodiments of Majesty in Henry II's France," in H. Duchhardt, R. A. Jackson, D. J. Sturdy (eds.), *European Monarchy: Its Evolution and Practice from Roman Antiquity to Modern Times* (Stuttgart, 1992), 127–153.

Burke, P., *The Fabrication of Louis XIV* (New Haven, 1992).

Burkert, W., *Structure and History in Greek Mythology and Ritual* (Berkeley and Los Angeles, 1979).

Cabrol, F., and H. Leclercq (eds.), *Dictionnaire d'archéologie chrétienne et de liturgie.* 15 volumes (Paris, 1907–1932).

Canguilhem, G., *The Normal and the Pathological.* Translated by C. Fawcett and R. Cohen (New York, 1989).

Cannadine, D., and S. Price (eds.), *Rituals of Royalty: Power and Ceremonial in Traditional Societies* (Cambridge, 1987).

Carroll, S., *Noble Power During the French Wars of Religion: The Guise Affinity and the Catholic Cause in Normandy* (Cambridge, 1998).

Carrithers, M., S. Collins, and S. Lukes (eds), *The Category of the Person: Anthropology, Philosophy, History* (Cambridge, 1985).

Carruthers, M., *The Book of Memory: A Study of Memory in Medieval Culture* (Cambridge, 1990).

Cassirer, E., *The Individual and the Cosmos in Renaissance Philosophy.* Translated by M. Domandi (New York, 1963).

Castor, G., *Pléiade Poetics: A Study in Sixteenth-Century Thought and Terminology* (Cambridge, 1964).

Cave, T., *The Cornucopian Text: Problems of Writing in the French Renaissance* (Oxford, 1979).

Céard, J., *La Nature et les prodiges: L'insolite au XVIe siècle, en France* (Geneva, 1996).

Certeau, M. de, *Heterologies: Discourse on the Other.* Translated by B. Massumi. (Minneapolis, 1986).

———, *The Writing of History.* Translated by T. Conley. (New York, 1988).

———, *The Mystic Fable.* Translated by M. B. Smith. 2 volumes (Chicago, 1992).

Chartier, R., *The Cultural Uses of Print in Early Modern France.* Translated by L. Cochrane (Princeton, 1987).

———, *Cultural History: Between Practices and Representations.* Translated by L. Cochrane (Ithaca, 1990).

Charton-Le Clech, S., *Chancellerie et culture au XVIe siècle: les notaires et secrétaires du roi de 1515 à 1547* (Toulouse, 1993).

Chartrou, J., *Les Entrées solennelles et triomphales à la Renaissance, 1484–1551* (Paris, 1928).

Chastel, A., *Culture et demeures en France au XVIe siècle* (Paris, 1989).

Chiapelli, F., M. J. B. Allen, and R. L. Benson (eds.) *First Images of America: The Impact of the New World on the Old.* 2 volumes (Berkeley and Los Angeles, 1976).

Chinard, G., *L'Exotisme américain dans la littérature française au XVIe siècle* (Geneva, 1970).

Chirol, E., *Un premier foyer de la Renaissance en France: Le Château de Gaillon* (Rouen, 1952).

———, "L'Influence de Mantegna sur la Renaissance en Normandie," in *Actes du XIXe congrès international d'histoire de l'art* (1968): 240–247.

———, "L'Hôtel de Bourgtheroulde" and "Le Gros-Horloge," in *Connaître Rouen* (Rouen, 1970).

———, "La Renaissance à Rouen," in *Connaître Rouen* (Rouen, 1970).

———, "Heures et malheurs du château de Gaillon," in *Précis analytique des travaux de l'Académie des Sciences, Belles-Lettres, et Arts de Rouen* (1982–1983): 55–78.

Chirol, P., *Un siècle de vandalisme. Rouen disparu* (Rouen and Paris, 1929).

Clough, C. H., "Francis I and the Courtiers of Castiglione's *Courtier*," in *European Studies Review* 8 (1978): 23–70.

Cloulas, I., *Henri II* (Paris, 1985).

Cohen, G., "La Farce des Veaux," in *Mélanges de linguistique et de littérature romanes à la mémoire d'Istvân Frank* (Saarbrucken, 1957).

Cohn, N., *The Pursuit of the Millennium: Revolutionary Millenarians and Mystical Anarchists of the Middle Ages* (New York, 1970).

Colin, S., "The Wild Man and the Indian in Early 16th Century Book Illustration," in C. Feest (ed.), *Indians and Europe: An Interdisciplinary Collection of Essays* (Aachen, 1987), 5–36.

Colombier, P. du, "Les Triomphes en images de l'empereur Maximilien Ier," in J. Jacquot (ed), *Les Fêtes de la Renaissance.* 3 volumes (Paris, 1956–1975), 2: 99–112.

Comito, T., "Renaissance Gardens and the Discovery of Paradise," in *Journal of the History of Ideas* 32: 4 (1971): 483–506.

Corvisier, A., "Une Société ludique au XVIᵉ siècle: L'Abbaye des Conards de Rouen," in *Annales de Normandie* 2 (1977): 179–193.

Crouzet, D., *Les Guerriers de Dieu. La Violence au temps des troubles de religion, (vers 1525–vers 1610).* 2 volumes (Seyssel, 1990).

Dalby, D., and P. E. H. Hair, "A Tupi Vocabulary of the 1540s," in *Transactions of the Philological Society* (1966): 42–66.

D'Ancona, M. L., "The Iconography of the Immaculate Conception in the Middle Ages and the Early Renaissance," in *Monographs on Archaeology and Fine Arts* 7 (New York, 1957).

Daston, L., "Reviews on Artifact and Experiment," in *ISIS* 79 (1988): 452–467.

———, "Marvelous Facts and Miraculous Evidence in Early Modern Europe," in *Critical Inquiry* 18 (1991): 93–124.

———, "Objectivity and the Escape from Perspective," in *Social Studies of Science* 22 (1992): 597–618.

———, "Baconian Facts, Academic Civility, and the Prehistory of Objectivity," in A. Megill (ed.), *Rethinking Objectivity* (Durham, 1994), 37–63.

———, "Curiosity in Early Modern Science," in *Word & Image* 2 (October–December, 1995): 391–404.

Daston, L., and K. Park, *Wonders and the Order of Nature 1150–1750* (New York, 1998).

Davis, N. Z., *Society and Culture in Early Modern France: Eight Essays* (Stanford, 1975).

———, *Fiction in the Archives: Pardon Tales and their Tellers in Sixteenth-Century France* (Cambridge, 1987).

Dear, Peter, *Discipline and Experience: The Mathematical Way in the Scientific Revolution* (Chicago, 1995).

Delaruelle, L., *Guillaume Budé: Les origines, les débuts, les idées maîtresses* (Geneva, 1970).

Delisle, L., "Note sur un manuscrit des poésies de Pétrarque rapporté d'Italie en 1494 par Charles VIII," in *Bibliothèque de l'Ecole de Chartes* 61 (1900): 450–458.

Delumeau, J., *History of Paradise: The Garden of Eden in Myth and Tradition.* Translated by M. O'Connell (New York, 1995).

de Montaiglon, A., "La Sculpture française à la Renaissance. La Famille des Juste en France," in *Gazette des Beaux-Arts* 12 (November and December, 1875): 385–404 and 515–526.

De Montifaud, M., *Les triomphes de l'Abbaye des Conards avec une notice sur la fête des fous* (Paris, 1874).

Denis, A., *Charles VIII et les Italiens. Histoire et mythe* (Geneva, 1979).

Denis, F., *Une Fête brésilienne célébrée à Rouen en 1550 suivie d'un fragment du XVIᵉ siècle roulant sur la théogonie des anciens peuples du Brésil, et des poésies en langue tupique de Christovam Valente* (Paris, 1850).

Deschamps, P., "Un épisode de l'entrée de Henri II à Rouen. La Chevauchée des Conards et la 'Farce des Veaulx'," in *Précis analytique des travaux de l'Académie de Rouen* (Fécamp, 1971): 23–33.

———, "Les Entrées royales à Rouen," *Connaître Rouen* 3 (Rouen, 1976).

Desmont, M., "Le Port de Rouen et son commerce avec l'Amérique," in *Société normande de géographie* 33(1911): 403–419.

Despres, D., *Ghostly Sights: Visual Meditation in Late-Medieval Literature* (Norman, 1989).

Dewald, J., *The Formation of a Provincial Nobility: The Magistrates of the Parlement of Rouen, 1499–1610* (Princeton, 1980).

———, "The 'Perfect Magistrate': Parliamentaries and Crime in Sixteenth-Century Rouen," in *Archiv für Reformationsgeschichte* 67(1986): 284–300.

Dickason, O. P., "The Concept of *l'homme sauvage* and early French colonialism in the Americas," in *Revue française d'histoire d'outre-mer* 64(1977): 5–32.

Douyère, C., "Les Marchands étrangers à Rouen au XVIᵉ siècle," in *Revue des sociétés savantes d'Haute-Normandie* 76 (1974): 27–61.

Dubois, C.-G., *Celtes et Gaulois au XVIᵉ siècle. Le développement littéraire d'un mythe nationaliste. . . . Avec l'édition critique d'un traité inédit de Guillaume Postel: De ce qui est premier pour reformer le monde* (Paris, 1972).

Du Busserolle, J.-X. C., *Notice sur l'abbaye des Conards, Confrérie célèbre qui a existé à Rouen du quatorzième au dix-septième siècle, à Évreux, de 1345 à 1420* (Rouen and Paris, 1859).

Du Colombier, P., "Les Triomphes en images de l'empereur Maximilien Iᵉʳ," in Jacquot, *Les Fêtes de la Renaissance* 2: 99–112.

Dufay, P., "Ronsard par Henri Longnon," in *Revue de la Renaissance* 5 (Paris, 1913).

Dull, O. A., *Folie et rhétorique dans la sottie* (Geneva, 1994).

Dupont, F., "The Emperor-God's Other Body," in M. Feher, R. Naddaff, and N. Tazi (eds.), *Fragments for a History of the Human Body* (Zone, 1989), 396–419.

Éliade, M., "Le Myth du bon sauvage," *Nouvelle revue française* 32 (August, 1955): 229–249.

Elias, N., *The Court Society* (New York, 1975).

———, *The Civilizing Process.* 2 volumes (New York, 1978).

Elliott, J. H., *The Old World and the New, 1492–1650* (Cambridge, 1970).

———, "Renaissance Europe and America: A Blunted Impact?" in F. Chiappelli, M. J. B. Allen, and R. L. Benson (eds.), *First Images of America: The Impact of the New World on the Old.* 2 volumes (Berkeley and Los Angeles, 1976).

Enders, J., *Rhetoric and the Origins of Medieval Drama* (Ithaca, 1992).

Estancelin, L., *Dissertation sur les découvertes faites par les navigateurs dieppois* (Abbeville, nd).

Ettlinger, Leopold, "The Duke of Wellington's Funeral Car," in *Journal of the Warburg and Courtauld Institutes* 3 (1939–1940): 254–259.

Evans, R. J. W., *Rudolph II and His World: A Study in Intellectual History, 1576–1612* (Oxford, 1973).

Farge, J. K., *Orthodoxy and Reform in Early Reformation France: The Faculty of Theology of Paris, 1500–1543* (Leiden, 1985).

Febvre, L., "Une question mal posée: les origines de la réforme française et le problème des causes de la réforme," in *Revue historique* 161 (1929): 1–73.

————, "Civilisation: évolution d'un mot et d'un groupe d'idées," in *Pour une histoire à part entière* (Paris, 1962), 481–528.

————, *The Problem of Unbelief in the Sixteenth Century: The Religion of Rabelais*. Translated by B. Gottlieb (Cambridge, MA, and London, 1982).

Febvre, L., and H.-J. Martin, *The Coming of the Book: The Impact of Printing, 1450–1800* (London, 1976).

Feest C. (ed.), *Indians and Europe: An Interdisciplinary Collection of Essays* (Aachen, 1987).

Findlen, P., *Possessing Nature: Museums, Collecting, and Scientific Culture in Early Modern Italy* (Berkeley and Los Angeles, 1994).

Fisher, P., *Making and Effacing Art: Modern American Art in a Culture of Museums* (Oxford, 1991).

Flint, V. I. J., *The Imaginative Landscape of Christopher Columbus* (Princeton, 1992).

Floquet, A., "Histoire des Conards de Rouen," in *Bibliothèque de l'école des Chartes* 1 (1839): 105–123.

Ford, F. L., *Robe and Sword: The Regrouping of the French Aristocracy after Louis XIV* (Cambridge, 1953).

Foucault, M., *The Order of Things: An Archaeology of the Human Sciences* (London, 1970).

Fouquet, H., *Histoire civile, politique et commerciale de Rouen* (Rouen, 1875).

Fournée, J., "Les Thèmes iconographiques de l'Immaculée Conception en Normandie au moyen-âge de la Renaissance," in *Virgo Immaculata, Acta Congressus Mariologici-Mariani Romae anno MCMLIV celebrati*, Volume 15, *De Immaculata Conceptione in litteratura et in arte Christiana* (Rome, 1957).

Frazer, J. G., *The Golden Bough: A Study in Magic and Religion* (New York, 1950).

Freedberg, D., *The Power of Images: Studies in the History and Theory of Response* (Chicago, 1989).

Fréville, C. E. de, *Mémoire sur le commerce maritime de Rouen, depuis les temps les plus reculés jusqu'à la fin du XVIe siècle*. 2 volumes (Paris, 1857).

Frondeville, H. de, *Les présidents du parlement de Normandie, 1499–1790, Recueil généalogique établi sur la base du manuscrit Bigot, de la Bibliothèque de Rouen* (Rouen, 1953).

————, *Les Conseillers du parlement de Normandie au seizième siècle (1499–1594), Recueil généalogique établi sur la base du ms. Bigot de la Bibliothèque de Rouen* (Rouen, 1960).

Gadoffre, G., *La Révolution culturelle dans la France des humanistes: Guillaume Budé et François Ier* (Geneva, 1997).

Gaffarel, P., "Anciens voyages normands au Brésil," in *Bulletin de la Société de l'histoire de Normandie* 5 (Rouen, 1887–1890): 236–239.

————, *Histoire du Brésil français au seizième siècle* (Paris, 1878).

Galinsky, G. K., *The Herakles Theme: The Adaptations of the Hero in Literature from Homer to the Twentieth Century* (Oxford, 1972).

Ganon, F., "Le thème médiéval de l'homme sauvage dans les premières représentations des Indiens d'Amérique," in G.-H. Allard (ed.), *Aspects de la marginalité au Moyen Age* (Montreal, 1975), 83–99.

Garin, E., *Uomo del Rinascimento*. Translated by P. Burke (Paris, 1990).

Geary, P. J., *Furta Sacra: Thefts of Relics in the Central Middle Ages* (Princeton, 1978).

————, "Sacred Commodities: The Circulation of Medieval Relics," in A. Appadurai (ed.), *The Social Life of Things: Commodities in Cultural Perspective* (Cambridge, 1986), 126–191.

Gébelin, F., "Un Manifeste de l'école néo-classique en 1549: L'Entrée de Henri II à Paris," in *Bulletin de la Société d'Histoire de Paris* 51 (1924): 35–45.

Geertz, C., *Negara: The Theatre State in Nineteenth-Century Bali* (Princeton, 1980).

————, *Local Knowledge: Further Essays in Interpretive Anthropology* (New York, 1983).

Giesey, R., *The Royal Funeral Ceremony in Renaissance France* (Geneva, 1960).

————, "Models of Rulership in French Royal Ceremonial," in S. Wilentz (ed.), *Rites of Power: Symbolism, Ritual, and Politics since the Middle Ages* (Philadelphia, 1985), 41–64.

Ginzburg, C., "Charivari, associations juvéniles, chasses sauvages," in J. Le Goff and J.-C. Schmitt (eds), *Le Charivari*. Actes de la table ronde organisée à Paris (25–27 avril 1977) par l'École des Hautes Études en Sciences Sociales et le Centre National de la Recherche Scientifique (Paris and New York, 1981), 131–140.

————, *The Cheese and the Worms: The Cosmos of a Sixteenth-Century Miller*. Translated by J. Tedeschi and A. C. Tedeschi (New York, 1982).

————, *Clues, Myths, and the Historical Method*. Translated by J. Tedeschi and A. C. Tedeschi (Baltimore and London, 1989).

————, *Ecstasies: Deciphering the Witches' Sabbath*. Translated by R. Rosenthal (London, 1990).

————, "Représentation: le mot, l'idée, la chose," in *Annales* 46: 6 (novembre-décembre 1991): 1219–1234.

Gluck, D., "Les Entrées provinciales de Henri II," in *L'Information d'histoire de l'art* 10 (1965): 191–218.

Golenistcheff-Koutouzoff, É., "La Première traduction des «Triomphes» de Pétrarque en France," in *Mélanges de philologie, d'histoire et de littérature offerts à Henri Hauvette* (Paris 1934), 107–112.

Goody, J., *The Domestication of the Savage Mind* (Cambridge, 1977).

————, *Representations and Contradictions: Ambivalence Towards Images, Theatre, Fiction, Relics and Sexuality* (Oxford, 1997).

Gordon, A., "The Ascendancy of Rhetoric and the Struggle for Poetic in Sixteenth-Century France," in J. J. Murphy (ed.), *Renaissance Eloquence: Studies in the Theory and Practice of Renaissance Rhetoric* (Berkeley and Los Angeles, 1983), 376–384.

Gosselin, J.-E.-A., *Recherches sur les origines et l'histoire du théâtre à Rouen avant Pierre Corneille* (Rouen, 1868).

Grafton, A., *Joseph Scaliger: A Study in the History of Classical Scholarship* (Oxford, 1983).

————, *Cardano's Cosmos: The Worlds and Works of a Renaissance Astrologer* (Cambridge, MA, 2000).

————, *Bring Out Your Dead: The Past as Revelation* (Cambridge, MA, 2001).

Grafton, A., A. Shelford, and N. G. Siraisi, *New Worlds, Ancient Texts: The Power of Tradition and the Shock of Discovery* (Cambridge, MA, 1992).

Grafton, A., and L. Jardine, *From Humanism to the Humanities: Education and the Liberal Arts in Fifteenth- and Sixteenth-Century Europe* (Cambridge, MA, 1986).

Graham, V. E., "The Triumphal Entry in Sixteenth-Century France," in *Renaissance and Reformation* ns, 10 (1986): 237–257.

———, "The Entry of Henry II into Rouen in 1550: A Petrarchan Triumph," in K. Eisenbichler and A. Iannucci (eds.), *Petrarch's Triumphs: Allegory and Spectacle*, University of Toronto Italian Studies 4 (Ottawa, 1990), 403–413.

Greenblatt, S. J., *Renaissance Self-Fashioning from More to Shakespeare* (Chicago, 1980).

———, *Marvelous Possessions: The Wonder of the New World* (Chicago, 1991).

Greene, T. M., "Ritual and Text in the Renaissance," in the *Canadian Review of Comparative Literature* (June/September, 1991): 179–197.

Griffin, R., *Coronation of the Poet: Joachim du Bellay's Debt to the Trivium* (Berkeley and Los Angeles, 1969).

Gros, G., *Le Poète, la Vièrge et le prince du Puy: Étude sur la poésie mariale en milieu de cour aux XIVe et XVIe siècles* (Paris, 1992).

Guénin, E., *Ango et ses pilotes d'après des documents inédits, tirés des archives de France, de Portugal et d'Espagne* (Paris, 1901).

Guérin, L., *Histoire maritime de France depuis la fondation de Marseille, 600 ans avant J.-C., jusqu'à l'année 1850* (Paris, 1851).

Guéry, A., "Le Roi est Dieu, le Roi et Dieu," in N. Bulst, R. Descimon, and A. Guerreau (eds.), *L'État ou le roi. Les fondations de la modernité monarchique en France (XIVe-XVIIe siècles)* (Paris, 1992), 27–47.

Guillerm, L., *Sujet de l'écriture et traduction autour de 1540* (Lille and Paris, 1988).

Guiot, J.-A. André, *Les Trois siècles palinodiques ou histoire générale des palinods de Rouen, Dieppe, etc.* 2 volumes (Rouen and Paris, 1898).

Guyon, J., "La Vente des tombes à travers l'épigraphie de la Rome chrétienne," in *Mélanges d'archéologie et d'histoire: Antiquité* 86 (1974).

Hale, J. R., "War and Public Opinion in Renaissance Italy," in E. F. Jacob (ed.), *Italian Renaissance Studies* (London, 1960), 94–112.

Hallowell, R., "Ronsard and the 'Gallic Hercules Myth,'" in *Studies in the Renaissance* 9 (1962): 242–255.

Hamon, A., *Jean Bouchet* (Paris, 1901).

Hanley, S., *The Lit De Justice of the Kings of France: Constitutional Ideology in Legend, Ritual and Discourse* (Princeton, 1983).

Hardy, G. Le, *De L'histoire du protestantisme en Normandie depuis son origine jusqu'à la publication de l'Edicte de Nantes* (Caen, 1869).

Hartner, W., "The Principle and Use of the Astrolabe," in *Oriens-Occidens* (Hildesheim, 1968).

Hartog, F., *The Mirror of Herodotus: An Essay on the Representation of the Other*. Translated by J. Lloyd (Berkeley and Los Angeles, 1988).

Harvey, H. G., *The Theatre of the Basoche: The Contribution of Law Societies to French Medieval Comedy* (Cambridge, MA, 1941).

Hathaway, B., *Marvels and Commonplaces: Renaissance Literary Criticism* (Ithaca, 1968).

Hawkins, R. L., *Maistre Charles Fontaine, Parisien* (Cambridge, MA, 1916).

Hay, D., "Italy and Barbarian Europe," in E. F. Jacob (ed.), *Italian Renaissance Studies* (London, 1960), 48–68.

Haydn, H., *The Counter Renaissance* (New York, 1950).

Hemming, J., *Red Gold: The Conquest of the Brazilian Indians* (Cambridge, MA, 1978).

Héron, A., *Deux chroniques de Rouen* (Rouen, 1900).

Hertz, R., *Death and the Right Hand*. Translated by R. Needham and C. Needham, introduced by E. E. Evans-Pritchard (London, 1960).

Herval, R., *Histoire de Rouen* (Rouen, 1949).

Higman, F. M., *Censorship and the Sorbonne: A Bibliographic Study of Books in French Censured by the Faculty of Theology of the University of Paris, 1520–1551* (Geneva, 1979).

Hobsbawm, E. J., and T. O. Ranger (eds.), *The Invention of Tradition* (Cambridge, 1993).

Hocart, A. M., *Kings and Councilors: An Essay in the Comparative Anatomy of Human Society*. Edited and introduced by R. Needham (Chicago and London, 1970).

Hodgen, M. T., *Early Anthropology in the Sixteenth and Seventeenth Centuries* (Philadelphia, 1964).

Howse, D., "Navigation and Astronomy," in *Renaissance and Modern Studies* 30 (1986): 60–86.

Hüe, D., "Un nouveau manuscrit palinodique, Carpentras, Bibliothèque Inguimbertine n° 385," *Le Moyen Français* 35–36 (1995): 175–230.

————, *La Poésie palinodique à Rouen (1486–1550)* (Paris, 2002).

Hughes, D. O., "Regulating Women's Fashion," in G. Duby and M. Perrot (eds.), *A History of Women in the West*. Volume 2, C. Klapisch-Zuber (ed.) *Silences of the Middle Ages* (Cambridge, MA, and London, 1992), 136–158.

Hughes, P. E., *Lefèvre: Pioneer of Ecclesiastical Renewal in France* (Grand Rapids, MI, 1984).

Huppert, G., "The Trojan Franks and Their Critics," in *Studies in the Renaissance* 12 (1965): 227–241.

————, "The Idea of Civilization in the Sixteenth Century," in A. Molho and J. Tedeschi (eds.), *Renaissance Studies in Honor of Hans Baron* (De Kalb, 1971), 759–769.

————, *Les Bourgeois Gentilshommes: An Essay on the Definition of Elites in Renaissance France* (Chicago, 1977).

Husband, T., *The Wild Man: Medieval Myth and Symbolism* (New York, 1980).

Jacquot, J. (ed.), *Les Fêtes de la Renaissance*. 3 volumes (Paris, 1956–1975).

Jardine, L., and A. Grafton, *From Humanism to the Humanities: Education and the Liberal Arts in Fifteenth- and Sixteenth-Century Europe* (Cambridge, MA, 1986).

Jardine, N., "The Forging of Modern Realism: Clavius and Kepler Against the Sceptics," in *Studies in History and Philosophy of Science* 10 (1979): 141–173.

Jeanneret, M., "The Vagaries of Exemplarity: Distortion or Dismissal?" in *Journal of the History of Ideas* 59:4 (October 1998): 565–579.

Jenn, J.-M., F. Jenn, J.-P. Babelon, and A. Erlande-Bradenbourg (eds), *Le Roi, la sculpture et la mort: Gisants et tombeaux de la Basilique de Saint Denis*, in *Archives departmentales de la Seine-Saint-Denis, bulletin* 3 (June, 1975).

Johnson, W., "Essai de critique interne des livres d'entrées français au XVIe siècle," in Jacquot, *Fêtes de la Renaissance*, 3: 187–200.

Joly, A., *Étude sur la vie et les œuvres de Jean Marot* (Caen, 1865).

Jouanna, A., *Ordre social. Mythes et hiérarchies dans la France du XVIe siècle* (Poitiers, 1977).

Joukovsky, F., *Orphée et ses disciples dans la poésie française et néo-latine du XVIe siècle* (Geneva, 1970).

———, "L'Empire et les barbares dans la Galerie François Ier," in *Bibliothèque d'humanisme et renaissance* 50 (1988): 6–27.

Jowitt, C. E., *Old Worlds and New Worlds: Renaissance Voyages of Discovery* (University of Southampton, 1995).

Jung, M.-R., *Hercule dans la littérature française du XVIe siècle. De l'Hercule courtois à l'Hercule baroque* (Geneva, 1966).

Kadir, D., *Columbus and the Ends of the Earth: Europe's Prophetic Rhetoric as Conquering Ideology* (Berkeley and Los Angeles, 1992).

Kantorowicz, E. H., "The 'King's Advent' and the Enigmatic Panels in the Doors of Santa Sabina," in *Arts Bulletin* 26/4 (December, 1944): 207–231.

———, *Laudes Regiae: A Study in Liturgical Acclamation and Medieval Ruler Worship* (Berkeley and Los Angeles, 1946).

———, "*Deus Per Naturam, Deus Per Gratiam*: A Note on Medieval Political Theology," *The Harvard Theological Review* 45 (1952): 253–277.

———, *The King's Two Bodies: A Study in Medieval Political Theology* (Princeton, 1957).

Kastner, L. E., "Les Grands rhétoriqueurs et l'abolition de la coupe féminine," in *Revue des langues romanes* 45 (1903): 289–297.

Kaufmann, L. F., *The Noble Savage: Satyrs and Satyr Families in Renaissance Art* (Ann Arbor, 1984).

Kelley, D. R., *Foundations of Modern Historical Scholarship. Language, Law, and History in the French Renaissance* (New York and London, 1979).

Kinser, S., "Temporal Change and Cultural Process in France," in A. Molho and J. Tedeschi (eds.), *Renaissance Studies in Honor of Hans Baron* (De Kalb, 1971), 703–755.

Kipling, G., *Enter the King: Theatre, Liturgy, and Ritual in the Medieval Civic Triumph* (Oxford, 1998).

Knecht, R. J., "The Court of Francis I," in *European Studies Review* 8 (1978): 1–22.

———, *Francis I* (Cambridge, 1982).

Konigson, E., *L'Espace théâtral médiéval* (Paris, 1975).

————, "Le Masque du démon, phantasme et metamorphoses sur la scène médié-vale," in O. Aslan and D. Babet (eds.), *Le Masque du rite au théâtre* (Paris, 1985), 103–117.

Lafon, A., and A. Marcel, *L'Hôtel de Bourgtheroulde à Rouen* (Paris, 1888).

Langer, U., "A Courtier's Problematic Defense: Ronsard's 'Responce aux injures'," in *Bibliothèque d'humanisme et renaissance* 46 (1984): 343–355.

————, *Divine and Poetic Freedom in the Renaissance* (Princeton, 1990).

Lang-Verte, A., "Quelques triomphes figurés dans l'art normand, du XVᵉ au XVIᵉ siècle," in *Bulletin des amis des monuments Rouennais* (Rouen, 1935–1938): 179–186.

Latour, B., "Visualization and Cognition," in *Knowledge and Society* 6 (1986): 1–40.

————, *We Have Never Been Modern* (Cambridge, MA, 1993).

Lauvergnat-Gagnière, C., *Lucien de Samosate et le lucianisme en France au XVIᵉ siècle: athéisme et polémique* (Geneva, 1988).

Leach, E. R., *Political Systems of Highland Burma: A Study of Kachin Social Structure* (Boston, 1965).

Lebègue, R., "La Vie dramatique à Rouen de François I à Louis XIII," *Etudes sur le théâtre français* (Paris, 1978) 2: 85–112.

Le Cacheux, P., *Bulletin de la Société de l'histoire de Normandie* 14 (1925–1930): 203–209.

Lecoq, A.-M., *François Iᵉʳ imaginaire. Symbolique et politique à l'aube de la Renaissance française* (Paris, 1987).

Lefranc, A., *Histoire du collège de France: depuis ses origines jusqu'à la fin du premier empire* (Paris, 1893).

————, "Les Commencements du Collège de France (1529–1544)," in H. V. Lindan and F. L. Ganshof (eds.) *Mélanges d'histoire offerts à Henri Pirenne*. 2 volumes (Brussels, 1926).

Le Goff, J., and J.-C. Schmitt (eds), *Le Charivari*. Actes de la table ronde organisée à Paris (25–27 avril 1977) par l'École des Hautes Études en Sciences Sociales et le Centre National de la Recherche Scientifique (Paris and New York, 1981).

Le Roy Ladurie, E., *Carnival in Romans* (New York, 1979).

————, *L'état royal de Louis XI à Henri IV, 1460–1610* (Paris, 1987).

Lestringant A., and A. Picard (eds.), *Société de l'Histoire de Normandie. Mélanges*, Treizième Série (Rouen and Paris, 1937).

Lestringant, F., "Fictions de l'espace brésilien à la Renaissance: L'exemple de Guanabara," in F. Lestringant and J. Christian (eds.) *Arts et légendes d'espaces: Figures du voyage et rhétoriques du monde* (Paris, 1981), 205–256.

————, *Le Huguenot et le sauvage. L'Amérique et la controverse coloniale en France, au temps des guerres de religion (1555–1589)* (Paris, 1990).

————, *L'Atelier du cosmographe, ou l'image du monde à la Renaissance* (Paris, 1991).

Lesueur, P., "Les Italiens à Amboise au début de la Renaissance," in the *Bulletin de la Société de l'Histoire de l'Art Français* 8 (1929–1930): 7–11.

Levi, A. C., *Barbarians on Roman Imperial Coins and Sculpture* (New York, 1952).

Lévi-Strauss, C., *Structural Anthropology* (New York, 1963).

Levin, H., *The Myth of the Golden Age in the Renaissance* (Bloomington, 1969).

Lovejoy, A. O., and G. Boas, *Primitivism and Related Ideas in Antiquity* (New York, 1935).

Lyons, J. D., *Exemplum: The Rhetoric of Example in Early Modern France and Italy* (Princeton, 1989).

MacCormack, S., "Change and Continuity in Late Antiquity: The Ceremony of *Adventus*," in *Historia* 21 (1972): 721–752.

———, *Art and Ceremony in Late Antiquity* (Berkeley and Los Angeles, 1981).

———, *Religion in the Andes: Vision and Imagination in Early Colonial Peru* (Princeton, 1991).

———, "Limits of Understanding: Perceptions of Greco-Roman and Amerindian Paganism in Early Modern Europe," in K. O. Kupperman (ed.), *America in European Consciousness, 1493–1750* (Chapel Hill and London, 1995), 79–129.

MacIntyre, A., *After Virtue: A Study in Moral Theory* (Notre Dame, 1981).

Maclean, I., "Foucault's Renaissance Episteme Reassessed: An Aristotelian Counterblast," in *Journal of the History of Ideas* 59 (1998): 149–166.

Madelaine, V., *Le Protestantisme dans le pays de Caux* (Paris, 1906).

Maillard, J.-F., "Postel et ses disciples normands," in *Guillaume Postel, 1581–1981, Actes du Colloque International d'Avranches, 1981* (Paris, 1985), 79–94.

Mâle, E., "L'Art symbolique à la fin du moyen âge," in *La Revue de l'art ancien et moderne* 19 (février, 1906): 111–126.

Marchant, A., *From Barter to Slavery: The Economic Relations of Portuguese and Indians in the Settlement of Brazil, 1500–1580* (Gloucester, MA, 1966).

Marin, L., *Portrait of the King.* Translated by M. Houle. (Minneapolis, 1988).

Marsden, C. A., "Entrées et fêtes espagnoles au XVIe siècle," in Jacquot, *Les Fêtes de la Renaissance* 2: 389–412.

Mason, P., "From Presentation to Representation: Americana in Europe," in *Journal of the History of Collections* 6 (1994): 1–20.

Massa, J. M., "Le Monde luso-brésilien dans la Joyeuse Entrée de Rouen," in Jacquot, *Les Fêtes de la Renaissance* 3: 105-116.

Mauss, M., *The Gift: Forms and Functions of Exchange in Archaic Societies.* Translated by I. Cunnison (New York and London, 1967).

———, "A Category of the Human Mind: The Notion of the Person, the Notion of the Self," translated by W. D. Halls, in M. Carrithers, S. Collins, and S. Lukes (eds.), *The Category of the Person: Anthropology, Philosophy, History* (Cambridge, 1985).

Mazouer, C., "Spectacle et théâtre dans la chevauchée des Conards de Rouen au XVIe siècle," in *Fifteenth Century Studies* 13 (1988): 387–399.

McClellan, A., *Inventing the Louvre: Art, Politics, and the Origins of the Modern Museum in 18th-Century Paris* (Cambridge and New York, 1994).

McCormick, M., *Eternal Victory: Triumphal Rulership in Late Antiquity, Byzantium, and the Early Medieval West* (Cambridge and Paris, 1990).

McGowan, M. M., "Forms and Themes in Henry II's Entry into Rouen," *Renaissance Drama* 1 (1968): 199–252.

————, *Ideal Forms in the Age of Ronsard* (Los Angeles and Berkeley, 1985).

Mialet, H., "Do Angels Have Bodies: The Cases of William X and Mr. Hawking," *Social Studies of Science* 29 (1999): 551–582.

Mitchell, B., *The Majesty of the State: Triumphal Progresses of Foreign Sovereigns in Renaissance Italy (1494–1600)* (Florence, 1986).

Mollat, M., *Le Commerce maritime normand à la fin du Moyen Age: Étude d'histoire économique et sociale* (Paris, 1952).

————, *Histoire de Rouen* (Toulouse, 1979).

————, "Mue d'une ville Médiévale (environ 1475–milieu du XVIᵉ siècle)," in M. Mollat (ed), *Histoire de Rouen* (Toulouse, 1979), 145–178.

Mollat, M., and J. Habert, *Giovanni et Girolamo Verrazano, navigateurs de François Iᵉʳ* (Paris, 1982).

Montaiglon, A. de, "La Sculpture française à la Renaissance: la famille des Juste en France," in *Gazette des Beaux-Arts* 12 (November and December, 1875): 385–394 and 515–526.

Montaigne, J.-M., *Le Trafiq du Brésil. Navigateurs Normands, Bois-Rouge et Cannibales pendant la Renaissance* (Rouen, 2000).

Moss, J. A., "The Rouen Puy d'Amour, 1543–1547," in *Kentucky Romance Quarterly* 27 (1980): 391–411.

Muir, E., *Civic Ritual in Renaissance Venice* (Princeton, 1981).

Mullaney, S., "Strange Things, Gross Terms, Curious Customs: The Rehearsal of Cultures in the Late Renaissance," in S. Greenblatt (ed), *Representing the English Renaissance* (Berkeley and Los Angeles, 1988), 65–92.

Needham, R., *Against the Tranquility of Axioms* (Berkeley and Los Angeles, 1983).

Neuschel, K. B., *Word of Honor: Interpreting Noble Culture in Sixteenth-Century France* (Ithaca and London, 1989).

Newcomer, C. B., "The Puy at Rouen," in *Publications of the Modern Language Association of America* 31, ns 24 (March, 1916): 211–231.

Nicholls, D., "Social Change and Early Protestantism in France: Normandy, 1520–62," in *European Studies Review* 10 (1980): 279–308.

Nicoll, A., *Masks, Mimes and Miracles: Studies in the Popular Theatre* (New York, 1963).

Nietzsche, F., *Genealogy of Morals* (New York, 1969).

Norton, G. P., *The Ideology and Language of Translation in Renaissance France and their Humanist Antecedents* (Geneva, 1984).

Oakley, F., *Omnipotence, Covenant, and Order: An Excursion in the History of Ideas from Abelard to Leibniz* (Ithaca, 1984).

Oberman, H. A., "The Shape of Late Medieval Thought: The Birth Pangs of the Modern Era," in C. Trinkaus and H. Oberman (eds), *The Pursuit of Holiness in Late Medieval and Renaissance Religion* (Leiden, 1974), 67–92.

————, *The Impact of the Reformation* (Grand Rapids, 1994).

————, *The Harvest of Medieval Theology: Gabriel Biel and Late Medieval Nominalism* (Grand Rapids, 2000).

O'Connor, E. D. (ed.), *The Dogma of the Immaculate Conception: History and Significance* (Notre Dame, 1958).

Olmi, G., "Science-Honor-Metaphor: Italian Cabinets of the 16th and 17th Centuries," in O. Impey and A. MacGregor (eds.), *The Origin of Museums: The Cabinet of Curiosities in Sixteenth- and Seventeenth-Century Europe* (Oxford, 1985), 1–17.

Ong, W. J., "From Allegory to Diagram in the Renaissance Mind: A Study in the Significance of an Allegorical Tableau," in *The Journal of Aesthetics & Art Criticism* 17 (1959): 424–440.

———, *The Presence of the Word: Some Prolegomena for Cultural and Religious History* (New Haven, 1967).

———, *Ramus: Method, and the Decay of Dialogue from the Art of Discourse to the Art of Reason* (Cambridge, MA, 1983).

Orgel, S., *The Illusion of Power: Political Theater in the English Renaissance* (Berkeley and Los Angeles, 1975).

Orth, M., "The Triumphs of Petrarch Illuminated by Godefroy Le Batave (Arsenal Ms. 6480)," in *Gazette des beaux-arts* 104 (December 1989): 197–206.

Ouin-Lacroix, Ch., *Histoire des anciennes corporations d'arts et métiers et des confréries Religieuses de la capitale de la Normandie* (Rouen, 1850).

Oursel, M., *Notes pour servir à l'histoire de la Réforme en Normandie au temps de François Ier* (Caen, 1913).

Ozment, S., "Mysticism, Nominalism, and Dissent," in C. Trinkaus and H. Oberman (eds.), *The Pursuit of Holiness in Late Medieval and Renaissance Religion* (Leiden, 1974), 67–92.

Pagden, A., *The Fall of Natural Man: The American Indian and the Origins of Comparative Ethnology* (Cambridge, 1982).

———, *European Encounters with the New World: From Renaissance to Romanticism* (New Haven and London, 1993).

Panofsky, E., *Tomb Sculpture: Four Lectures on its Changing Aspects from Ancient Egypt to Bernini* (New York, 1964).

Panofsky, E., and F. Saxl, "Classical Mythology in Mediaeval Art," *Metropolitan Museum Studies* 4 (1933): 228–280.

Parent, A. (ed.), *La Renaissance et le Nouveau Monde* (Quebec, 1984).

Paxton, F. S., *Christianizing Death: The Creation of a Ritual Process in Early Medieval Europe* (Ithaca, 1990).

Pellegrin, E., *Manuscrits de Pétrarque dans les bibliothèques de France* (Padua, 1966).

Petit de Julleville, L., *Histoire du théâtre en France, Les comédiens en France au moyen age* (Paris, 1885).

Phelan, J. L., *The Millennial Kingdom of the Franciscans in the New World* (Berkeley and Los Angeles, 1970).

Philipot, E., "Les 'sieurs d'ais' confrérie dramatique rouennais des XVe et XVIe siècles," in *Romania* 39 (1910): 93–95.

Pianzola, M., *Les Français à la conquête du Brésil (XVIIe siècle), Les Perroquets jaunes* (Paris and Geneva, 1991).

Picot, E. *Notice sur Jacques Le Lieur, échevin de Rouen, et sur ses heures manuscrites* (Rouen, 1913).

Pomian, K., *Collectors and Curiosities: Paris and Venice 1500–1800*. Translated by E. Wiles-Portier. (Cambridge, 1990).

Pottier, A., "L'Entrée de Henri II à Rouen," in *Revue de Rouen, ns* 5 (1835): 29–43; 85–108.

Pouchelle, M.-C., "Des peaux de bêtes et des fourrures. Histoire médiévale d'une fascination," in *Le temps de la réflexion* 2 (1981): 403–438.

Pradel, P., *Michel Colombe, le dernier imagier gothique* (Paris, 1953).

Prentout, H., "La Réforme en Normandie et les débuts de la Réforme à l'Université de Caen," in *Revue Historique* 114 (1913): 285–305.

———, *Histoire de l'Université de Caen* (Caen, 1932).

Quérière, E. de la, *Notice sur diverses antiquités de la ville de Rouen* (Rouen, 1825).

———, *Dissertation sur les portraits de François Ier et de Henri VIII existant à l'hôtel du Bourgtheroulde* (Rouen, 1828).

Reeves, M., *The Influence of Prophecy in the Later Middle Ages: A Study in Joachimism* (Oxford, 1969).

———, "The Development of Apocalyptic Thought: Medieval Attitudes," in C. A. Patrides and J. Wittreich (eds), *The Apocalypse in English Renaissance Thought and Literature: Patterns, Antecedents and Repercussions* (Ithaca, 1984), 40–72.

———, *Prophetic Rome in the High Renaissance: Period Essays* (Oxford, 1992).

Reid, D., "Carnival in Rouen: A History of the Abbaye des Conards," in *The Sixteenth Century Journal* 32 (2001): 1027–1055.

———, "The Triumph of the Abbey of the Conards: Spectacle and Sophistication in a Rouen Carnival," in Joëlle Rollo-Koster, *Medieval and Early Modern Ritual: Formalized Behavior in Europe, China and Japan* (Leiden, Boston, Köln, 2002), 147–173.

Reinach, A., "Les Têtes coupées et les trophées en Gaule," *Revue celtique* (1913): 38–60; 253–286.

Reiss, T. J., *Knowledge, Discovery and Imagination in Early Modern Europe: The Rise of Aesthetic Rationalism* (Cambridge, 1997).

Rice, E. Jr., "The Patrons of French Humanism," in A. Molho and J. Tedeschi (eds.), *Renaissance Studies in Honor of Hans Baron* (De Kalb, 1971), 689–702.

Richard, P., "Rouen and the Golden Age: The Entry of Francis I, 2 August 1517," in C. Allmand (ed.), *Power, Culture and Religion in France* (Woodbridge, 1989), 117–130.

Rigolot, F., "Montaigne: European Reader of America," in *Diogenes* 164 (1993): 1–12.

Ritter, G., and J. Lafond, *Manuscrits à peintures de l'école de Rouen: Livres d'heures normands* (Rouen, 1913).

Robillard de Beaurepaire, E. de, *Les Puys de Palinod de Rouen et de Caen* (Caen, 1907).

Roche, Louis P., *Claude Chappuys (?-1575), Poète de la cour de François Ier* (Paris, 1929).

Roelker, N. L., *One King, One Faith: The Parlement of Paris and the Religious Reformations of the Sixteenth Century* (Berkeley and Los Angeles, 1996).

Rollo-Koster, J., *Medieval and Early Modern Ritual: Formalized Behavior in Europe, China and Japan* (Leiden, Boston, Köln, 2002).

Root, D., "The Imperial Signifier: Todorov and the Conquest of Mexico," in *Cultural Critique* 9 (Spring, 1988): 197–219.

Roncière, C.-M. de La, *Histoire de la marine française.* 3 volumes (Paris, 1914).

Rossi, P., *Francis Bacon: From Magic to Science* (Chicago, 1968).

———, "Society, Culture, and the Dissemination of Learning," in S. Pumfrey, P. Rossi, and M. Slawinski (eds.), *Science, Culture and Popular Belief in Renaissance Europe* (Manchester, 1991), 143–175.

Rousse, M., *Le Théâtre des farces en France au Moyen Age,* Volume 5, *Textes de farces, documents d'archives.* Typescript thesis (Reims, 1983).

Rubin, M., *Corpus Christi: The Eucharist in Late Medieval Culture* (Cambridge, 1991).

Rummel, E., *The Humanist-Scholastic Debate in the Renaissance and Reformation* (Cambridge and London, 1995).

Sahlins, M., "The Apotheosis of Captain Cook," in M. Izard and P. Smith (eds.), *Between Belief and Transgression: Structuralist Essays in Religion, History and Myth.* Translated by J. Leavitt (Chicago and London, 1979), 73–102.

Salmon, J. H. M., *Society in Crisis: France in the Sixteenth Century* (New York, 1975).

———, "Storm over the Noblesse," in *Journal of Modern History* 53 (1981): 242–257.

Samaras, Z., *Le Règne de Cronos dans la littérature française du XVIe siècle* (Paris, 1983).

Saulnier, V. L., "Sebillet, du Bellay, Ronsard: L'Entrée de Henry II à Paris et la révolution poétique de 1550," in Jacquot, *Les Fêtes de la Renaissance* 1: 31–59.

Saunders, H. S., *All the Astrolabes* (Oxford, 1984).

Schalk, E., *From Valor to Pedigree: Ideas of Nobility in France in the Sixteenth and Seventeenth Centuries* (Princeton, 1986).

Schechner, R., *Between Theater & Anthropology* (Philadelphia, 1985).

Scheller, R., "Imperial Themes in Art and Literature of the Early French Renaissance: The Period of Charles VIII," in *Simiolus* 12 (1981–1982): 5–69.

———, "Ensigns of Authority: French Royal Symbolism in the Age of Louis XII," in *Simiolus* 13 (1983): 75–141.

———, "Gallia cisalpina: Louis XII and Italy 1499–1508," in *Simiolus* 15 (1985): 5–60.

Schiffman, Z. S., *On the Threshold of Modernity: Relativism in the French Renaissance* (Baltimore and London, 1991).

Schmitt, J.-C., *Ghosts in the Middle Ages: The Living and the Dead in Medieval Society.* Translated by T. L. Fagan (Chicago, 1998).

Schneider, R. A., *The Ceremonial City: Toulouse Observed 1738–1780* (Princeton, 1995).

Schneider, R. G., "Le Thème du triomphe dans les entrées," in *Gazette des beaux-arts* 1 (1913): 85–106.

Schulz, H., *A Study of the Moralités in the La Vallière Manuscript, Bibliothèque Nationale, Ms. Fr. 24341.* Typescript thesis (Toronto, 1982).

Scobey, D., "Anatomy of the Promenade: The Politics of Bourgeois Sociability in Nineteenth-Century New York," in *Social History* 17 (May, 1992): 203–228.

Screech, M. A., *Ecstasy and The Praise of Folly* (London, 1980).

———, *Laughter at the Foot of the Cross* (London and New York, 1997).

Sealy, R. J., *The Palace Academy of Henry III* (Geneva, 1981).

Setton, K. M., *Christian Attitude Towards the Emperor in the Fourth Century* (New York, 1941).

Seward, D., *Prince of the Renaissance: The Life of François I* (London, 1974).

Shapin, S., "Pump and Circumstance: Robert Boyle's Literary Technology," in *Social Studies of Science* 14 (1984): 481–520.

Shapin, S., and S. Schaffer, *Leviathan and the Air-Pump: Hobbes, Boyle, and the Experimental Life* (Princeton, 1985).

Silver, L., "Paper Pageants: The Triumphs of Emperor Maximilian I," in B. Wisch and S. Scott Munshower (eds.), *"All the world's a stage . . ." Art and Pageantry in the Renaissance and Baroque* (University Park, 1990), 292–332.

Simone, F., *The French Renaissance: Medieval Tradition and Italian Influence in Shaping the Renaissance in France*. Translated by H. G. Hall (London, 1969).

Slaughter, M., *Universal Languages and Scientific Taxonomy in the Seventeenth Century* (Cambridge, 1982).

Smith, P., *The Anti-Courtier Trend in Sixteenth-Century French Literature* (Geneva, 1966).

Souchal, G., "Le Mécénat de Charles d'Amboise," in *Les Informations d'histoire de l'art* (May-June, 1972): 176–181.

Stallybrass, P., and A. White, *The Politics and Poetics of Transgression* (London, 1986).

Starn, R., "Seeing Culture in a Room for a Renaissance Prince," in L. Hunt (ed.), *The New Cultural History* (Los Angeles and Berkeley, 1989), 205–232.

Starn, R., and L. Partridge, *A Renaissance Likeness: Art and Culture in Raphael's Julius II* (Berkeley and Los Angeles, 1980).

Stewart, S., *On Longing: Narratives of the Miniature, the Gigantic, the Souvenir, the Collection* (Baltimore, 1984).

Strayer, J., "France: The Holy Land, the Chosen People, and the Most Christian King," in T. Rabb and J. Seigel (eds.), *Action and Conviction in Early Modern Europe: Essays in Memory of E. H. Harbison* (Princeton, 1969), 3–16.

Strong, R. C., *Art and Power: Renaissance Festivals, 1450–1650* (Suffolk, 1984).

Struever, N., *The Language of History in the Renaissance* (Princeton, 1970).

Supple, J. J., *Arms Versus Letters: The Military and Literary Ideals in the 'Essais' of Montaigne* (Oxford, 1984).

Tilley, A., *The Literature of the French Renaissance* (New York, 1959).

Todorov, T., *The Conquest of America: The Question of the Other*. Translated by R. Howard (New York, 1984).

Tracy, J. D., "Against the 'Barbarians': The Young Erasmus and His Humanist Contemporaries," in the *Sixteenth Century Journal* 11:1 (1980): 3–22.

Trapp, J. B., *Essays on the Renaissance and the Classical Tradition* (Vermont, 1990).

Trexler, R. C., *Public Life in Renaissance Florence* (Ithaca, 1980).

Tribby, J., "Body/Building: Living the Museum Life in Early Modern Europe," in *Rhetorica* 10 (1992): 139–163.

Turner, A. J., *Early Scientific Instruments: Europe, 1400–1800* (London, 1987).

Turner, V. W., *The Ritual Process: Structure and Anti-Structure* (Chicago, 1969).

Versnel, H. S., *Triumphus: An Inquiry into the Origin, Development and Meaning of the Roman Triumph* (Leiden, 1970).

Vincent, C., "La confrérie comme structure d'intéraction: l'exemple de la Normandie," in *Le mouvement confraternel au Moyen Age. France, Italie, Suisse*. Actes de la Table Ronde organisée par l'Université de Lausanne avec le concours de l'École Française de Rome et de l'unité associée du CNRS École Française de Rome (Geneva, 1987), 111–131.

———, *Des Charités bien ordonnées. Les confréries normandes de la fin du XIIIᵉ siècle au début du XVIᵉ siècle* (Paris, 1988).

Wainwright, G., *Eucharist and Eschatology* (London, 1971).

Watts, P. M., "Prophecy and Discovery: On the Spiritual Origins of Christopher Columbus's 'Enterprise of the Indies'," in *The American Historical Review* 90 (February, 1985): 73–102.

Weber, H., *La Création poétique au XVIᵉ siècle en France: de Maurice Scève à Agrippa d'Aubigné* (Paris, 1956).

Weill, G., *Vie et caractère de Guillaume Postel*. Translated by F. Secret (Milan, 1987).

Weinstein, D., "Millenarianism in a Civic Setting: The Savonarola Movement in Florence," in S. Thrupp (ed.), *Millennial Dreams in Action* (The Hague, 1962), 187–203.

Weiss, N., "Note sommaire sur les débuts de la Réforme en Normandie (1523–1547)," in *Congrès du millénaire normand* 1 (Rouen, 1911): 193–205.

———, *La Chambre ardente* (Geneva, 1970).

Weiss, R., "The Castle of Gaillon in 1509–10," in *Journal of the Warburg and Courtauld Institutes* 16 (1953): 1–12.

West, D., "Medieval Ideas of Apocalyptic Mission and the Early Franciscans in Mexico," in *The Americas* 45:3 (January, 1989): 293–313.

Westman, R., "The Astronomer's Role in the Sixteenth Century: A Preliminary Study," *History of Science* 18 (1980): 105–147.

———, "Proof, Poetics, and Patronage: Copernicus's Preface to *De Revolutionibus*," in Westman and Lindberg (eds.) *Reappraisals of the Scientific Revolution* (Cambridge, 1990), 167–205.

Westman R., and D. Lindberg (eds.) *Reappraisals of the Scientific Revolution* (Cambridge, 1990),

Williamson, A. H., "Scots, Indians and Empire: The Scottish Politics of Civilization 1519–1609," in *Past & Present* 150 (1996): 46–83.

Wind, E., "'Hercules' and 'Orpheus': Two Mock-Heroic Designs by Dürer," in *Journal of the Warburg and Courtauld Institutes* 2 (1938): 206–218.

Winter, P. M. de, "Vision of the Apocalypse in Medieval England and France," in *Bulletin of the Cleveland Museum of Art* (September, 1983): 396–417.

Wintroub, M., "The Looking Glass of Facts: Collecting, Rhetoric and Citing the Self in the Experimental Natural Philosophy of Robert Boyle," *History of Science* 35 (1997): 189–217.

————, "Civilizing the Savage and Making a King: The Royal Entry Festival of Henri II (Rouen, 1550)," the *Sixteenth Century Journal* 29 (1998): 467–496.

————, "Taking Stock at the End of the World: Rites of Distinction and Practices of Collecting in Early Modern Europe," *Studies in History and Philosophy of Science* 30 (September 1999): 395–424.

————, "L'ordre du rituel et l'ordre des choses: l'entrée royale d'Henri II à Rouen (1550)," *Annales: Histoire, Sciences Sociales* 56 (March–April, 2001): 479–505.

Wisch, B., and S. Scott Munshower (eds.), *"All the world's a stage . . . " Art and Pageantry in the Renaissance and Baroque* (University Park, 1990).

Wittgenstein, L., *Philosophical Investigations.* Translated by G. E. M. Anscombe (New York, 1968).

Wood, J. B., *The Nobility of the Election of Bayeux, 1463–1666: Continuity Through Change* (Princeton, 1980).

Yates, F. A., *Astraea: The Imperial Theme in the Sixteenth Century* (London, 1975).

————, *The French Academies of the Sixteenth Century* (New York, 1988).

Yu-Ling Liou, E., "Cardinal Georges d'Amboise and the Château de Gaillon at the Dawn of the French Renaissance," Ph.D. diss., Pennsylvania State University, 1997.